History

20th Century World

Authoritarian and Single-Party States

PEARSON
BACCALAUREATE

BRIAN MIMMACK   DANIELA SENÉS   EUNICE PRICE

PEARSON

Pearson Education Limited is a company incorporated in England and Wales, having its registered office at Edinburgh Gate, Harlow, Essex, CM20 2JE. Registered company number: 872828.

www.pearsonbaccalaureate.com

Pearson is a registered trademark of Pearson Education Limited

Text © Pearson Education Limited 2010

First published 2010

20 19 18 17 16 15 14 13 12
IMP 10 9 8 7 6 5 4

ISBN 978 0 435032 64 7

Edited by Chris McNab
Designed by Tony Richardson
Typeset by Tony Richardson
Original illustrations © Pearson Education Limited 2010
Illustrated by Oxford Designers & Illustrators, TechType and Tony Richardson
Cover design by Tony Richardson
Picture research by Joanne Forrest Smith

Cover photo © Alamy Images: Mary Evans Picture Library

Printed in Malaysia, CTP-KHL

Acknowledgements

The authors and publisher would like to thank the following individuals and organizations for permission to reproduce photographs:

(Key: b-bottom; c-centre; l-left; r-right; t-top)

akg-images Ltd: 118; Alamy Images: 259b, Alex Fairweather 171, Interfoto 194, J Marshall – Tribaleye Images 252br, Julio Etchart 251bl, Peter Horree 250l, Premiergraphics 258, Rod McLean 262b, The Art Archive 144; Bob Row: 50t; British Cartoon Archive, University of Kent www.cartoons.ac.uk: David Low published in the *Evening Standard* on 22 December 1939 130c, Michael Cummings published in the *Daily Express* 29 September 1961 235, Raymond Jackson published in the *Evening Standard* on 23 June 1967 240t, Solo Syndication 240c, Solo Syndication / David Low 130b, 133; Camerapress: 60t, Charles Paynter 178t, Gamma / Eyedea / Mohammad Eslamirad 262t, Gammar / Umar Leyla 61bc, Keystone France 40, TIO 202; Corbis: 147t, Bettmann 30, 47, 56, 102cr, 151, 173, 175, 234, 260tr, Bob Krist 58, Brian A. Vikander 260br, epa / Alejandro Ernesto 53, Hulton-Deutsch Collection 102c, 102bl, 102bc, 106cl, 260bl, Lester Cole 61cl, Lucien Aigner 129tl, Madeleine Répond 61bl, Owen Franken 93, Reuters 188, 251t, Reuters / Granma / Handout 66, Swim Ink 142, Sygma / Apis 214, Sygma / Carlos Carrion 48, Underwood & Underwood 102cl, Wally McNamee 169; Fred Halla: 210; Getty Images: 9, 76, 94, 102br, 106b, 158, 217, 255, AFP 17, 35, 45, 182t, Bloomberg 260cl, epa / Maxim Shipenkov 256, Popperfoto 50b, 160, Time & Life Images 119cl, Time & Life Pictures 29, 43, 129tr, 242cr; GNU Free Documentation License: Wikipedia: 25, 26; Instituto Nacional Juan Domingo Perón, de Estudios e Investigaciones Históricas, Sociales y Políticas: 41; iStockphoto: 261; James Fitzpatrick: 252c; Magnum Photos Ltd: 60b; Masoud Kipanga: 205; Nathan Mpangala: 209; Pat Oliphant: 182b; Pearson Education Ltd: The Illustrated London News Picture Library 146b; Photoshot Holdings Limited: 83c, 83b, 119cr, UPPA 97, 139; Sophie Grillet: 206; Special Collections at the University of Miami Libraries: 38; Stefan R Landsberger Collection/ http://chineseposters.net: 78, 95, 159tl, 159tr, 176, 177, 253tr/1, 253c/3, 253cl/2, 253bl/4, 253bc/5, 253br/6; Tom Burns/Threadless.com: 259t; Tony Burciaga, 'Last Supper of Chicano Heroes' mural provided by courtesy of Professor Carlos G. Vélez-Ibáñez, Arizona State University: 252bl; TopFoto: ullsteinbild 61c, 61cr, 61br, 85, HIP/ Keystone Archives 174, RIA Novosti 106cl, 238, Roger-Viollet 63, The Granger Collection 117, The Granger Collection, New York 150, Topham 199, Topham/AP 248, Topham Picturepoint 242cl, Ullsteinbild 219; Vladimir Tsesler: 257c

All other images © Pearson Education Limited.

The publisher and authors would also like to thank the following for permission to use © material:

From 'Cuba c. 1930–1959' by Louis A. Pérez, found in *Cuba: A Short History* by Leslie Bethell (ed.), Cambridge University Press, 1993, used by permission; *Cuba: Between Reform and Revolution* by Louis A. Pérez, © Louis A. Pérez, Oxford University Press, 1988; *Cuba Betrayed* by Fulgencio Batista, Vantage Press, 1962; *Cuba: Anatomy of a Revolution* by Leo Huberman and Paul Sweezy, Monthly Review Press, 1960, used by permission; *Castro* by Sebastian Balfour, © Sebastian Balfour, published by Longman an imprint of the Pearson Group, 1990, used by permission; Extract from a speech by Fidel Castro in Santiago de Cuba, 3 January 1959. From Marxist Internet Archive; Extract from a transcript of a press conference given by Fidel Castro at Havana Presidential palace on 27 February 1959; *Socialism and Man in Cuba* by © Ernesto Guevara, 1989, 2009 by Pathfinder Press, used by permission; From *Inside the Revolution: Everyday Life in Socialist Cuba* by Mona Rosendahl, © Mona Rosendahl, Cornell University Press, 1997, used by permission; From *Fidel Castro and the Quest for a Revolutionary Culture in Cuba* by Julie Marie Bunck, Pennsylvania State University Press, 1994; From *Child of the Revolution: Growing Up in Castro's Cuba* by Luis M. Garcia, Allen & Unwin Australia, 2006; Poem *Cuban Poets no Longer Dream* by Herberto Padilla; From *Culture and Customs of Cuba* by William Luis, Greenwood Press, 2001, reproduced with permission of ABC-CLIO, Santa Barbara, CA; Extract from a speech by Fidel Castro in Havana on 1 May 1980; From *Fidel Castro* by Robert E. Quirk, © 1993 by Robert E. Quirk, used by permission of W.W. Norton & Company, Inc; From *Cuba in Revolution* by Antoni Kapcia, © Antoni Kapcia, Reaktion Books, 2009, used by permission; From *The Cuban Revolution: Origins, Course, and Legacy* by Marifeli Pérez-Stable, Oxford University Press, 1993, used by permission; Extract from a letter to the Secretary of State, 25 February 1947, found in *The Critical Phase in Tanzania 1945–1968* by Cranford Pratt, Cambridge University Press, 1976, used by permission; From *Tanganyika, Legislative Council Official Report*, 34th Session, vol. 1, col. 5, 14 October 1958, found in *The Critical Phase in Tanzania 1945–1968* by Cranford Pratt, Cambridge University Press, 1976, used by permission; From *The Critical Phase in Tanzania 1945–1968* by Cranford Pratt, Cambridge University Press, 1976 used by permission; From *Freedom and Unity* by Julius Nyerere, Oxford University Press, 1966; From 'Constitution-making in Tanzania: The role of the people in the process' by Chris Maina Peter, Professor of Law, University of Dar es Salaam, Tanzania, August 2000; From Charter of the Organization of African Unity, 1963, used by permission of the African Union; From The Arusha Declaration, 5 February 1967, by Ayanda Madyibi from: Marxist Internet Archive, used by permission; Chart from *The Journal of Modern African Studies* by Michael F. Lofchie, Cambridge University Press, used by permission; From *Freedom and Socialism* by Julius Nyerere, Oxford University Press, 1968; Short extract from: *Daily News*, 7 November 1973; 'Cotton Production Tanzania 1964–1985', used by permission of the United States Department of Agriculture; 'Tanzania Economic Indicators for 1967–1984', adapted from U. Lele, *Agricultural Growth, Domestic Policies, the External Environment and Assistance to Africa: Lessons of a Quarter Century*, MADIA Discussion Paper II, World Bank Washington, 1989, used by kind permission of the World Bank; 'Expansion of the Education Sector between 1971 and 1991' from *Tanzania: Ministry of Education and Culture; Tanzania Public Expenditure Review: The Role of Government*, World Bank, 1994, used by kind permission of the World Bank; 'Expansion of the Health Sector in Tanzania between 1969 and 1992', *Tanzania: Ministry of Health; Tanzania Public Expenditure Review: The Role of Government*, World Bank, 1994, used by kind permission of the World Bank; From 'Nyerere No Great Leader, But Ensured Poverty For Tanzania' by Simon Barber, from *Business Day*, 27 October 1999; Extract from lyrics of tango *Cambalache* by Enrique Santos Doscepolo, 1934, translated by John Kraniauskas, Duke University Press, used by permission; From *Argentina: What Went Wrong?* by Colin M. MacLachlan, © Colin M. MacLachlan, Greenwood Publishing Group, 2001, reproduced with permission from ABC-CLIO, Santa Barbara, CA; From *Mañana es San Perón: A Cultural History of Perón s Argentina* by Mariano Ben Plotkin, Scholarly Resources, 2003, used by permission of the author; From *Perón and the Enigmas of Argentina* by Robert D. Crassweller, © Robert D. Crassweller. W.W. Norton, 1987, used by permission of W.W. Norton & Company, Inc; From *Perón: A Biography* by Joseph Page, Random House USA, 1983; From *Sindicalismo y Peronismo: Los comienzos de un vinvulo perdurable* by Hugo del Campo, CLACSO, Buenos Aires, 1983; Extract from a statement by Juan Domingo Perón, November 1943, from *Authoritarian Argentina: The Nationalist Movement, Its History and Its Impact* by David Rock, University of California Press, 1995; From *Politics and Education in Argentina, 1946–1962* by Mónica Esti Rein, © Mónica Esti Rein, M.E. Sharp, 1998; From *Culture and Customs of Argentina* by David William Foster, Melissa Fitch Lockhart and Darrell B. Lockhart, Greenwood Press, 1998, reproduced with permission of ABC-CLIO, Santa Barbara, CA; From *Gender, Agency, and Change: Anthropological Perspectives* by Victoria Ana Goddard (ed.), Routledge, 2000, an imprint of Taylor Francis Group, used by permission; From 'Evita and Propaganda: Selling an Argentinian Dictatorship' by William Shannon © 2000, found on the Mail Archive; From *A Brief History of Argentina* by Félix Luna, © Félix Luna, Planeta, 1995; From 'What the People Want: State Planning and Political Participation in Peronist Argentina, 1946–1955', by Eduardo Elena, from *Journal of Latin American Studies*, 37, Cambridge University Press, 2005, used by permission; From a speech by Juan D. Perón, 20 August 1948, found on the Fordham website; From a speech given by Juan D. Perón to a group of intellectuals in 1947 found on newsmatic.e-pol.com.ar; From *Nasser: The Last Arab* by Said Aburish, © Said Aburish, Duckworth, 2004; From *Nasser* by Anthony Nutting, Constable & Robinson, 1972; From *Revolutionaries* by Eric Hobsbawm © Weidenfeld &Nicolson, 1973, an imprint of the Orion Publishing Group, London; From *Nasser* by Anne Alexander, Haus Publishing, 2005; From *Nasser* by Robert Stephens, © Robert Stephens, Penguin Books, 1973; From *A History of the Middle East* by Peter Mansfield, © Peter Mansfield, Penguin Books UK, 1991; From *The State of Africa* by Martin Meredith, © Martin Meredith, The Free Press, 2006; From 'Egyptian Cinema' by Viola Shafik, found in: *Companion Encyclopaedia of Middle Eastern and North African Film* by Oliver Leaman (ed.), Routledge, 2007, a member of the Taylor Francis Group, used by permission; From *Stalin: A Political Biography* by Isaac Deutscher, © Isaac Deutscher, Oxford University Press, 1966; From an article by Ferdinand Mount, found in *The London Review of Books*, reproduced with permission of *The London Review of Books*; From *Stalinism* by Graeme Gill, © Palgrave Macmillan, 1998, reproduced with permission of Palgrave Macmillan; From *The Soviet Century* by Moshe Lewin, © Moshe Lewin, Verso Books, 2005, used by permission; From *Comrades* by Robert Service, Macmillan, 2007, used by permission of Pan Macmillan; From *A History of Twentieth-Century Russia* by Robert Service, Penguin, 1999, used by permission of The Penguin Group; From *The Whisperers* by Orlando Figes, Penguin, 2007, used by permission of The Penguin Group; Chart from *The Soviet Union 1917–1991* by Martin McCauley, Pearson, 1993, used by permission of Pearson Education Ltd; Chart from *An Economic History of the USSR* by Alec Nove, © Alec Nove, 1969, used by permission of Penguin Books; Chart from *The Economic Transformation of the Soviet Union 1913–1945* by R.W. Davies, M. Harrison and S.G. Wheatcroft (eds), Cambridge University Press, 1994; From *A History of the Soviet Union* by Geoffrey Hosking, © Geoffrey Hosking, HarperCollins, 1992; From *Soviet Politics 1917–1991* by Mary McAuley, © Mary McAuley, Oxford

Websites
There are links to relevant websites in this book. In order to ensure that the links are up to date, that the links work, and that the sites are not inadvertently linked to sites that could be considered offensive, we have made the links available on the Pearson Hotlinks website at www.pearsonhotlinks.com.

Contents

Introduction

How will this book help you in your IB examination?

This book will help you prepare for Paper 2 (Route 2) in the International Baccalaureate History exam by equipping you with the knowledge and skills you need to demonstrate in your examination. It focuses on Topic 3 – 'Origins and development of authoritarian and single-party states' – one of the five topics in Paper 2. It addresses six of the states that feature as material for detailed study in the History Guide. These case studies also constitute relevant material for the different Higher Level regional options.

Included in the book are chapters on each of the selected states. There is also a chapter on how to approach Paper 2 questions, offering essay-writing techniques, and a chapter on history and Theory of Knowledge (ToK). By working through these chapters, you will gain an understanding of the aims of the IB History course, as well as the skills that are reflected in the structure and assessment objectives of Paper 2.

Information for students

What are the aims and assessment objectives of the IB History course?

Whether you are studying history at Higher or Standard Level, you need to take a broad view of how past events have brought us to where we are today. The awareness of how events that are separated by both time and space are nevertheless linked together in cause and effect is one of the most important qualities to be developed during the IB History course. For example, you need to understand what circumstances and methods brought a particular leader to power and analyze the part played by similar factors in the rise of leaders from other regions.

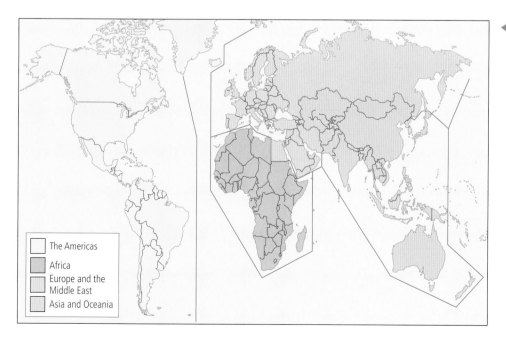

◀ Map of the IB regions.

The Americas

Africa

Europe and the Middle East

Asia and Oceania

Although this book is essentially designed as a textbook to accompany Paper 2, Topic 3 (Authoritarian and Single-Party States), as you work through it you will be learning and practising the skills that are necessary for different papers. This book also covers the assessment objectives relevant to Paper 2. Specifically, the assessment objectives focus on the following skills:

Assessment objective 1: Knowledge and understanding

You will learn how to recall and select relevant historical knowledge, and demonstrate detailed and in-depth understanding of processes of cause–effect and continuity–change.

Assessment objective 2: Application and interpretation

You will learn how to apply historical knowledge as evidence and show awareness of different approaches to, and interpretations of, historical issues and events.

Assessment objective 3: Synthesis and evaluation

You will learn how to evaluate and appreciate the reasons and ways in which opinions and interpretations differ and to synthesize these using evidence.

Assessment objective 4: Use of historical skills

You will develop the ability to structure an essay answer, using evidence to support relevant, balanced and focused historical arguments.

IB Learner Profile

When the IB set out a course curriculum, they have in mind certain qualities that they want a student to develop. These are not abstract ideas; everything you learn and do as part of the IB programme contributes to the development of these qualities. These objectives apply to the study of history.

Through the study of the topics in this book, you will become more knowledgeable about the world around you, become a critical inquirer, and make connections between events and across regions. You will be encouraged to take an investigative approach, gathering and analyzing evidence and producing logical, well-argued answers. Be prepared to change your mind; if you hold a particular opinion about an issue, find out about different points of view. It is useful to reflect on how the material you have learned and the skills you have acquired are relevant to areas other than history, and how they help you deal with your understanding of, for instance, global issues.

What this book includes

This book addresses one of the five topics of History Paper 2. You are required to prepare for two topics and answer one question from each of the selected topics. The book provides you with detailed information on all the themes you need to study for each of the state leaders included. The content of the book will also be useful to the Higher Level Regional Option Paper 3, as the selected states are relevant to the history of their respective regions. In addition, the material included in each chapter can be used to assist you in the choice and research of suitable topics for the Internal Assessment (IA – Historical Investigation) or the History Extended Essays (EE).

The book includes:

- Timelines of events for each leader, to help you put him into context.
- Analysis, origins, ideology, form of government, organization, nature and domestic policies relating to each of the regimes included.
- Primary and secondary sources, including reference to historiographical approaches relevant to each major theme.
- Examples of students' responses to let you reflect on their content and approach.
- Examiner's comments that explain the strengths and weaknesses of students' responses, and make recommendations on how the different students' answers could have been improved.
- Examiner's hints to help you understand what is expected for each type of question and plan your answers accordingly.
- Review sections to help you summarize the main points from each chapter and expand your knowledge.
- A chapter on how to approach Paper 2 questions and develop essay-writing skills and techniques.
- A chapter on ToK to help you think about the links between the study and writing of history and other areas of knowledge.

How this book works

In addition to the main text, there are a number of coloured boxes in every chapter, each with its own distinctive icon. The boxes provide different information and stimulus:

ToK Time

These boxes will enable you to consider ToK issues as they arise and in context. Often they will just contain questions to stimulate your own thoughts and discussion.

ToK Time
In groups, discuss the following questions in relation to the policies towards the arts under Fidel Castro.

Interesting facts

These boxes contain interesting information that will add to your wider knowledge, but which does not fit within the main body of the text.

Monoculture economy
The agricultural practice of producing or growing one single crop over a wide area.

Examiner's hint

These boxes can be found alongside questions, exercises and worked examples. They provide insight into how to answer a question in order to achieve the highest marks in an examination. They also identify common pitfalls when answering such questions and suggest approaches that examiners like to see.

● **Examiner's hint**
This section has provided you with information about Castro's social policies. It has addressed the status of women, education, the role of the arts, religions and the treatment of minorities.

Examiner's comments

These boxes can be found after student answers. They include an assessment of how well a question has been answered, along with suggestions of how an answer may be improved.

> **Examiner's comments**
>
> Here is a very interesting opening, which shows a comprehensive understanding of the rise of single-party and authoritarian states. The student also shows some understanding of the conditions against which Perón came to power. From what is offered in this introductory paragraph, it is expected that the candidate will follow by providing information about which particular sectors found Perón's promises appealing and more detail as to the reasons why this was so. For example, what did Perón mean by 'social justice'? What specific promises did he make in relation to these goals? To whom were these promises directed? Which 'ideological pronouncements', if any, did Perón make?

Online resources

Online resources boxes indicate that online resources are available that relate to this section of the book. These resources might be extension exercises, additional practice questions, interactive online material, suggestions for IA, EE and revision, or other sources of information. Some of the content on this site may be password protected for copyright reasons. When prompted for a password, please use the ISBN or title exactly as shown.

 To access Worksheet 2.1 on 'Cambalanche', please visit www.pearsonbacconline.com and follow the on-screen instructions.

Weblinks

Relevant websites are recommended in the Further Reading section at the end of the book. On these webpages you will find video material and background information to support the topic.

Review boxes

These boxes are found at the end of each chapter and summarize the main points to be considered.

REVIEW SECTION
This chapter has examined the rise to power of Juan Domingo Perón and his rule of Argentina, looking at his three presidential terms. It has focused on: • The conditions and methods that led to Perón's rise to power. • The methods used to consolidate power. • The nature, implementation and effects of his social, political and economic policies. • Peronist culture, propaganda and education. • The nature and extent of opposition.

TOPIC 3 – THEMES AND EXAM TIPS

This chapter will introduce Topic 3: 'Origins and development of authoritarian and single-party states'. It examines the nature of these states, along with the major themes listed in Topic 3. It then looks at the structure of the exam and the kind of exam questions that you may be asked, before giving advice on how to write a good essay answer in the exam.

What constitutes an authoritarian or single-party state?

To be classed as an authoritarian or single-party state, a country or state will have:

- only one legal political party
- a leader often chosen by/from the military following a coup
- a leader or group who controls the state even though there may, in theory, be other parties.

Jeane Kirkpatrick, the US Ambassador to the United Nations, once said during the early 1980s that an authoritarian state was different from (better than!) a totalitarian state, because there was a chance that it would eventually move towards democracy. Of course, this view was expressed during the Cold War and she was differentiating between single-party states that were on the side of the USA and those on the side of the USSR. For example, Nicaragua, under the dictatorship of Somoza, was considered to be authoritarian by the USA but Cuba was considered to be totalitarian.

In general, authoritarian or single-party states have the following characteristics in common:

- Little or no freedom of speech
- No freedom of assembly (unable to hold meetings without the approval of the government)
- No freedom of movement – often, individuals need documents or even internal passports to move around inside the country
- No freedom to travel abroad
- No independent judicial system
- All sources of information are censored
- Any opposition to the regime is harshly punished
- A leader whose popularity is reinforced by a personality cult.

Not all such states have these characteristics and some may be more or less oppressive than others. All, however, will exercise strict control over the freedom of the people and will use a variety of methods to hold on to power.

In many states, the age of Kings and Emperors ended with World War I, and short-lived experiments with democracy gave way to a new kind of all-powerful leader. The authoritarian or single-party states and leaders that you study will be examples taken from the 20th century. This century was one of the most bloody in history, and included two major world wars and ideologies that subordinated the needs of the individual to the needs of the state.

Left and right wing

Exam questions on Topic 3 may sometimes ask about 'left-wing' and/or 'right-wing' states or leaders. Although these terms have their origin in the French Revolution, they are still used today to describe political parties, movements or ideas.

Left wing: We use 'left wing' to describe single-party leaders and states that are either communist or socialist. Nasser, Stalin, Mao, Nyerere and Castro would all be 'left wing'.

Right wing: Although some of the fascist leaders of the 20th century began their political careers as members of socialist parties, we consider fascist leaders and states to be right wing. Examples would include Hitler, Mussolini and Franco. Their policies were often supportive of capitalism as an economic system. They were also ultra-nationalist and, in some cases, promoted religion as a way to unite the people and to gain the support of the Church. They were also vehemently anti-communist.

Fascism

Name given by Mussolini to the movement he led in Italy from 1922. The term is commonly used to identify other right-wing regimes such as German Nazism and Spanish Falangism. It is characterized by extreme nationalism, hostility to democracy, respect for collective organizations, the cult of the leader and army-like discipline. Fascism is also anti-communist and anti-liberal.

Right-wing ideologies

The best-known examples of 20th-century right-wing ideologies were **fascism** in Italy and Nazism in Germany. They emerged in very similar circumstances. In Germany there was despair associated with defeat in World War I, and in Italy the perception of a 'mutilated victory' that had not been worth the cost of that war. Although they began with **socialist** programmes intended to appeal to the lower classes (the workers, the small farmers and the skilled craftsmen), both ideologies became more conservative as they sought the support of the middle classes. Inevitably, enemies were treated harshly and dissent was not tolerated. Under Hitler, the racial aspects of his ideology led to the attempted extermination of the Jews in Europe.

There were also right-wing ideologies among military-backed leaders in other countries, such as Juan Perón in Argentina or General Franco in Spain. These do not fit so easily into the 'fascist' mould, but they were strongly nationalistic and considered **communism** to be a serious threat.

Left-wing ideologies

One of the most widespread ideologies of the 20th century was communism. It was born out of industrialization in the 19th century and based upon the writings of Karl Marx and Friedrich Engels. This ideology promised a society in which all people were equal and in which the state would 'wither away', as it had no need to control or to legislate when there was no private property to protect. Under Lenin and Stalin, the Soviet Union created a template for all other communist states in the 20th century. Neither leader claimed to have reached the goal of communism or 'Great Harmony', as it was called by Mao Zedong. Yet the road to this paradise on earth was a difficult one and so, they believed, justified the application of harsh measures.

There were significant variations in the nature of left-wing single-party states. They ranged from the violent and complete dictatorship of Stalin to that of Gamal Nasser of Egypt, who was vehemently anti-communist and followed an ideology tempered with capitalism. One characteristic all these leaders had in common, whether from the left or the right, was their belief that they alone had the knowledge and the will to bring about the ideal state. Note also that apart from Italy under Mussolini, most of the examples of authoritarian or single-party states in the 20th century were republics, for example: Portugal under Salazar, Hungary under Bela Kun, Spain under Franco and so on. Many of the single-party states were created in the post-monarchical vacuum after a strong leader had been overthrown or had abdicated.

Socialism

The roots of socialism and communism were very similar. The Social Democratic Parties of Germany and Russia, for example, were originally based on the writings of Karl Marx, with the more radical members splitting off at a later stage to form communist parties. What did develop in Europe, especially after World War II, was what may be called Modern Socialism. This had the following characteristics:

- the redistribution of wealth through taxation
- the state ownership of major industries such as steel and coal
- the state ownership of 'monopolies' such as transport, communications, water etc.
- free health care and free education for all.

In many countries, these criteria became known as the 'welfare state' based on the belief that the government should ensure a basic standard of living for all its citizens.

The stages of communism

The classic Marxist interpretation of history can be broken down into distinct stages determined by which class owned the wealth of the state and the 'means of production'.

These stages can be seen as:

Primitive communism: meaning the prehistoric hunter-gatherer communities in which there was no monopoly over the means of production. In other words, people worked together to find food and shared their resources. This was viewed by Marx as some kind of early communism.

Feudalism: this stage came about when settled, agricultural-based communities developed into kingdoms and powerful rulers took ownership of the land and the people who farmed it.

Capitalism: commercial activities such as trading in manufactured goods became a greater source of wealth than land, especially after the Industrial Revolution. The powerful merchant/business/bourgeoisie class came into being and political systems became more democratic.

Communism: Marx predicted that the workers (proletariat) would rise up against the capitalist owners of the means of production (factories and businesses) and would replace the democracy of capitalism with the true democracy of the workers' state. In this state, private property would no longer exist and the people would contribute their skills, taking only what they needed. This situation would then lead to a 'withering away of the state', as there would be no need for laws to protect wealth and property as all would be communally owned.

Lenin knew that the establishment of a communist state in the USSR would not be achieved quickly and he was prepared to fail and try again (as when he abandoned War Communism and replaced it with the NEP in 1921). It was expected that there would be a series of attempts and the maxim would be 'try, fail, fail better'. Lenin also considered the stage between 'post-capitalism' and the achievement of communism to be 'socialism'. Khrushchev predicted that communism would be achieved by 1980, although Brezhnev settled for calling the USSR a 'developed socialist state'.

Examiner's hint

It is a good idea to think broadly about the topic of single-party and authoritarian states. Begin by studying individual leaders, but don't forget to place them in their historical context. When you study Stalin, for example, be aware of what is going on elsewhere at the same time. Historical events are interconnected and have a huge influence upon each other. When you look at Mao and the Great Leap Forward, it is worth checking what was happening in the USSR and the Eastern Europe states at the same time. These communist countries were trying to increase production levels and their methods were not so different. Nasser and Fidel Castro of Cuba were contemporaries and both needed the support of the USSR, even though one actually put communists in prison whilst the other declared himself to be a 'Marxist-Leninist'.

What themes should you study?

The IB History Guide outlines three major themes for Topic 3:

Origins and nature of authoritarian and single-party states

This theme asks you to look at the rise to power of authoritarian and single-party leaders or the emergence of authoritarian or single-party states. You need to consider what kind of circumstances made it possible for this to happen and what kind of methods were used by the leader to take power.

Establishment of authoritarian and single-party states

This theme asks you to look at the leader or the state once power has been assumed and other political parties or groups have been suppressed. You need to consider how power is maintained, probably through the use of popular policies and/or terror.

Domestic policies and impact

This theme asks you to look at the way the state is actually structured and what kind of policies are carried out. You need to consider what kind of programme is put into practice and how economic and social policies are created and implemented. You will also need to know something about the role of women (always an interesting aspect of regimes that took power when women had fewer rights than men), attitudes towards religion and the kind of culture that developed inside the state.

How is the exam structured?

The paper

The exam for Paper 2 consists of five topics, each with six questions. You have to answer two questions, each taken from a different topic.

The questions

For each topic, three out of the six questions will be 'named' questions. This means that, in Topic 3, three of the questions will refer to particular states or leaders. These will be chosen from the list included in the 'Material for Detailed Study' listed under Topic 3 in the IB History Guide. For example:

> *Analyze the methods used by either Castro or Mao to maintain his position as the ruler of a single-party state.*

For each topic, two out of the six will be 'open-ended' or general questions. This means that you can choose any suitable example that you have studied. For example:

> *Examine how and why one leader of a single-party state was able to make a successful bid for power.*

For each topic, one out of the six questions will ask about 'social, economic or gender issues'. For example:

> *Discuss the role and status of women in two single-party states, each chosen from a different region.*

Notice that in this final question, it asks for two examples but they must come from different regions.

Command terms

At the start of each question, there will be a 'command term'. This refers to the way the question is asked. A comprehensive list of command terms, with explanations, is given in the IB History Guide.

For example:

Analyze: Break down in order to bring out the essential elements or structure.

Compare and contrast: Give an account of similarities and differences between two (or more) items or situations, referring to both (all) of them throughout.

Discuss: Offer a considered and balanced review that includes a range of arguments, factors or hypotheses. Opinions or conclusions should be presented clearly and supported by appropriate evidence.

Evaluate: Make an appraisal by weighing up the strengths and limitations.

Examine: Consider an argument or concept in a way that uncovers the assumptions and interrelationships of the issue.

To what extent: Consider the merits or otherwise of an argument or concept. Opinions and conclusions should be presented clearly and supported with appropriate evidence and sound argument.

(All definitions taken from the IB History Guide © IBO, 2009)

Doing the exam

Preparation

If you are planning to answer a question from Topic 3, it is best to revise at least two leaders, preferably from different regions and, if possible, different ideologies. Make sure that you know enough to be able to answer questions that may come up on the different themes.

Writing an exam essay

Choosing the question

You will have five minutes' reading time before the exam officially begins. You may not write during this time, but you can read the questions and think about how you could answer them. Read the questions carefully and choose the two that are best suited to the material you have revised. Make sure they are from different topics. Take your time and, if you need to discuss more than one leader, see if you can choose appropriate examples. If a question asks you, 'To what extent do you agree…' see if you can challenge the assertion.

Timing

You have probably had plenty of practice at writing history essays, and so you can use the same technique in the exam. The only difference is that you will only have 90 minutes for two essays, or 45 minutes per essay.

Planning

No matter how desperately you want to start writing, always take five minutes of your time to plan your answer. This can make a huge difference to the quality of your answer and help you to know where you will end up before you start to write! A good plan or outline is more than just a list of facts that you can recall. It should help you to organize your ideas and to think through arguments.

For example, how would you plan your answer to this question?

> *Compare and contrast the economic and social policies of two single-party leaders, each chosen from a different region.*

Take a look at these student samples and see if you agree with the examiner's comments.

STUDENT PLAN 1 – SALLY

Examples – Mao and Stalin

Mao – Land reform, Five Year Plans, Cooperatives, Collectives, Communes, Backyard furnaces, Hundred Flowers, Antis, Cultural Revolution.

Stalin – Collectivization, Five Year Plans, Industry, Purges, Terror, Culture.

Examiner's comments

This is not much of a plan, but more of a brainstorm. Sally has jotted down all the policies she can think of and will use the lists as a reminder to mention all these points. She has not made it clear to herself how she will compare and contrast the two leaders she has chosen.

STUDENT PLAN 2 – PETER

Examples – Mao and Stalin

For comparison:

Both wanted rapid industrialization and based this on a planned economy (give examples… refer to Five Year Plans)

Both had largely agricultural economies and a population that worked on the land – land reform was followed by collectivization in both cases

Both had huge labour resources – big populations

Both wanted more education – literacy campaigns in both states

Both wanted more women in the workforce

Both used terror to ensure the policies were carried out (but terror is not 'a domestic policy')

Both used propaganda campaigns to get the population working with them… speak bitterness, 100 flowers, antis.

For contrast:

Mao wanted to develop the countryside and the town together in the Great Leap Forward (GLF); Stalin wanted the countryside to finance the industrialization of the USSR. Link to different interpretations of Marxism.

Stalin wanted to urbanize, to create a proletariat; Mao wanted to 'walk on two legs' (a reference to the GLF)

Stalin wanted to re-arm (Plan #3); less important for Mao

Stalin was isolated; Mao had the help of the USSR to train his workers

Stalin wanted to do away with the role of the Orthodox Church, especially in the countryside; religion was less important for Mao except for Christian missionaries, who were associated with imperialism.

Examiner's comments

Peter has a much better plan. He has not simply jotted down a lot of key facts, but has focused on answering the question and using a comparative structure. He has also been careful to include only social and economic policies. Stalin and Mao make a good choice, because they have similar policies, so there is a lot to compare, but also less to contrast. Don't worry too much about this; the examiner will be looking for a nicely structured answer that is reasonably balanced (so not only comparison or not only contrast), but don't feel that if you have five comparisons you must also have five contrasts! Of course, your plan could be even shorter than Peter's, and you could use your own abbreviations to save time. Similarly, you may prefer to draw a spider-gram or a 'mind map'. Whatever helps you to plot your journey through to the conclusion is fine, as long as you figure it out before you start to write.

How to structure your essay – and some do's and don'ts

An exam essay is really no different from a class or a homework essay, except that you have to write it without access to sources and within a given time period.

Do's:

- Do read the question very carefully and make sure that you can answer it. If a specific time period is mentioned, do you have enough material to cover it all? If the question asks about social and economic policies, do you know enough about both?
- Do answer the question that is asked on the exam paper and not a similar one you prepared earlier!
- Do plan your answer and include this plan on your exam answer sheets.
- Do begin with an introduction and always refer to the question in the introduction.
- Do define any key words such as 'totalitarian' or 'authoritarian' if the question mentions these.
- Do use a comparative structure if the question asks you to compare and contrast. (Look at Peter's plan; he will be writing about both Mao and Stalin at the same time and not simply listing Stalin's policies and then listing those of Mao.)
- Do include DATES! When you are writing about why something happens, you will usually need to refer to what came before (cause and effect), and so knowing the order in which events happen is very important.
- Do refer to the question in each paragraph, to make sure that your answer stays focused.
- Do finish with a conclusion that sums up your arguments.
- Do include some reference to different historical interpretations, if this is appropriate.

Don'ts:

- Don't write down everything you know about a topic; you need to select only relevant material.
- Don't leave out facts and dates. Your arguments need to be supported, so saying that Castro used guerrilla tactics to come to power is fine, but you need to support this statement with evidence of how he did this.
- Don't just list what historians say about a topic; use historiography to support your arguments not replace them.
- Don't use quotations to replace your arguments. If you use quotations, explain why and link them to your arguments.
- Don't use 'I think…' or 'In my opinion…' but instead write, 'It is clear that…' or 'Given the evidence, it can be seen that…' Try to keep an 'academic' tone to your writing.

Introductions and conclusions – don't neglect these!

Introduction

There is no formula for a good introduction. While some students will state very clearly how they will structure their answers, others may simply give some relevant background and their thoughts on the question. Examiners will want to know that you have understood the question and have grasped its implications. Think of it as a 'first impression', leading the examiner to think 'Good, they are on the right track'. Also, if you are answering an 'open-ended' question that may, for example, ask about the rise to power of a leader, then you can state here what time period you will focus on. In the case of Nasser, for instance, would you begin in 1952 or 1948 or earlier? Also, are there terms that need to be defined? If so, it is a good idea to do this in the introduction.

Conclusion

Here is your chance to make a 'lasting impression'. You will need to summarize your arguments concisely, but not by repeating them one by one – this is tedious and doesn't add much to your answer. If you have a nice quotation that is relevant (make sure it is!) and sums up your argument, then use it in the conclusion. It may spark the examiner's interest and leave a good impression. For example, if you were writing about Nasser, it may be relevant to mention that Zhou Enlai said that Nasser had died of a 'broken heart' (see the chapter on Nasser).

Plan ahead!

See if you can get access to previous examination papers so that you can become familiar with the kind of questions that will be asked. Then, think about how you would answer them. Work in a group and come up with plans for typical questions.

2 JUAN PERÓN AND ARGENTINA

Peronism is one of the most controversial topics in Latin American history. Historians have tried to unravel why the ideas and image of Juan Domingo Perón have been so passionately defended, or rejected, since his reign. They have studied Perón's rise and fall to understand why, both during his 18-year exile as well as after his death, he has continued to influence Argentine history and politics.

This chapter focuses on the rise to power and rule of Juan Perón in Argentina. It addresses the reasons and ways in which Perón came to rule in 1946 and covers the domestic policies implemented in the country during his two consecutive terms in office (1946–52 and 1952–55). It also looks at the reasons for his fall in 1955, and refers to his third presidency between 1973 and 1974.

Juan Perón

Timeline – 1895–1976

1895 Juan Domingo Perón is born in Lobos, province of Buenos Aires.

1911 Perón starts his military training.

1919 Eva Duarte (Evita) is born in Los Toldos, province of Buenos Aires.

1930 A coup involving the Argentine armed forces led by General Uriburu, with the participation of Perón, overthrows President Hipólito Yrigoyen. The 'Infamous Decade' begins.

1936 Perón is appointed military attaché to the Argentine embassy in the Republic of Chile.

1939 Perón leaves Argentina for Europe on a military mission. Outbreak of World War II (1939–45). Argentina proclaims its neutrality.

1941 Perón returns to Argentina and is promoted to the rank of colonel.

1943 A military coup against President Castillo is organized by the Grupo de Oficiales Unidos (GOU; United Officers' Group). One of its leading figures is Colonel Perón, who becomes Secretary of Labour and Welfare.

1944 Perón meets Eva Duarte at a fundraising event for the victims of an earthquake in the province of San Juan. Argentina breaks off diplomatic relations with Japan and Germany. General Farrell becomes President. Perón is appointed Minister of War and Vice-President.

1945 Perón is pushed out of office and imprisoned in the island of Martín García. Five days later, hundreds of thousands of workers march to Casa Rosada to demand Perón's release.

1946 Perón wins elections for the presidency.

1947 Women are granted the right to vote.

1949 A new constitution strengthens the power of the President, allows for his re-election and incorporates social rights.

1951 Perón is re-elected President with a huge majority.

1952 Eva Perón dies.

1955 An attempted coup by the Argentine navy is crushed by forces loyal to Perón. In September, a coup by all three branches of the armed forces leads to the 'Liberating Revolution'. Perón resigns and goes into exile.

1958 Presidential elections are held. Perón orders the Peronists to make a **blank vote**. Arturo Frondizi is elected President.

 Blank vote
A blank vote means the voter does not endorse any candidate in an election or other kind of democratic process.

The Great Depression
Economic crisis that
began in the USA in 1929
with the collapse of the
stock market, and which
led to the financial ruin
of banks in Europe and
the USA and impacted
on economies worldwide
during the 1930s.

1962	Frondizi is overthrown and replaced by José M. Guido, President of the Senate.
1963	Arturo Illia is elected President.
1966	A coup led by General Juan Carlos Onganía overthrows President Illia.
1970	General Onganía is deposed and replaced by Roberto M. Levingston.
1971	President Levingston is deposed and replaced by General Alejandro A. Lanusse.
1972	Perón makes a brief visit to Argentina.
1973	The Peronist Party wins elections in March. Hector Cámpora becomes President. Perón returns to Buenos Aires in June. Cámpora resigns and Perón is elected President in September.
1974	Perón dies in July. His third wife, Isabel, succeeds him. Terrorism from right and left escalates, leaving hundreds dead. There are strikes, demonstrations and high inflation.
1976	Isabel Perón is overthrown by a military coup.

Section I:
Historical background and the road to the presidency

Figure 2.1
Map of Argentina.

Argentina, the largest country in Latin America after Brazil, achieved its independence from Spain in 1816. The Argentine economy in the 19th and early 20th centuries developed based on the export of food such as wheat and meat and the importation of manufactured and luxury goods, largely coming from Europe. Industrial development was mostly restricted to meatpacking and refrigerating factories to facilitate the exports of food to distant markets. The arrival of immigrants from Europe provided the country with a rural working class and skilled urban labourers, which in turn fuelled a continuous increase in agricultural output. European – and later US – capital was invested in developing the Argentine railways and meatpacking, communications and service industries, and Buenos Aires became a major port for exports. The ruling class in the country represented the land owning families who defended the economic agro-exporting model, which enjoyed a sustained level of growth until the **Great Depression** of 1929.

The Infamous Decade (1930–43)

As a result of the Depression, the prices of commodities plummeted and by 1933 they were at 50 per cent of their 1928 level. The drop in prices was less severe for manufactured than industrial goods. This situation eroded the **terms of trade** for Argentina, and it was not long before the country faced difficulties in affording the importation of the industrial and luxury goods which it did not produce.

The economic problems affecting the nation contributed to political instability and in 1930 caused the overthrow of the Unión Cívica Radical (UCR; Radical Party) democratic government, led by **Hipólito Yrigoyen**, by army officers with popular support. This event was followed by a period of autocratic conservative rule known as the 'Infamous Decade', which, despite its name, extended for 13 years. Argentine Presidents came to office either through *coups d'état* or fraud in elections.

The period inaugurated by the 1930 coup brought many changes to the Argentine economy and society. Although the immediate economic effects of the Depression were relatively short-lived, it became clear that there was a need to overcome the country's economic vulnerability. The governments after 1930 began to develop national industries to substitute importations and reduce dependency. With the outbreak of World War II in 1939, the idea that Argentina needed to gain economic independence was strengthened.

During the Infamous Decade, traditional political parties were banned from participating in elections; opponents to the regime were persecuted, imprisoned and tortured. Corruption was widespread. People lost faith in the political system and rejected the prevailing corruption and government impunity.

ToK Time

The tango music and dance is universally associated with Argentina, though it is more representative of the city of Buenos Aires, its capital. Tango originated towards the end of the 19th century, and was first danced among men in the brothels and ports of Buenos Aires. Read through the lyrics below, then tackle the questions that follow, thinking generally about the relationship between the arts and politics.

Today no one gives a damn
whether you are straight or bent!
Ignorant, scholar, crook,
kind or con!
Whatever! No matter!
Great professor or dunce,
who cares!
No lesser, no betters,
the immorals have made us all the same
(…)
And, like a mule,
you may work night and day,
but you are just the same
As the man who lives off others,
the man who kills, who cures,
who lives by breaking the law.

From the lyrics of tango 'Cambalache', composed by Enrique Santos Discépolo in 1934. Quoted in Gabriela Nouzeilles and Graciela Montaldo (eds), *The Argentine Reader: History, Culture and Politics*, 2002

Questions

a) What is the message of 'Cambalache'? The word is used in Argentina and Uruguay to refer to shops that sell all kinds of second-hand products. Why do you think the author chose this word as a title for his tango?

b) Can you think of other examples of songs that express critical views of specific historical events or periods? How effective has social criticism been when channelled through the arts? To what extent are political and social criticisms legitimate roles of the arts?

The international context

To better understand the context of Perón's rise to power, you need to be aware of the events that were happening in the world between 1930 and his election as President of Argentina in 1946. We have already mentioned the impact of the Depression on the Argentine economy, and how it led to a revision of its economic model in favour of a policy of import substitution. The economic problems that began in 1930 and the plans to industrialize Argentina exposed the gaps between the rich and the poor. Rural workers arrived in the cities hoping to find jobs in factories, but lived and worked in very precarious conditions. The fear that the new social and economic conditions would make communism attractive to these

Terms of trade
Relationship between the prices at which a country sells its exports and the prices paid for its imports.

Hipólito Yrigoyen (1852–1933)
The first Argentine President elected by universal male suffrage. He represented the Radical Party (UCR). Yrigoyen ruled between 1916 and 1922 and, after a four-year rule by another member of his party, was re-elected in 1928. The rule of the UCR between 1916 and 1930 represented the first time in Argentine history when the middle class played important political roles. Under Perón, the UCR party became his main opponent.

To access Worksheet 2.1 on 'Cambalache', please visit www.pearsonbacconline. com and follow the on-screen instructions.

● **Examiner's hint**
Paper 2 questions will not focus on the foreign policies of the selected leaders. However, it is very difficult to understand how and why Perón came to power in 1946 without considering some of the most relevant ideas and events at the time. You may have already referred to some of these in your lessons.

sectors also played a role in the support for Perón, as we will later examine. Moreover, the outbreak of World War II in 1939 encouraged belief in the idea that Argentina needed to break away from international economic dependence and achieve self-sufficiency.

In the political field, the emergence of ideologies such as fascism in Italy and Nazism in Germany, with their contempt for democracy and support for nationalist ideals, also contributed to the circumstances in which Perón rose. There were many Argentines who were disappointed at the fake and corrupt democracy of the Infamous Decade, which had not brought effective solutions. They were attracted to the European models of government, which at the time seemed to have improved the social and economic situation in countries like Italy and Germany.

Origins and nature of authoritarian and single-party states – Argentina

This section analyzes Perón's rise to power. It addresses the structural problems of Argentina at the time, as well as the immediate events surrounding his rise (1943–46) in an attempt to explain how and why he became President of Argentina in 1946.

Why did Perón come to power?

There is no straightforward answer to the above question, and several issues need to be considered. Long-term conditions, which we have briefly considered, were of great importance in making Juan Perón an appealing figure to the Argentines. An analysis of the circumstances in which he appeared on the political scene in 1943 also contributes to understanding the short-term factors behind his rise.

Long-term factors

The reasons why Perón came to power are related to the social, political and economic structures of Argentina. The governments of the Infamous Decade were unpopular for many reasons. We have already noted the lack of genuine democracy and the widespread corruption prevailing during those years. At a political level, we could add that the middle class felt their voices were not heard; intellectuals felt politically frustrated, since they couldn't voice their thoughts and were unable to fight against fraud and **nepotism**. Yet the working class lacked the organization – and perhaps even the political awareness – to fight against this system, while the middle class had not yet found a leading figure to organize the opposition.

Nepotism
Favouritism shown in business and politics on the basis of family relationships.

Juan Perón is best known as the first political figure to address effectively the many problems of the working class. Governments before 1943 had done very little to grant the social legislation that protected workers in other countries. No laws protecting workers' rights existed, to the advantage of employers. Labour movements and socialist parties had had limited political participation and had not brought about significant changes in these conditions.

SOURCE A

In the initial stages of industrialisation, characterised by under-capitalised small scale industry, makeshift machinery, poorly designed buildings and a tendency to cut corners, workers laboured under marginal conditions. Dust, chemical fumes, stench and dangerous solvents assaulted the health of workers. Packinghouse floors covered with blood, entrails and excrements made for ghastly work. Men who carried meat to the freezers covered their faces

and hands with rags or old newspapers so that the fresh blood would not freeze on their bodies. Rheumatism disabled many packinghouse workers within five years. Child labour resulted in prematurely aged and wizened children. Employers, accustomed to the grim reality of factory life, demonstrated little concern for the health and comfort of their employees… In rural areas conditions differed but presented their own hardships. Low wages, payment in script, inadequate food, and conditions of semi-servitude could all be found.

From Colin M. MacLachlan, *Argentina: What Went Wrong?*, 2001

STUDENT STUDY SECTION

QUESTIONS

a) **What, according to Source A, were the social problems of Argentina in the 1940s?**

b) **On the basis of the evidence in Source A, imagine you are a trade union leader in 1940. What demands would you present to the government? Why?**

Another structural problem of Argentina was that Buenos Aires ruled over the country. This rule was not only in political terms, but also in economic terms. The railroads designed by the British in the 19th century connected the provinces to Buenos Aires, but not the provinces to each other. Hence the industrial boom was heavily concentrated around Buenos Aires (with some industrial areas in cities like Córdoba and Rosario – see map on p.10). All this led the provinces to be economically and socially backwards compared to Buenos Aires. The levels of malnutrition and illiteracy were far higher in the interior; the rural workers lived far apart, as roads were still very few. These circumstances pushed them to Buenos Aires, where they found poor living and working conditions. Such long-term factors played a significant part in explaining Perón's rise, as they relate to the promises and proposed solutions he made during his ascendancy and rule.

Short-term factors

The events and circumstances surrounding the emergence of Perón on the political scene relate to two main areas: 1) the outbreak of World War II and its impact on Argentina; 2) the action of a military secret society, the Grupo de Oficiales Unidos (GOU; United Officers' Group).

Argentina and World War II

When World War II broke out in 1939, Argentina declared its neutrality in the conflict. Great Britain welcomed this declaration because, as neutral vessels, the Argentine ships could continue to sail and supply Allied Europe without facing attacks from the enemy. However, after its entry into the war in 1941, the USA began to put pressure on the Argentine government to break diplomatic relations with the **Axis**. The Argentines were divided between those who wanted to declare war against the Axis and those who felt that Argentina should maintain its tradition of neutrality. Although there was a small group who sympathized with the Axis, represented, for example, by certain circles in the armed forces, they did not openly express this and tended to join those who favoured neutrality.

On 4 June 1943, the military intervened in the political life of Argentina again, leading a coup that overthrew President Ramón S. Castillo and ended the Infamous Decade. The ostensible aim was to prevent another fraudulent election from taking place. However, there were other reasons for the coup. Some sectors of the armed forces had grounds to believe that the candidate who would have won the elections by fraud had intentions of declaring

Axis
The alliance of Germany, Japan and Italy and their allies. The enemy of the Axis is referred to as the Allies, which consisted primarily of Great Britain, the USA and the Soviet Union, with Italy switching sides to the Allies in 1943.

war against the Axis. The armed forces interfered in political life to prevent this from happening and to continue with the position of neutrality. This position was interpreted both within the country and by the USA as an implicit support of the Axis.

The GOU

The group that led the coup was represented by a secret society known as the GOU, of which Colonel Juan D. Perón was a founding member. They were young officers from middle- and lower-class families of anti-communist, ultra-catholic and nationalist ideas. The ideas of the GOU responded to the situation in Argentina in the early 1940s:

- They claimed they had come to end corruption and fraud and to restore the Argentine constitution.
- They believed that Argentina had to develop its national industry and strengthen its defences.
- Fearful of the possible expansion of communism after the end of World War II, they considered it was better to introduce improvements in the living and working conditions of employees from above, to avoid them being attracted by left-wing ideas.
- At an international level, they defended the idea that Argentina should remain in a position of neutrality towards the war and resisted US pressure to declare war on the Axis.

But although they had a set of aims, it was only with Perón that these aims became a programme of action to address the specific problems of Argentina. His participation was fundamental for the government to gain civilian support. His role within the government that emerged from the 1943 coup became an important factor in this rise.

SOURCE B

On June 5, one day after taking power, the new government issued a proclamation, probably written by Perón, making public its objectives. According to this proclamation, the principal problem of the country, whose resolution the new authorities took it upon themselves to solve, were: immorality in public administration, the absence of God in public schools, the excessive power of 'usurious capital' to the detriment of national interests, the lack of moral authority of the judicial system, and the Communist threat. The military authorities also stressed the importance of industrial development as a prerequisite for attaining 'economic independence'.

From Mariano Ben Plotkin, *Mañana es San Perón: A Cultural History of Perón's Argentina*, 2003

● **Examiner's hint**
Exam questions on authoritarian and single-party states may ask how and why a leader came to power. To analyze the reasons (why), you should focus on the long- and short-term factors that explain his rise. In the case of Perón, it would be important to look at the characteristics of the background against which he rose: a discredited democracy; a working class that lacked representation and labour legislation; the rise of industrialization, etc. You also could assess the significance of World War II in creating circumstances that were favourable for Peron's rise and address the ideas Perón represented and how they related to the issues described above.

> **STUDENT STUDY SECTION**
>
> **QUESTIONS**
> a) **What principles of the GOU are reflected in Source B?**
> b) **How do they relate to the problems Argentina faced between 1930 and 1943? Which sectors of society do you think found these principles appealing? Why?**

How did Perón rise to power?

We have now learnt about some of the problems Argentina faced, such as its discredited democracy, the difficulties of an agro-exporting economy and the rise of an urban working class on the eve of industrialization. We have analyzed how these factors led to the collapse of the system implemented in the Infamous Decade, and to the success of the military coup in 1943. These issues have helped us understand the circumstances that played a part in

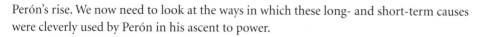

Perón's rise. We now need to look at the ways in which these long- and short-term causes were cleverly used by Perón in his ascent to power.

Colonel Perón did not occupy the presidency of the Republic in 1943. This was held for three days by General Arturo Rawson, who was replaced by General Pedro Pablo Ramírez and, in March 1944, by Edelmiro Farrell, a supporter of Perón.

Perón: Secretary of Labour and Welfare

The process of industrialization that began in the early 1930s caused a rush of **internal migration** – that is people moving within a country – from the countryside to the major cities in search of employment in the factories. This exponential growth met with severe problems in terms of housing and the very poor living conditions for those arriving to join the urban workforce, many of whom did not find jobs fast enough. Consequently, slums developed outside the industrial areas of the large cities, but the government provided them with very little social assistance. Also, trade unions were poorly prepared to absorb the masses of workers, of whom only a limited number had unionized before 1943. The urban and rural workers, now consisting largely of native Argentines rather than immigrants, felt their interests and needs were not taken into account either by the government or by the trade union leaders. This is significant because native Argentines, as opposed to immigrants, could vote. Remember, Perón was legitimately elected President for his three terms in office.

The military coup of 1943 placed Perón in the Labour Department, an institution that did not have significant political weight. In November that year, it was raised to the status of Secretariat of Labour and Welfare by unifying different welfare agencies and putting them under Perón's control, with the aim of centralizing them and making the new Secretariat more efficient. His work as Secretary of Labour and Welfare, from November 1943 to October 1945, achieved far more for the workers than anything the unions had achieved since 1930. Instead of repressing the workers, as the government had done in the past, or allowing them to be attracted by the leftist political parties, Perón listened to them and acted upon their demands and needs. His reforms included:

- Improvement in labour legislation (such as the establishment of labour courts to rule in conflicts between employers and employees).
- Regulations against arbitrary job dismissal.
- The right to paid holidays for workers.
- Regulations covering the apprenticeship of minors.
- Retirement benefits for workers.
- New syndicates were created for those economic activities that had not been unionized before.
- Commissions were formed by representatives of workers and employers to negotiate matters related to work conditions and pay.
- Wages were increased.
- The passing of the Peasant Statute: for the first time, rural workers were unionized and their working and living conditions subject to the law rather than to the goodwill of their employers.
- Other measures included the freezing of the rent paid on fields to the owners and the suspension of peasants' evictions.

Perón offered a new vision as regards labour. He said that in labour issues there were three actors: the workers, the employers and the state, and all should have a say. He made sure he was seen as the creator and producer of all reforms and changes (see Source C following).

● Examiner's hint

If asked how a leader came to power, you should focus on the methods he or she used. In other words, if the problems of the working class were a condition that supported Perón's rise, you should now analyze what he did in relation to such a condition and how those methods or policies contributed to his political achievements. Did he use legal methods? Did he make use of force? You could also refer to events that may have either weakened the opposition or strengthened Perón's position.

Internal migration into the cities

It is estimated that the population living in the industrial area of greater Buenos Aires increased by one million between 1936 and 1945.

SOURCE C

If a law was to be proposed, Perón made the announcement. When delegations came to discuss the matter, Perón addressed them. When the law was signed, it was his hand that held the pen. If there was a ceremony that could be worked up, it was held in his office. If a gesture was desired to tilt a strike negotiation to the side of labour, it was Perón who would visit the premises and be photographed chatting with the strikers. If union leaders had to be coaxed, it was to Perón's office that they were invited… As time went on the entire national movement came to be seen as the personal and sole achievement of Perón, a movement in which Perón led and the labour leaders struggled to maintain his pace. He was using them, not the reverse.

From Robert D. Crassweller, *Perón and the Enigmas of Argentina*, 1987

● **Examiner's hint**

Some of the leaders you have studied or will study are charismatic; others are not. This word refers to whether people see a leader as somebody who is set apart from the rest of the people because of his exceptional personal qualities or his exemplary actions, both of which inspire loyalty among his followers. Consider why Perón could be considered a charismatic leader. Think of how you would justify the idea that Perón was charismatic (you can find examples throughout this chapter). Analyze the role charisma played in Perón's rise and rule, and consider how this information can help you demonstrate your understanding of Perón. Have you studied any other charismatic leader? Explain the nature of the leader's charisma.

STUDENT STUDY SECTION

QUESTIONS

a) **Looking a Source C, explain the meaning and significance of the sentence 'He was using them, not the reverse.'**

b) **Perón later referred to his years as Secretary of Labour as his 'charismatic years'. What do you think he meant by this? To what extent do you agree with this description?**

In exchange for the recognition of these rights and the mediation of the Secretariat, which often benefited the workers over the employers, Perón expected the unions to recognize government leadership over their affairs. Before the end of the year, Perón had made significant progress in his attempt to militarize the trade unions, that is, to make them respond to the government. The most important central labour organization at a national level was the Confederación General del Trabajo (CGT; General Confederation of Labour), which was founded in 1930. Shortly before the 1943 coup, it split into CGT1 and CGT2, responding to political differences in the leadership. Perón dissolved the CGT2, claiming that it was dominated by communists. He restructured the CGT1 as one single union that responded to him.

SOURCE D

At this point Perón in no way controlled the CGT or the labour movement. The colonel had no punitive mechanism at his disposal and could not enforce the loyalties of organised labour. But what he could do and did do was bind labour's recently acquired privileges to his tenure in office. Union leaders understood perfectly well that if Perón lost power, the progress they had been making would swiftly deteriorate.

From Joseph Page, *Perón: A Biography*, 1983

STUDENT STUDY SECTION

QUESTIONS

a) **How does Source D explain the ways in which Perón benefited from his position as Secretary of Labour?**

b) **What limitations does Source D identify in Perón's influence over the workers?**

How did Perón's work as Secretary of Labour contribute to his rise?

There are two main reasons why Peron's role in the Secretariat of Labour strengthened his position. First, the fact that Perón fulfilled many of the demands of the unions meant that traditional left-wing parties, which claimed to represent the interests of the workers, lost their appeal. Workers realized that it was more likely that conflicts would be resolved and demands met if they went to Perón and accepted his role in the negotiations. Second, and equally important, was the extent to which Perón was personally associated with the newly acquired rights. This meant that the workers – who feared the loss of their benefits – became unconditional supporters of Perón. The working class had been transformed from a potential threat to a strong and compliant source of support. Perón's political alliance with organized labour became a fundamental instrument in his rise to power.

There was also a significant event that gave Perón the opportunity to go beyond the circle of labour relations into an area of higher profile, that of social aid. Early in 1944, a devastating earthquake hit the northern province of San Juan (see map, p.10). Perón led, organized and attended fundraising campaigns to assist the victims of the earthquake. This event had an unexpected but equally significant ramification. It was at one of these fundraising events that he met actress **Eva Duarte**, who played a fundamental role in Perón's rule.

Eva Duarte (1919–52)
Eva Duarte was born in the small village of Los Toldos in 1919. At the age of 15, Eva decided to move to Buenos Aires to become an actress and had some success as a radio star. When she met and later married Colonel Perón, her life changed dramatically and she became an important political figure in her own right.

Perón: Minister of War and Vice-President

In January 1944, Argentina abandoned its neutrality and broke relations with the Axis. Argentina only declared war on the Axis in 1945, the year the war ended. This shift in policy led to President Ramírez's resignation and the appointment of General Edelmiro Farrell as President. As a consequence of these changes in cabinet, Perón took office in the War Ministry (without abandoning his position of Secretary of Labour), which had been under the command of now President Farrell.

Perón launched a massive expansion of the armed forces. He increased both the army's size and its budget: the army's manpower tripled by 1945 and army expenditure more than doubled between 1943 and 1945. He ordered the purchase of new military equipment, expanded local factories for the production of military material, raised officers' pay and improved military barracks and living quarters. These policies gained Perón the support of the army. In July 1944, Perón also became Vice-President of Argentina.

Eva Perón

The Peronist ideology

You now have an understanding of the background against which Perón came to power and of how these circumstances relate to the actions of Perón within the government. To understand his rise, you should also study his ideas and assess how and why they became appealing to the Argentine people. It is important to keep in mind that the rise of Perón, unlike that of some of the other single-party leaders you may study, is completed with his election as President of Argentina in February 1946. In this context, it becomes important to understand why his thoughts became appealing to a majority of voters.

Although there are hundreds of writings, speeches and recorded interviews with Perón, historians and political analysts have always found it very difficult to agree in their interpretations of Perón's ideas and aims. Even if there are some prevailing ideas on the role of the state, such as the importance given to economic independence, and to political sovereignty and social justice, there also are contradictions in some of his thoughts.

SOURCE E

Peronism is humanism in action; Peronism is a new political doctrine, which rejects all the ills of the politics of previous times; in the social sphere it is a theory which establishes a little equality among men, which grants them similar opportunities and assures them of a future so that in this land there may be no one who lacks what he needs for a living, even though it may be necessary that those who are wildly squandering what they possess may be deprived of the right to do so, for the benefit of those who have nothing at all… That is Peronism. And Peronism is not learned, nor just talked about: one feels it or else disagrees. Peronism is a question of the heart rather than of the head.

From a speech by Juan D. Perón, 20 August 1948

STUDENT STUDY SECTION

QUESTIONS

Read through Source E, and answer the following questions:

a) **What do you understand by 'Peronism is humanism in action'?**

b) **What, according to this source, are the aims of Peronism?**

c) **Which problems of Argentina in the early 1940s is this source addressing? Explain your answer fully.**

d) **Using this source, discuss who you think Peronism appealed to and who may have had grounds to reject these ideas?**

The influences on Peronist thought

In many ways Peronism was not a new ideology, but rather borrowed concepts from existing organizations and ideologies. The army, contemporary European right-wing experiences, Catholicism and socialism were all possible sources of many Peronist ideas.

The influence of the army

One great influence on Perón was his time serving in the military. Life in the army gave Perón the opportunity to travel across Argentina and to witness the hardships of the provinces first hand. This experience made Perón very aware of the conditions of inequality in the country. He came to the conclusion that if those conditions were not redressed by the government, a violent revolution following the **Bolshevik** example could follow.

Military values also played a part in shaping Perón's thoughts. Discipline and a sense of 'spiritual unity' – the idea that one single thought had to dominate the entire group and that disagreement should not be tolerated – were important to him. As you will see, his domestic policies were planned accordingly.

The influence of Catholicism

The members of the GOU were Catholics and, as such, shared with the Catholic Church in Argentina the view that the conditions of the working class needed attention. They also believed that remedying social injustice was an effective tool to prevent the expansion of revolutionary ideologies such as Marxism, which were strongly anti-religious. Perón

Bolshevik
The Bolshevik revolution that occurred in Russia in 1917 established the first Marxist government. Bolshevism promoted a form of communism aimed at a violent revolution to overthrow capitalism.

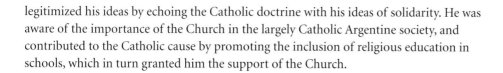

legitimized his ideas by echoing the Catholic doctrine with his ideas of solidarity. He was aware of the importance of the Church in the largely Catholic Argentine society, and contributed to the Catholic cause by promoting the inclusion of religious education in schools, which in turn granted him the support of the Church.

The influence of contemporary ideologies

Perón's trip to Europe between 1939 and 1941 allowed him to come into contact with the Nazi regime in Germany and with Mussolini's fascism in Italy. He imitated some of the aspects of these right-wing ideologies which, at the time of Perón's visit, were experiencing popularity at home. In the same way as Perón felt attracted by some features of European fascism, he rejected **Marxist** ideas as well as liberalism. He preferred to describe his movement as a 'Third Position'.

 Marxism
The political and economic philosophy of Karl Marx (1818–83) and Friedrich Engels (1820–95), in which the concept of class struggle – the motor of history – plays a central role in explaining the development from bourgeois oppression under capitalism to a socialist and ultimately classless society by means of revolution.

SOURCE F

[In Europe, Perón] not only came to appreciate firsthand the achievements and organization of the Fascist regime, but he also personally witnessed the horrors of immediate post-Civil War Spain. Perón never hid his admiration for Mussolini, not even for Hitler… From Fascist Italy, Perón learnt some practical ways in which the masses could be organised and controlled. As he himself would say in Conducción Política, *'The value of the people … does not reside in the number of men who are organized. Its value resides in the rulers who lead the people, because action is never generated by the mass or by the people, but by the rulers who lead them. The mass goes wherever its rulers take it; otherwise, it overflows and God forbid!'*

From Mariano Ben Plotkin, *Mañana es San Perón: A Cultural History of Perón's Argentina*, 2003

SOURCE G

Perón rejected the two orthodox political-economic systems of the time, capitalistic liberalism and Marxism, and proposed an alternative of his own: the 'Third Position,' equidistant between capitalism and communism and opposed to them both. He presented this concept as part of a new national project that included the social integration of the masses and the transformation of Argentina's economic infrastructure. In his words: 'We have a third position, in which we do not wish the individual to be exploited in the name of either capital or the state. We want the individual… not to be an instrument serving the appetites of capital or the state.'

From Mónica Esti Rein, *Politics and Education in Argentina, 1946–1962*, 1998

STUDENT STUDY SECTION

QUESTIONS

a) How, according to Source F, was Perón influenced by his experiences in Europe?

b) According to Sources F and G, what importance did Perón attribute to leadership?

c) In what ways was Perón's rejection of liberalism related to the conditions of Argentina in the early 1940s?

d) You may be familiar with other leaders who have declared their opposition to both Marxism and liberalism. How does their ideology compare to that of Perón?

You have now seen which ideas contributed to the formation of Peronist thought. You have learnt where Peronism stood in relation to liberalism and Marxism. The most effective way to summarize Perón's ideology is to refer to the three Peronist principles: social justice, economic independence and political sovereignty.

Social justice: The integration of the working classes

Peron made constant reference to the concept of 'social justice'. Like many of the elements in Peronist thought, this was not a new idea. The term refers to the idea that wealth or privileges in a society had to be distributed to achieve a fairer order.

In order to avoid huge gaps between the different social classes, Perón thought that the state should share and distribute wealth with discipline. In Perón's words: 'We aim at eliminating class struggle, replacing it by a fair agreement between workers and employers under the law which derives from the state.' Most of the labour reforms carried out by the Secretariat of Labour and Welfare were attempts to bring about social justice.

SOURCE H

In our trade unionist work – says a metallurgic worker – we witnessed incredible things as from 1944: the labour legislation which in the past had not been regarded was now respected; there was no need to go to Court to obtain holidays; other labour legislation such as the recognition of factory representatives and the reassurance that they would not be fired, etc, etc had immediate and rigorous enforcement. Internal relations between industrialists and workers completely changed in nature. Owners were disconcerted while the workers were astonished and cheerful. The Secretariat of Labour and Welfare had become a power for the organization, development and support of the working class. It did not operate as a state regulation above the classes, but rather as a state ally of the working class.

Translated from Hugo del Campo, *Sindicalismo y Peronismo: Los comienzos de un vínculo perdurable*, 1983

STUDENT STUDY SECTION

QUESTIONS

a) **To what extent does Source H reflect the principle of social justice? Explain your answer fully.**

b) **With reference to its origins and purpose, assess the value and limitations of Source H to an historian studying the influence of the working class on the rise of Perón.**

Political sovereignty: The role of the state in society

In the light of the social conflicts that needed to be addressed, Perón gave great importance to the role of the state. Under the governments that had preceded the 1943 coup, the state had represented the interests of a specific social class, the landowners. Perón proposed a change in how the state stood in relation to the different social classes. It was the role of the state to determine the aims of the country and mobilize all necessary resources to achieve them. The state stood above all social classes and was understood as the engine of progress. As such, it had to play an active part in social and economic developments, mediating where interests clashed.

SOURCE I

[The aim is to] improve the standards of living of the workers but without tolerating social conflict… I shall not allow free rein to the agents of destruction and unrest, who are often not even Argentines but foreigners. I have working class issues completely under control, not by force but through agreements. Don't believe we are anti-capitalists. We are not.

From a statement by Juan Domingo Perón in November 1943, quoted in David Rock, *Authoritarian Argentina: The Nationalist Movement, its History and its Impact*, 1993

STUDENT STUDY SECTION

QUESTIONS

a) **What is the message of Source I?**

b) **Identify the 'agents of destruction and unrest' to whom Perón referred.**

c) **What elements of the Peronist ideology surface in this source?**

Economic independence: An appeal to nationalist elements

To prevent crises like the one experienced in the 1930s, Perón believed that Argentina needed to become economically independent. This focus raised two main issues: the achievement of autarky (self-sufficiency) and the **nationalization** of foreign companies operating in Argentina. The mechanism for achieving economic independence was to centralize economic activity in the hands of the state. The model proposed by Perón was one in which Argentina would develop a national industry to satisfy its domestic needs and demands. To do this, **protectionist** policies had to be applied and foreign-owned companies nationalized.

SOURCE J

The Peronist economic reform had two main purposes. One was to preserve the country's resources from the appetites of foreign interests and to put them at the service of the state. The other was to divide up those resources fairly so that there would be no excessively wealthy people at the expense of excessively poor ones. Policy directors did not speak of socialism, of course, but rather of the social reform of the capitalist system: the capitalist system would remain in place but it would be restricted by state management.

From Mónica Esti Rein, *Politics and Education in Argentina, 1946–1962*, 1998

STUDENT STUDY SECTION

QUESTIONS

a) **Why, according to Source J, did Perón favour nationalization of foreign companies?**

b) **In what ways does Source J relate the concept of economic independence to the principles of social justice and political sovereignty?**

c) **'Promises of improved social and economic conditions win more support for would-be single-party rulers than ideological pronouncements.' How far do you agree with this claim?**

Nationalization
The acquisition by the state of property previously owned by private individuals or companies.

Protectionism
Government policies promoting home industries by preventing the competition of foreign goods. The importation of foreign goods is checked or discouraged by the imposition of duties (tariffs), quotas or other regulations.

● **Examiner's hint**
Questions that ask that you to assess the validity of a claim require that you first show understanding of the claim itself. In the case of Question C below, you need to show that you understand the difference between the promises made and the ideological pronouncements. Do you consider Perón offered both? If so, which were they? Which of them was more effective in winning support? It will not be enough to say that you agree, in Perón's case, that promises of better conditions gained him more support than explanations of his ideological stance. You will need to give specific examples of both and analyze why one became more effective than the other. You may consider them both to have been equally important, but again, you will have to explain why and how.

● **Examiner's hint**
An introduction is an opportunity for you to show the examiner you have understood the question. In this sense, the introduction here would have benefited from an explicit definition of 'ideological pronouncements'.

Read the following introduction from a student essay:

Student Answer – *Michael*

It is often said that crisis situations lead to the rise of authoritarian states. These situations include the negative outcome of wars, economic problems and civil unrest. The Argentina of the 1940s, however, was not a country in economic ruins; its population was not being affected by the course of World War II and, although there were social problems, the situation was not one of instability. Yet, between 1946 and 1946 Juan Perón organized a political party that promised to bring about changes that a significant part of society considered attractive enough to support. With limited ideological pronouncements and a wider use of promises of social justice and economic independence, Perón won the Presidential elections in 1946. To what extent did Perón's promises play a more important role than the ideological pronouncements in gaining support for his movement?

Examiner's comments

Here is a very interesting opening, which shows a comprehensive understanding of the rise of single-party and authoritarian states. The student also shows some understanding of the conditions against which Perón came to power. From what is offered in this introductory paragraph, it is expected that the candidate will follow by providing information about which particular sectors found Perón's promises appealing and more detail as to the reasons why this was so. For example, what did Perón mean by 'social justice'? What specific promises did he make in relation to these goals? To whom were these promises directed? Which 'ideological pronouncements', if any, did Perón make?

The road to the presidency: October 1945 to February 1946

Perón became the President of Argentina in February 1946, elected by universal male suffrage. This victory had its roots in many of the issues you have studied: the conditions of Argentina, the methods used by Perón to address these conditions, and his gathering support. But the period from 17 October 1945 to February 1946 requires separate analysis. It is here we see how and why Perón became a near-mythical figure.

In March 1945, as we have seen, the government of President Farrell declared war on Germany and Japan. This decision was taken at a time when there was little doubt about the Allied victory in the conflict. It increased the unpopularity of the 1943 government, which had hesitated to break relations with the Axis powers and had taken so long to declare war on the Axis. Neutrality had always been viewed as implicit support for Germany rather than the consequence of the traditional isolation of Argentina. Elections could not be postponed much longer as violent outbreaks and demonstrations against the government took place in several cities. Yet the rising status of Colonel Perón and his accumulation of power worried several sectors of society.

Who opposed Perón and why?

Industrialists and businessmen disliked the effects of Perón's labour legislation and claimed it had raised the costs of production. They frowned at Perón's reference to a strong state, as they sensed state interference in the economy of the country and feared more government intrusion. Landowners, by contrast, saw their traditional relations with the rural workers affected by the Peasant Statute. Socialist or communist trade unionists felt they were losing influence, as Perón favoured the establishment of parallel unions loyal to him.

Traditional political parties – which had been suspended in 1943 – demanded free elections. At the same time, they worried that Perón would become the official candidate and use the state apparatus, including the media and the labour organizations, to win power. Intellectuals, university teachers and newspapers that had suffered censorship and bans questioned President Farrell and the growing power of Perón, and accused them of wanting to establish a fascist dictatorship in Argentina.

By 1944, Perón was living with Eva Duarte, at that time an actress. Traditionalist Catholic members of the armed forces were unhappy with Perón's 'lack of morals'. They also questioned his revolutionary style, and many complained that he was concentrating too much power in his hands.

SOURCE K

In view of his failure to attract business groups to his heterogeneous coalition, and aware that in such circumstances the working class sector's support was crucial, Perón radicalised his speech. He began to characterise his base of support as 'the people', while referring to the opposition as the 'oligarchy'. With the approach of the February elections, it became obvious that Perón was succeeding in displacing the terms of the debate from the political to the social sphere.

From Mariano Ben Plotkin, *Mañana es San Perón: A Cultural History of Perón's Argentina*, 2003

STUDENT STUDY SECTION

QUESTIONS

a) **Look up the term 'oligarchy'. Find out how it was used and why it had such negative connotations in Peronist Argentina.**
b) **Explain 'Perón was succeeding in displacing the terms of the debate from the political to the social sphere.'**

As a response to pressure from within and outside the armed forces, on 8 October 1945 the government announced that Perón had resigned from all his positions. Farrell agreed to Perón's dismissal, but allowed him to address the people 'for the last time' from the balcony of the Secretariat of Labour and Welfare and on a nationwide radio broadcast.

SOURCE L

We set our incorruptible and untameable position against the oligarchy. We think that the workers should trust themselves and remember the emancipation of the working class is in the workers' own hands... We will prevail within a year or within ten, but we will prevail... I put myself at the service of the people, and I am willing to serve it with all my energies... And if some day, to awake that faith, it is necessary, I will join a union and I will fight from below. Victory does not come through violence; it is conquered with intelligence and organization... I ask, therefore, the maximum of tranquillity from all the workers of the country; tranquillity and calm is what we need to continue structuring our organizations and make them so powerful that in the future they may become invincible. I ask for order so that we can continue ahead in our triumphant march but if necessary, some day I might request war.

From Juan D. Perón's farewell speech on 10 October 1945

Plaza de Mayo

Plaza de Mayo is the square that stands before the government house. It is an historic site in Buenos Aires, and was where the first patriotic government was declared, in 1810. Ever since, it has been a centre of political expression.

Descamisados

It is uncertain who coined this term. Joseph Page attributes it to the newspaper *La Epoca* in its account of the events of 17 October. Regardless of who invented the term, it was soon adopted by Perón to refer to his followers.

The events of 17 October

Perón's resignation did not appease the opposition, who saw in his speech a strategy to get his followers to oppose the measure. On 12 October, a civilian demonstration against the military regime demanded that power be passed to the Supreme Court of Justice and elections held immediately. At the same time, members of the armed forces who opposed Perón demanded that he be arrested. The colonel was sent to an island off the coast of Buenos Aires, Martín García.

That night it seemed that anti-Peronist and anti-workers forces would prevail. However, the CGT announced a general strike for 18 October, making no explicit reference to Perón but calling for action in defence of the labour legislation. The day before the strike, on 17 October, thousands of workers abandoned their posts and began to march towards the centre of Buenos Aires to demand the release of the 'colonel of the people'.

Buenos Aires had never seen such a thing. The city had a very formal dress code in the 1940s: everyone in town wore hats, dark suits and ties. Even the workers carried their work clothes in a bag and wore suits and hats when they had to go downtown. Suddenly, on 17 October, thousands of people in their work clothes and with bare heads began to move into the most residential neighbourhoods of Buenos Aires, on their way to the Casa Rosada (Pink House), the seat of the Argentine government, to demand Perón's release. It was a very hot spring day; to the shock of the neighbours, they freshened up in the fountains of the **Plaza de Mayo**. It was as if a different Argentina, one the higher classes had excluded, had suddenly emerged. Thousands of citizens, who until then had not dared occupy the public spaces of Buenos Aires, now appeared. They were Perón's followers, his *descamisados* ('shirtless') as they were called thereafter. Participants shouted 'We want Perón' and refused to disperse to their homes until they saw him.

It is of relatively minor importance whether the demonstration of 17 October was organized by the CGT, if Eva Perón played a leading part in it, or whether it was a spontaneous event. What is of great significance is that those people in the plaza had found a leader and were able to put so much pressure on the government to force its hand and obtain the release of Perón.

Look at the photograph above. Describe the image to the rest of your class, taking one of the following roles: a) a participant in the demonstration in support of Perón; b) a member of the elite in Buenos Aires; c) a member of the government in October 1945. Other students should describe the photograph from the other perspectives.

Account for the similarities and differences in these descriptions.

Questions

a) 'Context is all'. To what extent are our experiences of events determined by the context in which we live? What constitutes such context?

b) What are the implications of all of the above for the study of history?

SOURCE M

My father was a socialist, we were in the plaza… It was dark now and people lit newspapers and used them as torches. The night air and the humidity of the river could be felt on the skin. It was almost 10 o'clock and I looked at my father, as if saying: 'It is cold; let's go home.' He gave me one of those looks that one never forgets as if saying: 'Nobody moves from here!' The arrival, the liberation of Perón was imminent. I was in the centre of a scene that divided the history of Argentina in two.

Extract from an eyewitness's account of the events of 17 October

---

STUDENT STUDY SECTION

QUESTIONS

a) **What is the message of Source M?**

b) **In context, what is the significance of 'My father was a socialist'?**

c) **With reference to its origins and purpose, assess the value and limitations of Source M and the photo in the ToK box above to an historian studying the impact of the events of 17 October.**

The government, fearful of the reaction of the crowd, ordered Perón's release and brought him before the people to show he was well. Perón addressed 150,000 people who had gathered in Plaza de Mayo. He was greeted by an ovation that lasted 15 minutes. After he spoke, they all went home.

A mass of people gathered in Plaza de Mayo on 17 October 1945.

SOURCE N

I also give the first embrace to this great mass, which represents the synthesis of a feeling that was dead in the republic: the true civility of the Argentine people. You are the people… This is the true celebration of democracy, represented by the people who have walked for hours to come to demand that the government respects their authentic rights… As from this hour, historic for the Republic, may Colonel Perón become the link to make the brotherhood of people, the army and the police unbreakable; may this union be eternal and infinite so that our people do not only possess happiness, but may be able to defend it with dignity… Workers! Be united; today more than ever… Every day, we shall incorporate into this enormous body the unruly and discontented so that, along with us, they be merged into this patriotic and beautiful mass that you form.

From speech by Juan Perón to the people gathered at Plaza de Mayo, 17 October 1945

STUDENT STUDY SECTION

QUESTIONS

Looking at Source N:

a) **Explain 'You are the people.' To whom was Perón referring?**

b) **How would you describe the tone of Perón's speech?**

c) **With reference to its origins and purpose, assess the value and limitations of this source for an historian studying the events of 17 October.**

d) **How does this source help you understand the significance of 17 October and the reasons why it went down in Argentine history as 'Loyalty Day'?**

The events of 17 October sealed the relationship between Perón and the workers. They had first supported him to maintain their legal and economic gains, but somehow Perón emerged from the events strengthened and as the potential future President of Argentina.

SOURCE O

*It caused us a lot of pain to find out he had been detained, but we considered ourselves
unable to do much about it because we were just beginning to awake, after many years, in
this country. Our conscience began on 17th of October. We started to believe something which
Perón proclaimed daily and that was that we had the right to be respected as people. Because
of this, although we believed ourselves helpless, we felt we could do something about it: rescue
Perón from the clutches of the oligarchy and put him in the place he belonged and make lasting
justice. We had never experienced the idealism we then had in the country. I never thought
there would be so many people in the Plaza.*

Extract from the testimony of a worker who participated in events on 17 October 1945

STUDENT STUDY SECTION

QUESTIONS

a) **What light does Source O throw on the conditions of workers before Perón?**

b) **According to Source O, what was the significance of the events of 17
October? What, according to the worker, changed since?**

The elections of February 1946

Following the events of 17 October, Perón began to campaign for the presidency. He did
not have a party structure of his own, but obtained the support of the Labour Party (which
named him as a candidate), of the Peronist trade unions and of the Unión Cívica Radical
Junta Renovadora (UCRJR; Renewed Board of the Civil Radical Union), a part of the UCR
radical party.

The opposition to Perón, Unión Democrática (UD; Democratic Union), had two main
problems. First, it lacked cohesion. It was a very heterogeneous organization, which included
conservatives, communists, socialists and a faction of the UCR. It had the support of the
different sectors of society that were opposed to Perón's policies and methods, such as the
landowning classes, many industrialists, businessmen and members of the middle class.
Although they represented different sectors and interests, this worked against the UD
because it was difficult for the party to agree on specific proposals that would please all
represented sectors. Also, the UD candidate, radical José P. Tamborini, lacked popular appeal.

The second problem for the opposition was the figure of the US ambassador in Argentina,
Spruille Braden. Just before the elections, Braden published the **Blue Book** in which he
described Perón as a Nazi agent. Braden openly supported the opposition to Perón, but
his support of the UD played against their interests. Perón responded with the Blue and
White Book (the colour scheme based on the national colours of Argentina). He accused
the USA of interfering in the domestic policies of Argentina. Perón criticized the opposition
by saying that they were not only 'oligarchic', but that they were associated with foreign
imperialists and, consequently, were 'anti-fatherland'. With a view to the elections that were
announced for February 1946, Perón managed to portray himself as a leader who defended
the gains in social justice and who could safeguard the nation against the imperialists,
which he identified with the UD and Braden.

Two months before the elections, the government granted a Christmas bonus to all workers,
together with other social benefits. The employers complained that they did not have the
time to make provisions for this extra pay and the UD supported them in their claim. This
situation also helped Perón for two reasons. First, it appeared that if he lost the elections,
these and possibly other benefits would be lost. Second, it weakened the appeal of socialist

Blue Book
This document aimed at
showing there had been
links between Argentina
and the former Axis. A
major contributor was
US Ambassador Spruille
Braden, who was working
in the US Department
of State. The document
was presented with blue
covers, which explains why
it became known as the
Blue Book.

and communist parties, which as part of the UD became associated with the denial of rights to workers.

Perón won the elections held in February 1946 by 55 per cent of the votes.

STUDENT STUDY SECTION

QUESTIONS

Consider the following task: 'Analyze the conditions and methods of Perón's rise to power.' Read the examiner's hint for guidance.

Now consider the following question: To what extent is organization more important than ideology in the rise of single-party states? Read the conclusion of the student essay below.

Student Answer – Angela

Conclusion:

During his rise, Perón did not make his ideology too clear. He referred to certain concepts such as 'economic freedom', 'social justice' and 'political independence', but he used these terms in a relatively loose way. He did not explain clearly and explicitly how he meant to attain these ideological objectives. On the other hand, he made intensive use of trade unions, the Labour Party and mass rallies to spread his popularity, as shown both by the events of 17 October 1945, and his victory in the 1946 elections. For Perón, organization played a greater role than ideology.

Examiner's comments

This conclusion focuses on the question clearly and shows which ideological elements and which organizational aspects played a role on the rise of Perón. The candidate comes to a conclusion, that organization played a greater role. Perhaps the conclusion could have been more specific as to how exactly organization contributed to Perón's rise: why were the roles of the trade unions, Labour Party and the mass rallies significant? Why did ideological considerations seem less important at this stage?

● **Examiner's hint**

Some Paper 2 questions ask you to refer to the conditions and the methods that explain the rise of a leader. These questions provide you with an opportunity to demonstrate analytical skills and explain how the conditions determined the methods used. In the specific case of Perón, you could identify the lack of faith in leadership after the Infamous Decade as a condition, and then explore the methods used by Perón to appear as someone prepared to lead and produce changes. Consider, for example, how the events of 17 October contributed to the rise to power of Perón.

Section II:
The rule of Juan Perón (1946–55)

Now that you are familiar with how and why Perón came to power, this section will explain how he consolidated his position after the elections. It will also look at the social, political and economic policies of his first and second presidencies (1946–52 and 1952–55). It will analyze the impact of domestic policies on culture and education; the status of women; the nature and extent of opposition; and Perón's religious policies.

Perón's consolidation of power

Together with the presidency, Perón obtained a majority in the **Argentine parliament**. But this did not mean his position in power was secure.

Argentine parliament ⓘ
Under the 1853 constitution, Argentina adopted a presidential system. Legislative power was held by a parliament divided into two chambers: the Chamber of Deputies and the Senate. Members of both chambers were elected by universal male suffrage and represented the different provinces into which the country was divided.

SOURCE A

The Peronist and UCRJR coalition elected all of the national senators except two. In the chamber of deputies, where minority representation was constitutionally ordained, it still won an astonishing two-thirds majority. And in the provinces it won governorships and legislative majorities everywhere except in Corrientes. No such broad mandate had ever been given in

Argentina… In an electoral context that required more in the way of coalition management and sacrifice than had any other, the parties of the UD had generally been unable to agree on joint tickets for national offices below the presidential level and for provincial offices. They therefore ran separate tickets for these and they lost everything to the Peronist coalition, whose own serious unity problems were less extreme.

From Robert D. Crassweller, *Péron and the Enigmas of Argentina*, 1987

● **Examiner's hint**
Paper 2 questions ask about the methods used by leaders to come to power. They may have used force, legal methods or a combination of both. Perón's rise was inaugurated with a military coup in 1943 and ended with his election as President in 1946. How would you then explain the methods used by Perón? How do the methods used by Perón compare to those used by other leaders you have studied?

STUDENT STUDY SECTION

QUESTIONS

a) What reasons does Source A above give for the defeat of the UD?

b) According to Source A, how decisive was Perón's victory in the elections?

As President, Perón began to work towards consolidating his position. Victory in the polls had granted him something more important than a majority in the Chambers or the control of the provinces. His victory was legitimate; he was a constitutional President elected in one of the cleanest elections in Argentine history. Even when demonstrations of support had crowded the streets of Buenos Aires, Perón knew he owed much of his success to the CGT, which had backed him on 17 October, and to the Labour Party, which had served Perón as a political platform to win the elections. Perón did not have the support of the entire armed forces, as those sectors that had been suspicious of him remained so. The same could be said about the civilian population. Although Perón was now President, his position was not fully secured.

The first measure Perón took to consolidate his position was to dissolve all the forces that had supported him in the campaign, including the Labour Party. He replaced them with a single party, the Partido Unico de la Revolución (PUR; Sole Party of the Revolution), later to become the Partido Justicialista or Peronista. This party was under his personal control and became part of the state apparatus.

The dissolution of the Labour Party was met with resistance from their leaders, but they could do little to prevent it. The President of the Labour Party, Luis Gay, who was also Secretary General of the CGT and had supported Perón's rise, was removed from the leadership of the CGT in 1947. Cipriano Reyes, a Labour Party leader who had been until then an unconditional supporter of Perón, formed an independent Labour bloc in the Chamber of Deputies. From his seat, he accused Perón of wanting to become a dictator. In 1948, when his term as deputy came to an end, he was arrested and tortured. Reyes remained imprisoned until Perón's fall in 1955.

The Peronist Party naturally had to respect Perón's leadership. Candidates for the different offices, such as Governors, Deputies and Senators, were appointed by Perón without consultation or internal elections. Once elected to parliament, Peronist representatives had to vote with the party rather than follow their conscience.

Next, Perón moved to discipline the unions. He ordered all trade unions to become members of the official CGT. Those unionists who opposed the measure were persecuted and imprisoned. By 1948, Perón had consolidated his leadership over the party and the trade unions had been united under the CGT.

Labour Party leader, Cipriano Reyes.

Political policies

During Perón's rule, the state apparatus grew in size and influence, centralizing decision-making and policy implementation. Although parliament was never closed under Perón, it became very difficult for the opposition to influence government policies.

● **Examiner's hint**

The section of Paper 2 this book prepares you for is 'Origins and development of authoritarian and single-party states'. Argentina under Perón did not strictly fit the definition of a single-party state. Other political parties continued to exist under Perón; parliament remained open and elections took place as stated by the constitution. Perón's efforts to centralize decision-making and to limit the role of the opposition show that Peronist Argentina qualifies better as an authoritarian state. The prevailing viewpoint of the Peronists was the belief that people need authority and discipline and those should come from an executive power that centralizes authority. However, Peronism has been categorized as a single-party ideology by those historians who have argued that opposition existed in name only and Perón ruled as if it did not exist. Read about the treatment of opposition under Perón to come to your own conclusions on the matter.

Political parties found it very difficult to work in Congress. This was partly because of problems within the opposition parties. It took the Radical Party a long time to overcome the rift created by UCRJR support for Perón in 1946. Unable to compromise and form a joint front against Peronism, each party adopted different strategies, ranging from abstention to obstruction and open confrontation, none of which advanced their cause. The opposition had limited access to the media and the press, and their meetings were frequently disbanded by the police. The opposition was also more influential amongst more experienced politicians, as most of the Peronist representatives were new to parliamentary life, but they were unable to make their experience count in any significant way. Some radical leaders who voiced their anti-Peronism passionately were expelled from the legislative body or even jailed. Three members of the Supreme Court of Justice were accused of malfeasance, impeached and convicted. New judges were appointed and the Court was 'Peronized'.

SOURCE B

A protest march against Perón takes to the streets of Buenos Aires.

QUESTION

What is the message conveyed by Source B?

During Perón's first term in office, the Secretariat of Information was established with the aim of controlling the outputs of journalists. The government implemented censorship against some publications, such as the socialist newspaper *La Vanguardia*. National newspapers *La Nación* and *La Prensa*, which were critical of the regime, had their supply of paper restricted. The government bought newspapers, magazines and radio stations to use them for propaganda.

SOURCE C

Between 1943 and 1946, 110 publications in the country were forced to close, although many simply continued to publish underground. In 1949, when La Nación *published information about the torture of those who opposed Peronism, the government forces immediately went to work to make it nearly impossible for the paper to continue to be published. They subjected the offices to bogus inspections in an effort to find justification for closing it down, and they attempted to curtail the connection between the newspapers and those who provided them with paper. Official radio programs were established to refute the daily editorials that emerged on the pages of* La Prensa *and* La Nación. *In 1951 Perón's patience with* La Prensa *ran out. It was decided that the newspaper, the most prestigious one in the city with the highest circulation and the one considered by many to be the most credible, was shut down. The newspaper reappeared later in the year under a new pro-Perón directorship.*

From David William Foster, Melissa Fitch Lockhart and Darrell B. Lockhart, *Culture and Customs of Argentina*, 1998

QUESTIONS

a) **What methods of controlling the press are described by Source C?**

b) **Why do you think the government chose to use 'bogus inspections' or cut the connections with the providers of paper?**

c) **Is there evidence in this source that the pressure on the media was not as effective as expected?**

RESEARCH ACTIVITY

In groups, find additional information about the methods used by Perón to control the media.

Civil servants had to become members of the Peronist Party to keep their jobs. Education, as we shall later discuss, was also subjected to state control. Criminal laws were passed to discourage expressions of dissent and participants in any strike that the government declared illegal were punished.

SOURCE D

I don't understand why Perón insisted in imposing a repressive apparatus when, no doubt, the 1946 elections had been a high point in an electoral career that continued to rise. Some offer a psychological explanation, attributing to him an authoritarian Nazi mind. I do not think that is enough. What motivated Perón – despite his personal innate optimism – was that he thought popularity would be exhausted and he would need his repressive apparatus at some point in time. But of course these are guesses. Perón failed to recognize that this apparatus existed.

Talking to him [in 1970], I explained that there was imprisonment, torture and excesses, but he always had explanations to offer. When – desperate because I was unable to establish a common ground for discussion – I said 'Look, general, I was held captive and tortured', he looked amazed and said 'Where?', as if he was about to tell off the superintendent at that very moment.

From an interview with Argentine historian Félix Luna

STUDENT STUDY SECTION

QUESTIONS

a) **Compare and contrast the views on the treatment of opposition expressed in Sources C and D.**

b) **With reference to its origin and purpose, assess the value and limitations of Source D for an historian studying the treatment of opposition to Perón.**

Perón's star continued to rise. The Peronists won the parliamentary elections held in 1948 with 62 per cent of the votes. That year, Perón obtained approval to call for a Constituent Assembly to reform the constitution. The majority in parliament and the new constitution enabled him to continue with the reforms by legal means. Although the 1948 political successes can be partly explained by the limited opportunities of the opposition to reach the population, a more likely explanation lies in the social and economic benefits people enjoyed and which were attributed to Perón at a personal level.

The 1949 constitution

Perón claimed that the new social rights and the reinforced role of the state had to be incorporated in the constitution. A convention to carry out the constitutional reforms was elected and formed by a majority of Peronists and a minority of radicals. The other parties had not obtained sufficient votes to appoint representatives.

The 1949 constitution did not create an entire new order, but introduced changes to the original constitution of 1853. One of the most important changes was the reform of Article 77 to allow the President to stand for immediate re-election. Prior to 1949, a President had to step down at least for one term before he could be re-elected. This reform eliminated that obstacle, although at the time Perón claimed he had no intention of running for re-election.

The approval of the new constitution demonstrated once more that the strategies used to limit Perón were not effective. The radicals withdrew from the debates of the convention to express their disagreement with the Peronist character of the document. The convention, now populated by the Peronists alone, passed the constitution, which remained in place until 1956.

The nature of the 1949 constitution was nationalist and emphasized the strong role of the state. The state had a right to intervene – and even monopolize – certain economic areas, such as foreign trade. In other words, the state could decide what should be imported and exported and fix the prices. Other elements of the constitution included the following:

- It gave a special place to the family; this was seen positively by the Catholics. The state had a duty to protect the institution of marriage and to assist mothers and children. The elderly were the legal responsibility of their families.

- All public services were now nationalized and put under the control of the state, which would either buy or expropriate those in private or foreign hands.
- All sources of energy, such as oil, coal and gas, were also national property and could not be sold.
- Property and capital, according to the constitution, had to fulfil a social role and belong to those who would work them. This article ended the inviolability of private property and opened the possibility of implementing policies leading to the redistribution of land.

STUDENT STUDY SECTION

QUESTIONS

a) **Explain to what extent the 1949 constitution reflected the aims of a 'politically sovereign, socially just, and economically independent nation'.**

b) **Make a list of the political policies implemented by Perón. To what extent did each of them contribute to strengthen the role of the state?**

c) **Explain why, despite parliamentary representation, the opposition seemed unable to limit the power of the government? Remember to refer to both the actions of the opposition and those of the government. Make reference to specific examples.**

Social policies

It was in the field of social policies that Argentina experienced the deepest changes under Perón. When looking at the conditions that explained the rise of Perón, you have examined the social problems of the new working class as well as the problems of the Argentine infrastructure. You have also analyzed the work of Perón as Secretary of Labour. This section will evaluate the social policies implemented under Perón in an attempt to establish the extent to which they explain the support for the regime.

Based on the idea of making the state an instrument to achieve social justice, the social policies of Peronism aimed at redressing the existing gaps between rich and poor, and between Buenos Aires and the rest of the country. When Perón came to power, the limited social aid offered by the government was very inefficient. There was consensus among different political parties as well as the Catholic Church that the system needed to undergo reforms.

As in other areas, the Peronist government acted with the idea of centralizing social policies to make them more efficient. Until then, independent charitable institutions – which received economic support from the state as well as private donations – and trade unions channelled social work to reach where the state did not offer solutions. Perón was determined to centralize the social policies and aid and to ensure they became accessible to all Argentines. The trade unions opposed this plan, as they were reluctant to lose control of the money they had at their disposal for social policies directed at their members. Perón was essentially a pragmatist and was not prepared to lose the support of the unions. So, in 1948, he decided to centralize social aid through a new and parallel organization, the Fundación Eva Perón (FEP; Eva Perón Foundation). The FEP was organized and led by Perón's wife, Eva.

Eva was also the creator of many of the social policies implemented. The FEP's work focused on many different areas, such as the welfare of children and the elderly; healthcare; housing; recreation; the provision of working tools. Educational facilities, hospitals equipped with modern technology, and houses were built in working-class suburbs. Orphanages, elderly homes and workers' resorts were inaugurated. In addition, a nursing school was established to meet the training demands of the hospitals. Sanitation campaigns were organized, including a hospital train that travelled across Argentina to detect cases of malnutrition, perform surgery, carry out vaccination campaigns and implement other forms of preventive medicine. Also, individuals who wanted to gain a skill could receive training from the government and all the necessary equipment to work.

SOURCE E

By the end of the 1940s [the FEP] exceeded, in size, in influence, and in general significance, most of the ministries of the government. Its assets exceeded $200 million. It had 14,000 permanent employees, including thousands of construction workers and a staff of priests. It acquired for distribution to the poor fantastic amounts of supplies, such as 200,000 cooking pots, 400,000 pairs of shoes, 500,000 sewing machines. Its flood of revenues came from many sources. Labor unions donated cash and goods made in the factories where members worked. The first few weeks of a pay raise would be donated to the foundation. The CGT contributed three man-days (later reduced to two) of salary for every worker it represented. A tax on lottery and movie tickets and a levy on casino revenues and admissions to horse races were fruitful… There were also a few cases of contributions that came by way of extortion.

From Robert D. Crassweller, *Perón and the Enigmas of Argentina,* 1987

STUDENT STUDY SECTION

QUESTIONS

a) What light does Source E throw on the significance of the work of the FEP?

b) How does it describe the relationship between the FEP and the trade unions?

c) In what ways is the organization and operation of the FEP consistent with the Peronist principles you have studied?

Eva made it clear that the work of the FEP was not charity; the organization aimed at giving people enough of what was rightfully theirs to restore their self-esteem. To respond to all their demands, and coordinate the efforts of the FEP, Eva Perón worked very long hours and was personally involved in many of the logistical aspects of the campaigns. She read the letters that asked for assistance and received hundreds of people in her office.

SOURCE F

There were groups of workers; union leaders; peasant women with their children; foreign journalists; a gaucho family with their ponchos, the man with his long and silky huge black whiskers; there were refugees from behind the Iron Curtain; people who had come from post-war Europe; intellectuals and university professors from the Baltic States; priests and monks; fat, clamorous and sweaty middle-aged women; young clerks and football players; actors and people from the circus… [And] in the midst of this apparent chaos, this noisy and confused kermesse, Evita listened to whatever was asked of her, from a simple demand for increased wages, to an entire industry-wide settlement and along the way a request for a place for a family to live, furniture, for a job in a school, food… Evita was inexhaustible. She kept the momentum of this show running for hours, often well after nightfall.

From Victoria Ana Goddard (ed.), *Gender, Agency, and Change: Anthropological Perspectives,* 2000

SOURCE G

Photograph showing Eva Perón receiving petitions at the FEP.

The Peronist social policies contributed to many improvements in Argentine society. However, the FEP also played a significant part in shaping the cult of Eva Perón, who became known as the 'lady of hope', 'the mother of the innocent' and, later, 'the spiritual leader of the nation'. The cult of Eva bordered on religious adoration, particularly after her death in 1952. She publicly subordinated herself to Juan Perón, saying she liked to think of herself as bridge between Perón and the masses. But the truth is that Eva was second to none after President Perón.

To access Worksheet 2.2 on Perón's social policies, please visit www. pearsonbacconline.com and follow the on-screen instructions.

STUDENT STUDY SECTION

QUESTION
Consider the following question: 'Assess the impact of Perón's social policies on Argentina up to 1955.'

Sample Answer – *Arturo*

Perón promised to improve the living conditions of the workers and he did. Most occupations were unionized, extending rights to workers such as paid holidays and the right to a minimum wage. Hospitals and schools were opened in regions that had had limited access to health and education in the past. The Foundation led by his wife, Eva, extended benefits to people who had until then been neglected by the state and more traditional charity institutions. People wanting to work were given tools and land. Rents were made more affordable and new housing projects offered many the opportunity to have their first homes.

Examiner's comments

This paragraph makes reference to many of the social policies implemented by Perón. However, it is not enough for you to show that you know which policies were implemented. To answer this question effectively, you are required to show the impact they had. In other words, you need to show which social problems existed before Perón, which specific policies were implemented to address those problems and, finally, you need to assess their effect. A more effective approach to this question would be to take the policies individually in order to assess their impact on Argentine society.

Status of women

As soon as he came to power, Perón made it clear that he wished to improve the social and political status of women. In 1946, women were excluded from political participation – they could neither vote nor be elected. They were also subjected to different forms of exploitation at work, such as receiving lower salaries than men for similar jobs. This inequality, together with the prevailing idea in many sectors of society that the woman's place was in the home, meant that by 1947 more than 60 per cent of women did not work outside their homes.

It was not until Perón came to power that women were granted the right to vote and be elected, although the idea had been expressed by both radicals and socialists in the past. In 1947, a law that enabled all women in Argentina to vote was passed. Argentine women voted for the first time in the presidential elections of 1951, in which Perón was elected for a second term.

Perón aimed at expanding his base of support. The new legislation contributed immensely to this end; 90% per cent of the women registered voted in 1951 and Perón obtained 64 per cent among female voters. The second reason to incorporate women in political life was that, as mothers, they were essential for taking Peronism into the home.

SOURCE H

To be a Peronist for a woman means, above all, fidelity to Perón, subordination to Perón, and blind confidence in Perón… All of us [women], with no exception, from the one who considers herself to be the humblest, to the one who is considered by her companions to be the most efficient and the smartest, are not, nor expect to be, anything else but General Perón's helpers.

From a speech by Eva Perón in 1951, quoted in Mariano Ben Plotkin, *Mañana es San Perón: A Cultural History of Perón's Argentina*, 2003

STUDENT STUDY SECTION

QUESTIONS

a) What, according to Source H, was the role of women in Perón's government?

b) To what extent is Source H consistent with the Peronist ideology? Explain your answer fully.

A female branch of the Peronist Party, the Partido Peronista Femenino (PPF), was formed under Eva's command. The PPF appointed delegates who were then personally instructed by Eva Perón to travel across the country to affiliate other women to the party.

Although the political status of women improved, women did not experience a significant change in their role in society. Peronist principles shared with Catholicism the value given to the role of the family and, within it, to women as mothers and wives. Therefore unlike, for example, Cuba under Castro, where women were mobilized to join the workforce, there was no massive campaign for women to join the labour force in Argentina.

SOURCE I

It would be a mistake, however, to think that Peronism freed women from their traditional roles in society. They were given political rights, it is true, but their real standing in society did not change radically. Women continued to figure in textbooks as mothers caring for their children, their workplace usually the home, and their business the family. Eva Peron herself explained to Argentine women what a woman's purpose should be. In a section headed 'The Home or the Factory' in her book **La razón de mi vida***, the president's wife explained that a woman's place was in the home.*

From Mónica Esti Rein, *Politics and Education in Argentina, 1946–1962*, 1998

STUDENT STUDY SECTION

DISCUSSION ACTIVITY

Using these sources and your own knowledge, discuss the view that single-party states allow women to play a fuller role in society. You may refer to the status of women in other single-party regimes you have studied.

Education, the arts and propaganda

This section analyzes the policies implemented by Perón to address the problems in the field of education. It also addresses the relationship between the Peronist government and intellectuals and the use of propaganda made by the former.

Education

Perón was very critical of the education system he had inherited. Although the level of illiteracy in Argentina had been historically low, particularly when compared to other countries in the region, access to education was limited by several factors. There were economic factors, but there was also the fact that, particularly in the provinces of the interior, schools were few and far apart.

Like other aspects of life under Perón's rule, education and culture came under state control. The aim to build a 'new Argentina' required a revolution in the education system. Two areas of education had to change: access to the system and the ideas that education taught.

La razón de mi vida
This book, published in 1951, is often presented as Eva's autobiography. However, the focus is not her life and it would be more accurate to see it as a political manifesto that explains Peronism and the reasons for the policies that the government implemented. In this work, Eva showed total devotion and submission to Perón. The book became compulsory reading in Argentine primary schools.

To access Worksheet 2.3 on Eva Perón and the role of women, please visit www.pearsonbacconline.com and follow the on-screen instructions.

● **Examiner's hint**
A good starting point for this activity would be to define what you understand by 'a fuller role in society'. Were improvements in women's political rights reflected in a wider participation in society? If women entered the workforce in greater numbers as a result of government policies, did it necessarily mean their role in society was 'fuller'? Some regimes may offer you the possibility of focusing on specific cases of women who played a significant part, such as Eva Perón in Argentina or Celia Sánchez and Vilma Espín in Cuba. But to what extent are these cases representative of the role of women in general?

In order to achieve his aims, Perón promoted a centrally planned and organized education system. The Perón administration expanded existing schools to host more pupils, while it also led a campaign to build new schools where they were needed. The government offered free transportation to and from schools for those living far from an educational centre. It provided free meals for students and granted scholarships. Vocational schools and schools for adults were opened; public universities were made free. A wide range of educational options became available to people who until then had been marginalized from these opportunities. The budget allocated to education increased steadily during the Peronist years.

New textbooks for all levels of education were commissioned by a committee of experts. These textbooks all had to include: the words of the national anthem; the preamble to the 1949 constitution; the declarations of political and economic independence and reference to 'People's Loyalty Day' (17 October 1945). After 1952, Eva Perón's *La razón de mi vida* ('My Mission in Life') became mandatory reading.

Teachers who did not declare themselves Peronist soon found themselves out of the system. In 1945, Perón said: 'I have always said that we do not want to mix politics with teaching, but I have also always thought that in Argentine schools… we cannot tolerate the activities of those who do not agree with the National Doctrine that the people have adopted in order to construct their present happiness and the future greatness of the Fatherland.'

SOURCE J

The committee obviously took its mandate seriously: to propose a way of developing new books that would reflect 'the new Argentina' and its values. These books were supposed to convey clear Peronist messages wrapped in a great deal of nationalist rhetoric. The value system reflected by these books was dictated by the committee; the books' authors had no outlet for personal expression, and certainly no possibility of criticizing what happened in the country. Another related decision by the education ministry concerned the preparation of new teacher's guides and other didactic aids. The ministry resolved that these, too, should accord with the regime's stated goal of transmitting the values of the Peronist doctrine to the young. This indicates that the Peronization process was comprehensive and well thought out; the Peronist education system also provided for the political indoctrination of the teachers, so that they could fulfill their function as indoctrinators of the students.

From Mónica Esti Rein, *Politics and Education in Argentina, 1946–1962*, 1998

SOURCE K

Cover of a textbook used in a primary school. The title of the book is *Privileged*.

The arts, media and censorship

Perón promoted the development of a 'national art', understood as one based on the Argentine customs and traditions and which could become a vehicle for the transmission of Peronist values. He encouraged the intellectuals and artists to join him in the effort of creating a national culture, one that reflected the values of political sovereignty and which took the role of unifier of all voices in the field. The work of artists and intellectuals was coordinated by government institutions.

SOURCE L

I hope that you [the intellectuals] organize yourselves as a society; I hope that you unify, no matter what you think, what you feel, and what you want; but that you fulfil your role within the orientation the state will no doubt fix.

From a speech given by Juan D. Perón to a group of intellectuals in 1947

The decision to reinforce nationalist concepts led the government to legislate that at least half of the music played in radio stations, clubs, cafés, etc. had to be by Argentine composers and singers. There was a genuine boom in Argentine cinema in the late 1940s and 50s. A new law regulating the film production industry was passed in 1947 and workers and actors were unionized. Argentina's first international film festival was held in the city of **Mar del Plata** in 1954. Also, the Peronist government granted subsidies and loans to film-makers to promote the industry.

As with teachers, many actors and directors who did not express their support for Perón were forbidden to work. At other times, rather than ban the production of a movie, the government would not provide the producers with the necessary film to finish their work. But more than a visible censorship apparatus for the arts, what seemed to work under the Peronist system was 'self-censorship', meaning that authors and artists thought very carefully before they included anything that could sound vaguely anti-Peronist in their works.

Nevertheless, some actors and directors showed certain levels of criticism of the regime. Director Daniel Tinayre illustrated in his thriller **Deshonra** (1952) the achievements of the Peronist regime in relation to the improvements in prison policies, but still offered a critical view of life under Perón. However, as economic problems emerged and opposition to Perón increased after 1952, control of the arts became tighter.

 Mar del Plata
The choice of the city of Mar del Plata (see map on p.10) for the international cinema festival of 1954 was not innocent. Mar del Plata had been the beach resort of the oligarchy and, with the promotion of tourism for the workers, became the favourite destination for thousands of Argentines who had felt excluded from it before.

Deshonra and Argentine cinema
Argentine cinema experienced significant expansion during the 1950s, when some outstanding directors, actors and actresses opened a new era. During the Peronist years, there was strict censorship. Director Daniel Tinayre eluded the censorship of *Deshonra* by illustrating the improvements in prison policy under Perón while, in a more subtle manner, he transmitted the feeling of oppression experienced by society as a result of the Peronist regime.

Propanganda

Peronist propaganda aimed to illustrate the successes of the regime and reinforce Peronist values among the population. The radio – to which the opposition had restricted access – transmitted Perón's speeches and recounted his official events on an almost daily basis. The newsreels that were shown before the movies in cinemas became an effective tool of propaganda to highlight the achievements of the regime: inauguration of hospitals and schools, mass rallies, the work of the FEP, etc. Also, Perón's and Eva's words were compiled in books such as *The Peronists' Manual; Forces of the Peronist; Peronists, Let Us Meditate;* and *The Message of New Argentina.*

SOURCE M

Peronist magazines such as New Argentina *were filled with news and photos of the ruling couple and their activities, while the more sophisticated, well illustrated* Peronist World *presented current events through the eyes of the party. Both circulated widely, and had their own publishing houses that produced volumes of Perón's sayings or poems celebrating the New Argentina. Everybody, Peronist or not, constantly heard the words of the party song 'The Peronist boys' with its rousing refrain: 'Perón, Perón, how great you are; My general, how much you are worth; Perón, Perón, great leader, you are the First Worker.'*

From William Shannon, 'Evita and Propaganda: Selling an Argentinian Dictatorship', 2000

STUDENT STUDY SECTION

QUESTIONS

a) **What, according to Source M, were the aims and methods of Peronist propaganda?**

b) **Explain the reference to Perón as 'the First Worker'.**

Mass rallies were used by Perón to demonstrate support for the regime. On every 1 May and 17 October, Plaza de Mayo became crowded with supporters, who patiently waited for Perón and his wife Eva to come out on a balcony in the Pink House and greet the audience as *Compañeros!* (companions), smiling and with open arms. On those occasions, they asked people if they were happy with the government, a question which was answered with a 'Yes, my general!' every time. This display aimed at demonstrating the massive support the regime enjoyed, legitimizing its right to rule.

Juan Perón addresses a mass rally.

Argentine poster reading: 'Worker. Oppressed Yesterday. Dignified Today. 1st May. Secretariat of Labour and Welfare'.

STUDENT STUDY SECTION

QUESTIONS

a) **What is the message conveyed by Source N?**

b) **How effective do you consider Peronist propaganda was in obtaining the loyalty of his followers? How effective do you consider it was to gain the support of anti-Peronists? Explain your answers fully.**

c) **Now consider the following question: 'Examine the role of education and the arts in Argentina under Perón.' Once you have reflected on the question, read the examiner's hint.**

● **Examiner's hint**
Before you can examine the role of education and the arts, you should think of the wider picture: What role did the government want these areas to play in Argentina? Then, you can consider whether they played such roles or, alternatively, whether they became areas that reflected weaknesses of the regime. For example, if the role of education was to indoctrinate people, you can evaluate the extent to which this was achieved and the challenges it faced. Or, if the arts had a mission to portray a new model of nationhood, consider whether they were also used to express dissent.

Economic policies

The end of World War II found Argentina in an advantageous economic situation. It was a producer of raw materials at a time when the European economies were still recovering from the war. Also, it was a creditor nation, having accumulated revenues in its foreign accounts from its exports during World War II. With plentiful natural resources and demands for Argentine goods, the context in which to implement changes of direction in the economy was a positive one. However, the policies that were put into practice did not necessarily bring about the desired changes.

Economic aims

Perón's economic policies echoed his political ideas. The state played a large part in the economy. It aimed at achieving economic independence for Argentina through autarky, the transfer of foreign-owned companies to the state and the repatriation of foreign debt. Nationalism promoted the development of industries, including armament and heavy industry, which also aimed at obtaining full employment rates.

To access Worksheet 2.4 on Peronist propaganda, please visit www. pearsonbacconline.com and follow the on-screen instructions.

The policies implemented included:

- The promotion of industrialization by the use of protectionist measures such as restrictions of imports.
- State subsidies were implemented to assist in the development of new industries.
- The purchase and nationalization of all railroads, gas companies and power plants in foreign hands by the use of wartime profits.
- Control of river and air transportation, which was taken away from private companies and put under state control.
- State control of exports of meat, grains and other important primary products. This policy meant the state bought directly from the producers at a fixed price and sold the products in foreign markets at international prices with significant profit.
- State control of imports, through a similar system as the one described for imports.
- State control of currency exchange.
- Nationalization of the Central Bank of Argentina, which designed the policies that all public and private banks in the country had to follow.

SOURCE O

In essence the state had enormous involvement in the economic life of the country. The number of public agents increased considerably and the regulations became more and more oppressive as the economic policy suffered some difficulties. Campaigns began to be made for a decrease in the cost of living, for price regulation, for subsidies for specific activities such as bakeries or cold storage companies, or for the punishment of 'unscrupulous' merchants who increased prices. It is evident that the state had so great a presence in the economic life that it would not be exaggerated to say that the policy of Perón was purely statist.

From Félix Luna, *A Brief History of Argentina*, 1995

STUDENT STUDY SECTION

QUESTIONS

a) **What, according to Source O, were methods used by the government in economic matters?**

b) **Explain 'the policy of Perón was purely statist'.**

Between 1946 and 1948, the Peronist economy achieved a certain level of success. The construction industry expanded, pushed mainly by government investments in public works. Exports, led by agricultural products, also experienced an increase in the immediate post-war years, and allowed for the importation of the necessary equipment to promote industrialization. Living standards, particularly those of the working class, improved. For the first time in history, in 1948 Argentina's industrial production surpassed its agricultural output. But this situation spelled problems in the near future.

One of Perón's major interests was to keep the purchasing power of the working class high. In order to ensure this, he increased salaries irrespective of whether the different economic sectors experienced improvements that would pay for the rise. He also put into effect measures to keep prices low, including price controls and the revaluation of the national currency. The attempt to keep prices low at a time when people were getting higher salaries led to many problems. First, the rise in the salaries pushed producers' costs up – salaries are a critical part of production cost. Second, because producers could not increase their prices, they either stopped producing or decided to sell part of their output on the black market at higher prices that would cover their increasing costs better. Finally, although the revaluation of the national currency made imports more accessible, it affected the exporting sector as

Argentine products became more expensive. Therefore, although workers earned more money, they were not necessarily better off.

The harsh conditions imposed on farming – the control of exports, the revaluation of the peso and high levels of taxation – led to a decrease in agricultural production. In turn, the reduced production had a negative impact on the industrialization of Argentina, a country that depended on revenues from exports to pay for the importation of capital goods, such as machinery, to achieve industrial progress. It also contributed to the rising levels of prices and inflation, and forced the government to review its public spending levels.

Another problem that forced a review of the economy by 1951 was related to the companies that had been bought by the state. They often lost money and increased state expenditure.

The economy under review

After 1951, the emerging economic problems called for a review of policies. Among other measures, regulations over agricultural exports were made more flexible, to promote their growth. In addition, in 1951 the government began a policy to attract foreign investments, something that would have been unthinkable in the not so distant years of nationalizations. The fact that Perón was prepared to change what had constituted one of the founding ideas of his movement, and to accept the participation of US capital in the exploration and exploitation of the Argentine subsoil, speaks volumes about his pragmatism. But it also showed how gravely the economy had been affected and how his economic plan had failed to achieve the aims of autarky and nationalism. The opposition lost no time in making severe criticisms of the Peronist economy, particularly the decision to attract foreign capital for loans and investments. They reminded Perón that his 1949 constitution explicitly prohibited the transfer of energy resources to foreign hands.

Perhaps one of the greatest mistakes of the Peronist economy was the belief that the comparative advantages enjoyed by Argentina in the early years of the regime would continue indefinitely. Europe recovered sooner than the Peronist economists would have liked; wartime profits were largely spent in the nationalization of companies. And, against Perón's own calculations, the Cold War did not develop into a Third World War that would have placed Argentina again as a supplier of primary products. These miscalculations played a significant role in bringing about the severe economic problems that contributed to the rise of opposition and unrest.

SOURCE P

◀ Workers in an Argentine automobile factory.

SOURCE Q

Peronism's goal of an autarchic 'New Argentina' – as a familiar slogan went, a 'politically sovereign, socially just, and economically independent nation' – was pursued along similar lines across the globe. Scholars have most often compared Perón to European fascists like Franco or Mussolini, and indeed the Peronists also saw themselves as pursuing a nationalist third-way between the extremes of capitalism and communism. But there were many other experiments with both state planning and 'third-way' politics. Perón can be placed alongside other 'Third-World' advocates of national planning such as Nehru, Sukarno, Nkrumah, Kubitschek and Nasser to illuminate this important dimension of twentieth-century history.

From Eduardo Elena, 'What the People Want: State Planning and Political Participation in Peronist Argentina, 1946–1955', *Journal of Latin American Studies*, 2005

● **Examiner's hint**

Paper 2 demands that you are familiar with regimes that represent different ideologies and which come from different regions, as questions may ask you to compare and contrast them. It is therefore useful that you try to think across regions and ideologies when studying leaders. You can help yourself by preparing charts that compare and contrast different areas, such as their political, social and economic policies; the nature and extent of opposition; their aims and methods, etc. Preparing the charts is a good revision exercise and you can always refer back to them when writing essays or studying for the IB exam.

STUDENT STUDY SECTION

QUESTIONS

a) **What is the message of Source P? To what extent do you consider it to be a fair representation of the economic achievements of Perón? Explain your answer fully.**

b) **In Source Q, to what extent do you agree with the view that Perón's economic policies pursued similar lines to other single-party regimes in the world? Explain with reference to other authoritarian or single-party states you have studied.**

Section III:

The rise of opposition, and the fall and return of Perón

This section aims at analyzing the nature and extent of opposition to Peronism, particularly after 1952. It also looks at the government's response to that opposition and the events that led to Perón's downfall in September 1955.

As we have seen, by the end of his first presidency Perón had made great accomplishments in improving the living conditions of workers. The economy, however, began to experience problems and Perón was forced to make changes. The economic problems after 1951 became a contributing factor to the rise of opposition.

Under Perón, a significant part of the middle class did not experience an increase in living standards, as they were affected by measures such as the freezing of rents that had given them an additional source of income in the past. The landowning class of Argentina had seen state intervention significantly reduce the revenues of their exports. While some industrialists benefited from the Peronist protectionist policies, others were concerned about the tight control on imports. A number of trade unions organized strikes against the economic policies, especially as the impact on the living standards of the working class began to be felt. There was pressure from businessmen for the government to limit the concessions and improvements made to the workers' conditions in exchange for an increased investment in their enterprises. At a political level, negotiations were opened to attract foreign investments to help overcome some of the financial difficulties. As we have seen, these were heavily criticized by the opposition, however, who were quick to show how these policies contradicted the very essence of Peronism's emphasis on political sovereignty. The Peronist dream of a united nation was showing signs of rifts.

The government's reaction to this situation also contributed to the rise of opposition. The administration increased the persecution of opponents, limited freedom of speech even further and reinforced the cult of the leaders Eva and Juan Perón. Back in 1951, a proposal that Eva Perón run as Perón's Vice-President in the elections caused resistance among the traditionalist armed forces as well as the middle and upper classes, who saw in Eva someone much more reactionary than Juan. Whether Eva stepped down as a consequence of pressure on Juan Perón, or due to the fact that she was by then terminally ill with cancer, is difficult to tell.

Despite Eva's move out of politics, the armed forces expressed their general discontent in September 1951, when General Benjamin Menéndez led an attempted coup. The move failed and revealed that the conditions to overthrow Perón were not yet ripe. Yet it also made it evident to the government that all was not well. The President declared an 'internal state of war', which enabled him to suspend constitutional freedoms and increase his power in an attempt to control the situation.

Photograph showing people queuing to pay tributes to Eva Perón in Buenos Aires, July 1952. Almost 2 million people from all across the country went to the Congress to pay tributes to Eva, all wearing black as a sign of mourning.

Eva Perón died on 26 July 1952, a few weeks after her husband was sworn in as President of Argentina for the second time. Her death was devastating to her supporters. It also deprived Perón of someone who had guaranteed popular support at a time of economic difficulties, inflation and shortages of goods. The cult of Eva, promoted by the state, increased after her death, and became one of almost religious proportions, irritating the Catholic Church and the more traditional sectors of the armed forces. Catholic groups began to organize themselves politically and Juan Perón felt threatened. He imprisoned priests and accused them of interfering with politics. Next, he closed Catholic newspapers and banned religious processions.

SOURCE A

Certainly one of the factors contributing to Perón's electoral victory was the Church's almost explicit directions to Catholics to vote for the Peronist coalition. And it is equally certain that Perón's fall in September 1955 cannot be divorced from his deteriorating relations with the Church. Although this deterioration dated from the beginning of the 1950s, it was most critical in the period from November 1954 until the overthrow of the regime. Once his regime was well established politically and he felt secure, Perón seemed to think he no longer needed the ideological and moral support of the Church… Thus, the two ideologies, Peronism and Catholicism, competed for the hearts of the Argentines. Conflict between state and Church became inevitable, and it was expressed initially by mutual verbal attacks. In the last months of his presidency, Perón canceled the various privileges that the Catholic Church enjoyed, and published a series of laws designed to push the Church out of its central position in Argentine life. He abolished compulsory Catholic religious instruction in the state schools (which he had instituted himself at the beginning of his presidency), introduced a divorce law, legalized the country's brothels, and topped it all off by proclaiming the separation of church and state.

From Mónica Esti Rein, *Politics and Education in Argentina, 1946–1962*, 1998

Jockey Club

The Jockey Club was founded in 1882 by a generation of Argentine leaders who admired European culture and wanted to create a social centre. Although originally aimed at organizing the sport of horse racing, its members coordinated numerous fundraising activities and charity events which raised significant funds, particularly before Perón rose to power.

Corpus Christi Day

A Catholic celebration that honours the Eucharist, the ceremonial wine and bread that believers consider to be the actual body and blood of Christ.

In April 1953, a bomb exploded during a demonstration organized by the CGT in support of Perón, causing five casualties. The event gave way for Peronist extremists to attack – with unprecedented violence in the Perón era – the **Jockey Club**, a symbol of the oligarchy, as well as the headquarters of the Socialist, Radical and Conservative parties.

Yet, the largest expression of dissent came in June 1955, on **Corpus Christi Day**. There was an incident in which Catholics were accused of having burnt an Argentine flag; they claimed it had been done by the police to incriminate them. Whatever the truth, it was the catalyst for violence. The navy and the air force bombarded the surroundings of the presidential palace. The attempt against Perón's life failed, but caused hundreds of casualties among the civilian population. In a violent reprisal, supporters of Perón set fire to churches and other buildings that represented anti-Peronism.

In an unexpected turn of events, instead of persecuting and imprisoning the opposition, Perón offered his resignation to reconcile the nation. He also dismissed some of the most uncompromising members in his government. The opposition, however, was not attracted to Perón's offer of reconciliation and did not believe his offer to resign for the good of the nation. They saw it as a strategy by Perón to deceive them.

The reasons why Perón chose not to react have been a matter of contention. One explanation suggests that Perón, a military man himself, refused to move against comrades of the armed forces. It is also claimed that he was well aware of his weak situation and decided not to do anything that would antagonize his enemies further and risk losing the support of the sector of the army that remained loyal to him. Finally, it could be argued that Perón knew the end of his days was coming and refused to do anything that could develop into more chaos and, potentially, a civil war between Peronists and anti-Peronists.

On 31 August, the CGT organized a massive rally in support of Perón. Irritated by the opposition's rejection of his offer of pacification, and strengthened by the show of support for him, he declared:

SOURCE B

To violence we will reply with a greater violence. With our excessive tolerance we have won the right to suppress them violently. And from now on we establish as a permanent rule of conduct for our movement: any person who in any place tries to disturb the public order in opposition to the constituted authorities, or contrary to the law or the constitution, may be killed by any Argentine… The watchword for all Peronists, whether as individuals or within an organization, is to reply to a violent action with one more violent. And when one of ours falls, five of theirs will fall.

From a speech pronounced by Juan D. Perón on 31 August 1955, quoted in Robert D. Crassweller, *Perón and the Enigmas of Argentina*, 1987

STUDENT STUDY SECTION

QUESTIONS

a) **Explain the message in Source B.**

b) **What reasons can you suggest to explain the tone and content of this speech?**

c) **It is claimed that Peron's greatest mistakes in dealing with the August crisis were to abandon his position of mediator and violently take sides. To what extent do you agree with this view? What other reasons can you provide to explain Perón's failure to keep himself in power?**

The 'Liberating Revolution' and the fall of Perón

On 16 September 1955, after confrontations between Peronist workers and the armed forces, Perón's government fell and was replaced by a military junta, which led the 'Liberating Revolution'. A few days later, Perón abandoned the country, seeking asylum in Paraguay. That event started an exile that would last until 1973.

SOURCE C

Photograph of Plaza de Mayo taken on the triumph of the Liberating Revolution, September 1955.

STUDENT STUDY SECTION

QUESTIONS

a) What is the significance of the photograph in Source C?

b) Who do you think attended the celebrations? Explain the reasons for your answer.

ToK Time

As we have seen, Plaza de Mayo became a symbol of Peronist Argentina on 17 October 1945. From then on, Peronist supporters considered it their public space and every anniversary of 17 October and on Labour Day (1 May), they marched to see President Perón and participate in celebrations. That same Plaza witnessed a massive demonstration in support of the Liberating Revolution that overthrew Perón in 1955. In the 1970s it became a symbol of another type of demonstration. Look at the photograph below:

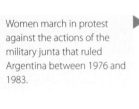

Women march in protest against the actions of the military junta that ruled Argentina between 1976 and 1983.

The photograph above represents the 'Mothers of Plaza de Mayo' or 'Madres de Plaza de Mayo'. See what information you can find about the origins of the group, their aims and their role in the history of Argentina.

To what extent does the study of the public demonstrations help us understand historical processes and events?

Think of other mass demonstrations of historical relevance that you have studied. Are there significant differences in the way societies express either their discontent or their approval across time and in different cultures?

STUDENT STUDY SECTION

Why did Perón fall in 1955?

Different answers have been offered to explain why Perón fell. In groups, explain which of the following interpretations you agree or disagree with, providing reasons and examples to support each of the arguments. Select the three reasons your group considers most important and compare your choice to those of the other groups. Individually, use the material to write an answer to the question above. You can add any other reason you may consider relevant using supporting evidence.

- During his government, Perón relied more on popular support than on well-established policies.

- He attempted to solve the problems with policies that went against what Peronism had stood for.
- The centralized, authoritarian model had exhausted itself.
- He used repression and violence to maintain himself in power.
- His economic policies failed.
- His propaganda, though successful with the sectors that supported him, failed to appeal and persuade the anti-Peronists.
- The anti-clerical campaign he initiated caused resistance among earlier supporters.
- It was entirely Perón's decision not to fight to keep himself in power.

The return of Perón

Background

Following his overthrow in 1955, Perón spent almost 18 years in exile. After years of living in different Latin American countries, in 1960 he settled in Madrid, in the Spain of **General Francisco Franco**. During his exile, Perón and the Peronist party remained proscribed in Argentina.

This situation did not imply that Perón had ceased to influence Argentine politics. He was constantly consulted by politicians, trade union leaders and other public figures. He had the power to influence election results by either demanding that his followers voted blank or by suggesting which candidate he was prepared to endorse, which almost guaranteed by itself the victory of the politician in question. It was not until 1973, however, that he was able to return to his country.

Perón's return to power

The immediate preparations for the return of Perón began when the military government of **General Alejandro A. Lanusse** decided to call for democratic elections for the year 1973. At the time, Argentina was suffering economic problems that caused social unrest. Also, guerrilla groups of Peronist orientation operated in the country with Perón's implicit approval. The demand that Peronists be allowed to participate in elections not only came from the party members and followers; many other people joined in this demand, in the belief that only Perón's return could normalize political life.

Although Lanusse lifted the ban on political parties to allow the participation of the Peronist Party, he decreed that only those Argentines who were living in Argentina could run as candidates, a measure that excluded Perón, who lived in Spain. Nonetheless, a Peronist coalition won the elections carrying the Cámpora–Solano Lima ticket, defeating UCR leader **Ricardo Balbín** in March 1973. Perón was now free to return.

But what he was to find was a movement divided. Peronism was no longer the politically homogeneous organization that he had created. It was instead divided into several factions that opposed one another; all of which hoped to count on Perón's support.

Perón's return was awaited with great anxiety by his supporters. It is estimated that nearly two million people, coming from all corners of Argentina, gathered to welcome him in the Ezeiza Airport area on 20 June 1973. The event ended in a bloodbath. The different factions of the movement confronted one another in what became known as the 'Ezeiza massacre', which left, according to official figures, 13 dead and hundreds injured.

General Francisco Franco (1892–1975)
Spanish dictator who ruled Spain from after the Spanish Civil War (1936–39) to his death in 1975. His government was strongly nationalist, anti-communist and ultra-Catholic. He can be used to answer Topic 3 open questions.

Ricardo Balbín (1904–81)
Leader of the UCR, Balbín was presidential candidate for the party in several elections and competed against Perón as well as other politicians after him. As a member of the parliament in Perón's times, he firmly opposed the President and was consequently persecuted, expelled from parliament and imprisoned on several occasions.

General Alejandro A. Lanusse (1918–96)
General Lanusse was the de facto President of Argentina between 1971 and 1973. After he came to power, he began preparations to allow free elections and the return of democracy. He was aware of the fact that no democratic government could rule with stability if the Peronists did not participate in the election process.

SOURCE D

Cartoon by Bob Row, 2006. ▶

STUDENT STUDY SECTION
QUESTION
What is the message of Source D?

The Ezeiza massacre caused the resignation of President Cámpora, his Vice-President and the President of the Senate (third in the line of succession). The immediate consequence was the scheduling of new elections, with Perón as a candidate. As expected, Perón defeated the UCR in September 1973, winning by almost 62 per cent of the votes. Unlike 1952, when he decided not to have Eva Perón accompanying the presidential ticket, this time his third wife, Isabel Martínez Perón, became Vice-President of Argentina.

Photograph showing President Perón. Next to him is his wife and Vice-President, Isabel Perón.

Perón's third presidency (September 1973–June 1974)

Two issues dominated Perón's third, brief presidency. First, the economic problems of the country, and second, the hostility between different groups that called themselves Peronist.

In relation to the economy, the government tried to curb inflation and the rising number of strikes by promoting a 'Social Pact' between workers, employers and the state, but results were poor. Inflation, goods shortages and a black market continued to affect people's living standards. As for the clashes between different factions, Perón was unable to appease them as he had hoped. After the Ezeiza massacre, he had shifted his support to the Peronist trade unions. On 1 May 1974, during the traditional celebration for Labour

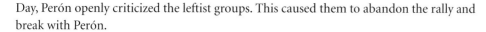

Day, Perón openly criticized the leftist groups. This caused them to abandon the rally and break with Perón.

On 12 June, Perón made his last public speech in a rally organized by CGT in his support.

SOURCE E

Confronted with deceit and violence, we shall impose the truth, which is worth much more. We do not want anyone to fear us; we want, instead, to be understood. When people are persuaded of their destiny, there is nothing to fear. Neither truth, nor deceit nor violence, nor any other circumstance can influence people in a negative way, just as nothing will influence us to change our direction which, we know, is the direction of the fatherland. Each one of us must become a maker, but he must also become a preacher and a surveillance agent of control to perform the task and neutralize the negative that exists in those sectors which have not yet understood and will have to understand.

From a speech by Juan D. Perón on 12 June 1974

STUDENT STUDY SECTION

QUESTIONS

a) What is the message of Source E?

b) To whom is this speech addressed? Explain your answer fully.

c) Which elements of Peronist thought appear in this speech? Can you identify new elements? Explain your answer fully.

Juan Domingo Perón died on 1 July 1974. His wife Isabel took office. Without Perón, her government was unable to bridge the differences and control the various Peronist factions. Additionally, the economy was hit by an international crisis caused by a rise in the price in oil. Argentine exports decreased; inflation and unemployment rose significantly; labour conflicts and strikes were widespread. Guerrilla groups spread violence and terror across the country. The military launched operations to search for terrorists in different regions of the country, while the government seemed to be unable to control the situation. Some political parties called for the removal of the President, while there were increasing rumours that there would be another military coup.

On 24 March 1976, President Isabel Perón was overthrown by a joint military coup led by the army, the navy and the air force. The 'Process of National Reorganization', as it became known, launched one of the darkest eras in the history of Argentina.

STUDENT STUDY SECTION

Consider the following question: Assess the importance of social and economic factors in causing opposition to authoritarian regimes.

Student Answer – Arnold

The economic factors were highly responsible for the downfall of Perón in 1955. His attempt to industrialize Argentina went against the traditional economic pattern of the country and gained him the opposition of the landowning class, who were affected by Perón's strict control of exports. It was the government that bought the raw material to be exported, fixing the price and the quantity that could be sold to third countries. This meant that producers received less money and, consequently, decided to lower their production. This increased the prices at home and also decreased the government's incomes from taxation and exports to the extent that Perón was forced to review his policies towards the sector. However, by then prices had risen and affected the purchasing power of the workers who began to protest to gain increases in their pay.

The economic measures also affected industrialists, who saw their production costs rise because of government intervention in favour of the working class. They were also negatively affected by the limitations on importations which meant they sometimes lacked the materials for specific production cycles. This increased opposition to Perón.

Examiner's comments

The candidate shows a good level of knowledge of the economic measures taken by Perón and he also knows how they affected Argentina. However, analysis of the relations between the economic issues and the rise of opposition is limited. For example, the answer shows awareness of specific economic policies that the landowning class opposed, and of their reaction to the strict government control. But there is limited explicit analysis of how important these factors were in creating opposition to Perón. The focus of the analysis should be on how the opposition developed and how it affected Perón, rather than on the reasons why opposition emerged.

REVIEW SECTION

This chapter has examined the rise to power of Juan Domingo Perón and his rule of Argentina, looking at his three presidential terms. It has focused on:

- The conditions and methods that led to Perón's rise to power.
- The methods used to consolidate power.
- The nature, implementation and effects of his social, political and economic policies.
- Peronist culture, propaganda and education.
- The nature and extent of opposition.

3 FIDEL CASTRO AND CUBA

Cuba is one of the few countries in the world that remains communist in its ideology. Ever since 1959, historians have tried to explain the reasons why Fidel Castro was able to rise and maintain himself in power for so long, in spite of often adverse domestic and international circumstances.

A Spanish colony until 1898, and a republic strongly linked to the USA after its independence in 1902, Cuba did not seem to offer the conditions for a successful communist revolution. Other countries in the region suffered deeper political, social and economic problems. Yet events between 1953 and 1959 contributed to the rise of Fidel Castro and his 26th of July Movement.

This chapter deals with the rise to power and the rule of Fidel Alejandro Castro Ruz (b. 1926) in Cuba. It focuses on the conditions against which he came to power, addresses the methods used in his rise and analyzes domestic policies up to 2000.

 Fidel Castro

Timeline – 1926–2008

1926 Fidel Alejandro Castro Ruz is born in Biran, south-eastern Cuba.

1933 President Gerardo Machado is overthrown by the head of the army, Fulgencio Batista.

1934–44 Fulgencio Batista controls the country through puppet governments.

1934 The Platt Amendment is abolished. USA retains a naval base in Guantánamo Bay and trade agreements between the nations remain in place.

1940 Batista becomes President. A new constitution is adopted.

1944–48 Partido Auténtico (Authentic Party) leader, Ramón Grau San Martín, becomes President.

1948–52 Authentic Party leader Carlos Prío Socarrás rules Cuba.

1952 Batista seizes power in a coup against Prío Socarrás.

1953 Castro leads the Moncada assault against a military garrison. He is sentenced to 15 years in prison.

1955 Castro is granted amnesty and leaves Cuba.

1956 Castro returns from Mexico, leading the *Granma* expedition. He launches a military campaign against Batista in the **Sierra Maestra** mountains.

1958 USA withdraws assistance to President Batista. Batista's final offensive against the rebels ends in failure.

1959 Batista flees the country. Castro's troops enter Havana and a provisional government is set up. Fidel Castro becomes Prime Minister in February. Expropriation and nationalization of businesses begins.

1960 Castro nationalizes foreign companies. USA abolishes Cuban sugar quota and begins an economic blockade. Castro establishes diplomatic and commercial relations with the Soviet Union.

1961 The Bay of Pigs invasion is repelled. USA breaks diplomatic ties with Cuba, and Castro announces the socialist character of the revolution.

1962 Cuban Missile Crisis. USA imposes a trade embargo on Cuba.

1963 Castro makes his first visit to the Soviet Union.

 ToK Time
At the time of writing this book, Fidel Castro had transferred power to his brother Raúl, but has continued to be a leading voice in Cuban affairs. What, if anything, do you know about Fidel Castro? Can you find any recent information in the newspapers about Cuba? To what extent do you think your previous knowledge and opinions of Castro and Cuba can influence your study of this chapter?

Sierra Maestra
Mountain range in the south-east of Cuba, in the Oriente province.

1967	Ernesto 'Che' Guevara is killed in Bolivia.
1968	Castro announces the Revolutionary Offensive.
1970	The 'Ten Million Zafra' programme fails to achieve its target.
1976	Under a new constitution, Castro assumes the title of President of the State Council, and becomes head of state, head of government, and commander-in-chief of the armed forces.
1980	Massive Cuban emigration of approximately 125,000 people to the USA from the Mariel port.
1991	Cuba begins 'Special Period in Times of Peace' programme following the end of Soviet aid to Cuba.
1995	Castro visits China for the first time.
1998	Castro welcomes Pope John Paul II in the pontiff's historic visit to Cuba.
2006	Castro announces a temporary transfer of power to his brother, Raúl Castro.
2008	Castro resigns as President.

Figure 3.1
Map of Cuba.

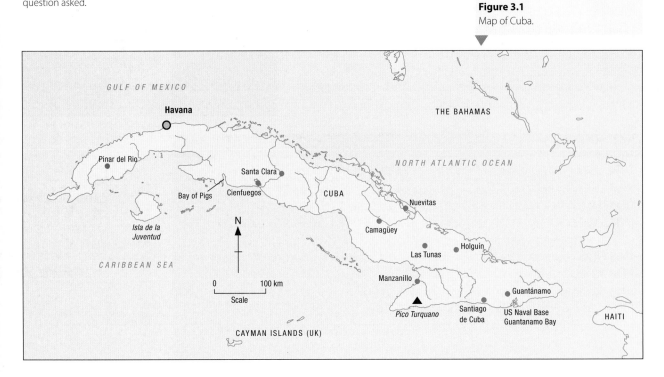

Section I:

Origins and nature of authoritarian and single-party states – Cuba

No doubt Fidel Castro played a large part in the success of the Cuban revolution in 1959, and in retaining power for almost 50 years. It is also true, however, that particular historical conditions created the background against which Castro became an appealing option to many and an indisputable force to others.

This section aims at analyzing the contributions of Fidel Castro to the success of the Cuban revolution in January 1959, as well as the part played by the historical, political and economic circumstances against which he rose to power.

Background

Cuban independence

After many years of struggle, and with the aid of the USA, Cuba shook off Spanish rule in what became known as the Spanish–American War (1898). The Treaty of Paris (1898) between Spain and the USA granted the territories of Puerto Rico, Guam and the Philippines to the USA in exchange for money. Spain also lost sovereignty over Cuba, which was placed under military occupation by the USA for five years. In 1902, the Republic of Cuba was declared. Yet Cuba was not fully sovereign. By the Platt Amendment annexed to the Cuban constitution, the USA kept the right to intervene in Cuba's finances and foreign relations. The Platt Amendment not only aimed at preventing the influence of third-party countries in Cuba, but also at guaranteeing US control of Cuban affairs. In the following years, until its abolition in 1934, the Platt Amendment was used on several occasions by the USA to intervene in Cuban internal affairs and protect US economic interests on the island.

Economic and social aspects

The USA's interests in Cuba were protected by policies that benefited American investments in the island. US capital played an important part in the exploitation of Cuban national resources. Known as 'the sugar bowl of the world', Cuba was a **monoculture economy**. Although it also produced tobacco, coffee and rice, it was the production of sugar that provided the most important income for the republic. Washington bought a significant percentage of Cuban sugar production at prices higher than those set by the international market. In exchange, Cuba was to give preferential access to American products. Cuba was not an industrialized nation and depended on the revenues from exported sugar to buy the necessary manufactured goods and oil. The development of Cuban service and utility industries, such as gas, electricity, communications, railways and the banking system, relied upon large amounts of US investment. Although there were economic advantages for Cuba in these agreements, they also meant that the Cuban economy was tied to the USA. If Washington decided to reduce the quantity of sugar bought from Cuba, the economy of the island would be seriously affected.

Cubans enjoyed a better standard of living than workers in other regions of the continent, but there were many social and economic problems that affected them. The living conditions for workers were precarious. Wages were low, housing was limited and access to health and education not available to all. Few rural areas possessed running water or electricity. Illiteracy was widespread, reaching 50 per cent in certain parts of the countryside. Sugar workers were seasonal; this meant there were months when they did not have steady employment. The ownership of land and of the sugar mills was largely concentrated in the hands of the upper class and foreign companies.

Monoculture economy
The agricultural practice of producing or growing one single crop over a wide area.

STUDENT STUDY SECTION

RESEARCH ACTIVITY

To understand the social and economic situations against which Castro rose to power, it is important that you are familiar with the role played by foreign companies as well as with the importance of sugar to the Cuban economy.

In groups, find information about some of the different foreign companies operating in Cuba before the revolution. Assess their impact on the Cuban economy and society. Research the importance of sugar before the revolution and the reasons why it began to lose economic value throughout the 20th century.

Fulgencio Batista

Political aspects

Between independence and revolution, Cuba was led by a series of governments that showed high levels of corruption and limited success in solving economic problems and social inequality. By 1934, the armed forces under the command of General Fulgencio Batista controlled the nation by the appointment of puppet Presidents. In 1940, Batista himself became President of Cuba and ruled until 1944.

Between 1944 and 1952 there was a return to democracy, but corruption continued to dominate every branch of the government, while Cuba faced inflation and unemployment. On 10 March 1952, Batista returned to the political stage and overthrew President Carlos Prío Socarrás. He suspended the constitution to rule as a dictator.

The rule of Fulgencio Batista (1952–59)

During Batista's period as President, political corruption continued to reign, and at shocking levels. As economic problems worsened, social and political unrest developed. Batista moved from making concessions to using repression to maintain control of the country.

One of the reasons why the Cuban economy worsened was the decline in sugar prices on the international sugar market. As the price of sugar dropped, Cuba found it more expensive to purchase the goods it did not produce at home. This situation is known as the 'deterioration of the **terms of trade**'. However, because of its international obligations with the USA, Cuba could not successfully develop an industry to substitute its imports, a measure many Latin American countries had taken by the end of World War II (see previous chapter). The rise in the cost of imports led to shortages and inflation. Furthemore, the rise in the price of oil affected transportation and the operation of sugar mills, increasing unemployment to an alarming 17 per cent during the late 1950s, to be combined with a 13 per cent level of underemployment and low wages for those who were employed.

Under these circumstances, opposition to Batista's dictatorship intensified. The rural workers, poorly housed and under-educated, did not support the regime. Urban workers were affected by the economic problems of inflation and unemployment, and student unions demanded freedom and democracy. The higher social classes, who were losing their purchasing power and whose businesses were being affected by the atmosphere of economic uncertainty, were another source of opposition to Batista. Opposition, however, was not organized and had not yet found a leading figure.

The rise of opposition to Batista

One of the factors that contributed to the rise of Castro was the fact that the Cuban political parties did not seem to offer a genuine alternative to the existing order. The Authentic Party and the Orthodox Party were two main political parties in Cuba before the revolution. The communists were represented by the PSP, the Popular Socialist Party.

Partido Auténtico (full name: Partido Revolucionario Cubano or Cuban Revolutionary Party)

Founded in 1934, this party's platform had socialist and nationalist elements. It defended the rights of workers to be represented by trade unions. Nationalism was expressed in its motto 'Cuba for the Cubans'. However, Presidents Ramón Grau San Martín (1944–48) and

Terms of trade
Relationship between the prices at which a country sells its exports and the prices paid for its imports.

Carlos Prío Socarrás (1948–52) were Authentic Party leaders who ruled during one of the most corrupt and undemocratic periods in Cuban history.

Partido Ortodoxo (full name: Partido del Pueblo Cubano or Cuban People's Party)

Born from a split of the Authentic Party, this party was founded in 1948 by Eduardo Chibás, who coined the party's motto 'Integrity against Money'. It played an important role in the denunciation of the corruption in Cuban politics. Its aims were to end government corruption and to nationalize US-owned companies. Orthodox leader Chibás was considered to be a solid presidential candidate, but he committed suicide in 1951. Fidel Castro was a member of the party until he formed his own organization, the 26th of July Movement.

The Partido Socialista Popular (PSP; Popular Socialist Party)

The PSP was Cuba's communist party. Founded in 1925, it suffered persecution and was banned from participating in elections several times. In 1953, Batista banned the PSP again.

SOURCE A

The Auténtico and Ortodoxo parties proved incapable of responding effectively to Batista's seizure of power. The Orthodox were leaderless and the Auténticos could not lead. After 1952 Cuba's two principal parties became irrelevant to a solution of the political crises. Both parties, to be sure, condemned the violation of the 1940 Constitution, but neither party responded to the army usurpation with either a comprehensive program or compelling plan of action.

From Louis Perez Jr., 'Cuba c. 1930–1959' in Leslie Bethell (ed.), *Cuba: A Short History,* 1993

STUDENT STUDY SECTION
QUESTION
Why, according to Source A, was opposition to Batista ineffective?
RESEARCH ACTIVITY
Find information on Eduardo Chibás' ideas and roles. Explain how and why he decided to end his life.

The greatest challenge for the government would not come from any of the more traditional Cuban parties. It would come instead from the rise of Fidel Castro as leader of a totally new movement.

Section II:
The Cuban Revolution and the rise of Fidel Castro

Fidel Alejandro Castro Ruz was born in 1926 in the eastern province of Oriente. His father, an immigrant from Spanish Galicia, owned sugar plantations in the region. In 1945, Castro enrolled in law school in Havana and soon joined the Orthodox Party. He was an outstanding orator, who had an exceptional memory for everything he read and heard; he was also a fine athlete. All of these factors helped him gain popularity and support within the party. In 1952, Castro planned to run for a seat in Congress, but elections were never held, as

ToK Time

If you were to write a biography of Fidel Castro, what would you include? Would this choice be affected by the context in which you would be using the biography? In other words, is there a history of Castro the leader, one of Castro the student, another of Castro the family man or is everything relevant to understand the influence of a leader on historical events? Explain your answer fully.

When you need to find the biography of a historical character, where do you go? Do you go to Wikipedia? Evaluate the usefulness of the entry for Fidel Castro in Wikipedia. Is knowledge that is collectively produced in any sense 'better' than a biography written by one person? How much of one's knowledge depends on interaction with other knowers?

a result of Batista's coup against Prío Socarrás. From the very beginning Castro showed his opposition to the rule of Batista and in 1953 he tried to depose him for the first time. When analyzing the role played by Fidel Castro in the Cuban revolution, three stages must be taken into consideration:

- The attack against the Moncada Barracks (1953), which provided him with an opportunity to be known by fellow citizens and launch the 26th of July Movement.
- The landing of the *Granma* expedition (1956), which marked the beginning of the armed struggle at a national level.
- The campaign in the Sierra Maestra (1956–59), which ended with his Rebel Army's victorious entry into Havana city in January 1959.

The Moncada assault (1953) and the birth of the 26th of July Movement

On 26 July 1953, a group of approximately 140 men dressed in military uniforms attacked a military garrison in Cuba known as the Moncada Barracks. Most of them were members of the Partido Ortodoxo, and they were led by Fidel Castro, his brother Raúl and **Abel Santamaría**. Moncada is situated in Santiago de Cuba, in the Oriente province, and was chosen for several reasons. It was the second-largest military garrison in the country and had large supplies of ammunition that Castro hoped to seize. Also, Oriente was one of the regions with the greatest social unrest, which Castro thought would provide popular support for the attack. Moreover, the distance between Santiago de Cuba and Havana (see map on p.54) ensured that if Batista's troops were sent from the capital to defend the building, there would be enough time to complete the takeover. Finally, the timing of the attack coincided with a popular celebration in the streets of Santiago, so Castro hoped to find fewer soldiers in the garrison.

The aim of the operation was to obtain weapons that would help spark a general insurrection against Batista. Castro believed that if the attack was successful and his men acquired weapons, they would gather massive popular support for the uprising.

Abel Santamaría (1927–53)

A member of the Orthodox Party, Santamaría met Castro in 1952 and, like him, rejected Batista's coup. He was captured and tortured to death by Batista's forces after the Moncada raid.

Picture of the Moncada Barracks.

The attack had been carefully planned, but several last-minute problems complicated the work of the rebels. Although the surprise factor was intended to play in the rebels' favour, the army managed to defend the building successfully. Almost half of the rebels who participated in the attack were killed; many were captured and tortured to death, including Abel Santamaría. Fidel and Raúl Castro managed to escape, but were soon captured by Batista's forces and imprisoned.

Batista decided to make the trial of the rebels a great show of strength. He wanted Cubans to see how determined he was to crush any opposition to the regime, in the hope that it would work as a deterrent. Fidel Castro, a lawyer, decided to defend himself at the trial. Although Castro's own trial took place in a separate room and attendance was restricted, his speech **'History will absolve me'** became not only his defence, but a programme for the political and social reform of the country.

SOURCE A

There are two hundred thousand peasant families who do not have a single acre of land to cultivate to provide food for their starving children…

A revolutionary government with the backing of the people and the respect of the nation, after cleaning the various institutions of all venal and corrupt officials, would proceed immediately to industrialize the country, mobilizing all inactive capital, currently estimated at about 500 million dollars, through the National Bank and the Agricultural, Industrial and Development Bank, and submitting this mammoth task to experts and men of absolute competence, completely removed from all political machinations, for study, direction, planning and realization… A revolutionary government would solve the housing problem by cutting all rents in half; by providing tax exemptions on homes inhabited by the owners; by tripling taxes on rented homes; by tearing down hovels and replacing them with modern multiple-dwelling buildings; and by financing housing all over the island on a scale heretofore unheard of; with the criterion that, just as each rural family should possess its own tract of land, each city family should own its home or apartment… Finally, a revolutionary government would undertake the integral reform of the educational system, bringing it in line with the foregoing projects with the idea of educating those generations who will have the privilege of living in a happy land.

From Fidel Castro, 'History will absolve me', 1953

STUDENT STUDY SECTION

QUESTIONS

a) **How effective do you think the speech was in identifying Cuba's problems?**

b) **Explain why you consider that 'History will absolve me', once printed and circulated among the Cubans, became an appealing speech.**

Consequences of the Moncada assault

The Moncada assault marked the foundation of Castro's political movement, '26th of July', named after the day of the attack. The rebels became known as the 'Generation of the Centenary', as 1953 marked the hundredth anniversary of the birth of Cuban hero, **José Martí**.

Fidel Castro became the only political leader who not only complained about Batista's dictatorship, but who was also ready to do something about it. Although the rebels were the aggressors, Batista's excesses in repression, torture and persecution affected his image and allowed Castro and his men to emerge as martyrs of the dictatorship.

In 1954, in an attempt to legitimize his rule, Batista held elections and ran as presidential candidate. With Castro in prison, the PSP banned and no effective opposition to his candidature, Batista used the elections to claim that he had been rightfully chosen by the people. The following year, among some other concessions made to appear democratic, Batista allowed political parties to regroup and released many political prisoners, including

Fidel Castro and other prisoners leave prison after Batista's amnesty.

the leaders of the Moncada raid. Fidel Castro was now a free man and went into exile in Mexico to prepare the revolution.

Despite Batista's efforts to appear democratic, demonstrations in Cuba grew in size and led to armed clashes in towns and cities. Different revolutionary organizations spread through the countryside, promoting rural insurgence, sabotaging property across the island and organizing **guerrilla** groups. Communications and the delivery of food to towns and cities were often disrupted. Sugar production dropped as a consequence of acts of sabotage against sugar mills, oil refineries and railroads. Political parties – with the exception of the 26th of July Movement, which believed change in Cuba would only come after the use of force to overthrow Batista – demanded elections but Batista refused to hold them.

On 2 December 1956, Fidel Castro returned to Cuba and launched the next stage of the struggle that would take him to power.

Guerrillas

An irregular military force fighting small-scale, fast-moving actions against conventional military and police forces. Guerrilla tactics involve constantly shifting points of attack, sabotage, and terrorism. The strategy of the guerrilla is to wear down the enemy until he can be defeated in conventional battle or sues for peace. (The word 'guerrilla' means 'little/small war' in Spanish.)

Rebels disembarking from *Granma*.

The *Granma* expedition (1956)

In 1956, Fidel and Raúl Castro returned from exile aboard the overcrowded and poorly equipped yacht *Granma*. They landed on the southern coast of Oriente with some 80 rebels who had been recruited in Mexico.

The voyage was rough, as the *Granma* was heavily laden with men and weapons, and supplies of additional oil to enable it to reach the shores of Cuba. The radio failed and the engines were poor, so *Granma* reached Cuba two days behind schedule. The urban arm of the 26th of July Movement, under the command of **Frank País**, had prepared a strike in Santiago de Cuba in support of the landing, but coordination was affected by the delay in the *Granma*'s arrival. Castro also failed to make contact with those who had prepared land support for the operation. Spotted by government forces, Castro and his men landed in a swamp and were forced to leave supplies and ammunition behind. They were ambushed at Alegría del Pío and those surviving (only 12 of the original 82-man crew) dispersed and hid in the Sierra Maestra to regroup and emerge as the Rebel Army.

Anti-government rebellions led by several groups in the cities continued throughout 1957 and 1958, and included an attempt to seize the presidential palace and murder Batista. Although it failed, it showed the President how difficult it had become to maintain himself in power. Batista struggled desperately to control the situation, but his response was so violent that it embittered the people against him.

The cast of characters

Fidel Castro was not alone on the road to power. Although he was the leading figure, many men and women contributed to the success of the 26th of July Movement. Some of them played an important part in the struggle for power; others continued to work in the revolutionary government. Study these photographs and biographical details carefully. You will find reference to these characters throughout the chapter.

Frank País (1934–57)
Student leader who fought against Batista since the 1952 coup and who joined the 26th of July Movement. He led the movement while Castro was in exile. His brutal murder in 1957 at the age of 23 led to one of the largest general strikes in Cuba.

▲ Raúl Castro

▲ Vilma Espín

▲ Camilo Cienfuegos

▲ Ernesto 'Che' Guevara

▲ Haydée Santamaría

▲ Celia Sánchez

Raúl Castro – Fidel's younger brother Raúl took part in the attack on the Moncada Barracks, was imprisoned with Fidel and later exiled to Mexico, from where he helped prepare the *Granma* expedition. Since 1959, he has acted as Fidel's right-hand man and has served in many key positions, such as head of the (Cuban) Communist Party, Minister of Defence and Vice-President of the Council of State. He was appointed President in 2008 after his brother resigned for health reasons.

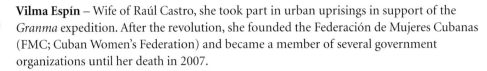

Vilma Espín – Wife of Raúl Castro, she took part in urban uprisings in support of the *Granma* expedition. After the revolution, she founded the Federación de Mujeres Cubanas (FMC; Cuban Women's Federation) and became a member of several government organizations until her death in 2007.

Camilo Cienfuegos – A survivor of the *Granma* expedition, Cienfuegos was responsible for many of the victories of the guerrillas in the Sierra Maestra. With the success of the revolution, he became head of the armed forces, but died in an aeroplane accident in 1959.

Ernesto 'Che' Guevara – A medical doctor born in Argentina, Guevara travelled throughout Latin America widely and became convinced that the region needed a solution to its poverty and corruption. He met the Castro brothers in Mexico and joined the *Granma* expedition. He was a leading figure in the Sierra Maestra fighting and became an icon of the revolution. After the revolution, he was responsible for the purges of Batistianos and other opponents. He also acted as head of the Bank of Cuba and Minister of Industry. Persuaded of the need to spread the revolution worldwide, he travelled to Congo in 1965 in support of a revolution, which ended in failure. In 1967 he was killed in Bolivia.

Haydée Santamaría – A member of the 26th of July Movement and sister to Abel. Together with her friend Melba Hernandez, she was one of the few women to participate in the Moncada assault. She then became responsible for distributing copies of Castro's 'History will absolve me' speech. Her role in the development of a Cuban culture after the revolution was fundamental. In 1959 she founded Casa de las Américas, a key literary institution of Cuba, which was visited by leading intellectuals and artists from all over the world. She committed suicide on 26 July 1980.

Celia Sánchez – A close friend of Fidel and an early member of the 26th of July Movement, she was responsible for providing land support for the *Granma* expedition. Once in Sierra Maestra, she contributed to the founding of the female 'Mariana Grajales' army. She occupied different government positions until her death in 1980.

SOURCE B

Bombs exploded in the capital. Two stores were attacked and in the exchange between police and the assailants, three uniformed men were killed and several wounded. Twenty civilians died. On interurban and rural transportation lines, drivers of trucks and buses, as well as automobile passengers, were attacked and killed. When the strike failed, the terrorists sabotaged the electric companies and plants, throwing many rural cities into darkness. For three days a section of Old Havana had no lights. To make repairs more difficult, the aggressors blew up one of the main outlets which used special cables not found in the Cuban market.

From Fulgencio Batista, *Cuba Betrayed*, 1962

STUDENT STUDY SECTION

QUESTIONS

a) **According to Source B, which methods were used by the rebels to fight?**

b) **With reference to its origins and purpose, assess the value and limitations of Source B to an historian studying the nature of the Cuban Revolution.**

In the Sierra Maestra mountains (1956–59)

Support for Castro and the rebels by the people from the Sierra Maestra increased with time, and varied from supplying the army with food and shelter to joining the rebels. There were several reasons why people all across Cuba felt attracted to the 26th of July Movement. First, peasants got to know a totally different type of army to the national army Batista had often used to suppress unrest. Castro's forces did not steal from the peasants and always paid for the food they were given. They respected women, put their medical doctors at the service of the peasants, taught them to read and write and even helped in the household chores. Any soldier breaking this code was sentenced to death. Peasants received more from the Rebel Army than they had ever received from the Cuban government.

Another factor that contributed to the popularity of and support for the Rebel Army was that their leaders explained what they were fighting for and what kind of new society they were hoping to achieve. The most important element in the new programme was the Agrarian Reform. The 26th of July Movement promised peasants an end to the ownership of large estates by a small sector of society or companies, and committed themselves to a fairer distribution of the land.

The rebels made use of the radio to spread their message and news about events in the Sierra. Radio Rebelde ('Rebel Radio') began to broadcast from 'the territory of Free Cuba in the Sierra' in 1958. People tuned in because they relied more on the news from Radio Rebelde than on the government media. Castro himself addressed the people on Radio Rebelde in a style that everyone understood. He also made sure people found out what government censorship was hiding from them about the fight against Batista.

Fidel Castro talks with local people. What is the message of this photo?

News about the progress made in the Sierra Maestra encouraged urban support for the revolution. Workers in towns and cities joined the revolution underground. They printed leaflets in support of the rebels and condemning Batista. They planted homemade bombs to blow up government installations, railways and public buildings, and sabotaged telephone lines, electricity stations and gas services. They assassinated those they believed to be enemies of the revolution.

SOURCE C

In the two-year period from Christmas, 1956, when the twelve men were alone on the mountain top until Batista fled and his army surrendered on January 1, 1959, nearly all classes of the population had identified themselves, in varying degrees, with the July 26th Movement. Some became an integral part of it because they believed in its revolutionary program; others made common cause with it because it had become the most effective force in the struggle to overthrow Batista.

To offset this overwhelming superiority in men and weapons, the revolutionary army had three advantages: (1) the battle was to be on its home grounds, a terrain of rugged mountains and treacherous jungle made to order for guerrilla warfare and defensive fighting; (2) unlike the government soldiers, the rebel soldiers weren't paid for fighting – they fought for something they believed in; (3) their leaders were men of outstanding ability – inspiring, humane, and master strategists in guerrilla warfare.

The rebel leaders' humanity – and excellent strategy – were illustrated in the order to the revolutionary army that captured soldiers were to be treated with kindness, their wounded given medical attention.

From Leo Huberman and Paul Sweezy, *Cuba: Anatomy of a Revolution*, 1960

STUDENT STUDY SECTION

QUESTIONS

a) **What light does Source C throw on the reasons why the 26th of July Movement and the Rebel Army gained support across the country?**

b) **What other reasons can you provide to explain the success of the Rebel Army?**

Fighting in itself did not guarantee the success of the revolution. The 26th of July Movement also needed to make alliances with other political parties and define the future of Cuba after the fall of Batista. Castro, aware of such needs, made contact with leaders from different political parties. By 1958, under the Pact of Caracas, the vast majority of the opposition recognized the leadership of Fidel Castro in the struggle to overthrow Batista. The Pact of Caracas included all the main political parties and organizations, even the communist PSP, which had remained critical of the Moncada attack and Castro's leadership until then. The pact was a heavy blow to Batista, as it openly exposed his political isolation.

To what extent did Batista contribute to the success of the revolution?

The success of the guerrilla war was due in part to the excesses of the incumbent regime. The police and the army imprisoned and tortured anyone they suspected of being a rebel or having helped rebels. This policy led to the death and imprisonment of many innocent men and women. To reduce support for the rebels, Batista ordered peasants to evacuate whole areas of the countryside, and those who remained behind were treated as traitors. In an attempt to wipe out rebels who could not be seen in the thick jungle, entire plantations were set on fire, causing the peasants to lose their crops. The government wanted to frighten citizens so that they would not help the rebels, but instead people were drawn to the rebels, in hatred of the government. Batista not only pushed people away from him, but also away from more moderate opposition into the arms of Fidel Castro, the 26th of July Movement and the Rebel Army.

Batista launched a major attack against the guerrillas in the Sierras in July 1958, but the campaign failed. Soldiers, fearful of the guerrilla forces and often isolated from relief, deserted in massive numbers or surrendered to the rebels without firing a shot. The weapons and equipment left behind by deserting soldiers were used by the resistance.

Elections were held in 1958 but Batista's candidate, Andrés Rivero, was fixed to win. This outcome disappointed the few who still hoped for a democratic solution to the conflict. For the same reasons, Rivero did not obtain US backing. In disagreement with Batista's violent actions, the USA imposed an arms embargo on Cuba in March 1958. The US position complicated government access to weapons and ammunitions and had a demoralizing effect on the army.

Batista still refused to negotiate. He rejected a proposal from the USA for him to capitulate to a caretaker government, to which the USA could give military and diplomatic support in order to prevent Fidel Castro coming to power. US officials feared Castro might turn to communism.

To access Worksheet 3.1 on the success of the Cuban revolution, please visit www.pearsonbacconline.com and follow the on-screen instructions.

GROUP DISCUSSION

You have now read about the reasons why support for Castro grew and about Batista's mistakes and miscalculations. In groups, discuss the relative importance you think each factor had in contributing to the fall of Batista and the rise of Castro.

Now consider the following question: **How and why did Fidel Castro come to power in Cuba?**

Under 'why' (reasons) you are being asked about factors that contributed to Castro's rise. These could include an analysis of the economic and social problems in Cuba before 1959; the failure of previous governments to address these issues and the consequences of that failure; the greed and corruption prevailing in society; the suspension of the 1940 constitution after 1952; the part played by Batista; and the reasons why Castro was appealing to different sectors of the Cuban population, among other relevant factors. Be careful not to produce a narrative of the historical background; you should focus on the links between Castro's rise and each condition you select. You may want to go back to the period before 1953 (for example, to explain the economic problems of Cuba), but the focus should remain on Castro and the events as from 1953.

The second part of the question asks you to explain how Castro came to power; that is, the methods he used.

Read the following paragraph on how Castro came to power:

Student Answer – *Antonio*

Fidel Castro was seen as someone who could bring genuine change to Cuban society. His promises to end corruption in the government and to produce a fairer society were of great importance to gain him the support of peasants in the Sierras. The fact that his soldiers helped with the harvest and taught the peasants to read and write also showed that they meant to bring about genuine change in society. Castro was seen as a hero and that helped his rise.

Examiner's comments

This paragraph focuses on a specific example of Castro's methods – his popular appeal. The candidate shows he understands how the conditions against which Castro rose were used to present his movement as one prepared to bring about genuine change, explaining how Castro's men related to the peasants and using specific examples to prove a point. However, this response could offer a deeper level of analysis. For example: why were the promises to end corruption and bring about justice of such importance? To whom? Castro was certainly not the only opponent to the government who believed in the need for such change, so what made him different? Was it perhaps the fact that he had dared act upon his beliefs in the Moncada assault? Who saw Castro as a hero? Why did this contribute to his rise?

REVISION ACTIVITY

Make a list of the methods used by Fidel Castro. Can you think of specific examples for each of the methods listed?

● **Examiner's hint**

This is a two-part question. It asks you to explain why (reasons) and how (methods) Castro came to power. Both aspects of the question must be addressed and you need to show clear knowledge and understanding of both reasons and methods.

● **Examiner's hint**

It is not sufficient to show that you know which methods Castro used in his rise to power. You also need to explain how they contributed to his rise. A paragraph explaining the events of the Moncada assault will not be an effective way to address how Castro came to power. You will need to explain the significance of the event in Castro's road to power by, for example, explaining how the use of force in Moncada enabled the Cuban population to identify Castro as a leader of the opposition who was prepared to act in order to change the situation.

The triumph of the revolution

After the success against Batista's forces in the Sierra, Castro believed the time had come to spread the war to the other Cuban provinces. He trusted Camilo Cienfuegos, Raúl Castro and Che Guevara to lead the campaigns. As they moved around, they were joined by more volunteers, marching at night or under the rain to hide from Batista's planes. By Christmas 1958, the city of Santa Clara, capital of the province of Las Villas, had been taken. Raúl and Fidel Castro marched towards Santiago de Cuba, while in Havana rebel leaders increased their acts of sabotage and their attacks against army installations. Politically isolated and unable to control the situation, Batista fled Cuba on 1 January 1959. The army refused to continue fighting against the rebels and an immediate ceasefire was ordered. Soon after, Fidel Castro and his *barbudos* ('bearded men') entered Havana and established a provisional government.

One explanation for Fidel Castro's rise to power can be found in his charisma. In an attempt to explain the sources of authority (i.e. why a leader was obeyed by the people), sociologist Max Weber defined the characteristics of charismatic leadership. He considers authority to come from the fact that the leader is set apart from the rest of the people because of his exceptional personal qualities or his exemplary actions, which inspire loyalty among his followers.

Eric Selbin in *Modern Latin American Revolutions* analyzes the part played by charisma in revolutions. He states that charismatic leaders promote and make the revolutionary process possible by their ability to represent the people's needs and aspirations in a vision of the future. Charismatic figures represent the potential for rejecting an old order, creating attractive future possibilities for the people.

STUDENT STUDY SECTION

Analyze the following sources and answer the questions below each.

SOURCE D

Photograph taken at a speech given by Fidel Castro in January 1959. The man behind Castro is Camilo Cienfuegos.

QUESTION
What is the message in Source D?

SOURCE E

Revolutionary leaders reached ascendancy in spectacular fashion, and en route were endowed with proportions larger than life. Already in 1959 the leaders of the revolution had become the stuff of legends and lore, the subjects of books and songs, of poems and films. Revolutionaries were celebrities, folk heroes, and the hope of the hopeful.

Extract from Louis A. Pérez Jr, *Cuba: Between Reform and Revolution*, 1988

QUESTIONS

a) **Why do you think that, according to Source E, the leaders of the revolution were the 'hope of the hopeful'?**

b) **Refer back to Source D and to Castro's 'History will absolve me' speech (Section II, Source A). How do you think these sources relate to the idea of charismatic leadership? Explain your answer fully.**

> Charismatic leaders are good communicators. They appeal to people's feelings and needs. In the next sections, you will study some of Fidel Castro's speeches. When you do, pay attention to the elements in the speech that relate to the ideas above.

SOURCE F

Castro thus stepped into a power vacuum that was not entirely of his making. He had skilfully seized the opportunities offered by a conjunction of historical conditions that were unique to Cuba. His success, moreover, owed as much to his imaginative use of the mass media as to the guerrilla campaign… By 1959 Castro had become the repository of many disparate [different] hopes for Cuba's regeneration. As he had made his slow triumphal way by road from Santiago to Havana, he was treated as the last in the long line of Cuban heroes – the last, because, unlike the others, he had survived and prevailed.

From Sebastian Balfour, *Castro*, 1990

QUESTIONS

a) **Explain the meaning of 'Castro had become the repository of many disparate hopes for Cuba's regeneration'?**

b) **Which opportunities do you think had been 'skilfully seized' by Castro?**

c) **Discuss the part played by the use of the mass media and the guerrilla campaign in Castro's success in the revolution. Explain your answer fully.**

d) **How does Castro's rise compare to that of other leaders you have studied? Did they come to power by the use of force? Were they, like Juan Perón, elected by the people? Did they, like Castro, come to power as a consequence of a fight against a dictatorial system?**

Section III:

The rule of Fidel Castro

Fidel Castro came to power certain that Cuba needed not only a new government, but a new order. This new order had to be based on Cuba's economic independence. The influence of the USA on Cuban affairs had brought, in Castro's view, many of the economic and social problems affecting the nation. It was not enough to have put an end to Batista's corrupt dictatorship. Just as Cubans wanted their political rights back, they also wanted better living conditions. Redistribution of land, improved working conditions and better wages were only a few of the demands people expected Castro and his men to address. Living standards needed to be raised; health and education made accessible to all. The question was how to meet these demands in the shortest period of time.

This section explains how and why Fidel Castro moved from being a member of the provisional government to becoming the undisputed leader of Cuba.

The consolidation of power (1959–62)

In order to consolidate the revolution, Castro made use of several methods between 1959 and 1962. First, he removed the people associated with Batista's regime. Next, he consolidated the position of the 26th of July Movement within the provisional government. Third, he launched reforms to show that the revolution lived up to its promises, and to gain support. Finally, he exploited the idea that Cuba was threatened by the USA and appealed to the people's sense of nationalism.

Citizens who had served in the Batista government and armed forces were now imprisoned, their properties confiscated as they were brought to trial. They were either executed or given long prison sentences. The trials took place with little time to assess the real participation in the Batista regime of each of the people involved, and they did not conform to the standards of justice. As such, they were criticized not only in Cuba but also in the USA for not offering human rights guarantees to the prisoners. Those who believed justice had not been done were told that the revolution was endangered by these people and that 'immediate justice' was more necessary than a fair trial.

The provisional government established in January 1959 was formed by a significant number of liberals. They hoped to moderate the left-wing elements, which included the rebels of the 26th of July Movement as well as members of the PSP, the Cuban communist party. The government was led by moderates Manuel Urrutia as President and José Miró Cardona as his Prime Minister. Castro set up an office outside the presidential palace, at the Havana Hilton hotel, as commander of Cuban armed forces.

In spite of the provisional government representing many political sectors, real authority was in the hands of Fidel Castro from the very start. He was seen everywhere and heard by everyone. His almost daily speeches appealed to people's hopes for a new Cuba, based on the grand ideas of the leaders of the independence and the ideals of social justice, economic security and political freedom. He approached people in a way that Cuba had never experienced before, going out into the streets and travelling across the country to meet them face to face. It was not uncommon to see Castro spending an afternoon in a rural village discussing who should repair tractors or fixing refrigerators for the people.

Six weeks after the provisional government took over, Prime Minister Cardona unexpectedly resigned. Fidel Castro stepped in as Prime Minister. Next, in July 1959, President Urrutia resigned because he was opposed to the increasing influence of communists in the government, as well as to Castro's refusal to hold elections. He was replaced by Osvaldo Dorticós, who remained President until the 1976 constitution was passed.

Castro's appointment as Prime Minister enabled the revolution to move quickly, implementing reforms that led to the transformation of the country into a communist state by the end of 1961. He was supported in this move to the left by the members of the PSP.

SOURCE A

Personal turnovers in the government, in part voluntary, in part forced, increased quickly thereafter. Liberals and moderates resigned, or were forced out, their places taken by loyal fidelistas and members of the PSP. At the time, senior administrative positions in the Ministry of Labour were filled by the PSP. The presence of the PSP in the armed forces was also increased. Party members received teaching appointments at various Rebel Army posts in Havana and Las Villas. The appearance of the PSP in the armed forces, in turn, led to wholesale resignation and, in some cases, arrest of anti-communist officers. In October, Raúl Castro assumed charge of the Ministry of the Revolutionary Armed Forces (MINFAR), and forthwith launched a thorough reorganization of the military, distributing key commands to only trustworthy officers. By the end of the year, anti-communism had become synonymous with counter-revolution.

From Louis A. Pérez Jr, *Cuba: Between Reform and Revolution*, 1988

STUDENT STUDY SECTION

QUESTIONS

a) **With reference to Source A and your own knowledge, account for the increasing influence of the PSP in the revolutionary government.**

b) **What is the significance of the policies implemented by Raúl Castro?**

c) **What are the implications of 'by the end of the year, anti-communism had become synonymous with counter-revolution'?**

Castro and his supporters introduced dramatic changes in the organization of the political parties in Cuba. In 1961, various revolutionary organizations that had acted against Batista were unified under the Integrated Revolutionary Organizations (ORI), which aimed to provide the government with a political party of its own. The ORI was formed by the 26th of July Movement (led by Castro), the PSP and the Directorio Revolucionario (Revolutionary Directorate), a revolutionary student organization. The following year, ORI became the Partido Unido de la Revolución Socialista de Cuba (PURSC; United Party of the Socialist Revolution of Cuba) under Castro's leadership. In 1965, the Party was renamed Partido Comunista Cubano (PCC; Cuban Communist Party).

The PCC remains the only officially authorized political party in Cuba and has ruled since 1965, as other existing political parties in Cuba cannot participate in elections. The PCC began to publish its own newspaper, *Granma*, and developed its youth branch (Young Communist League) and children's organization (the José Martí Pioneers).

SOURCE B

Since we feel that we have already reached a stage in which all types of labels and things that distinguish some revolutionaries from others must disappear once and for all and forever and that we have already reached the fortunate point in the history of our revolutionary process in which we can say that there is only one type of revolutionary, and since it is necessary that the name of our party says, not what we were yesterday, but what we are today and what we will be tomorrow, what, in your opinion, is the name our party should have? The Communist Party of Cuba! Well, that is the name that the revolutionary conscience of its members, and the objectives of our revolution, our first central committee adopted yesterday, and that is quite proper.

From a speech by Fidel Castro at the inaugural meeting of the PCC, 1965

STUDENT STUDY SECTION

QUESTIONS

a) **What reasons does Fidel Castro give in Source B for the foundation of the PCC?**

b) **What other reasons can you suggest to explain the foundation of this party?**

RESEARCH ACTIVITY

In groups, carry out research on the history of the *Granma* newspaper. Find out information about its relationship with the Cuban state. Also, discuss why you think the PCC formed a youth branch and a children's organization.

Huber Matos (1918–)

A former teacher and member of the Orthodox Party who joined the Rebel Army against Batista. He played a leading part in the Sierra Maestra days in the taking of Santiago de Cuba. In the early stages of the revolution he was appointed commander of the army in the province of Camagüey. Soon after that, he began to express his opposition to the radicalization of the revolution and was arrested by Castro. He spent 20 years in prison and was subjected to physical and psychological tortures. When released in 1979 he fled to Miami, where he has become a leading voice of the Cuban dissidence and published his memoirs, *How the Night Came*.

The growing influence of the PCC and of communist ideas in the government was looked at with some suspicion, even within Castro's inner circle. While men like Raúl Castro and Che Guevara welcomed the revolution's turn to the left, not everyone supported this shift.

One of the people who opposed the turn to the left was **Huber Matos**, a leader of the 26th of July Movement. He decided to resign as Military Chief of Camagüey – where he enjoyed immense popularity – because he opposed the increasing influence of communist ideas in the revolution and also objected to Castro's refusal to set a date for elections in Cuba. The resignation of someone who had played a leading role in the revolution would have been a great embarrassment for Castro. Also, there was fear that Matos' attitude could encourage more dissidence within the movement. After failing to persuade Matos not to resign, Castro ordered Camilo Cienfuegos to inform Matos that he was under arrest and would be tried for conspiracy and treason against the revolution.

Shortly after his visit to Camagüey, Cienfuegos' plane disappeared in an accident. The bodies of the passengers and the remains of the aircraft were never found. There are several theories that propose that Castro had Cienfuegos eliminated. One claims that Cienfuegos had also expressed his concerns about the communist nature of the reforms. Another theory claims that what disturbed Castro above all was Cienfuegos' popularity. The Cuban government has always explained these events as an accident. Matos was accused of treason and sentenced to 20 years' imprisonment. He was released after he fulfilled his sentence and left Cuba in 1979.

The reforms of 1959–62

SOURCE C

*We will not forget our peasants in the Sierra Maestra and those in the interior of the country…
I will never forget those country people and as soon as I have a free moment we will see about
building the first school city with seats for 20,000 children. We will do it with the help of the
people and the rebels will work with them there. We will ask each citizen for a bag of cement
and a trowel. I know we will have the help of our industry and of business and we will not
forget any of the sectors of our population.*

*There will be freedom for all men because we have achieved freedom for all men. We shall never
feel offended; we shall always defend ourselves and we shall follow a single precept, that of
respect for the rights and feelings of others.*

From a speech by Fidel Castro in Santiago de Cuba, 3 January 1959

STUDENT STUDY SECTION

QUESTIONS

a) **What, according to Source C, were Castro's aims?**

b) **How did he plan to achieve them?**

c) **In your view, who is the speech addressed to? Explain your answers fully.**

The speech above (Source C) was one of many of similar tone delivered by Castro
immediately after the overthrow of Batista, focusing on the challenges ahead and the
proposed solutions. If you refer to a complete version of the 'History will absolve me'
speech, you will be able to identify many similarities with this speech. Castro offered every
sector of society what they needed: work for the unemployed, land for rural workers,
improved working conditions for the urban workers. The middle class were promised they
would be able to become professionals; women that they would be able to work in equal
conditions to men. Castro concentrated on his role as a man of action, designing policies to
bring about these changes.

The most significant of the measures in this period was the Agrarian Reform Act, which
aimed at making the distribution of land more equitable, agriculture more efficient and
Cuba less dependent on sugar. The act, which had been promised by the rebels in the
Sierra Maestra days, restricted the land that could be owned; anyone having more than the
established limit had that extra part **expropriated** and received **bonds** as compensation.
Expropriated land was to be organized in **cooperatives**. The Act also nationalized the land
in foreign hands and ended both Cuban and foreign ownership of large estates, while still
allowing private medium- and small-sized farms. These would be the targets of the second
(1963) and third (1968) Agrarian Reform laws.

The act was opposed by property owners affected by the reform, and was widely criticized
in the Cuban press. It also raised alarm in the USA, as the companies affected saw it as a
confiscatory measure and refused to settle for the compensation in Cuban bonds that was
offered. Washington began to consider cutting the sugar quota in retaliation.

Other reforms included an increase in wages and the reduction of rents. These created great
enthusiasm amongst the lower classes but, again, antagonized the middle and upper classes.
Foreign-owned companies began to face waves of strikes as workers took advantage of a
more favourable political situation to demand increases in wages and improved working
conditions. They found support in the new government, which intervened in many of the

Expropriation
Taking property out of an
owner's hands by public
authority.

Bond
An official document
issued by a government
or a company to show
that you have lent them
money that they will pay
back to you at a fixed
interest rate.

Cooperative
An association that is
managed by the people
who work in it.

conflicts, often in favour of the workers. Some foreign companies were threatened with expropriation, accused of representing countries that had provided Batista with weapons.

Import taxes were imposed on 'luxury goods' with several aims. Making these goods more expensive aimed at reducing their imports so that less money was spent on them by Cubans. But also, with the money raised with these taxes, the government hoped to invest in industrialization and the diversification of the economy (i.e. break with the sugar monoculture). This again affected the USA, which saw its sales to Cuba decrease by as much as 35 per cent.

To improve the living conditions, the government began to work on education and health reforms. Later in this chapter, you will be offered a detailed analysis of the literacy campaign of 1961.

● Examiner's hint
The study of a leader's rise to power requires considering the links between the conditions that contributed to his rise, the promises made in response, and the eventual policies implemented. You should be able to assess the extent to which the promises made addressed the problems of the country, and whether the policies implemented were effective in fulfilling those promises. Once you have completed the table opposite, see if you can produce a chart for other leaders you have studied.

STUDENT STUDY SECTION

You have now examined the conditions of how and why Castro came to power. You have also analyzed the promises he made to the Cuban population and some of the reforms implemented in the period 1959–62. Copy and complete the following chart to help you establish the links between these three factors. There are some suggestions already inserted to help you get started; add as many rows as you consider necessary until you have addressed as many aspects as you can. Compare your chart with others in your group.

CONDITION	PROMISE	POLICIES
		Agrarian Reform
Illiteracy		
	Economic independence	

Effects of the reforms

The reforms announced between 1959 and 1962 had several results. First, they allowed Castro and the PSP to become more popular among many sectors of society and to consolidate their position in the government. Many Cubans therefore became less concerned about when Castro would call for elections and restore the constitution. They seemed to accept the idea that it was first necessary to dismantle the old political, social and economic systems.

Yet there was a certain level of resistance to the changes, as small groups opposed the pace of the revolution and took up arms in some parts of the country. Local opposition was controlled by the government and did not lead to major crises, particularly because at this stage Castro still allowed those against the revolution to leave the country. Between January 1959 and October 1962, approximately 250,000 people left Cuba, including former *batistianos*, middle-class citizens who feared the radicalization of the revolution, and members of religious congregations who disliked the communist nature of the reforms.

Castro was less successful in dealing with opposition from the USA. Relations between Havana and Washington deteriorated dramatically between 1959 and 1962. Two major incidents developed in these years, the Bay of Pigs invasion (1961) and the Cuban Missile Crisis (1962).

American–Cuban relations (1959–62)

Even before 1959, Fidel Castro had made it clear that he believed Cuba needed to develop its economy outside the shadow of the USA. When US interests began to be affected by Cuban policies, Washington pressed other countries to prevent economic aid from reaching the island. Castro then ordered the expropriation of US property in Cuba. In turn, Eisenhower cancelled the sugar quota, a measure which extended into an economic embargo that was intensified in October 1960, after all US banks in Cuba had been confiscated.

While tensions between the USA and Cuba increased, Cuban relations with the USSR improved. Probably encouraged by the direction of the early reforms, in May 1960 the Soviets established formal diplomatic relations between the two countries. (Previously, relations between Cuba and the USSR had been severed as a consequence of Batista's coup in 1952.) Trade agreements were signed and Cuba found a new market for its sugar production. The USSR also granted Castro loans to purchase industrial equipment and weapons. It was not long before the USSR promised to help Cuba 'prevent an armed United States intervention against Cuba'.

The Bay of Pigs Invasion (1961)

While Cuba was cementing its relationship with Moscow, Washington contemplated a plan for the invasion of the island. The plan aimed at using Cuban exiles, trained as a paramilitary force, to return to Cuba and overthrow Castro. This was the origin of the Bay of Pigs invasion of April 1961.

President J.F. Kennedy (1961–63) had promised a tough attitude against the penetration of Marxism in Latin America. He approved the plan, which had been devised during President Eisenhower's administration (1953–61). Cuban exiles trained in Guatemala and Nicaragua in preparation to invade Cuba to start a popular uprising against Castro. US troops were not to be directly involved in the invasion. The Cuban Revolutionary Council, an anti-Castro group led by former Prime Minister Miró Cardona, now exiled in the USA, was ready to take over and form a provisional government after the fall of Castro.

The operation was a failure on many levels. When the troops landed in Bay of Pigs (Playa Girón), Cuban forces led by Castro himself defeated them and imprisoned more than 1,000 participants. The hope that the invasion would spark spontaneous uprisings against Castro revealed that the significance of his reforms had not been fully understood by Washington.

Fidel Castro emerged from Bay of Pigs more powerful than before. The victory against the USA made Cubans conclude that Castro was definitely making Cuba a stronger country, and the credibility of the revolution was reinforced. The image of Castro leading the resistance against the invasion added a new dimension to his hero-worship and reinforced Cuban nationalism. In addition, the Bay of Pigs episode gave Castro what he needed to demand increasing commitment to the revolution: a visible enemy. In the face of this, Cubans needed to remain united and accept the leadership of Castro in preparation for another attack. A final implication of the Bay of Pigs was that it tempted the USSR to establish stronger military ties with Cuba, and a military presence within Cuba itself.

The Cuban Missile Crisis (1962)

The next incident between Cuba and the USA came with the Cuban Missile Crisis of October 1962, when Washington and Moscow confronted each other over the Soviet placement of nuclear missiles on the island. The crisis took the world to the brink of

To access Worksheet 3.2 on cartoon analysis and the Cuban revolution, please visit www.pearsonbacconline.com and follow the on-screen instructions.

● **Examiner's hint**
Paper 2 will not ask specific questions on the foreign policies of leaders. In the case of Fidel Castro, however, it becomes very difficult to understand his domestic policies without making some reference to Cuban relations with the USA and USSR. Although no question will ask about Cuba's relations with other countries, you need to have some understanding of events like the Bay of Pigs invasion and the Cuban Missile Crisis to grasp the changes in, for example, Cuba's economy.

To access Worksheet 3.3 on Fidel Castro, Agrarian Reform and the USA, please visit www.pearsonbacconline.com and follow the on-screen instructions.

nuclear war. After 13 days of tense negotiations, the Soviets removed the missiles and dismantled the sites in Cuba. In exchange, the USA removed its own nuclear missiles from Turkey and made a promise that it would not invade the island. Although this pledge was good news for Cuba, Castro was faced with the disappointment that the Soviets would no longer defend his island.

STUDENT STUDY SECTION
RESEARCH ACTIVITY **Find information to help you understand the context against which the Bay of Pigs incident and the Cuban Missile Crisis took place. What do you know about the Cold War? How was Cuba affected by this conflict?**
CLASS DISCUSSION **With your class, discuss whether the Bay of Pigs incident and the Cuban Missile Crisis strengthened or weakened Castro's position in Cuba. Find material to support your views. This could include treatment of these events in the Cuban press, public speeches, popular songs, etc.**

● **Examiner's hint**
If a Paper 2 question asks you to discuss issues relating to the consolidation of power, answers on Castro should only include events up to 1962.

By 1962, Fidel Castro had freed himself from the *batistianos* and the liberals in government. He had also extinguished revolts in the provinces and implemented revolutionary domestic policies. No other figure from the revolution seemed to be in a condition to dispute his authority. Furthermore, he emerged from this period with a more radical position by accepting Soviet assistance, and also making public that he was a Marxist-Leninist. In December 1961, for example, he declared 'I am a Marxist-Leninist and shall be one until the end of my life.'

Fidel Castro's ideology

It is often discussed whether Castro had always intended to align the revolution with Marxism or whether this was the product of US policies that pushed Cuba into the arms of the USSR. It was not clear in 1959 that Cuba would soon adopt a communist ideology. The inclusion of liberals in the provisional government, for example, seemed to indicate that all the revolution was hoping to change was tyranny for democracy. Also, in 1959 Castro seemed little inclined to commit himself to any specific ideology or detailed programme, and he publicly denied any relation between the 26th of July Movement and the communists. He refused to answer questions about which global political ideology matched his own. Any observance of a fixed set of principles, such as communism, would have restricted the methods at Castro's disposal.

SOURCE D

The 26 July movement which is a truly revolutionary movement, which wants to establish the economy of the country on a just basis, which is a revolutionary movement and at the same time a democratic movement with broad human content, was established in Cuba, its ranks were swelled by many people who previously had no political alternative and who inclined toward parties with radical ideas. The 26 July movement is one with radical ideas, but it is not a communist movement, and it differs basically from communism on a whole series of basic points. And those in the 26 July movement, both Raúl and Guevara, like all the others, are men who agree very closely with my political thinking, which is not communist thinking. The thinking of the 26 July movement is not communist thinking.

From a transcript of a press conference given by Fidel Castro at Havana Presidential Palace on 27 February 1959

Section IV:
Castro in power: Economic policies and their impact

Fidel Castro aimed to make Cuba an economically independent and industrialized nation. However, the Cuban economy was to remain linked to the decisions and policies of other nations. The US **embargo**, the economic dependence on the Soviets and the impact of the subsequent collapse of the USSR on Cuba helped shape Castro's different economic policies. Although these policies were claimed to uphold the aims of the revolution, Cuba responded to the internal and international challenges with different – and at times contradictory – instruments.

This section analyzes the economic policies adopted by Cuba after 1962 in order to assess their levels of success in achieving the revolutionary aims.

The influence of Che Guevara: Moral incentives and voluntarism

A revolutionary who played an important part in the design of Cuba's economic policies was Che Guevara. He occupied the positions of President of the National Bank of Cuba and, later, Minister of Industries. With the revolution in power, Guevara believed it was time to leave capitalism behind and adopt communism. He favoured a **centrally planned economy**, with an emphasis on moral incentives and self-sacrifice. By this he meant that people should work for the ideals and values of the revolution rather than for personal gains. Moral incentives included **socialist emulation**, party membership and state recognition, amongst others. All workers were to receive equal pay; overtime would not be

paid for, as workers were expected to cover it voluntarily as their personal contribution to
the revolution.

Guevara aimed at creating a new consciousness, and with it a 'new man' prepared to
sacrifice himself for a higher good – a society ruled by the principles of the revolution.

SOURCE A

*We are doing everything possible to give labour this new status of social duty and to link it on
the one side with the development of a technology which will create the conditions for greater
freedom, and on the other side with voluntary work based on a Marxist appreciation of the fact
that man truly reaches a full human condition when he produces without being driven by the
physical need to sell his labour as a commodity.*

*This is not a matter of how many pounds of meat one might be able to eat, nor of how many
times a year someone can go to the beach, nor how many ornaments from abroad you might
be able to buy with present salaries. What is really involved is that the individual feels more
complete, with much more internal richness and much more responsibility.*

From Ernesto Guevara, 'Socialism and Man in Cuba', 1965

SOURCE B

Ernesto 'Che' Guevara at work
with Cuban locals. ▶

STUDENT STUDY SECTION

QUESTIONS

a) **What, according to Source A, were the aims of the revolution? How does this
speech compare to Castro's 'History will absolve me' speech?**

b) **What is the message of Source B? How do you think this photograph relates
to Source A?**

c) **In groups, discuss the ideas presented by Guevara in 'Socialism and Man in
Cuba'. Can you identify any source of inspiration for Guevara's ideas? Who
do you think they were appealing to and who might have opposed to them?
Justify your answers.**

The push to transform the Cuban economy into a communist one continued after 1961. In 1962, Cuba changed the national currency and anyone caught with their savings in banks that did not belong to the state lost them overnight. In the cities, rents – which had been reduced by 50 per cent in 1959 – were abolished. This meant that those people living in a property that they did not own virtually became property owners overnight. In 1963, a second Agrarian Law reduced again the amount of land that could be owned by a single person or entity, to prevent the existence of 'rich' peasants. After 1963, the state owned 70 per cent of the land, the rest being small farms, which were expropriated in 1968.

But the economic plans to increase productivity met several obstacles. First of all, Cuba faced a lack of specialized personnel and technicians, many of whom had left the country since the revolution. This deficit meant that the assessment of problems and the implementation of solutions was limited. Also, moral incentives were not efficient in raising productivity levels and tackling poor-quality work and absenteeism. Farmers in collective farms were forced to sell their product to the state at very low prices. They consequently lost motivation to produce more than what they needed to survive. As a result, sugar production levels were very low and government plans to diversify away from the cultivation of sugar did not compensate for the drop in those levels.

Determined to advance the industrialization programme, the government continued to buy machinery from the USSR and Eastern European nations and to increase its debt. Cuba was again trapped in trade relations of subsidized sugar in exchange for goods and, by 1964, it had to return to intensive sugar production to reduce debt.

The Revolutionary Offensive (1968)

In March 1968, Castro launched the 'Revolutionary Offensive' to move Cuba further towards a communist state and remove the last vestiges of capitalism from the island. The Offensive emphasized the ideas of Guevara's 'new man', in which work was a social duty rather than a way to achieve personal aims. Under the Revolutionary Offensive, Castro ordered the expropriation of all remaining privately owned enterprises, such as family stores, restaurants, handicraft stores, grocers, service shops and street vendors. All of these were to be owned and managed by the state and put at the service of a centrally planned economy. Farmers' markets were eliminated. Self-employment was banned, as it was seen as pursuing individualist aims.

The Offensive did not achieve an increase in productivity, but instead produced administrative chaos as the number of government agencies needed to organize the different fields of production and sales grew exponentially. Also, the return to the policy of moral incentives was met with high levels of absenteeism and vagrancy.

The 'Year of the Ten Million' (1970)

In order to solve the problems left by the revolutionary offensive in 1969, Castro announced that he intended Cuba to break its previous sugar production record and reach a 10 million ton output in 1970. The campaign aimed to obtain from the harvest enough money to pay off Cuban debts to the USSR and, by selling surplus sugar, make investments to achieve economic diversification. In Castro's words, it was 'a liberation campaign'.

With 1970 becoming the 'Year of the Ten Million', the *zafra* (sugar season) became another battle for Cuban pride. It was intended to show those who remained sceptical about the revolution that it could attain its dreams. The campaign became a crusade that mobilized the entire population and became a political test for Castro.

In order to achieve the 10 million tons target, and aware that the appeal to voluntarism and solidarity had not guaranteed results in the past, Castro appealed for the 'militarization' of labour (organized and disciplined like an army). Students, conscripts, law breakers, emigrants awaiting their turn to leave the island – all worked cutting cane side by side as 'volunteers'. The armed forces occupied the sugar-producing regions and were put in charge of the sugar mills. Castro himself was seen cutting cane in street posters, to motivate people to work. To increase productivity, bars and theatres were closed and even Christmas and New Year celebrations were cancelled.

SOURCE C

Propaganda poster used in 1970. It reads 'And where shall we be on January 2? AT THE SUGAR CANE!'

y dónde estaremos el 2 de enero ?
EN LA CAÑA !

STUDENT STUDY SECTION

QUESTIONS

a) What is the message of Source C?

b) What do you think was the purpose of the poster?

c) How does it help you understand the nature of the campaign?

Despite the fact that the entire nation had been put at the service of the campaign, and that a record harvest of 8.5 million tons was reached, Castro was forced to admit that they had been unable to reach the 10 million tons target. Deep harm had been inflicted on the economy. The agricultural machines had been over-used; agricultural production of crops other than sugar had suffered; other economic areas such as forestry and fishing had seen important losses. Rather than raise the morale of Cubans, the campaign had exhausted them and made them sceptical. The soldiers, for example, who had been mobilized to oversee operations, had felt their status diminished – they had been used to cut cane when they had been trained to defend the nation.

Because the campaign had been given so much importance, its failure was a terrible blow for Castro not only at an economic but also at a political level. In an address to the nation on 26 July 1970, he admitted that the campaign's failure was due to the administrative apparatus rather than the ordinary citizens' commitment. In doing so, and by offering his resignation to a crowd that cheered his name, Fidel Castro managed to survive the political effects of the failure. The price he had to pay was the abandonment of Guevara's ideas of solidarity, voluntarism and self-sacrifice, and the acceptance of a greater economic dependency on the USSR.

Farmers' markets were reinstated. State-owned companies were given enough autonomy to take some daily decisions without having to go through the state bureaucracy. Material incentives, such as pay for overtime work, were introduced. However, Cuba continued to suffer similar economic problems.

The end of the 1970s brought new levels of recession. Cuba was badly hit by the international economic situation as the USSR cut the price it paid for Cuban sugar. Unemployment, debt and policies that limited consumption led to increased discontent, which contributed to the 1980 **Mariel** exodus, when 125,000 abandoned Cuba for the USA.

Mariel
Mariel was one of Cuba's emigration ports. Built between 1762 and 1768 on the Mariel Bay in the province of Pinar del Río, it soon became an important deep-water port and integral to the country's economy.

The Rectification Campaign (1986)

In 1986, Castro blamed the more liberal measures that had been adopted in the past for the present economic problems. He consequently advocated a return to the values of solidarity and voluntarism under the 'Rectification Campaign'. The aim was to 'rectify errors and negative tendencies' linked to the relaxation of communist principles after 1970.

Under the Rectification Campaign, farmers' markets were again banned; bonuses and extra pay were abolished and self-employment was discouraged. Farm cooperatives were given new emphasis as, under a new Agrarian Reform Act, the percentage of land managed by independent farmers dropped to 2 per cent. Labour discipline was enforced and the workers lost many union rights.

The economic results of the Rectification Campaign were poor. Productivity fell; absenteeism at work increased. Reduced supplies of milk, oil, textiles and sugar led to an increase in their prices. Parallel or black markets reappeared to offer goods that were difficult to obtain, or that had been added to the list of rationed products. Transport and electricity rates also increased and affected the population's living standards. But Cuba had not yet seen the worst.

The Special Period (1991)

The dissolution of the USSR in 1991 was, in Castro's words, 'the most unfavourable international economic juncture ever faced by the Cuban economy in the entire history of the Revolution'. The 30-year period in which the USSR had become central to Cuba's economy and social development ended suddenly and unexpectedly. Soviet technicians left Cuba as hundreds of projects were abandoned. Subsidized goods, oil, access to international loans and everything the USSR had provided to Cuba were finished.

As a result, Castro announced Cuba had entered a 'special period in peacetime'. Cubans faced new levels of rationing as basic goods disappeared from the market. With Soviet oil gone, the need to save energy limited the working hours of the population, imposed long black-outs and restricted public transport.

SOURCE D

Large cuts had been made in food rations, and gasoline, electricity and other goods and services were in short supply. Food was scarce. People were not starving, but they could definitely not eat as much as they had before and they complained that there was no lard or cooking oil and that the food therefore had no taste. A disease was spreading that affected the eyes and the legs of many people and that was later diagnosed as caused by the drastic drop in food intake.

From Mona Rosendahl, *Inside the Revolution: Everyday Life in Socialist Cuba,* **1997**

STUDENT STUDY SECTION

QUESTIONS

a) **What does Source D reveal about the state of the Cuban economy during the Special Period?**

b) **To what extent can it be argued that the Special Period demonstrated that the Cuban revolution had failed in its economic aims?**

In order to adjust to the new scenario, and in response to growing unrest at home, new policies were implemented:

- A large percentage of state-owned farms began to be run as worker-managed cooperatives in an attempt to increase levels of productivity.
- In an effort to attract capital and diversify economic activities, Cuba was opened to international business. Foreigners were invited to join the state in the development of certain areas of the economy, such as tourism, mining and energy. Tourism in particular developed positively.
- In 1993 it was made legal for Cubans to buy and sell US dollars in an attempt to attract dollars from the relatives of Cubans overseas. The fact that Cubans could now buy and sell dollars freely had a positive impact on the demand for goods and contributed to the reactivation of the economy.
- Farmers' and handcraft markets reappeared and some level of self-employment and private businesses was allowed. The state aimed at saving money by reducing some subsidies and increasing taxes.

By 1994, those who had predicted the collapse of the regime were again proved wrong, as Cuba was showing some signs of economic recovery. Sugar had been replaced by tourism.

STUDENT STUDY SECTION

Fill in the following chart by identifying the aims of the different economic programmes you have studied in this section and listing their successes and failures. It will be useful revision before you approach the next exercises.

POLICY	AIMS	ACHIEVEMENTS	FAILURES

QUESTION

Consider the following question: 'Fidel Castro's government tried to promote economic development, but his policies did not succeed.' To what extent do you agree with this view?

Now read the following introduction to the question above:

● **Examiner's hint**
An effective approach to this question requires that you first show that the revolutionary government sought to generate economic growth. Because the question does not ask you to focus on a specific period, it would be a good idea to decide, before you start writing, which specific policies you plan to address. For each of the selected policies, you should show how the government hoped it would produce economic growth and then decide the extent to which this was achieved.

Student Answer A – *Jenna*

Fidel Castro came to power in Cuba in 1959 with the aim of making radical changes to the country. He promised to end inequality, corruption and the economic dependency on the USA. With these aims, he implemented economic policies to generate economic growth. These policies included the nationalization of industries and banks, the passing of an Agrarian Reform Act and the development of national industries. However, they did not bring about economic growth. Castro's attempt to increase the production of sugar to pay for the industrialization of the country did not succeed, as shown by the failure to reach the target of the 10 million tons of sugar in 1970. Also, after the revolution Cuba began to depend on the USSR and, with the collapse of that state, Cuba entered a very difficult economic period.

Examiner's comments

This introduction shows specific knowledge of the aims and policies of Castro's economy and the candidate is aware of the need to assess them. More could have been done to show explicitly which period/policies are treated in the essay and the attempt to assess the 10 million tons campaign could have been left for the essay itself.

Now read the following conclusion to the question above:

Student Answer B – *Jenna*

The Cuban revolution did not produce the promised economic growth. Under Fidel Castro, Cuba continued to experience the problems caused by economic dependence and the consequences of the collapse of the USSR on the island were devastating. Castro was equally unable to develop a national industry that would make Cuba more self-sufficient and the country was never really able to reduce the influence of the sugar market on the national economy. Economic policies increased the shortage of goods, which made the living standards of the population drop, as seen during the Rectification Campaign. Although the Cuban population gained access to land to work and houses to live in, the levels of economic recession were very high at different times, as shown by the analysis of the late 1970s. All in all, the economic policies of Cuba never brought economic growth.

Examiner's comments

This conclusion is very focused on the demands of the question. It also makes reference to specific arguments which, presumably, have been developed throughout the essay. Make sure you do not introduce new arguments and new evidence in your conclusion because there will be no time for you to develop the ideas. Use the conclusion to round up the supporting arguments you have presented in the essay with a clear focus on how they have helped answer the question before you.

Now read the following question: 'To what extent were the economic aims of the revolution achieved by Fidel Castro's government by 1990?'

- **In what ways is this question similar/ different to the previous one?**
- **How would you approach it?**
- **Think of the arguments you could develop and which examples you would be using to illustrate each point made.**

● **Examiner's hint**
This question requires a more specific treatment of the aims of the revolution and you will need to identify them early in your essay.

Section V:
Social policies

The revolution aimed to introduce social justice and allow all sectors of society to have equal opportunities. Reforms in health, education, and the treatment of women and of minorities were implemented, among other areas. Some of these reforms clashed with Cuban traditions and culture. Therefore, the arts played a fundamental role in designing a new Cuban culture in which, for example, the role of women as workers was promoted.

The following section analyzes two significant areas of social policy: the status of women and education. It evaluates the parts played by the FMC and the literacy campaign to change the status of women and promote education. It analyzes the relationship between the Cuban government and the arts to understand the attempt to transform Cuban culture through revolutionary values. It also addresses the relationship between the revolution and religious and racial groups.

Status of women

The status of women in Cuba by 1959 was different from that in many Latin American countries. Women were given the right to vote as early as 1934. The 1940 constitution also granted them equality before the law: women could not be discriminated against at work and were to receive equal pay for equal work. Yet although women were allowed to vote, study, work and even sue for divorce, pre-revolutionary Cuba remained in many ways a traditional society. Only a few occupations, such as teaching and nursing, were considered to be appropriate for women in the pre-revolutionary years. Women often faced discrimination at work, as the jobs with greater responsibility went to men. In the middle and upper classes, men preferred women to stay at home to look after their families rather than join the workforce.

The defence of the rights of women at work was largely a response to Cuba's economic needs. To achieve modernization, and in order to produce record harvests, women needed to become an active part of the workforce. This implied having to fight against two main problems: discrimination against women at work and finding how to make women's role in the workforce and the household compatible.

To address the first problem, new legislation was passed reinforcing the equal rights of men and women to access all types of jobs. Women were offered training at technical and professional levels to prepare themselves for posts with greater responsibility. They entered fields that had so far been almost exclusively all-male, such as construction, biotechnology and IT. In the rural areas, the Agrarian Reform acts opened the opportunity for women to work in areas that had also been limited to men, such as driving and repairing tractors. In the towns and cities, an increasing number of daycare centres for working mothers were made available so that women could become part of the workforce.

Under Castro, women were expected to leave their families and homes for long periods and work in 'Agricultural Legions', cutting cane and harvesting coffee and other crops. There was pressure on women to be efficient workers, participate in political life, volunteer to serve the revolution while at the same time fulfil their responsibilities as wives, mothers and housewives.

Cuba nevertheless remained a very patriarchal society. Women were expected to fulfil their roles as housewives, but men refused to share household responsibilities or live with potentially economically independent women. This conflict proved difficult to manage and resulted in many women giving up work and in entire families leaving Cuba.

In the 1970s, a new 'Family Code' was put in place. It stipulated equality of sexes both at home and at work. Men were to share in the household duties and the education of children; not doing so was seen as the exploitation of women. The presence of women in the workforce, however, remained lower than government expectations, a fact that even Castro was forced to admit.

SOURCE A

◀ Photograph showing a peasant woman ready for work.

SOURCE B

◀ A group of Cuban women enjoy a music class, c. 1965.

Case study: The Federación de Mujeres Cubanas (FMC)

The FMC was created by Vilma Espín (wife of Raúl Castro) in 1960 with the aim of helping women integrate into the revolution. It trained women to take up new jobs in farming, construction and teaching, among others. The FMC also organized many aspects of the campaign against illiteracy, and created and ran successful health programmes. FMC women joined 'Sanitary Brigades' that travelled to the rural areas to deliver vaccination campaigns, and they also served as social workers. The FMC worked with the Ministry of Education in the design of new textbooks to be used in revolutionary Cuba. In them, women were portrayed as committed workers and soldiers. Former domestic workers were trained to work as seamstresses or cooks, and they received education in history, geography and the new laws of revolutionary Cuba. Housewives were also taught in FMC headquarters so that they could complete their schooling.

Assessment

The policies aimed towards encouraging the equality of women seem to have been more geared towards increasing the size of the Cuban workforce than towards gender equality. More than 600,000 Cubans, many of whom were middle-class professionals, left the island in the 1960s. In order to fill up these vacancies, Cuban women trained for jobs and professions that had been denied to them in the past, and women played an important role in the success of literacy and health campaigns.

Yet despite the work of the FMC, the government could not achieve the levels of female employment it had hoped for. Furthermore, the low number of women in decision-making positions and in the higher levels of the PCC leads us to question whether the government really intended equality between the sexes or was merely creating policies to ensure their economic goals.

Student Answer – *Chang*

Castro's Cuba aimed at making a significant change in the lives of women. It expected to incorporate women into the revolution and the workforce. Several women played important roles in the government, such as Celia Sánchez and Vilma Espín. The latter founded the Federation of Cuban Women, which was the institution that led the policies for women in Cuba. Although Castro tried to limit the traditions which demanded women to be mothers and wives above all, he did not succeed and Cuban women were forced to be housewives, mothers, workers and party members, so they were not truly liberated by the revolution.

Examiner's comments

The candidate has missed the opportunity to define what 'a fuller role' is meant to be. He has an implicit understanding, however, of the idea that women had to play multiple roles and seemed to be worse off. Perhaps this introduction would be clearer if the candidate had omitted the specific examples mentioned and tried to establish the context: what is meant by a 'fuller role'? What was the situation of women at the time of the revolution? In general terms, in which areas were women allowed to play a fuller role and where were they limited by the revolution?

● Examiner's hint

In order to answer this question, you should start by explaining what you understand by 'a fuller role in society'. It is not only about whether more women were allowed in the workforce, but it is also about what their role was in that workforce. You could also use your research about some important women of the revolution and discuss whether the fact that they seemed to have played a 'fuller role' was the exception or the rule in Castro's Cuba.

SOURCE C

◄ Female soldiers of the Cuban armed forces seen here marching on parade.

Education

Cuba's access to education in the pre-revolutionary years varied significantly across geographical regions, becoming more restricted in the rural areas. It was also limited by economic status. Cuba had one of the highest illiteracy rates in Latin America. It reached 24 per cent among children under 10 and was high in the adult population as well. Public education was poor, while access to university was limited to those who could afford it and lived near one of the few universities in the island.

Case study: The literacy campaign

As he rose to power, Castro had promised Cubans improvements in education. During the years in Sierra Maestra, the Rebel Army taught children and adults alike to read and write.

Under the slogan of 'If you do not know, learn; if you know, teach', 1961 was declared 'The Year of Education' and Castro promised to end illiteracy within the year. To achieve this aim, he needed to solve two initial problems: lack of schools and lack of teachers. To solve the shortage of buildings, military barracks were turned into educational complexes, while new schools were built all across the country, particularly in the rural areas. Between 1959, when Castro began his policy of school expansion, and 1962 more schools were built than in the previous 58 years of Cuban history.

To produce more educators for the literacy campaign, Castro implemented a training programme for 271,000 teachers. To reach all areas, they were sent across the country to teach people in their homes. Literate citizens were expected to act as 'literacy volunteers' in their free time. They were dressed in an olive-green uniform and were also sent to the countryside to teach the peasants. These *brigadistas*, as they were known, lived with rural families during the campaign.

The Year of Education brought the entire Cuban population into a joint patriotic effort. By 1962, illiteracy had dropped to 4 per cent. The success of the campaign was spectacular and, as such, it increased the hopes in the revolution.

The aims of the literacy campaign had been twofold. First, it sought to fight illiteracy among the poor. Second, it also aimed to make the middle-class literate youth familiarize themselves with the living conditions and hardships of the poor, and to act in response to the values of the revolution: service and self-sacrifice. Their work in the literacy campaign opened their eyes to the 'other Cuba', and thousands of volunteers emerged from the experience totally transformed. The illiterate peasants, in turn, learnt what the revolution could do for them and were given another reason to support it.

SOURCE D

[The aim] was no longer simply to raise the level of basic knowledge and skills, but to foster the creation of a new man; a socialist man, honest, selfless, devoted to the community, and freed from greedy and corrupt bourgeois inclinations… The overall purpose of education at all levels is to produce better Communists, men and women, unconditionally loyal to the party and party leadership.

From Julie Marie Bunck, *Fidel Castro and the Quest for a Revolutionary Culture in Cuba*, 1994

STUDENT STUDY SECTION

QUESTIONS

a) **What is the message of Source C on p.85?**

b) **What does Source D reveal about the purpose of education in Cuba?**

c) **Explain the meaning and the significance of 'to foster the creation of a new man'.**

Education in communist Cuba

The shift towards communism in 1961 affected education. That year, all private schools were nationalized, boarding schools opened and a large scholarship programme for gifted and committed students was established. Participants were selected by the government, who often decided the subject areas in which particular students should specialize. Free time had to be used in 'intellectually valuable choices', such as volunteer work.

Teachers who did not support the revolution lost their jobs, and the new ones who came to replace them soon realized students acted as spies. On the other hand, teachers who supported the regime were rewarded with training in the USSR and Eastern Europe, where communist values were reinforced. New textbooks were adopted and teaching focused on the history of the revolution and the lives of heroes: Fidel, Che and Camilo (on first-name terms). Libraries were purged of what was considered to be inappropriate material. In Castro's words: 'The task of the schools… is the ideological formation of revolutionaries, and then, by means of the revolutionaries, the ideological formation of the rest of the people.'

SOURCE E

It doesn't take me long to discover that despite my initial reservations, I am going to enjoy school after all. We sit at our uncomfortable wooden desks learning to recite an alphabet where the F is for Fidel, the R for rifles and the Y is for the Yankees. Learning about Fidel and rifles and why we should hate the Americans can sometimes take up a fair amount of the school day, even in primary school. As we get older, more and more time is taken out for what my parents describe with growing alarm as indoctrination.

From Luis M. Garcia, *Child of the Revolution: Growing Up in Castro's Cuba*, 2006

STUDENT STUDY SECTION

QUESTIONS

a) **According to Source E, what were students expected to learn?**

b) **Explain the message in 'the F is for Fidel, the R for rifles and the Y is for the Yankees'.**

c) **Explain the meaning of 'what my parents describe with growing alarm as indoctrination.'**

d) **To what extent does Source E support Castro's view that schools had to provide the 'ideological formation of revolutionaries'?**

The arts

The revolution's new order aimed to change Cuban culture. Castro believed that Cuban culture before the revolution had been marked by foreign influence and that truly nationalist values had not been established. He therefore founded many organizations aimed at developing a Cuban culture based on nationalist and revolutionary values. These organizations coordinated the different policies to ensure the arts reflected and encouraged these values.

Among the early measures taken to end foreign influence was the translation of English terms into Spanish, such as on all wrappers and labels. Terms such as 'struggle', 'battle', 'victory' and 'enemy' were used to explain different events, from the campaign against illiteracy to the harvest season. Visual images of what constituted the ideal man and the ideal woman were based on the revolutionary heroes of the wars against Spain, as well as the revolutionary war against Batista.

The National Ballet and the Instituto Cubano de Arte e Industria Cinematográficos (ICAIC; Cuban Institute of Arts and Cinema Industry) were created in 1959. Two years later, the Unión de Escritores y Artistas de Cuba (UNEAC; Union of Artists and Writers of Cuba) was formed. Its declaration stated that 'The writer must contribute to the revolution through

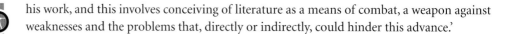

ToK Time

'Language shapes the way we see the world.' By making reference to the emergence of a revolutionary culture, discuss the extent to which you agree with this quotation.

his work, and this involves conceiving of literature as a means of combat, a weapon against weaknesses and the problems that, directly or indirectly, could hinder this advance.'

Case study: The *PM* affair and 'Words to the intellectuals'

PM (1961) was a short film documenting Afro-Cubans dancing and enjoying themselves. It was considered to show a decadent aspect of Cuba, and was accused of being counter-revolutionary and was eventually censored. The censorship of *PM*, a truly apolitical film, angered many Cuban writers and artists who had been enthusiastic supporters of the revolution. They feared that the government, and particularly Castro, would direct culture by dictating the themes and content of their work. In response to these concerns, Castro organized the First Congress of Cuban Writers and Artists, from which UNEAC emerged.

At this congress, Castro gave a speech that has become an essential document in the study of the history of the arts in the revolution. His objective was to enforce revolutionary discipline and to mobilize support for the regime. This speech, known as 'Words to the intellectuals', defined the responsibilities of artists in times of revolution when Cuba was being threatened by the enemy (the Bay of Pigs invasion had taken place earlier that year). The intellectuals were no longer free to create what they wanted; they were at the service of the revolution and had to work to strengthen its values.

In this speech, Castro made another point very clear. Art had a purpose, and this purpose was dictated by the needs of the revolution. An artist had to be a revolutionary first; he could not paint or write about what he wanted, he had to do it in such a way that the masses – the focus of the revolution – would receive a clear message. In other words, inspiration had to come from what the revolution demanded from the artist.

SOURCE F

The Revolution should maintain a majority, not only of revolutionaries, but also of all honest citizens. The Revolution should only turn away those who are incorrigible counter-revolutionaries. And, the Revolution must have a policy for that part of the population so that everyone in that sector of artists and intellectuals who are not genuinely revolutionary may find that they have a space to work and to create within the Revolution; and that their creative spirit will have the freedom to express itself. This means that within the Revolution, everything; against the Revolution, nothing. This is a general principle for all citizens; it is a fundamental principle of the Revolution.

From Fidel Castro, 'Words to the intellectuals', 30 June 1961

STUDENT STUDY SECTION

QUESTIONS

a) What is the significance of 'This means that within the Revolution, everything; against the Revolution, nothing'?

b) To what extent is Castro's speech consistent with his policies? Explain your answer fully.

In the light of these new directives, the arts were to promote revolutionary values. Poets wrote to encourage people to work in the *zafra* or the coffee harvest; novels described women who were role models at work and at home; films highlighted the achievements of the revolution, such as Manuel Herrera's *Girón*, which represented the Bay of Pigs incident, or Jorge Fraga's *Me hice maestro* (*I Became a Teacher*).

The arts came under even closer supervision after the Revolutionary Offensive was launched in 1968. The economic problems, the demoralizing effect of the death of Che Guevara and the need to stimulate people to achieve the 10 million tons sugar target demanded an even greater control of intellectuals and artists.

The Padilla affair and the 'grey years' (1971)

In 1971, conflict between the writers and the government broke out again over the work of poet Heberto Padilla, who had become disappointed with the revolution. In 1968, Padilla was awarded the UNEAC poetry prize for his work *Fuera del juego* (*Out of the Game*), which contained poems critical of the revolution. These appeared at a very sensitive time in Cuba, since the 10 million tons harvest programme had just failed and Castro was prepared to be far less tolerant towards dissent. Padilla was put under arrest and tortured. He was given a confession he had to learn and deliver in a staged public trial. The confession admitted to the charges of being an enemy of the revolution and Padilla was made to accuse his wife and friends of being counter-revolutionaries.

Padilla's detention and trial had an enormous impact not only in Cuba, but among intellectuals worldwide who had supported the revolution. Numerous artists intervened on Padilla's behalf and asked Castro to respect freedom of expression. Many of them broke away from the revolution.

The Padilla affair was followed by what became known as the 'grey period', in which artists were afraid to produce anything that could be interpreted as counter-revolutionary. Closer surveillance of their actions and work was carried out by the state and extended to other forms of academic and scientific activities.

SOURCE G

Cuban poets no longer dream
(Not even at night).
They close their doors to write alone.
But suddenly the wood creaks…
Hands seize them by the shoulders,
Turn them about,

Put them face to face with other faces
(Sunk in swamps, burning in napalm).
The world flows over their mouths.
And the eye is obliged to see and see and see.

'Cuban Poets no Longer Dream', poem by Heberto Padilla (trans. by Daniela Senés)

STUDENT STUDY SECTION

QUESTIONS

a) **In pairs, discuss the message of the poem and the reasons why it was seen as contrary to revolutionary values.**

b) **To what extent do you consider the poem reflected the atmosphere in which artists and intellectuals worked in Cuba?**

Little has changed in Cuba ever since. The 1976 constitution established that 'there is freedom of artistic creation as long as its content is not contrary to the revolution', echoing Castro's 'Words to the intellectuals' speech. (For more on the 1976 constitution, see Section VI on p.91.) Although there have been times when censorship appeared to loosen, most

ToK Time
In groups, discuss the following questions in relation to policies towards the arts under Fidel Castro:

● To what extent can art change the way we understand the world?
● Should art be politically subversive? Or should it serve the interests of the community, or the state, or the patron or funding organization?

Cuban writers who dissented from the revolution found the only way of publishing their work was to have it smuggled out of the island. In 1998, Castro again accused film-makers who criticized Cuba's social and economic conditions of being counter-revolutionaries.

SOURCE H

In the case of Cuba, we have the one Latin American country that has overcome the lockstep of school failure, the absence of educational opportunity, and poverty. Cuba has gone a long way toward fulfilling the educational needs of children at all school levels and has adopted broad measures to provide sound health care and proper nutrition, indispensable ingredients in a comprehensive effort to achieve victory over a history of neglect.

From William Luis, *Culture and Customs of Cuba*, 2001

● **Examiner's hint**

Question b): If this were an open question in an exam, Fidel Castro would certainly be an appropriate example to use in discussing the quotation. In the treatment of Castro's educational policies you will find material to both agree and disagree with the statement. Discuss all views before you come up with a conclusion.

STUDENT STUDY SECTION

QUESTIONS

a) **What, according to Source H, were the educational achievements of Castro's Cuba?**

b) **'Single-party states use education to obtain support rather than to instil knowledge.' How far do you agree with this statement?**

To access Worksheet 3.4 on Castro's views on freedom and democracy, please visit www.pearsonbacconline.com and follow the on-screen instructions.

Treatment of religious groups and minorities

Cuba is considered a Catholic country. However, along with Catholicism, **Afro-Cuban religions** also have a great influence. There are also minorities of Protestants and Jews.

The relationship between religious congregations and the revolutionary government has been a complex one. When the revolution triumphed in 1959, some sectors of the Catholic Church welcomed the opportunity to achieve social justice. Others looked at it with suspicion, particularly as the revolution began to move to the left. Castro thought many of the congregations in Cuba represented foreign interests, as their members were Americans or Spaniards. Whenever bishops criticized the policies of the revolution, Castro accused them of abandoning their pastoral duties and getting involved in politics. The nationalization of schools following the Bay of Pigs incident, and the government's decision that religious education could only take place in churches, increased tension between the state and many religious leaders. Many congregations lived in what historian Antoni Kapcia called 'internal exile', that is, as invisible groups with limited or no influence. Some pastors, however, thought that the only way to attract people back to their churches was to participate in the campaigns of the revolution as volunteers, and they joined the *zafra*, health campaigns and other forms of voluntary labour.

In an attempt to show there was no room for putting religious beliefs before the revolution, the constitution of 1976 stated that: 'It is illegal and punishable by law to oppose one's faith or religious belief to the Revolution, education or the fulfilment of the duty to work, defend the homeland with arms, show reverence for its symbols and other duties established by the constitution.'

Afro-Cuban religions
These faiths are based on the religious beliefs of former West African slaves, and they have incorporated some aspects of Catholicism. As they were forced to adopt Catholicism during the Spanish rule of Cuba, these slaves hid their religious secrets inside the imagery of their masters' saints. *Santería*, or 'the way of the Saints', is the term slave owners used to refer to their slaves' worship.

The hardships experienced during the Special Period – which seemed to augur the end of the revolution – strengthened attendance of people in their churches. In 1998, Pope John Paul II paid an historic visit to Cuba. A strong anti-communist, the Pope addressed the lack of political freedom in Cuba but he also criticized the US economic embargo. As a sign of improved relations, the government modified the PCC statute and allowed religious people to join. The separation between state and Church, however, continued to exist and religious education remained forbidden in all schools.

As for racial relations, in the years before the revolution Afro-Cubans (approximately 50 per cent of the population) were discriminated against in education, work opportunities, shops and restaurants. Supporters of the revolution in Cuba claim it has eradicated racial discrimination. Those who disagree maintain that the revolution raised the living standards of the poor – which happened to include a significant number of non-whites – but that inequality between the races continues to exist. Evidence of this is found in the limited number of non-whites who occupy positions of power within the PCC or decision-making posts in the Cuban government.

STUDENT STUDY SECTION

QUESTION

Assess the role of social policies as factors explaining the consolidation and maintenance of power of Fidel Castro.

● **Examiner's hint**
This section has provided you with information about Castro's social policies. It has addressed the status of women, education, the role of the arts, religions and the treatment of minorities. You need to bear in mind you have approximately 50 minutes to answer this question. There will be no time to use everything you have studied. Spend a few minutes planning your answer and thinking which specific examples you will use to illustrate your arguments. Also, remember this question asks you to assess how the social policies helped Castro consolidate AND maintain power, so you need to ensure your answer addresses both aspects.

Section VI:
Political policies and propaganda

Previous sections have addressed how Fidel Castro consolidated his political power between 1959 and 1962 by a combination of legal methods and the use of force. From 1962, Castro continued to use this combination of methods to maintain himself in power. This section analyzes the structure of the government administration, the policies for dealing with the opposition and the use of propaganda.

The 1976 constitution

When Fidel Castro overthrew Fulgencio Batista, he said that elections would be held at the appropriate time, after Cuba had successfully replaced Batista's dictatorial system with the revolution. However, it was not until the year 1976 that a new constitution was given to the people of Cuba and elections were held for the first time. The constitution, which is still in effect at the time of writing, is communist in nature and explicitly recognizes the influence of the political and social ideas of Marx, Engels and Lenin. It establishes the importance of the PCC in the administrative structure of the country by stating that 'it is the highest leading force of society and of the state, which organizes and guides the common effort towards the goals of the construction of socialism and the progress toward a communist society.'

Elections in 1976 were the first ones to take place since the revolution, but the only party allowed to campaign was the PCC and all nominees to elections at any level were chosen by the party. Under the new constitution, Fidel Castro became head of state, replacing Dorticós. He was also Head of the Government, President of the Executive Committee of the Council of Ministers, First Secretary of the Central Committee of the PCC and Commander-in-Chief of the Armed Forces. As in the period before 1976, Castro remained personally involved in all governmental decisions. Although a legislative body – the National Assembly – was created and elected provincial and municipal authorities established, the 1976 constitution brought little change in practice. The National Assembly only met twice a year for a period of four to five days.

After 1976, however, there was some room to discuss issues such as crime-related problems and family legislation at a local level, and the contents of the laws passed reflected this to an extent. Yet freedom of association to protest against government policies does not exist. All mass media has been controlled by the state since the 1960s.

Another characteristic of the Cuban government that has prevailed over time is an excessive level of bureaucratization. The different social, political and economic plans launched in Cuba led to the creation a large public sector, which employs a vast proportion of the workforce in an inefficient bureaucracy, as seen with the implementation of policies such as the Revolutionary Offensive.

Treatment of opposition

Previous sections have addressed policies implemented to control opposition, such the use of show trials (Padilla affair) or the restrictions placed on people's freedom to express their views. The role played by the Comités de Defensa de la Revolución (CDR; Committees for the Defence of the Revolution), set up in 1960 to 'defend the revolution', is also significant for understanding how Castro has treated opposition. The committees were responsible for some social projects, but their primary role was to report counter-revolutionary activity. There were CDR in operation in every workplace, street block and inside residential buildings. Members were instructed to identify 'enemies of the revolution' and report on their activities. By the end of its first year, the CDR had more than 800,000 members and had become an important tool in government surveillance. By 1963, one third of the Cuban population worked for a CDR. It meant that the level of peer surveillance was very high, which intimidated people. Many Cubans, however, felt that being members of a CDR was a way to contribute to the goals of the revolution and to ensure that what they had gained by it would not be lost.

The use of force to control and repress opposition was clearly illustrated in the creation of the Unidad Militar de Ayuda a la Producción (UMAP; Military Units to Aid Production). Between 1965 and 1968, about 25,000 young men were sent to UMAP labour camps. Everyone opposing military service on whatever grounds was sent to these camps, together with a variety of other 'offenders': children of political prisoners; youngsters imitating US dress codes and tastes; homosexuals and political dissenters. All were sent to the labour camps to be 're-educated through the liberating effects of collective work'. The camps were finally closed in 1968 as a result of domestic and international pressure on Castro, although he continued to claim that he had made that decision himself.

One of the distinguishing features of Fidel Castro in his treatment of opposition is that he has, at different times, allowed the exodus of Cubans from the island. You have already seen in an earlier section of this chapter how this policy helped him consolidate his power between 1959 and 1962. That was not the only time when Castro tolerated, and to some extent encouraged, the opposition to leave the island.

Case study: The Peruvian embassy and the Mariel boatlift

Asylum
Granting a citizen of one country refuge in a foreign, sovereign state or its territory.

Economic problems in Cuba made 1980 a year of political challenge for Castro's leadership. In April that year, a bus full of Cubans crashed the gates outside the Peruvian embassy in Havana, the occupants seeking **asylum**. In the incident, a Cuban guard was shot. In response to the Peruvian embassy's refusal to hand over the asylum seekers, Castro withdrew all guards from the embassy. Soon after, more than 10,000 Cubans forced themselves into the building, demanding asylum.

'Let them all go!' shouted Castro at a rally in his support in Havana. The Cuban press treated them with disdain, and hundreds of supporters of Castro and the PCC staged demonstrations outside the Peruvian embassy to express their rejection of those seeking asylum, referring to them as 'scum'. Castro announced that anyone who wanted was free to leave the island. Soon after that, hundreds of boats of all sizes, rented by Cubans living in Florida, arrived to assist in the emigration of 125,000 Cubans in the Mariel boatlift. These *marielitos*, as they became known, were not only opponents to Castro or people wanting to be reunited with their relatives. Thousands of prisoners and mentally ill people were released by the government and forced to board the arriving boats.

The Mariel boatlift showed levels of discontent that had been unheard of in Cuba before. Despite demonstrations in support of Castro, it put into question the level of commitment of the people towards the revolution and its very legitimacy. It seemed the readiness to tolerate hardship in the name of the revolution was coming to an end. The relaxation of the legislation that allowed Cubans living overseas to return to visit their relatives had exposed thousands of Cubans to, at times exaggerated, stories of success and accomplishment of their visiting relatives. This contributed to create a feeling of disillusion at the revolution and its gains.

This crisis was also unique in other aspects. This was not the first time that Castro had used emigration as a valve to defuse conflict. In the early days of the revolution, thousands of Cubans, mostly middle class and professionals, left the island as the early manifestations of what would become a communist state appeared. But unlike these previous migration waves, the people leaving in 1980 were more economic than political emigrants.

Cuban refugees sailing out from Mariel port towards the USA. Overcrowding on many of the refugee boats made the trip extremely perilous.

SOURCE A

Of course, at first they took the refined bourgeois, the well-dressed landowner. And then they took the physician, the professional. And remember they took half of our country's doctors… Now it is very difficult, very difficult to take a doctor away, because the ones that stayed behind were the best ones, and doctors who trained along other lines, with a solidarity and human spirit, doctors who are not money-minded.

From a speech by Fidel Castro in Havana on 1 May 1980

STUDENT STUDY SECTION

QUESTIONS

a) **With reference to their origins and purpose, assess the value and limitations of the photograph above and of Source A to an historian studying the 1980 Mariel boatlift.**

b) **In pairs, find information about other times when Castro used emigration as a method to control or reduce opposition. How effective do you consider this method has been?**

Propaganda

Previous sections in this chapter have made reference to the use of propaganda in Castro's rise, consolidation and maintenance in power. Propaganda was used to mythologize the revolution and to create the cult of Castro. Ever since the founding of Radio Rebelde, Castro used Cuban radio and, later on, television to make the revolution a permanent presence in Cuban homes. Magazines such as *Bohemia* and newspapers like *Granma* were used to raise awareness of the ideals and actions of the government and increase commitment to its policies. In a Cuba where educational levels had increased so much, written propaganda was a very effective tool.

Castro relied on his skills as a speaker to create the image of an engaged leader, who fought for the ideals of the revolution in the Sierras, on the shores of Bay of Pigs, and at international and diplomatic conferences. His nationalistic speech, his appeal to the idea that Cuba's integrity was threatened by imperialism, and that it was essential for Cubans to remain united and follow the directives of the government, were fundamental in shaping the political system with which Castro has remained in power since 1959.

SOURCE B

He lectured to soldiers on military matters, schoolteachers on education, physicians on medicine, agronomists on plant cultivation, coaches on athletics, filmmakers on the art of the cinema, master chess players on the best opening gambits, poets and novelists on the guidelines of acceptable writing. These speeches served various purposes. He instructed, explaining the workings of the revolution to the Cuban people. He responded to some crisis, announced a new policy. He spoke almost daily, and on some days more than once. Each assembly provided an opportunity to 'mobilize the masses,' to assure popular support for him and for the revolution. He marked important landmarks in the history of his revolution – the landing of the Granma*, the defeat of Batista…, the attack on the Moncada barracks…*

From Robert E. Quirk, *Fidel Castro,* 1993

Propaganda was also used to rally support for new policies or to emphasize the successes of the regime by the use of posters like the ones below:

SOURCE C

'Long live Cuba. Free territory of America.' ▶

¡CUMPLIMOS!

¡TODOS A SALUDAR A LAS BRIGADAS VENCEDORAS!

This 1961 poster reads: 'We have accomplished it! Everyone to greet the victorious brigades!'

STUDENT STUDY SECTION

QUESTIONS

a) What, according to Source B, was the purpose of Castro's public addresses?

b) Explain the message in Source C.

c) What event does Source D make reference to? What message does it convey?

Fidel Castro – an assessment

The question of why Fidel Castro was able to remain in power for so long is one that has fascinated historians. They agree in the fact that there is a combination of factors which have made Castro's rule the longest personal dictatorship in the history of Latin America, but they differ in the relative importance given to each.

Some studies emphasize Castro's appeal to Cuban history and to the belief that the revolution was the continuation of the war for Cuban independence. They analyze the use made of events such as the Sierra Maestra campaign or the defeat of the USA at the Bay of Pigs to appeal to nationalism and unite the country behind him. Other researchers claim that what helped Castro most were his policies to promote social justice and equality of opportunities, which guaranteed him a significant level of support to overcome the crises that followed. There are also historians who claim the figure of Castro himself is the truth of the matter. His charisma, political skills and his capacity to turn defeat into success are some of the qualities mentioned.

Study the following sources and answer the questions in the Student Study Section:

SOURCE E

Yet Castro has also been an astute politician, playing world politics as easily as playing the domestic scene. Within Cuba he has often demonstrated a clever ability to read the popular mood, occasionally, as in 1970 in his criticisms of the disastrous zafra, acting as his own opposition, but also, in the early 1960s, recognising the popular demand for rapid social reform and mobilisation.

From Antoni Kapcia, *Cuba in Revolution*, 2008

SOURCE F

The main source of the inspiration and legitimacy of Castro's revolution, however, has been the Cuban nationalist tradition in its more radical version. Castro saw his movement as a culmination of a time-honoured struggle for independence and development stretching from the first revolt against colonial rule in 1868 to the student rebellion of the thirties. His own supreme self-confidence was based on the conviction that he embodied that struggle.

From Sebastian Balfour, *Castro*, 1990

SOURCE G

Nonetheless the Cuban government retained an undetermined level of popular support. For many citizens, breaking with the government meant breaking with their lives: they had grown up or were young adults during the 1960s when the social revolution engulfed Cuban society, and they had committed themselves to a new Cuba. Many others – particularly poor and non-white Cubans – remembered their plight before the revolution and feared a post-socialist Cuba that would disregard their welfare.

From Marifeli Pérez-Stable, *The Cuban Revolution: Origins, Course and Legacy*, 1993

● **Examiner's hint**

If you would like to use different historiographical interpretations when answering a question, it is important that you analyze the ways in which they help you answer the specific question asked. Examiners will not be impressed by the fact that you can remember the names of historians, but might place your answer in a higher markband if you make use of their interpretations to offer different explanations.

● **Examiner's hint**

The first task is to determine to what extent you consider the Cuban economy a 'successful one'. If you consider that the economic successes some sectors of Cuban society experienced are not a sufficient explanation as to why Castro remained in power for so long, then you will need to explain the reasons for your position. Only after you have shown why a successful economic policy is not the explanation for Castro's maintenance in power, can you offer alternative explanations, such as social policies, propaganda, the use of the party, or any other elements you consider to be a more appropriate explanation for Castro's longevity in power.

STUDENT STUDY SECTION

GROUP ACTIVITY

In groups discuss the views about why Castro maintained himself in power for so long. Look for examples that could be used to support each of the views presented above. Choose one of the views and present it to the other groups using relevant examples. Listen to their arguments for alternative explanations.

Can you think of other explanations as to why Fidel Castro was able to remain in power for so long? How would you illustrate your views?

Answer the following question, reading the examiner's hint opposite:

'A successful economic policy is the most important factor for a single-party ruler to remain in power.' To what extent does the rule of Fidel Castro support this view?

REVIEW SECTION

This chapter has examined Castro's rise to power and his rule of Cuba until 2000. It has focused on:
- **The conditions and methods that led to Castro's rise to power.**
- **The methods used to consolidate power after the success of the Cuban revolution.**
- **The nature, implementation and effects of his social, political and economic policies.**
- **The different methods used by Castro to deal with opposition.**

4   JOSEF STALIN AND THE USSR

One of the most important leaders of the **USSR** during the 20th century, Josef Stalin established the political and economic structure that remained in place until the collapse of the Soviet Union in 1991. This chapter will cover Stalin's rise to power and how he was able to consolidate his control of the USSR both before and after World War II.

▲ Josef Stalin

Timeline – 1879–1953

1879	Stalin is born on 21 December in the town of Gori in Georgia, Russia.
1894	Stalin enters Tiflis Theological Seminary.
1898	The Russian Social Democratic Labour Party (RSDLP) is established.
1899	Stalin is expelled from Tiflis Seminary.
1902	Stalin is involved in illegal political activity; he is arrested and exiled to Siberia.
1903	The RSDLP splits into Bolsheviks and Mensheviks.
1905	Revolution breaks out in Russia; Stalin meets Lenin for the first time.
1914	World War I breaks out.
1917	The March Revolution takes place in Russia; Tsar Nicholas II abdicates; Lenin returns to Petrograd in April; Stalin arrives in Petrograd and becomes one of the editors of *Pravda*. The Bolshevik Revolution takes place in October; Stalin is appointed Commissar for Nationalities.
1918	The Treaty of Brest-Litovsk is signed with Germany; civil war breaks out in Russia; Stalin is placed in charge of Red Army forces in Tsaritsyn.
1921	The New Economic Policy is introduced.
1922	The Union of Soviet Socialist Republics (USSR) is founded; Stalin is appointed General Secretary of the Communist Party.
1924	Lenin dies in January; the 'troika' oppose Trotsky; Stalin proposes his theory of 'Socialism in One Country'.
1925	Stalin opposes the Left Opposition.
1926	Stalin opposes the United Opposition.
1927	Stalin proposes the Five Year Plan and collectivization.
1929	Stalin opposes the Right Deviationists; forced collectivization takes place.
1930	Stalin makes his 'Dizzy with Success' speech.
1932–33	Famine in the Soviet Union.
1934	Kirov is murdered.
1936	The show trial of Zinoviev and Kamenev – both are executed; Tomsky commits suicide.
1937	Stalin purges the military; the beginning of the 'Great Terror'.
1938	The show trial of Bukharin and Rykov – both are executed.
1939	The Great Terror draws to a close; the Nazi–Soviet Pact is signed; World War II breaks out in Europe.
1940	Trotsky is assassinated in August.
1941	Operation *Barbarossa* begins on 22 June.
1943	Turning point of the war, as Germans are defeated at Stalingrad.
1945	Stalin meets with Churchill and Roosevelt in February at Yalta; war ends in Europe in May; post-war meeting at Potsdam with Attlee and Truman; the Red Army occupies much of Central and Eastern Europe; the atomic bomb is dropped on Hiroshima and Nagasaki in August; the war in the Pacific ends in September.
1948	The Berlin Blockade.
1949	The People's Republic of China is established.
1950	The Korean War breaks out in June.
1953	Stalin dies on 5 March.

The USSR
Known in 1918 as the Russian Socialist Federation of Soviet Republics (the Soviet Union), the name was changed to the USSR (Union of Soviet Socialist Republics) in 1922. Lenin achieved his aim of allowing each republic to be equal and also to have the right to secede if they chose to do so. In fact, of course, power lay in Moscow and secession was not allowed, certainly not after Stalin took over. In 1936, the number of republics was increased to 11: Russia, Ukraine, Belorussia, Georgia, Armenia, Azerbaijan, Kazakhstan, Kirgizia, Uzbekistan, Turkmenistan and Tadzikhistan.

The Bolsheviks
In 1903, at a conference held in London, there was a disagreement among the leaders of the Social Democratic Labour Party between those who favoured a broadly based mass party (Mensheviks) and those who wanted a small, 'vanguard' party that would lead the workers towards a revolution (Bolsheviks).

Section I:

Origins and nature of authoritarian and single-party states – the USSR

Josef Stalin was not primarily responsible for the establishment of a single-party state in Russia. He was a **Bolshevik** and a member of the political party that carried out the October Revolution, but it was Vladimir Ilyich Ulyanov (Lenin) who set up the structure of what became known as the USSR. Stalin is, however, associated with the consolidation of the USSR and it was his policies that became the model for all future communist states.

What was Stalin's background and what was his role in the establishment of a single-party state in Russia?

Stalin before the Bolshevik Revolution

One of the most notorious single-party leaders of the 20th century, Josef Vissarionovich Dzhugashvili (Stalin) was born in 1879 in Gori, Georgia. Although part of the Russian Empire, Georgians had their own language and culture, and for Stalin Russian was a second language that he always spoke with a heavy accent. Rebellious at school, he later attended a theological seminary; this was not an unusual path for intelligent but impoverished young men who wanted an education. Stalin became influenced, however, by **Messame Dassy**, a revolutionary group that wanted to secure Georgia's independence from Russia. Through this organization, he met socialists whose ideology was based on **Marxism**. Stalin was expelled from the seminary in 1899 and in 1901 he joined the **Russian Social Democratic Labour Party (RSDLP)** and became a professional revolutionary.

Messame Dassy
A secret organization that wanted Georgia to gain independence from the Russian Empire. It was also socialist in its politics.

Marxism
Based upon the writings of Karl Marx and Friedrich Engels, Marxism formed the basis of the political ideology of the Communist Party. Central to this ideology is the belief that history shows that whoever owns the means of production of wealth controls all aspects of society. In feudal times, for example, whoever owned the land controlled wealth and power and structured society to benefit themselves. When wealth shifted to those who owned the means of industrial production (the bourgeoisie or middle classes), social and political power also shifted to the middle classes. Marx predicted that the workers (the proletariat), whose labour was exploited by the bourgeoisie, would rise up to seize power and to establish the 'dictatorship of the proletariat'. This would lead to the final stage of communism, a time when there would be no private property and resources would be shared.

The Russian Social Democratic Labour Party (RSDLP)
This political party was set up in Minsk in 1898 and focused on the role of the workers (proletariat) in the overthrow of the autocratic system in Russia. Almost immediately, the leaders were arrested and sent into exile. Lenin, among others, went abroad.

Unlike leaders such as Lenin, Stalin did not go abroad into exile, but stayed behind in Russia and became involved in organizing strikes among factory workers. Arrested for this in 1902, Stalin was sent into exile in Siberia, although he was able to escape in 1904. He first met Lenin in Finland in 1905 and sided firmly with the Bolsheviks. Stalin was arrested several times by the Tsar's secret police, before finally, in 1913, being sentenced to exile for

● **Examiner's hint**
Exam questions in Topic 3 of Paper 2 will often ask about either the rise to power or the maintenance of power by a single-party leader, and Stalin can be a good example to choose. Do avoid using him, however, if the question asks about the emergence of a single-party state as, in the USSR, it was Lenin and not Stalin that established a single-party state.

life. Stalin remained in Siberia until 1917, when the overthrow of the Romanov dynasty led to the establishment of the Provisional Government and the subsequent release of all political prisoners.

What role did Stalin play in the 1917 revolution?

Stalin returned to Petrograd (St Petersburg) in 1917 when he became part of the editorial board of **Pravda**, a post he had previously held in 1913. He was also elected to the Central Committee of the Bolshevik Party.

The Bolsheviks were a minority party in the early months of 1917, but Lenin's leadership and events over the summer gave it a lot of publicity and a reputation for being the only party to oppose consistently Russia's involvement in World War I. Lenin, as the leader of the Bolsheviks, also strongly opposed any collaboration between the **Petrograd soviet** and the Provisional Government.

'Land, Peace and Bread' and 'All Power to the Soviets' became the catchphrases of the Bolsheviks, but these also signified a departure from the policies adopted before Lenin returned to Petrograd. As one of the editors of *Pravda*, Stalin was caught up in a struggle within the Bolshevik Party. Lenin criticized editorials that had supported the war and even accused Stalin of being a 'betrayer of socialism'. Stalin was quickly persuaded to change his approach, to abandon support for the Provisional Government and the war and to work towards the revolution. Despite his rather senior position within the party, Stalin did not take a leading role in the October Revolution, as the planning of this was mostly the work of **Trotsky** and Lenin.

SOURCE A

In the days of the upheaval, Stalin was not among its main actors. Even more than usual, he remained in the shadow, a fact that was to cause embarrassment to his official biographers and perhaps justified Trotsky in saying that 'the greater the sweep of events the smaller was Stalin's place in it'… But in spite of their best intentions and indubitable zeal, the official Soviet historians have not been able to write Stalin's name or anyone else's into the blanks left by the deletion of Trotsky's.

From Isaac Deutscher, *Stalin: A Political Biography,* 1966

STUDENT STUDY SECTION
QUESTIONS
a) **What does Source A tell you about Deutscher's views on Stalin?**
b) **What does he mean by 'official Soviet historians'?**
c) **What is significant about the date when this was first published?**

The Bolshevik Revolution

The October Revolution of 1917 marked the seizure of power by the Bolshevik Party. The traditional Soviet view of the events of October 1917 was that it was a popular uprising expertly led by Lenin and his supporters. Other interpretations suggest it was a *coup d'état* by a small group of determined revolutionaries with limited popular support. More recently, assisted by access to the Soviet archives, historians have leaned more towards interpreting the revolution as popular unrest combined with dynamic leadership from the Bolsheviks. This party of revolutionaries was able to harness enough support to get itself

Pravda
This was the newspaper of the Central Committee of the Communist Party. Its name means 'The Truth'.

Petrograd soviet
The Petrograd soviet was a council composed of representatives elected by the soldiers stationed in Petrograd and by ordinary workers. It was intended to represent the views of the proletariat. During the February/March (depending on the calendar) Revolution of 1917, the Duma refused to disband when asked to do so by the Tsar. Demonstrations in Petrograd, a mutiny by the army and growing discontent with the rule of Tsar Nicholas II led to his abdication. The Duma became the Provisional Government and it shared power with the Petrograd soviet that was set up in March 1917.

Leon Trotsky (Lev Bronstein) (1879–1940)
Lev Bronstein was a Marxist who became the first chairman of the St Petersburg soviet in 1905. This was quickly suppressed by the Tsar, but Trotsky (his *nom de guerre*) took up journalism and reported on the Balkan Wars of 1912–13. He was in New York when the February Revolution took place in 1917 and returned to Petrograd to hover on the edges of the Bolshevik Party, although he did not join until the summer. A brilliant strategist, he planned the October Revolution and became a close comrade of Lenin. By 1923, it was widely expected that he would also be Lenin's successor.

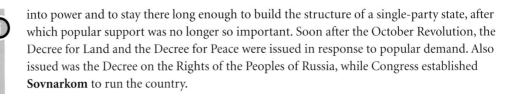

Sovnarkom (The Council of People's Commissars)
The overthrow of the Provisional Government meant that it had to be replaced by a temporary government until elections could be held. Sovnarkom was the name of the council made up of 15 commissars or ministers. Lenin was the Chairman, Trotsky was the Commissar for Foreign Affairs and Stalin was named the Commissar for Nationalities.

into power and to stay there long enough to build the structure of a single-party state, after which popular support was no longer so important. Soon after the October Revolution, the Decree for Land and the Decree for Peace were issued in response to popular demand. Also issued was the Decree on the Rights of the Peoples of Russia, while Congress established **Sovnarkom** to run the country.

Decree for Land

Although, according to Marxist doctrine, land would be held communally (or rather, no one would own it but all would share it), peasants had already taken over privately owned land and divided it up. Lenin saw this as a *fait accompli* and rather than try to rule against it, he made the land seizures legal by decreeing that, in theory, there would be no private ownership of land and that it would be 'held in common' by the people who farmed it. In practice, this meant that land owned by landlords (people who rented out their land to small farmers) and the Church would be taken away without compensation being paid for it. The land would then be divided among the peasants.

Decree for Peace

Russia would pull out of the war and begin negotiations for peace with Germany. It was also stated that there would be no more secret diplomacy conducted.

Decree on the Rights of the Peoples of Russia

This decree set up the structure for a federal state (in which different regions or republics would have their own independent rights over domestic policy) and it was followed by another decree in January 1918 that said any state wanting to leave (to secede from) the Soviet Union could do so.

While in Finland, where he had been hiding before the October Revolution, Lenin had written an important book, *The State and Revolution.* In this, he outlined his plans for a post-revolutionary Russia and indicated that he did not intend to share power with other parties. For Lenin, only one party knew how to proceed towards communism and it was up to the Bolsheviks to lead the way, to be the 'vanguard of the revolution'.

Lenin knew that elections for the Constituent Assembly had been promised by the Provisional Government and that the people expected these to take place, although he considered the Soviets to be more democratic than a parliament. Elections were held in November 1917, but the Bolsheviks did not gain enough seats to form a majority, and although Lenin allowed the Constituent Assembly to meet once in January 1918, he then closed it down. The Soviet Union did not turn into a single-party state overnight, but liberal parties were banned first and then, gradually, the more leftist parties were excluded from government until by 1921 all opposition was officially banned.

SOURCE B

…the closure of the Constituent Assembly, the suppression of other political parties, the elimination of press freedom and the establishment of party control over the soviets all occurred in the early years of Bolshevik rule. These moves effectively limited popular access to the political sphere … and by 1920 had rendered any notion of unfettered competitive politics impossible.

From Graeme Gill, *Stalinism*, 1998

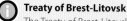

QUESTIONS

a) Find out what is meant by 'pluralism' in politics and discuss to what extent Lenin had decided by 1918 that this would not be put into practice in the Bolshevik state.

b) How far, do you think, was this rejection of pluralism a reflection of how the Bolsheviks believed that they were the party to lead the people towards communism?

The **Treaty of Brest-Litovsk** signed with Germany in March 1918 gave the people the peace for which they craved, but the price paid was very high and added to the discontent that was brewing among opponents of the Communist Party. Three years of brutal civil war followed and this led to radical policies being imposed in areas controlled by the Red Army. What now mattered most was that the revolution was secured and the **White and Green armies** were defeated. Meanwhile, the Tsar and his family were executed at Yekaterinburg in July 1918.

Stalin after the Bolshevik Revolution

In 1917, Stalin, now a well-established member of the Communist Party leadership, was appointed Commissar for Nationalities. Unlike Lev Kamenev and Grigory Zinoviev, two other leading members of the party, Stalin had supported the decision to take power in October and, unlike Trotsky, had been a long-standing member of the Bolshevik Party.

It was as Commissar for Nationalities, however, that Stalin had his first quarrel with Lenin. Lenin believed that the republics of the former Russian Empire would support a communist revolution and could be trusted to bind themselves willingly to the Soviet Union. Stalin took a more pragmatic view, however, and wanted to ensure that all the republics were tightly bound to the centre and to the Bolshevik Party. In *The Soviet Century*, Moshe Lewin explains that Lenin wanted a federation of fairly autonomous states but Stalin, influenced by his own experience as a Georgian and also by his experiences during the civil war, was convinced that the republics had to be ruled from a strong centre and with strict discipline.

SOURCE C

In four years of Civil War, we were obliged to display liberalism towards the republics. As a result, we helped to form hard-line 'social-independentists' among them, who regard the Central Committee's decisions as simply being Moscow's. If we do not transform them into 'autonomies' immediately, the unity of the soviet republics is a lost cause. We are now busy bothering about how not to offend these nationalities. But if we carry on like this, in a year's time we'll be verging on the break-up of the party.

Stalin quoted in Moshe Lewin, *The Soviet Century*, 2005

QUESTIONS

a) What did Stalin mean by suggesting the republics considered the Central Committee's decisions as 'simply being Moscow's'?

b) What does this source tell you about how Stalin behaved as Commissar for Nationalities?

Treaty of Brest-Litovsk
The Treaty of Brest-Litovsk was a very harsh peace treaty with Germany in which Russia (the Soviet Union) lost 32 per cent of its arable land, 26 per cent of its railways, 33 per cent of its factories, 75 per cent of its iron and coal mines, and 62 million of its total population. (McCauley, *The Soviet Union 1917–1991*, 1993)

White and Green armies
The White armies were composed of forces opposed to the Bolsheviks. These were not united in their aims and ranged from social revolutionaries to fervent monarchists who wanted the return of the Romanov dynasty. The Green armies were composed mostly of peasants and were especially active in the Ukraine. They were nationalistic and fought for regional independence. For the most part, the Greens would oppose both the Red and the White armies but, when required to choose a side, would more often side with the Reds, who had redistributed land to the peasants.

In 1922, the 'Georgian Question' brought this conflict to the surface. Georgia wanted to join the USSR as an independent republic and the Georgian Central Committee of the Communist Party complained they were limited in their autonomy and always overruled by the Transcaucasian Committee. According to Martin McCauley, Lenin had two irreconcilable aims because he wanted the republics to be independent but party organizations within them to be absolutely loyal to Moscow. Lenin suspected that Stalin wanted to restore centralized control that resembled Tsarist imperial ideology, and when the Treaty of the Union finally came into being in January 1924, Georgia did indeed enter as a member of the Transcaucasian Federation.

The Resolution on Party Unity, also known as 'the ban on factions', passed at the 10th Party Congress in 1921, tightened control over the party at all levels from the state down to the local branches. Stalin was to use this increasing control to good effect, as we shall see. In 1922, he was appointed General Secretary of the Party. He was now a member of the **Politburo**, the **Orgburo** and the **Secretariat**, the only leading member of the party to be in all three. This gave him a unique overview of the everyday running of the most powerful institutions in the Soviet Union.

The death of Lenin and Stalin's rise to power

The cast of characters:

▲ Grigory Zinoviev

▲ Lev Kamenev

▲ Leon Trotsky

▲ Nikolai Bukharin

▲ Alexei Rykov

▲ Mikhail Tomsky

Grigory Zinoviev – a Bolshevik since 1903 and a close comrade of Lenin. He was a member of the Politburo, the leader of the **Leningrad (Petrograd)** city and regional government and appointed the first Chairman of **Comintern** in 1919. Tried and executed in 1936.

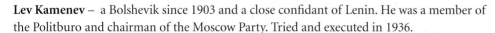

Lev Kamenev – a Bolshevik since 1903 and a close confidant of Lenin. He was a member of the Politburo and chairman of the Moscow Party. Tried and executed in 1936.

Leon Trotsky – Bolshevik only since 1917, but a brilliant orator and strategist. Planned the revolution in October 1917 and led the Red Army to victory in the civil war. Commissar for Foreign Affairs and then appointed Commissar for Military and Naval Affairs. On Stalin's orders, Trotsky was assassinated in Mexico in 1940.

Nikolai Bukharin – a Bolshevik since 1906, he was the editor of *Pravda*. He was in the Politburo and also on the committee of Comintern. Tried and executed in 1938.

Alexei Rykov – a Bolshevik since 1903, Deputy Chairman of Sovnarkom, Chairman of **Gosplan**. He was a moderate who favoured Lenin's New Economic Policy (NEP; see below). Tried and executed in 1938.

Mikhail Tomsky – a trade union leader who joined the Bolsheviks in 1906. A moderate who favoured the NEP, he was elected to the Politburo in 1927. In 1936, he openly criticized Stalin and then committed suicide.

These six staunch communists were to play a very important role in Stalin's rise to power.

What methods did Stalin use to come to power?

Lenin's health had not been good since he suffered an assassination attempt by Fanya Kaplan in August 1918. He never fully recovered and, in his early 50s, he suffered debilitating strokes in 1922 and 1923. Moshe Lewin considers Lenin's ill-health to have been crucial to Stalin's readiness to challenge him and suggests that without it Stalin would not have dared scheme against him too openly. As General Secretary of the Party, 'Stalin was charged by the Central Committee with supervising Lenin's medical treatment' and so was kept closely informed about Lenin's health (see Lewin, *The Soviet Century*, 2005).

Lenin reversed his most controversial economic policy, **War Communism**, in 1921 and replaced it with the NEP. War Communism provoked a lot of opposition from the peasants, but also from the soldiers and sailors of the Kronstadt naval base (an important source of support for the Bolsheviks in 1917). The so-called Kronstadt Uprising in March 1921 was harshly suppressed, but it made Lenin realize that he needed to turn back to a more moderate economic policy, the NEP.

The NEP was what Lenin referred to as 'one step back', meaning that War Communism had not only failed to introduce a communist economy into the Soviet Union but had plunged the country into economic chaos. A less radical and more moderate solution had to be found and so a 'step back' into capitalism was taken. The NEP retained state control of what were called the 'commanding heights', meaning heavy industry, transportation and so on, but small businesses could be privately owned. Peasant farmers who had suffered greatly under the grain requisitioning policies of the civil war were now allowed to keep any surplus produce after they had paid taxes in kind (in goods). Later, they were allowed to pay tax in cash and so to keep or sell their goods as they wished.

This proved controversial, but Lenin succeeded in putting the new Soviet state on a more stable economic footing. Yet the switch to the NEP was so controversial that the Resolution on Party Unity was meant to halt further discussion and opposition. Within the Politburo, Trotsky had been vocally opposed to the NEP, believing that it led away from and not towards the development of a socialist state.

By 1923, it was apparent that the NEP suited the peasants, as agricultural production (severely hampered by the war and War Communism) had recovered. Industrial growth

Leningrad etc.
In 1914, St Petersburg had its name changed to a more Russian- (and less German-) sounding Petrograd. This remained the name until the death of Lenin in 1924 when, in his honour, it was re-named Leningrad. The name was changed back to St Petersburg in 1991, after the fall of the USSR.

Comintern
Short for Communist International, an organization founded in Moscow in 1919 and dedicated to the global spread of communism.

Gosplan (State Planning Commission)
Set up in February 1921 to coordinate and organize the Soviet economy. It was very important in gathering statistics and allocating resources for the Five Year Plans. It continued to function until 1991.

War Communism
During the civil war, Lenin wanted to ensure that food grown in the countryside was delivered to the cities to feed the workers and to the army to feed the soldiers. In order to do this, he ordered the requisitioning of grain. In other words, peasants had to hand over the food they produced. Often, they were left with nothing, leading to widespread famine. Lenin extended this policy to introduce a system of barter to eliminate the need for cash. There was rationing, a ban on the private purchase and sale of goods, and major industries were nationalized. He thought these measures would serve two purposes, to win the war and also to proceed quickly towards a communist society.

10th Party Congress of 1921

At the 10th Party Congress that met in 1921, Lenin proposed the Resolution on Party Unity. This established that issues could be discussed at the level of the Central Committee, but once a decision had been made there could be no further discussion or disagreement. To pursue a different policy or to criticize party policy would be considered 'factionalism'. This method of imposing party unity is also referred to as 'democratic centralism'.

was much slower to recover, however, and there was a disparity between the cost of agricultural goods (cheap) and industrial goods (expensive). As a result, farmers produced less food. Trotsky viewed this as farmers (kulaks) holding the state to ransom, although Bukharin thought it was an economic trend that would resolve itself once industrial production speeded up and more goods led to cheaper prices. This event was referred to as the 'Scissors Crisis' because, on a graph, the decline in the cost of food and the increase in the cost of industrial goods intersected to look like an open pair of scissors. It deepened Trotsky's suspicion that the peasants were turning back to the old ways of producing food for profit.

Lenin's control of the Politburo weakened as his health deteriorated and he was less able to keep the Soviet Union on the course he had planned for it. In 1923, the leading Bolsheviks were divided over whether or not to support the NEP. Meanwhile, Lenin had lost the power of speech and could not maintain a united Politburo. When Lenin died in January 1924, it was the first time that the new Soviet state had to deal with the death of a leader and there was no ceremonial pattern to follow. There would be a state funeral, but it was also decided that Lenin would not be buried. His body was embalmed and displayed in a mausoleum, to become a place of pilgrimage for the Soviet people. Lenin's widow, Nadezhda Krupskaya, complained that he would not have wanted this, but her objections were brushed aside by Stalin, who set about turning Lenin into a god-like figure and himself into the closest and dearest disciple.

● **Examiner's hint**

When you read about Stalin's rise to power, it is tempting to see it all as inevitable. Stalin, the plotter, manages the downfall of Trotsky, his arrogant rival; astutely supports popular policies (NEP); moves almost seamlessly from the Right (with Bukharin) to the Left (against Bukharin); accuses enemies of 'factionalism'; fills the Politburo with supporters; and by 1929, is in sole charge of the Soviet Union. Could it all have been so easy? Beware of what is called '20/20 hindsight'! Sometimes we look back at events and everything seems to lead to one conclusion. Did Stalin plan it all so successfully? Luck probably played a part, but so did events over which he had no control, such as the War Scare of 1927 and popular unrest over the results of the NEP. To what extent did Stalin rise to power not only because of what he did, but also because of what happened in the Soviet Union? As you read through the following points, consider how Stalin both creates and takes advantage of opportunities to accumulate power.

Method 1: Stalin and Lenin

Stalin had fallen out of favour by 1923, for his boorish behaviour towards Krupskaya had convinced Lenin that the General Secretary of the Party was 'too rude'. Ill-health, however, meant that Lenin was unable to do more than to express his reservations about Stalin (and others) in his Testament. This was a series of memorandums written by Lenin between 1922 and 1923. They reflected on the personalities in the leadership of the Communist Party and on likely successors. Lenin had realized that Stalin was too powerful and recommended that he be removed from his post as General Secretary. The Testament was to be read at the 12th Party Congress in 1924, but it was decided to spare Stalin's feelings and to keep it quiet. Also, there was a feeling that the leadership had to appear united after Lenin's death. (The Testament was mentioned by Nikita Khrushchev in his secret speech in 1956, but remained 'buried in the archives' until 1989.)

Lenin already had concerns about Stalin's Russian chauvinism in his role as Commissar for Nationalities, and was intending to act on these when he suffered a major stroke in March 1923. After this, Lenin was more or less incapable of directing the Politburo and Stalin became alert for opportunities to assert his influence. Much has been written about this period from 1923 to 1924, and it seems that Stalin was aware of how much was at stake and was able to take advantage of the power vacuum far more effectively than any of his rivals. Stalin gave the oration at Lenin's funeral, but also gave Trotsky the wrong date for the ceremony so that he missed the funeral altogether. Trotsky therefore committed the cardinal sin of missing Lenin's funeral: he had been sunning himself in Sukhumi instead.

To expand the membership of the Party, Stalin began the 'Lenin Enrolment', which encouraged people to join as a mark of respect for the great leader. This policy also changed the nature of a party that had started as a deliberately small clique of leaders who would guide the masses. Now, the masses were being encouraged to join and to swell its ranks. From these masses would be chosen future members of the Central Committee and from his position as General Secretary, Stalin would oversee it all. Unlike the founding members who had argued with Lenin over interpretations of Marxism, the new membership could find a ready-made explanation of party policy in *The Foundations of Leninism* written by Stalin and published in 1924.

Method 2: Stalin and the removal of his rivals

Trotsky

Stalin and Trotsky had been considered likely successors to Lenin, although as we have seen by 1923 Stalin had fallen out of favour. Trotsky, with his legacy as the strategist of the October Revolution, his brilliant leadership of the Red Army during the civil war, and his considerable oratorical skills was best-placed to succeed Lenin in 1924. He lacked the will for a political fight, however, and was also unsure that, as a Jew, he would have the support necessary to lead the Soviet Union. Also, Trotsky failed to forge strong ties with his fellow members of the Politburo and made enemies by attacking the NEP and by advocating military-style leadership for the economy.

Neither Zinoviev nor Kamenev would support Trotsky in 1924 and both saw him as arrogant and overbearing. Along with Stalin, Kamenev and Zinoviev formed a *troika* (group of three) that planned to take over the leadership of the party once Trotsky had been removed. Trotsky lost support over his opposition to the NEP and his advocacy of '**permanent revolution**', and he resigned as Commissar for Military and Naval Affairs in 1925. He remained in the Politburo, but was no longer considered a potential leader for the party.

Zinoviev and Kamenev – the Left Opposition or the Left Deviationists

With Trotsky out of the way, Zinoviev, Kamenev and Stalin came to the fore. In 1925 there was considerable debate over whether or not to continue with the NEP. Did it favour the peasants over the workers? Kamenev and Zinoviev (known as the 'Left Opposition') argued that it did and so should be discontinued. Perhaps it is not surprising that the two leaders whose support lay in the two major cities of Moscow and Leningrad should have sympathized with the workers rather than the peasants. They faced the opposition of Bukharin who, on the contrary, argued that the NEP worked effectively to develop the economy of the USSR and so should be continued. It was at the 14th Party Congress in 1925 that Kamenev attacked not only the NEP, but also Stalin's policy of '**Socialism in One Country**'. The Central Committee was being filled with supporters of Stalin, however, and a vote was taken to remove Kamenev from the Politburo. This occurred when the membership of the Politburo increased to nine and Molotov, Kalinin and Voroshilov (all supporters of Stalin) were voted on. The *troika* was disbanded.

The Left Opposition became the United Opposition in 1926 when Kamenev and Zinoviev were joined by Trotsky. They were branded by Stalin as 'factionalists' (see the 10th Party Congress resolution in 1921) and expelled from the Central Committee and the Party. Trotsky was exiled to Alma-Ata in Kazakhstan. Kamenev and Zinoviev, knowing when they were beaten, repented and were allowed back into the Party.

Permanent revolution
Trotsky (and Lenin) had believed that the Russian Revolution would soon be followed by revolutions elsewhere. This would be good for Russia, as support would then be given by the more industrialized countries (e.g. Germany) to help modernize the Soviet Union. Meanwhile, within the Soviet Union harsh methods would have to be used to push it towards communism. Military discipline would be required to organize workers, and peasants would be forced to accept collectivization.

Socialism in One Country
By 1924, Stalin pointed out that the communist revolution had not succeeded elsewhere (by the end of the 1920s, Mongolia was the only other communist country) and it was unlikely to succeed in Germany or France, for instance, in the near future. The Soviet Union, therefore, had to depend upon its own resources and to focus on building socialism at home, an idea known as 'Socialism in One Country'. The methods Stalin would use to achieve this, however, were rather similar to the methods Trotsky proposed to achieve 'permanent revolution'.

The War Scare

This was the name given to a period of tension following alleged interference by the USSR in the British General Strike of 1926 and the general election of 1927. The War Scare reflected a fear that the Soviet Union was surrounded by enemies. There were many apparent threats. Britain broke off diplomatic relations in 1927 after a police raid on the Soviet trade delegation in London. Jiang Jieshi (the leader of the Guomindang in China) had turned against his communist allies and was killing them in what was known as the White Terror. Voikov, the Soviet envoy to Warsaw, was assassinated. It was highly unlikely that war would have been launched against the Soviet Union, but this was less important for Stalin than the fear created by the prospect of war.

Bukharin, Rykov and Tomsky – the Right Opposition or the Right Deviationists

Stalin demonstrated a change of heart in 1927 when he began to criticize the NEP and to advocate a harsher policy towards the peasants. The **War Scare** had led to another spell of hoarding by the peasants and a subsequent rise in food prices. Stalin was not prepared to tolerate this and spoke of the need to industrialize and to bring agriculture under the control of the state. This belief was directly contrary to Bukharin's idea that the NEP worked effectively by giving peasants the incentive to produce more. By 1928, Stalin had started a policy of grain requisitioning. The days of the NEP were numbered. Bukharin, Rykov and Tomsky were voted off the Politburo in 1929.

By 1929, Stalin had established his position as the most powerful member of the Politburo. He had undermined the authority of the Bolsheviks who had risen to power alongside him after the October Revolution. New members of the Politburo and close comrades of Stalin included Voroshilov, Mikoyan and Molotov. These three personalities were to remain alive (quite an achievement) and close to Stalin for the rest of his life.

◀ Stalin (left) and Voroshilov

▲ Anastas Mikoyan

◀ Molotov (right) and Stalin

SOURCE D

Stalin was the most violent of leading Bolsheviks. His terror campaigns in the civil war were gruesome. He adopted a military style tunic and knee-length black boots, and his soup-strainer moustache indicated a pugnacious man. At tactics and conspiracy he was masterful. He had reached dominance in the party before Trotsky, Zinoviev, Kamenev and Bukharin knew what had happened. There was no keeping a bad man down in the politics of the USSR.

From Robert Service, *Comrades*, 2007

ACTIVITY

Look at the list below and write a few lines on each of these headings to make sure you understand what each of them means. Sort the list into two columns, one under the heading 'Conditions' and the other under the heading 'Methods'.

- **Lenin's early death**
- **Lenin's Testament is kept secret**
- **Disagreements over the NEP**
- **The Lenin Enrolment**
- **The Foundations of Leninism**
- **Lenin doesn't seem to have a clear successor**
- **Trotsky seems easily outwitted by Stalin**
- **Permanent Revolution vs Socialism in One State**
- **Changing membership of the Politburo**
- **The War Scare of 1927**
- **The Scissors Crisis**

You may find it rather difficult to decide where to place some of these bullet points. How, for instance, do you choose where to put the War Scare of 1927? Was this a 'method' thought up and used by Stalin or a 'condition' that he used to his advantage?

QUESTION

For what reasons and by what methods was Stalin able to rise to power as the leader of the Soviet Union by 1929?

ESSAY INTRODUCTIONS

As we saw in previous chapters, the introduction to your essay is important. You need to show that you understand what the question is asking and to indicate how you will answer it. It is a good idea to refer to the question in your introduction.

Here are some samples of introductions for the essay question above.

Student Answer A – *Patrick*

Josef Dzhugashvili (named Stalin), was born in Georgia in 1879, he was the son of a shoemaker and the grandson of serfs. He soon became Marxist and in 1904 he joined the Bolshevik Party. He climbed up the ladder of the party and in 1917 he was the editor of *Pravda*. He became Commissar for Nationalities and was one of the main artisans of the creation of the USSR. He was also General Secretary of the Party's Central Committee since 1922 (a position considered as boring bureaucratic work by the other Revolutionaries) and a member of the Politburo. Before 1924, he was not a public figure but his internal influence was important.

Examiner's comments

This introduction is rather short and has too much narrative content. It does mention Stalin and gives some context to his emergence as leader, but it makes no mention of the essay question. It is a good idea to refer to the question in your opening paragraph. In this way, you will show the examiner that you are focused and that you will be answering the question. It also reminds you not to be too narrative in your approach.

● **Examiner's hint**

When you consider how single-party leaders rise to power there are several factors to bear in mind, including:

What conditions exist that allow leaders to centralize power? (In other words, are there opportunities that can be taken to enable leaders to seize power?)

What kind of methods do they use to get their hands on power?

Student Answer B – *Clara*

Lenin was for sure the strong commander of Russia till 1922, when he suffered his first stroke. After that, his leadership began to weaken, until his death on the 12th of January 1924. Before he died, though, it was clear to him that there would almost certainly be a struggle for power after he was gone. For this reason he wrote his Testament, in which he gave short portraits of his most probable successors, and their faults. He recognized five possible candidates: Trotsky, Zinoviev, Kamenev, Bukharin and Josef Stalin. Of these, it was Stalin who climbed to the top and became the main leader by 1929. Lenin had warned that although Stalin had great practical abilities, these were offset by his roughness and lack of consideration for his colleagues. Stalin, Lenin said, was 'too rude' and should be removed from his post as General Secretary of the Communist Party. Not only did Stalin manage to keep this quiet, he also managed to outmanoeuvre the other likely candidates for leader. How far, however, was his rise to the top a result of external reasons that Stalin was able to exploit or of Stalin's own political skills? This essay will examine both the reasons for and the methods by which Stalin came to power.

Examiner's comments

Clara's introduction is quite a lot better than Patrick's. She begins with a reference to Lenin and gives some relevant background before moving on to mention the essay question. This introduction makes a good impression by indicating that Clara will select relevant material and focus on Stalin's rise to power. Furthermore, she will address both 'reasons for' and 'methods' and so answer both parts of the question.

How you end your essay is also important! A good conclusion should sum up your arguments and, again, focus on answering the question.

Student Answer C – *Joanna*

Stalin's rise to power is mainly due to his political skills, his pragmatism, his populism, and his patience. Those skills were based on a strong propaganda, especially on the 'Cult of Lenin'. Propaganda leads the new uneducated base of the party to Stalin's cause, marginalizing his opponents. Stalin also benefited from the many errors of his opponent, particularly about Lenin's Testament. Stalin's rise to power left him in a position of entire control. He would soon become a strong totalitarian leader.

Examiner's comments

This is a rather short conclusion, but it does summarize the main points. It also refers to the question. It would be a good idea to say a little more about Lenin's Testament, however, as it needs to be made clear here why it was so important (was it more important than the use of 'factions', for instance?). Also, mentioning 'totalitarian' in the last sentence introduces an entirely new concept, perhaps not such a good idea.

Student Answer D – *Chris*

There is a great deal of controversy regarding how Stalin rose to power as many factors will have influenced events. On the one hand, as has already been mentioned, in many ways Stalin was lucky, benefiting from factors such as the premature death of Lenin and his rivals' weaknesses. In addition to this, Stalin benefited from circumstances such as the economic situation in the Soviet Union as well as the failure of revolution abroad. However, Stalin's triumph was not due just to good fortune and accidental circumstances. Indeed, it is not to be forgotten that Stalin's emergence as the single leader of the Soviet Union would not have been possible without his own ruthless political ability and his skill to take advantage of all the previously mentioned circumstances. As Bukharin once said, Stalin was 'an unprincipled intriguer who changed his theories at will in order to get rid of whomever he wished'.

Other aspects of Stalin's rise to power

Were his methods legal or illegal?

In some cases, single-party leaders use a combination of legal and illegal methods to come to power. For Stalin, what he did was entirely legal. He was an elected member of the Politburo, he was appointed to be General Secretary of the Communist Party and to the Orgburo. He had considerable power available to him because he held high office. When he accused his rivals of 'factionalism' he was applying a resolution that Lenin had proposed and that had been accepted by the 10th Congress of the Supreme Soviet in 1921. When his rivals were expelled from the Politburo, they were removed because the majority of the members voted for this. So, you could argue that Stalin's actions were quite legal.

Did he also respond to popular opinion?

Historians consider Stalin's ability to gauge public opinion and 'to give the people what they want' to be one of the important methods he used to establish himself in power. (Of course, clever use of propaganda can also be used to tell people what they want, and Stalin was able to use this very effectively.)

Since 1917, workers had looked for greater participation in the running of factories and an improved standard of living. The civil war had brought more hardship and to many the NEP was a betrayal of the revolution when it re-introduced the right to own small businesses and to hire labour. The prevalence of 'Nepmen' further angered workers, who saw these entrepreneurs or 'middle men' as exploiters of the working class. Stalin ceased to support the NEP once he had got rid of the Left Deviationists and, in doing so, he would also echo the grievances of the workers. The arguments raged inside the Central Committee (Zinoviev and Trotsky had both been expelled from the Politburo by now) and ended with Trotsky's expulsion to Alma-Ata and Zinoviev and Kamenev asking forgiveness.

Section II:
Stalin in power: Domestic policies and their impact

To access Worksheet 4.1 on Stalin's rise to power, please visit www.pearsonbacconline.com and follow the on-screen instructions.

Stalin's domestic policies

The Five Year Plans: 'The turn to the left'

In 1927, after several years of supporting the NEP, Stalin worked on an alternative economic system. This was the Five Year Plan, a model of economic planning that would eventually be adopted in almost every communist country during the 20th century. (See below p.114 for detailed outlines of each plan.)

A measure of central planning had been put in place by Lenin, and Gosplan was set up in 1921 to control the 'commanding heights' of industry that were to be nationalized under

Vesenkha (Supreme Council of the National Economy)

Set up in December 1917 to control the newly nationalized industries. It existed until 1932, when it was reorganized into different departments.

the NEP. Another organization that supervised nationalized industry was **Vesenkha**, set up in 1917.

Stalin believed that only through strict centralized control would the Soviet Union be able to achieve the level of production it needed to industrialize and urbanize. Since 1855, Russia had been attempting to achieve these twin aims, but with only limited success. Stalin was determined to succeed, however, where the Tsars had failed.

The Soviet economy was based on agriculture and it was agricultural exports that underpinned the economy. In order to industrialize, new technology needed to be imported from abroad, and to purchase this agricultural exports had to be increased. In other words, the Five Year Plan would be financed by agriculture, and the peasants, always unreliable in the eyes of the Bolsheviks, would have to work in the interests of the state. To achieve this, farms would have to be collectivized.

The collectivization of agriculture

The peasants were a force to be reckoned with, as they constituted more than 80 per cent of the population of the Soviet Union, but they were also a force to be crushed and bent to the will of the state. Bukharin had maintained that financial incentives would encourage peasants to increase production, but Stalin did not want to do this. He wanted to be sure that land and food production was under the full control of the state. Collectivization was also considered to be an important way to instil 'communalism' (people living and working together) and also to provide a workforce for the industrial cities.

In 1929, *kolkhozi* or collective farms were established to replace the individual farms owned by the peasants. Those who disagreed with or refused to go along with the orders of the party cadres were branded 'kulaks' and were severely punished. Norman Lowe states, 'It was probably in September, 1929 that Stalin was converted to total collectivisation' (*Mastering Twentieth Century Russian History*, 2002). Approximately 25 million small peasant farms were consolidated into 200,000 *kolkhozi* and hundreds of thousands of peasants became paid labourers on *sovkhozi* (state farms). By 1936, 90 per cent of all peasant households in the Soviet Union had been collectivized.

For Stalin, there were several advantages to collectivization:

- The USSR had an agrarian economy as most of its people lived in the countryside and worked the land, so collectivization gave state control to the main source of national wealth.
- Agriculture would 'pay tribute' to industry and cheap food could feed the cities and also be exported to finance the purchase of machinery from abroad.
- The authority of the Communist Party would be extended over the countryside and peasants would no longer be able to hold the state to ransom. Machine Tractor Stations were set up for a group of *kolkhozi*. Tractors and other machinery could be hired from these stations. Party officials were also based in the stations so they could check that party policies were carried out at a local level.
- Food production would be made more efficient and it would be easier to use machinery such as tractors on larger farms.
- Not all the peasants needed or wanted to stay in a collectivized countryside and the 'surplus labour' would be encouraged to leave and look for work in the cities.
- Collectivization would ensure state control over the production of food, which would be centrally planned like the rest of the economy.

Dizzy with Success

This is a reference to an article by Stalin published in *Pravda* in March 1930 that suggested collectivization had been pushed ahead too quickly by party officials who were 'dizzy with success'. The pace needed to be slowed down and so houses, small plots and animals would no longer be collectivized. Peasants left the collective farms at an alarming rate and planted the spring wheat. Once this had taken place, Stalin resumed collectivization.

Collectivization was not a popular policy and, in 1930, the shockingly poor harvest resulted in Stalin calling a temporary halt with his '**Dizzy with Success**' article in *Pravda*.

He also arranged for a small army of party activists known as the '25,000ers' to go to the countryside to encourage the peasants to follow party directives.

In the end, Stalin just wore opponents down and the disastrous famine in 1932–33 killed as many as 5–8 million people, particularly in the Ukraine. Although many historians would argue that the famine in the Ukraine was 'genocidal', Robert Service challenges this allegation by pointing out that the requisitioning quotas were cut three times during 1932 in response to evidence of widespread starvation. He also maintains that Stalin needed Ukrainian labour as much as he needed labour from elsewhere and that a deliberate policy of starvation would not have made economic sense (*A History of Modern Russia,* 2003). Grain requisitioning was, nevertheless, a brutal policy carried out regardless of the human cost.

SOURCE A

Collectivization was the great turning-point in Soviet history. It destroyed a way of life that had developed over many centuries – a life based on the family farm, the ancient peasant commune, the independent village and its church and the rural market, all of which were seen by the Bolsheviks as obstacles to socialist industrialization. Millions of people were uprooted from their homes and dispersed across the Soviet Union… This nomadic population became the main labour force of Stalin's industrial revolution, filling the cities and the industrial building sites, the labour camps and 'special settlements' of the Gulag.

The First Five Year Plan, which set this pattern of forced development, launched a new type of social revolution (a 'revolution from above') that consolidated the Stalinist regime: old ties and loyalties were broken down, morality dissolved and new ('Soviet') values and identities imposed, as the whole population was subordinated to the state and forced to depend on it for almost everything – housing, schooling, jobs and food – controlled by the planned economy.

From Orlando Figes, *The Whisperers*, 2007

STUDENT STUDY SECTION

QUESTION

What does Source A tell you about the impact that Stalin's policies had upon society in the Soviet Union?

SOURCE B

Table of statistics for grain production and procurement 1929–34 (millions of metric tons)

	Grain Production	Grain Procurement	Procurement as a % of production
1929	66.8	10.8	(16.2%)
1930	71.0	16.0	(22.5%)
1931	65.0	22.1	(34.0%)
1932	65.0	23.7	(36.5%)
1933	71.0	23.3	(32.8%)
1934	77.5	28.4	(36.6%)

Source: Martin McCauley, *The Soviet Union 1917–1991*, 1993

SOURCE C

Table of statistics for grain production (millions of metric tons) and grain export 1929–33

	Grain Production	Grain Export %
1929	71.7	0.18
1930	83.5	4.76
1931	69.5	5.06
1932	69.6	1.73
1933	68.4	1.69

Source: Alec Nove, *An Economic History of the USSR*, 1969, quoted in Norman Lowe, *Mastering Twentieth Century Russian History*, 2002

SOURCE D

Table of statistics for numbers of farm animals 1929–34 (million head)

	1929	1930	1931	1932	1933	1934
Cattle	67.1	52.3	47.9	40.1	38.4	42.4
Pigs	20.4	13.6	14.4	11.6	12.1	17.4
Sheep and Goats	147.0	108.8	77.7	52.1	50.2	51.9

Source: Alec Nove, *An Economic History of the USSR*, 1969, quoted in Chris Corin and Terry Fiehn, *Communist Russia under Lenin and Stalin*, 2002

STUDENT STUDY SECTION

QUESTIONS

Study the tables of statistics and answer the following questions:

a) What do these tables tell you about the rate at which the state procured grain from the peasants?

b) Is there a decrease in the level of procurement? Why did this take place, do you think?

c) What happens to the numbers of farm animals? Why does this happen?

d) If you look at the statistics for the levels of grain production in the two tables, you will see they are different. Why, do you think, is this so?

Peasants to proletariat

SOURCE E

For every thirty peasants who entered the kolkhozi, ten would leave the countryside altogether, mostly to become wage labourers in industry. By the early months of 1932, there were several million people on the move, crowding railway stations, desperately trying to escape the famine areas. The cities could not cope with this human flood. Diseases spread and pressure grew on housing, on food and on fuel supplies, which encouraged people to move from town to town in search of better conditions. Frightened that its industrial strongholds would be overrun by famine-stricken and rebellious peasants, the Politburo introduced a system of internal passports to limit the immigration to the towns.

From Orlando Figes, *The Whisperers*, 2007

Orlando Figes goes on to describe how the internal passports were also used to get rid of 'socially dangerous elements' that might rise up against the government. He also states that for many of the dispossessed, having no passport made them move often, seeking work illegally. In this mass movement, children were often abandoned. They were also abandoned by parents exiled to gulags who wanted to spare their children the same fate and, during the famine, by parents who could not feed them. 'They roamed the streets, rummaging through rubbish for unwanted food. They scraped a living from begging, petty theft and prostitution'.

Figes states that police figures showed that between 1934 and 1935, more than 840,000 homeless children were brought to the 'reception centres' and then sent to orphanages or the camps. In December 1934, Stalin passed a law stating that children over 12 could be treated as criminals and subject to the same punishments as adults, including execution. Figes states that between 1935 and 1940, more than 100,000 children between 12 and 16 were convicted of criminal offences.

The dark side of the Soviet Union during the 1930s is very bleak indeed, and both Figes and the British novelist Martin Amis, in his book *Koba the Dread*, describe the brutality of a system that was determined to forge a new utopia. Stalin (it is claimed) said that 'to make an omelette, you must break eggs', that 'if a man is a problem, no man, no problem'. His callousness is demonstrated over and over again, as well as that of his henchmen, who arrested, tortured, imprisoned and executed victims. These victims were often innocent people plucked at random for having the wrong name; being in the wrong place; having a powerful enemy. This 'randomness' was terrifying and meant that no one was safe.

The First, Second and Third Five Year Plans

The Five Year Plans were Stalin's answer to the problems created by the NEP. Only by taking full state control of the resources and the labour of the Soviet Union would industrialization be achieved. For Stalin, this policy would result not only in economic growth and economic self-sufficiency, but also in an increase in state control (party control) over the USSR and the creation of a disciplined proletariat. The theory of Marxism would be put into practice not from the bottom up but from the top down, which is why it is sometimes called the 'revolution from above' or 'the second revolution'. The Bolshevik Revolution had occurred in 1917, but now the conditions for a Marxist state would be put in place.

The First Five Year Plan (1928/29–32)

The First Five Year Plan was officially adopted in 1929, although it had unofficially begun in late 1928. It called for a massive increase in industrial output; this was highly ambitious for a country that did not have a workforce with the necessary skills. Stalin now set out to create a proletariat by moving large numbers of peasants from the countryside to the cities, or perhaps more accurately in some cases, to areas where cities would be built.

The aim of this plan was to 'increase the production of the means of production', in other words: to build iron and steel manufacturing plants; to build electric power stations; to build the infrastructure including railways; and to increase the production of coal and oil. This expansion would be the basis of the push for industrialization.

Listed here are some of the problems that Stalin faced with the Five Year Plan, along with the solutions that he came up with.

Problem	Solution
To access the necessary skills	Encourage skilled technicians and engineers to come from abroad on fixed-term contracts
To import the necessary technology	Pay for it by accumulating foreign exchange from the sale of grain
To persuade peasants to adapt to the discipline necessary for working in a factory, for example, getting to work on time	Introduce harsh labour laws to punish offenders
To prevent workers from leaving jobs they found too demanding and looking for work elsewhere	Introduce internal passports that prevented workers from changing jobs
To explain why the targets set by the Five Year Plans were not achieved	Change the statistics or blame the 'foreign experts'

STUDENT STUDY SECTION

RESEARCH ACTIVITY

Read through the 'problems and solutions' listed above. See what you can find out about when some of these measures were introduced.

The Second (1932–37) and Third Five Year Plan (1937–)

The focus in these two Five Year Plans shifted to the production of heavy industrial goods. The iron and steel plants were producing iron and steel, the electric power stations were providing electricity, but the country needed trains, trucks and tractors. Reflect for a moment on the European context of this period, when Hitler was focusing on the re-armament of Germany and many Central and Eastern European countries had right-wing authoritarian governments that were opposed to communism and the Soviet Union. For this reason, Stalin wanted to make sure that the Soviet Union would have the resources to re-arm, and so this emphasis became an important aspect of both the Second and Third Five Year Plans. (Note that the German invasion of the Soviet Union in 1941 interrupted the Third Five Year Plan.)

SOURCE F

Industrial production during the First and Second Five Year Plans

	1928	1932	1933	1936
Electric power (billion kWh)	5.0	13.5	16.4	32.8
Coal (million tons)	35.5	64.4	76.3	126.8
Pig iron (million tons)	3.3	6.2	7.1	14.4
Rolled steel (million tons)	3.4	4.4	5.1	12.5
Quality steel (million tons)	0.09	0.68	0.89	2.06
Cement (millon tons)	1.85	3.48	2.71	5.87
Locomotives (standard units)	478	828	941	1566
Tractors (thousand 15hp units)	1.8	50.8	79.9	173.2
Lorries (thousands)	0.7	23.7	39.1	131.5
Woollen fabrics (million linear metres)	101	89	86	102

Source: R.W. Davies, M. Harrison and S.G. Wheatcroft (eds), *The Economic Transformation of the Soviet Union 1913–1945*, 1994, quoted in Chris Corin and Terry Fiehn, *Communist Russia Under Lenin and Stalin*, 2002

● **Examiner's hint**
If you write an essay answer
to a question that asks about
the success or failure of Stalin's
economic policy, it is a good
idea to include some statistical
evidence. You do not need
to use all the statistics in the
table above, for instance, but
if you could show that the
production of coal increases or
the output of electricity goes
up, this can help support your
argument.

STUDENT STUDY SECTION

QUESTIONS

a) Why does the rate of growth in the production of goods increase quite slowly at first but quite significantly by 1936?

b) Why was the number of tractors produced so significant?

c) Look at what is listed in this table. Why are these goods so important to the Soviet Union during the 1930s? What kind of progress do they indicate?

d) What happens to the production of woollen fabric? What would this be used for? What does it suggest about what is not given importance in the Five Year Plans?

How did Stalin carry out the Five Year Plans?

Labour discipline

Many of the workers who came to the cities were peasants whose work routine varied in accordance with daylight hours and the seasons. Now, they needed to adjust to the demands of factory life and so had to arrive at work on time and stay until their shift was over. There were very harsh laws introduced that punished workers who were late or absent and that also made it a crime to break machinery or to take anything from the workplace. In the most extreme cases, these crimes were punished with execution. Early on during the First Five Year Plan, workers would move from one factory to the next looking for better conditions, but this practice was also forbidden. Workers had to have workbooks as a form of internal passport, and losing a job also meant losing your right to accommodation and food rations.

Managers were held responsible for meeting targets given to them by the state. If they failed to do so, they could be charged with 'sabotage' and accused of deliberately preventing the fulfilment of the Five Year Plan. This was a crime that could be punished with a death sentence. Both worker and manager sabotage quickly became an official excuse that could be used to explain the failure to meet the very ambitious targets set by the state.

Slave labour

It was during the 1930s that so many of the gulags were built. These were the labour camps where the kulaks were sent and also where hundreds of thousands of political prisoners were sent during the 'purges' (see Section III below, p.122). Conditions were so harsh that the majority of prisoners would die, often in their first year of captivity. The gulags were located in the most inhospitable areas of the Soviet Union, where winter temperatures fell as low as -50 degrees centigrade. They were remote from areas of habitation, and so difficult to escape from, and they were also located in areas rich in resources such as gold, uranium and coal. Free citizens would not have wanted to go and work in such places, but prisoners had no choice. When the growth of the Soviet economy during the Five Year Plans is measured, the contribution of the gulag prisoners has to be included as part of the terrible human cost.

Enthusiasm

There was clear enthusiasm among the workforce for many of Stalin's ambitious policies, although Robert Service maintains that the enthusiasts were in a minority. Even so, many

ToK Time

If you were asked to work hard or to put up with difficult circumstances so that conditions could be better for future generations, how, do you think, would you react? Would you do so willingly?

Consider the question of climate change, when we are asked to reduce energy consumption or even to become vegetarians so that we can secure the future of the planet at a time when we may not even be alive. What arguments can you think of to support and also to reject such a proposal?

Stakhanovites

Alexei Stakhanov was a coal miner who mined 106 tons of coal or 14 times his quota during a single shift in 1935. A movement was named after him to encourage all workers in the Soviet Union to work harder. It was very popular, with many workers attracted by the rewards such as extra rations, medals or even a motorcycle.

people believed in the importance of what they were achieving and were ready to tolerate extremely difficult conditions as they built, for instance, the city of Magnitogorsk. Here conditions were hardly better than in the gulags. Machinery was scarce but tremendous feats were achieved with man (and woman) power alone. Enthusiasts maintained that they were working for the country's future. This was not the 'alienated' labour that Marx had written about, but was the labour of people building a new world for themselves and for future generations.

Rewards

Workers were given different rewards or incentives for their efforts:

- Posters and party directives extolled the virtues of **Stakhanovites** and many were encouraged to try to emulate his success. They could receive food that was in short supply or even a motorbike for doubling or tripling their work quotas.
- League tables were published in all the factories, publicizing what each worker had produced in a week.
- Wages differentiated between skilled and unskilled workers.
- A good work record and party membership could lead to promotion for workers who had little formal education.

Propaganda

Stalin's speeches about the successes of the Five Year Plans were printed in *Pravda*. Yet the workers who actually built huge factories and electric power plants could see with their own eyes that the Soviet Union was industrializing and, indeed, catching up with the capitalist powers. Workers were told that the conditions in the capitalist countries were dire, and as this was the era of the Great Depression, newspapers carried photographs and articles about the food lines in New York and the hunger marches in London. What Stalin did not tell Soviet citizens, of course, was that in the Soviet Union prison camps were overflowing with people put there for no other reason than that their names had been added to a list. Like everything else, there were targets to be achieved for political prisoners.

For ideological indoctrination, Stalin's *Short Course on the History of the Communist Party of the USSR* was published in 1938 and, like the *Foundations of Leninism*, served as an introduction to the 'new' history of the Bolshevik Revolution.

STUDENT STUDY SECTION

QUESTION

How successful were Stalin's domestic policies?

In an essay asking you to assess the success of Stalin's domestic policies, you would need to refer to the Five Year Plans. How would statistics help you to support arguments for their success?

To help you put these statistics in perspective, consider the levels of economic growth – for comparison, check the GDP (Gross Domestic Product) of the USA or China or Russia between 1929 and 1937.

Don't forget that when you are asked a question like this in the exam, you must first consider what the aims were. When you think about the success of a policy, you need to ask yourself what the single-party leader intended. Then, you can look at the evidence and decide whether or not he achieved his goals. It is also worth looking more 'holistically' at the notion of 'success'. Was the policy successful for the citizens of the country concerned? Was the human cost of 'success' too much to bear?

In the case of Stalin's domestic policies, you would need to think about the following:

What did Stalin want to achieve when he devised the Five Year Plans? Use the following sub-headings to organize your evidence.

- His economic aims
- His social aims
- His political aims.

Was he able to achieve these aims?

Were his policies successful for the people of the Soviet Union:

- In the countryside
- In the city
- For the workers
- For the managers
- For the party members?

What was the cost? Was it worth it?

To access Worksheet 4.2 on the Soviet Union's industrialization under Stalin, please visit www.pearsonbacconline.com and follow the on-screen instructions.

Stalin's social policies

The role of women

The role of women had changed after the revolution, with opportunities opening up for careers as engineers and doctors, professions traditionally seen as the privilege of men. It is worth noting, however, that the upper echelons of the Communist Party did not have many women in its ranks and none appeared in the Politburo. By 1930, furthermore, Stalin wanted to restore more conservative values and this shift backwards became known as 'The Great Retreat'. The family once again became the central unit of society. The freedom afforded by revolution had to be reined in, as easy divorce had led to the abandonment of children and the ease of abortion threatened to halt population growth (although other reasons for this included poor nutrition, shortage of accommodation and exhaustion from hard work). To encourage population growth, abortion was made illegal in 1936, divorce was discouraged and women were rewarded with medals for giving birth to ten or more children. Moshe Lewin notes that, officially, there was a slight improvement in the birth rate in 1937, but that it fell again in 1939.

As well as being mothers and homemakers, women also had to play their part in the expansion of the Russian economy. On the collective farms, women were expected to work in the fields. This role was especially important during World War II, when men were drafted into the Red Army and many did not return from the war. In factories, women were expected to do the work of men and to take part in construction brigades, which helped to rebuild wartorn cities after 1945. Women were trained as pilots during the war and, unlike their counterparts in the USA and in Britain, they saw combat duties.

This poster shows women on a collective farm. The woman in the foreground is gathering corn and the women behind her are also working. Notice that the supervisors, however, are men.

Russian women fighter pilots of World War II. Women had been trained as engineers and technicians during the 1930s and it is not surprising that they were expected to be on active duty. Of course, the majority stayed at home to be an even more vital part of the workforce in factories and on collective farms.

Religion

The Russian Orthodox Church had for centuries been a strongly nationalistic mainstay of Russian society. Under Lenin, it was frowned upon to attend church and the demonization of religion was an important aspect of collectivization among the peasants, for whom religious belief was still very important. Churches were destroyed, bells hauled away to be melted down, priests were driven out along with the kulaks. Geoffrey Hosking argues, however, that centuries of religious worship could hardly be eradicated so easily and that in many cases, people formed 'underground' churches, meeting secretly (*A History of the Soviet Union, 1917–1991*, 1992). Similarly, in the areas where Islam was the dominant religion, most mosques closed and imams suffered the same fate as priests. Such practices as the veiling of women, fasting during Ramadan, polygamy, and travelling to Mecca on the *haj* were all forbidden. As in Christian communities, however, official prohibitions did not drive out religious belief but, rather, drove it underground.

When World War II broke out, Stalin changed his approach to the Church and used it to gather support from the people for the war effort. Religion was linked to nationalism and support for the defeat of the German invaders.

Art and culture

Stephen Lee suggests in *Stalin and the Soviet Union* that music in the USSR underwent something of a renaissance during the 1930s. The compositions of Prokofiev and Shostakovich, in particular, gained critical acclaim and would surely be considered among the finest music of the 20th century. No other dictatorship saw such a quantity of fine music. Stalin did not understand music but, clearly, he did not fear it either, although in the post-war period his taste grew more conservative and even Prokofiev and Shostakovich fell out of favour.

As summed up by Robert Service, 'Above all, the arts had to be optimistic' (*A History of Modern Russia*, 2003) and the school of Soviet Realism produced paintings that resembled propaganda posters intended both to entertain and educate the masses. Meanwhile, the writer Maxim Gorky returned to the Soviet Union in 1928, was feted by Stalin and provided with a large house in which to live. He was instrumental in establishing, in 1934, the First All-Union Congress of Soviet Writers to 'unite all writers supporting the platform of Soviet power and aspiring to participate in the building of socialism' (Hosking, *A History of the Soviet Union, 1917–1991*, 1992). In other words, the aim was to capture 'Soviet realism' in literature. Hosking explains how such novels revolved around a hero 'who appears from among the people, he is guided and matured by the party … and then leads his comrades and followers to great victories over enemies and natural obstacles in the name of the wonderful future that the party is building' (*A History of the Soviet Union 1917–1991*, 1992). *How the Steel Was Tempered* (1934), an autobiographical novel by Nikolai Alexeevich Ostrovsky, was from this genre and glorified the workers of the new Soviet Union. Another famous novel was written by Mikhail Sholokhov, *Quiet Flows the Don*. It focused on the heroic years of the revolution and civil war and gained an international reputation, with its author being awarded the Nobel Prize for Literature in 1965.

Writers who found favour with the regime were well looked after and led lives of privilege. Not all writers chose to follow the guidelines laid down, however, and Isaac Babel, Oscar Mandelstam, Anna Akhmatova and Boris Pasternak chose what Babel called 'the genre of silence'.

Sergei Eisenstein, the famous film-maker, produced epics such as *Ivan the Terrible*, recalling Russia's great leaders. The sequel to this film, however, was interpreted as being critical of Stalin and Eisenstein was criticized and dismissed from his post as the head of the Moscow Film School.

Sergei Eisenstein (1898–1948)
Best known for his film of the mutiny on the battleship *Potemkin* and for *October*, his account of the 1917 revolution, Eisenstein was one of the leading film-makers in the Soviet Union. He experienced mixed fortunes under Stalin, but was praised both for *Alexander Nevsky* (1938) and *Ivan the Terrible – Part One* (1943), both of which were strongly nationalistic. *Ivan the Terrible – Part Two* (1946), however, depicted the Tsar as a ruthless tyrant, and Eisenstein was strongly criticized. The film was banned and scenes that had been filmed for *Ivan the Terrible – Part Three* were destroyed.

ToK Time

Here are examples of the kind of art that was encouraged and discouraged under Stalin's rule. On the left we have an example of Soviet Realism and on the right, an example of the work of Kazimir Malevich.

Why, do you think, did Stalin prefer Soviet Realism? Which painting would be critically acclaimed today? Justify your answers.

Education and social mobility

One of the dilemmas that faced the revolutionaries in their efforts to transform the Soviet Union into a socialist state was how to address education. The children of the better-educated were more likely to go on to higher education, but appeared to perpetuate an elitist system. The difficulty lay in getting more people from poorer backgrounds into education. Under Lenin there was an attempt to make education more accessible, although the actual curriculum in schools did not change much. In 1928, it was pronounced that 65 per cent of those entering higher technical education had to be of working-class origin, a figure raised to 70 per cent in 1929, when 14 per cent of students had to be women. The percentage of working-class students in higher education went up from 30 per cent in 1928–29 to 58 per cent in 1932–33, and an effort was made to get rid of non-party lecturers and professors.

Already by 1931, the Central Committee was determined that students needed to be literate and have an understanding of basic science. By the mid 1930s, there were officially prescribed textbooks; tests and exams were restored; the teaching of history had to focus on political events and great men; uniforms were compulsory (including pigtails for girls); and fees were imposed for the three upper forms of secondary school.

But education was not just about book work and class learning. Back in the late 1920s, reforms took place to introduce closer links between education and practical work experience. As Hosking explains, 'The upper forms of middle schools were reclassified as *tekhnikuny*, or vocational training colleges, and by the end of 1930 all schools were required to attach themselves to an enterprise… The proportion of political instruction was also increased' (*A History of the Soviet Union 1917–1991*, 1992). Hosking mentions some of the side-effects of these reforms, with children as young as 11 working in coal mines or picking cotton for weeks on end. In other cases, factory managers found the attendance of children to be disruptive and tried to avoid having them present. Undoubtedly, the dismissal of schoolteachers who were not party members or who had, in most cases, simply been educated before the revolution, opened up opportunities for social mobility as younger 'red specialists' were given teaching posts. The party also realized it needed future leaders and selected these from factories, mines and state farms to study at technical institutes. 'According to Sheila Fitzpatrick, during the first Five Year Plan, some 110,000 Communist adult workers and some 40,000 non-party ones entered higher educational institutions in this way' (Hosking). The quota system imposed in 1929 was abolished in 1935. This change was probably due to questionable results as 'probably 70 per cent failed to complete their course' (McCauley, *The Soviet Union 1917–1991*, 1993).

Urbanization and more access to education often did lead to more social mobility as, for many people, opportunities they could hardly have imagined previously now appeared. Former peasants moved to cities where at least a few became managers and, if they were extremely fortunate, rose within the ranks of the party to lead privileged lives. As the Soviet Union made economic progress, it needed more managers and technicians, and at the end of the 1920s the importance of class meant that a humble background was advantageous. This was especially true during the period of the purges.

● **Examiner's hint**
An essay question like this is fairly common, as social change plays a significant role in a single-party leader's domestic policy. When you answer a question like this, however, it is important to include evidence of change. Always try to mention the names of artists or musicians and to know something about their work. Also, be sure that you discuss social policies and not political or economic policies.

STUDENT STUDY SECTION

QUESTION
Assess the impact of Stalin's social and cultural policies on the USSR up to 1941.

Here are some extracts from student essays discussing the impact of cultural change.

Student Answer A – *Leo*

Stalin also wanted to change Soviet culture. He liked art to be used for propaganda and preferred paintings that showed him with Lenin or surrounded by children, but he did not like modern art. He wanted people to read his books such as *The History of the Communist Party* and not novels and poetry. Stalin did like to attend the ballet and composers like Shostakovich were very popular. As long as artists and composers did what they were told to do, they were able to survive and they often lived in large apartments and were part of the elite of Soviet society.

Student Answer B – *Susan*

Another area in which there was change in Soviet culture was in the arts. Stalin understood the importance of music, literature and art and how these could be used to create a 'proletarian culture'. He approved of the music of Prokofiev and Shostakovich and encouraged their compositions. It is not very clear if these composers changed Soviet society in any way, but their music was considered to be very good, even outside the USSR. Also, concert tickets were cheap and everyone was encouraged to appreciate Russian composers, so it was also linked to encouraging nationalism. In literature, the works of Mikhail Sholokhov were available because they were written about the civil war and the revolution. Stalin did not like the poetry of Oscar Mandelstam, though, because his verses spoke about the Terror. By censoring such poetry, Stalin wanted to limit opposition. Stalin liked the people of the USSR to read novels and to look at paintings that were about the lives of workers and peasants, and the Writers' Union, for example, made sure that novelists knew what they had to produce.

What were Stalin's aims?

Securing his own position as the leader of the party and the state

Stalin had removed his rivals from the Politburo by the end of the 1920s. This did not mean that he was in complete control, however, and criticism from **Martemian Riutin** and associates in 1932 showed that Stalin's policies were not always popular with the Central Committee of the Communist Party. Although the 17th Party Congress in 1934 was named the Congress of the Victors, Stalin knew that the Second Five Year Plan had huge difficulties in meeting its targets and the human cost of collectivization was devastating for the countryside. Even more important, others knew this too and were not afraid to voice their concerns.

Defending the USSR

In Stalin's opinion, the USSR was a fragile state. It did not have a very developed industrialized economy and outside its borders there were many countries that feared the spread of communism. By the early 1930s, fascism was well-established in Italy and Nazism was on the rise in Germany. Both of these very similar ideologies had their roots in

Martemian Ivanovich Riutin (1890–1937)

Riutin criticized Stalin's overthrow of the collective leadership of the party, saying that this had led to ordinary people's disillusionment with socialism. The radical nature of collectivization had also contributed to Stalin's unpopularity with some leading cadres. Riutin was expelled from the party in 1930 and his associates were expelled in 1932, accused of trying to restore capitalism and of being kulaks. It is claimed that Stalin wanted the death penalty for Riutin, but that Kirov intervened. Riutin was sentenced to ten years' solitary confinement, but was shot in 1937.

● **Examiner's hint**
A common exam question will ask about the aims of single-party leaders and whether or not they were achieved. A typical question may look something like this: 'How successful were Stalin's domestic policies?'

Don't forget that when you have to assess the success of a leader's policies, it is important to start by stating what he intended to achieve. Another important consideration is that a leader may have achieved his aims but at a terrible cost, so was he 'successful'? As you read through this section, consider who may have benefited and who may have suffered from Stalin's policies. Then, when you get to the end, come back to this question and write an essay plan.

ToK Time
Stalin said, 'The death of one man is a tragedy, the death of millions is a statistic.'

Consider how this statement may or may not be valid today. Newspapers, the internet and television carry news stories that cover tragic events on a daily basis. Does the way news is communicated to us reflect Stalin's statement? Is this how we react to the news of a suicide bombing or a train crash?

socialism, but were vehemently opposed to communism. In a war, the USSR would need to defend its borders and have a well-trained and well-equipped army.

STUDENT STUDY SECTION

QUESTION

Now you have seen Stalin's aims, how did he go about achieving them and to what extent was he successful?

SOURCE G

Stalin put the matter vividly in 1931: 'To lower the tempo means to lag behind. And laggards [lazy people] are beaten. But we don't want to be beaten. No, we don't want it! The history of old Russia consisted, amongst other things, in her being beaten continually for her backwardness. She was beaten by the Mongol khans. She was beaten by the Turkish beys. She was beaten by the Swedish feudal lords. She was beaten by the Polish-Lithuanian nobles. She was beaten by the Anglo-French capitalists. She was beaten by the Japanese barons. She was beaten by all of them for her backwardness.'

From Robert Service, *A History of Modern Russia*, 2003

STUDENT STUDY SECTION

QUESTIONS

In Source G here, Stalin makes many references to Russian history. He does not mention communism at all. What does this suggest to you about how Stalin viewed the USSR? Was it a new, revolutionary state, do you think, or the latest manifestation of the Russian Empire? How would you support your answer?

Section III:
Stalin in power: Establishment and consolidation of authoritarian and single-party states

Methods: How did Stalin maintain power?
The Great Terror

The Great Terror of 1937–39 wasn't a domestic policy of Stalin, but it was woven into every aspect of the planned economy and was one of the most important methods by which domestic policies were achieved and opposition suppressed. Punishment was meted out to peasants who resisted collectivization; to factory workers who did not work hard enough; to managers who did not meet targets; and to party members who were considered too passive.

For Stalin, terror was one of his methods of ruling the Soviet Union. It made people afraid, and people who were frightened were more likely to be obedient. If instilling fear was his aim, he certainly achieved it. Even those who were not afraid of Stalin would be frightened of the dangers he told them existed. These included the fear of invasion, the fear of a counter-revolution and the fear of Stalin being removed from power by his enemies. The terror grew as Stalin became more powerful and surrounded himself with supporters in the Politburo and the Central Committee of the party. During the early 1930s, he still had to be cautious and his recommendation in 1933 that Riutin be executed was opposed by

Sergei Kirov. Events such as Kirov's murder in 1934 gave Stalin opportunities to purge the Leningrad Party and to introduce new laws. These included, as we have seen, the authority to execute children over 12, and he also removed any system of appeal so that a death sentence would be carried out immediately. It is unlikely that Stalin, without some suitable excuse, would have been able to step up the terror as he did.

The following is a brief list of the purges that were carried out during the 1930s.

- The purge of engineers and managers included the **Shakhty Trials**. The aim was to instil labour discipline and to punish anyone who could be blamed for a failure to achieve quotas.
- The purge of the Communist Party intended to ensure that all members were loyal to Stalin. The purging of the party began after Riutin's criticisms of Stalin's leadership.
- The purge of the leadership of the party that followed the death of Sergei Kirov.
- The **purge of the military** in 1937 that targeted the officers of the armed forces.
- Random quotas issued to local party branches with instructions that 'counter-revolutionaries', kulaks and 'Trotskyites' be imprisoned or executed. Party branches would receive orders to arrest a specific number of enemies of the state, whether these existed or not.

In June 1936, Zinoviev and Kamenev, who had been accused of having plotted Kirov's murder, were tried and executed. Stalin was now targeting influential Bolsheviks who had been members of the party leadership. Genrikh Yagoda, the head of the People's Commissariat for Internal Affairs (NKVD – the internal security police), objected to the execution of party leaders and then was criticized by Stalin for having started the terror four years too late (Lewin, *The Soviet Century*, 2005). In September 1936, he was replaced by Nikolai Yezhov , a close admirer of Stalin, who followed instructions to prise out enemies within the party. According to Robert Service, 681,692 persons were executed during the two years from 1936 to 1938 (*A History of Modern Russia,* 2003). Bukharin and Rykov were put on trial in 1938 and executed, having confessed to betraying the party. Service considers the unbridled terror to have had a negative impact upon the USSR's economy and its military and that even Stalin recognized that events had gone beyond his control by 1938. Slowly, the 'quotas' were reduced and, finally, Yezhov was demoted, imprisoned and executed in February 1939. It is not clear why Stalin slowed down the process of disposing of imagined enemies, but it is possible that the worsening situation in Europe meant that he had to shift his attention to foreign policy. Yezhov was executed as though to indicate that he had been over-zealous, and the Great Terror was described as the period of *Yezhovchina*.

Historians have argued over the numbers killed as well as the motivation that sparked the process. Mary McAuley, for instance, notes the difficulty of assessing the impact of the terror when the statistics are so unreliable. She also considers the difficulty of accumulating eye-witness memoirs when most people who wrote about their experiences were intellectuals. What, she asks, 'of the peasants and workers and the criminals' who were also imprisoned (McAuley, *Soviet Politics 1917–1991*, 1992)? She notes that Solzhenitsyn argued that the purges were symptomatic of Bolshevik ideology.

SOURCE A

Solzhenitsyn argues … if one believes that class origin determines behaviour and consciousness, if one believes that individuals' actions and ideas are determined by their social origins and that therefore members of the bourgeoisie cannot but act in a particular way, it is only logical to argue that they should be eliminated … the belief that revolutionary justice should be administered by those with a proper proletarian consciousness, and little else, allowed the riff-raff and sadists of society to staff the penal institutions.

From Mary McAuley, *Soviet Politics 1917–1991*, 1992

Sergei Kirov (1886–1934)
A close friend of Stalin, Kirov had taken over the administration of the Leningrad Party after the demotion of Zinoviev. A popular member of the leadership, Kirov had gained more votes than Stalin in the elections to the Central Committee in 1934. Soon after, he was murdered by Leonid Nikolaev who, it was alleged, was jealous because his wife had an affair with Kirov. The circumstances surrounding the murder were mysterious and there has always been a suspicion that Stalin ordered the murder, although no proof for this accusation has ever been found. He did use the opportunity, however, to purge the Leningrad Party and to arrest Kamenev and Zinoviev.

The Shakhty Trials
Named after the town in the Donbass coal-mining region where they took place, these were trials of 'foreign experts' and 'class elements' blamed for breaking machinery and sabotaging the Five Year Plan. Most likely, the breakage was the fault of unskilled workers, but 'experts' were convenient scapegoats. Public trials were held and 11 death sentences handed down, of which five were carried out.

The purge of the military
The purge of the military in 1937 cut a swathe through the officer ranks of the armed forces. In his unrelenting hunt for career officers who could not be trusted, Stalin executed thousands and put thousands more in prison. This was to lead to problems in 1941, when the early successes of the German invasion were partly due to the absence of experienced officers. It also influenced Britain's reluctance to pursue seriously an alliance with the USSR in 1939.

She then quotes Stanislaw Swianiewicz, a Polish economist who:

SOURCE B

…offers us a materialist explanation… Economic development necessitates the finding of resources for investment, for holding back consumption. How could this be done? One way to reduce consumption was to withdraw consumers from the market, place them in labour camps where they worked and consumed almost nothing… The labour camps, Swianiewicz argues, had an economic rationale.

From Mary McAuley, *Soviet Politics 1917–1991*, 1992

Memorial Society

Set up during the period of *perestroika* in the 1980s, this society tried to ensure that the victims of the purges were not forgotten. Its work seemed easier during the 1990s, for instance, than in more recent years, when Orlando Figes' *The Whisperers* was a forbidden publication in Russia. In the early 21st century, the officially approved image of Stalin was that of a great leader who had achieved economic growth and victory in World War II. Historical focus had to be on the positive rather than negative aspects of this rule.

Other historians such as Orlando Figes researched the 1930s in depth, accessing the archive of memoirs collected 'in collaboration with the **Memorial Society** organised in the late 1980s to represent and commemorate the victims of Soviet repression' (*The Whisperers*, 2007). He estimated that '25 million people were repressed by the Soviet regime between 1928 … and 1953. These 25 million – people shot by execution squads, Gulag prisoners, "kulaks" sent to "special settlements", slave labourers of various kinds and members of deported nationalities – represent about one-eighth of the Soviet population…'. Figes also comments on how, inevitably, in a regime that was so repressive, one survival method was for people to identify so strongly with Stalin that even their punishment could not shake their belief in his righteousness.

SOURCE C

Immersion in the Soviet system was a means of survival for most people, including many victims of the Stalinist regime, a necessary way of silencing their doubts and fears, which, if voiced, could make their lives impossible. Believing and collaborating in the Soviet project was a way to make sense of their suffering, which without this higher purpose might reduce them to despair. In the words of (another) 'kulak' child, a man exiled for many years as an 'enemy of the people' who nonetheless remained a convinced Stalinist throughout his life, 'believing in the justice of Stalin … made it easier for us to accept our punishments, and it took away our fear'.

From Orlando Figes, *The Whisperers*, 2007

SOURCE D

'… a true Bolshevik will readily cast out from his mind ideas in which he has believed for years. A true Bolshevik has submerged his personality in the collectivity, "the Party", to such an extent that he can make the necessary effort to break away from his own opinions and convictions… He would be ready to believe that black was white and white was black, if the Party required it.'

Yuri Piatakov quoted in Orlando Figes, *The Whisperers*, 2007

STUDENT STUDY SECTION
QUESTIONS
a) **How could you use Source C to support an argument that Stalin continued to be revered even by those he punished?**
b) **Why, do you think, did this happen?**
c) **How could you use Sources C and D to agree/disagree with the following assertion, 'Stalin had total control over the population of the Soviet Union'?**

The constitution of 1936

In 1936, Stalin revised the constitution of the USSR. It was, on paper, a document that was very democratic, as it guaranteed freedom of the press, freedom of thought, the right to public assembly and all other basic human rights. It also stated, however, that these rights would be guaranteed as long as they were in accordance with the interests of the workers. In this way, anything that was against 'the interests' of the workers' state was forbidden. In fact, everything that was not specifically allowed was forbidden. Even so, the constitution gave the impression or illusion that the USSR was a liberal state at a time when Stalin was increasingly concerned about its image abroad.

Popular policies

Many of Stalin's policies were popular and did buy him support. Stalin's rejection of the NEP in 1927, for example, struck a chord with workers, who felt that the Soviet Union had slipped back into capitalism. His punishment of kulaks was probably supported by peasants, who resented their richer neighbours, and many did not question the execution of leading Bolsheviks when they publicly confessed their guilt. The 1930s were also the decade when the population of the cities increased, and there were more opportunities for education and for job promotion. In 1926, 17.4 per cent of the population lived in cities, but this had increased to 32.9 per cent by 1939 (Lewin, *The Soviet Century*, 2005). Social mobility was a fact of life in Stalin's state, and the terror brought employment opportunities and even promotion for those who were not shot or sent to the gulags. In this way, the terror contributed to social mobility.

Stalin's cult of personality was also important in ensuring that his image and words were familiar to all Soviet citizens. Paintings, photographs and statues made Stalin recognizable throughout the Soviet Union and his speeches and messages were carried to the people by radio broadcasts and *Pravda*.

The use of language was also an integral part of the Stalinist system. Enemies were defined as kulaks and Trotskyists even if the former were not, by any stretch of the imagination, rich peasants or if the latter had never had any connection with Trotsky. This twisting of language didn't matter, because all that was important was to identify these people as counter-revolutionaries. Getty and Naumov stress that the same language was used in private as was used in public. Officials 'spoke Stalinist' 'as a matter of group conformity and even individual survival' (J. Arch Getty and Oleg V. Naumov, *The Road to Terror*, 1999).

ToK Time
Today, when a government censors information that is broadcast by TV stations or published either in newspapers or on the internet, we usually consider it to be rather authoritarian. Are there ever good reasons, do you think, for censoring information or, indeed, literature and films? For instance, would we accept censorship in a time of war? Are there other circumstances when it would be acceptable or is it always the right of citizens to have free access to all information?

Was Stalin a totalitarian leader?

To be a totalitarian leader implies total power and total control over the state. When Stalin ordered the purges of the party and the military, did he really have complete control over exactly what took place?

SOURCE E

Although by the end of the decade he was unquestionably the supreme leader, he was never omnipotent, and he always functioned within a matrix of other groups and interests.

From J. Arch Getty and Oleg V. Naumov, *The Road to Terror*, 1999

Getty and Naumov note that Stalin could not have acted alone in the purges; he had to have the cooperation of society, or at least, its tacit acceptance of these punishments. Having survived the upheavals of the famine, collectivization and rapid industrialization in the early 1930s, the leadership of the party may have congratulated itself at the Congress of Victors but, nevertheless, Stalin was dismayed by the votes cast for Kirov and began to doubt the continued support of his colleagues.

Getty and Naumov stress that communication was very difficult when all the regions of the Soviet Union did not have a telephone connection. Party officials had to struggle along poor roads on motorbikes carrying messages from the centre. What hope was there, then, of maintaining a close eye on what went on locally? This argument suggests that Stalin may have been a 'totalitarian' leader by aspiration, although practical problems meant that on occasions he fell short of being totalitarian in actuality.

Nature, extent and treatment of opposition

Stalin believed that he encountered a great deal of opposition and once stated that he trusted no one: 'I trust no one, not even myself.' It was also said that he had an inferiority complex and thought he was less educated, less intellectual and less popular than the other Bolsheviks. It is possible to dismiss Stalin as paranoid, imagining enemies around every corner, but was there real opposition to his bid for power and to his policies?

● **Examiner's hint**
If you are asked to consider the methods that Stalin used to stay in power (or to consolidate power), you can start your plan by making a list.

For example:
● Terror
● Propaganda
● Education and youth groups
● The centralized control of the party
● Popular, successful policies.
Once you have done this, you can include evidence to support your points and some analysis to determine which were the most important.

To access Worksheet 4.3 on opposition to single-party regimes, please visit www.pearsonbacconline.com and follow the on-screen instructions.

● **Examiner's hint**
When facing this question you probably think immediately of terror and the gulags. These were probably the main ways that Stalin dealt with his enemies, but don't forget that single-party rulers can also be proactive in getting rid of opposition by encouraging people to support themselves.

STUDENT STUDY SECTION

QUESTION

What was the extent of the opposition that Stalin faced?

Using the following list, consider what kind of opposition Stalin faced and when. Did Stalin respond to opposition or did he create it, do you think?

● Lenin	● Riutin
● Nadezhda Krupskaya (Lenin's wife)	● Kirov
● Trotsky	● Ordinary party members
● Kamenev and Zinoviev	● Workers
● Bukharin	● Peasants

Don't forget to consider 'extent', so think about how much opposition there was and where it came from.

Another kind of essay question could ask how Stalin actually dealt with opposition.

QUESTION

In what ways and with what success did Stalin deal with internal opposition to his regime?

To answer a question like this, it is a good idea to write a detailed plan, first outlining all the different kinds of opposition to Stalin. These could include the following:

● Opposition from within the party
● Opposition from the peasants
● Opposition from the workers
● Opposition from the Church.

Then consider the methods used to deal with each one and how successful they were. Also notice that the question has two parts: 'in what ways' and 'with what success'. You need to address both parts and so can structure your answer accordingly. Begin by mentioning the kinds of opposition Stalin had to deal with and then go on to discuss the 'ways' before ending with an assessment of how successful he was. Alternatively, you can begin by mentioning the kinds of opposition, going on to discuss how and with what success he tackled each one. As long as you answer the question (both parts), you can use whatever structure you prefer.

Form of government and ideology

The USSR followed the left-wing ideology of communism, although this was adapted by both Lenin and Stalin according to what they perceived to be the needs of the state. Stalin had become a committed Bolshevik as a young man. He had been prepared to break the law for his political beliefs and to spend many years in exile. He was a staunch advocate of the October Revolution and he fought to save the revolution during the civil war.

Furthermore, regarding how the Communist Party planned to run the country, Service mentions how Lazar Kaganovich produced a pamphlet 'on the party workings'. Kaganovich, 'already one of Stalin's close associates, spelled out the system of vertical command needed in the party-state if the communists were to enhance their power…' (*Comrades*, 2007).

According to Marxism, the proletariat were meant to rule, but in the Soviet Union this can hardly be said to have been true when the Communist Party had so much control. The excuse given for the 'dictatorship of the party' was that Russia was too backward and that the 'dictatorship of the proletariat' could not take place until people had been educated to have the correct values. This policy, of course, would require social engineering. Proletarians would have to be made and quickly!

STUDENT STUDY SECTION

- In the Secret Speech given at the 20th Party Congress in 1956, Nikita Khrushchev said that Stalin was not a 'Marxist'.
- Trotsky referred to Stalin as 'the gravedigger of the revolution'.
- Simon Sebag Montefiore wrote a book about Stalin and called it *The Court of the Red Tsar*.
- Robert Service stated that Stalin 'knew his Marxism and he was a dedicated Leninist' (*Comrades*, 2007).

QUESTIONS

a) **Four opinions have been expressed here about Stalin's political beliefs. See if you can find evidence in this chapter to support and/or oppose each one.**

b) **To what extent can Stalin be considered a Marxist?**

c) **To what extent can Stalin be considered a Leninist?**

d) **Is there a difference between a Marxist and a Leninist? How would you explain the difference?**

SOURCE F

Robert Service in Comrades *mentions how Alexander Herzen, a 19th-century Russian essayist, '… expressed fear of bloody revolution in his country. He thought that, if ever the peasantry rose against their masters, they might be led by some "Genghis Khan with the telegraph".' Service goes on to describe the Bolsheviks as 'Jacobins with the telephone and the machine gun'.*

Adapted from Robert Service, *Comrades*, 2007

STUDENT STUDY SECTION

QUESTIONS

a) **What was meant, do you think, by the phrase, 'Genghis Khan with the telegraph'? (A better way to describe it today, perhaps, would be 'Genghis Khan with a mobile phone'.)**

b) **Who were the Jacobins? Why, do you think, does Service compare the Bolsheviks to them?**

Lavrenti Beria (1899–1953)

Lavrenti Beria was Stalin's 'hatchet man'. He took over the leadership of the NKVD (the secret police) in 1938 after the dismissal of Yezhov. He remained close to Stalin, becoming a member of the Politburo in 1946. He was arrested and executed after the death of Stalin in 1953.

● **Examiner's hint**

When you consider all these points about Stalin's rule during the 1930s, you can see how he has many methods by which he consolidates his power. The structure of the party, as well as the ideology of Marxism-Leninism, are important to consider too, as these also enable Stalin to centralize power.

The structure and organization of government and administration

The governmental structure of the USSR was established by the constitution of 1922 and amended slightly by the constitution of 1936. In both, the hierarchical structure for both the soviets and the party were outlined. Each republic had a Congress of Soviets, which sent representatives to the Union Congress of Soviets that elected the Central Executive Committee. This body, divided into the Congress of the Union and the Congress of Nationalities, appointed the members of Sovnarkom. Similarly, the Communist Party had local branches that sent representatives to the Central Committee from which the Politburo was elected. It was imperative that members of the soviets, even at a local level, were members of the party and so the party dominated the government. It was the Politburo that was the policy-making organ and Lewin mentions that by the late 1930s, the Politburo in practice had become limited to a 'quintet' of Stalin, Molotov, Mikoyan, **Beria** and Malenkov. Indeed, it was often reduced to Stalin and Molotov consulting only each other (Lewin, *The Soviet Century*, 2005).

STUDENT STUDY SECTION
QUESTION
What does this paragraph tell you about the way power was centralized in the Soviet Union under Stalin?

Section IV:

Stalin after 1939 – the Great Patriotic War; the Cold War; domestic policies

Stalin's foreign policy up to 1941

Timeline – 1930–1941	
1930	Maxim Litvinov is appointed Commissar for Foreign Affairs.
1933	The USA establishes diplomatic relations with the USSR.
1934	The USSR joins the League of Nations.
1935	The Franco-Soviet Pact; Comintern orders cooperation with anti-fascist governments.
1936	The Spanish Civil War begins (1936–39); Germany signs the Anti-Comintern Pact with Japan.
1937	Italy joins the Anti-Comintern Pact.
1938	The Munich Conference; border conflict with Japan begins and ends in 1939.
1939	Molotov replaces Litvinov as Foreign Minister; the Nazi–Soviet Pact is signed; World War II begins; Poland invaded and divided between Nazi Germany and the USSR; the 'Winter War' with Finland begins in October.
1940	The Katyn Massacre; the 'occupation' of the Baltic States and Bessarabia.
1941	Operation *Barbarossa* – the German invasion of the USSR – begins.

The 1930s were a decade of great tension in Europe and the Far East. Authoritarian states had emerged across Eastern Europe as well as in Germany, Italy and Japan, although these three countries also had ambitions to expand into neighbouring, and more distant, countries to acquire empires. Stalin was not unaware of the threat posed by Germany and Japan to the security of the Soviet Union. In particular, Stalin feared a two-front war waged against Germany and Japan, and this became a real threat after these two countries signed the Anti-Comintern Pact in 1936.

Stalin's economic policies were certainly driven in part by his determination to re-arm his military forces and to prepare for war. The military leadership was also thoroughly purged, probably because he did not trust his officers and also because executions and imprisonment would instil fear and so guarantee loyalty in the event of war.

Maxim Litvinov

Vyacheslav Molotov

Maxim Litvinov was appointed the Commissar for External Affairs in 1930, and until he was replaced in 1939 he was the architect of Soviet foreign policy. At first glance, Litvinov had many of the characteristics of Stalin's victims: he was an 'old Bolshevik' who had joined the party in 1903; he was well-travelled and spoke many languages; he was married to an Englishwoman; and he was Jewish. Yet Litvinov survived possibly because his skills were needed in determining foreign policy, not an area of expertise for Stalin. It was Litvinov who proposed collective security for the USSR, resulting in its joining the League of Nations in 1934. He also favoured closer cooperation with anti-fascist governments, a policy approved by the Comintern in 1935, after which **Popular Front** governments were established in France and Spain and the **Second United Front** was set up in China.

The weakness demonstrated by the League of Nations over the Manchurian Crisis of 1931 and the Italian invasion of Abyssinia in 1935 damaged the reputation of 'collective security'. Perhaps a closer relationship with Britain and France was never very realistic, as Britain in particular did not relish an alliance with the USSR. The likelihood of such an alliance was also undermined by the events of 1938, when Stalin was not invited to attend the Munich Conference, although the USSR had an alliance with Czechoslovakia.

SOURCE A

Litvinov explicitly told the British delegation to the League [of Nations] that, if the Germans invaded Czechoslovakia, the 'Czechoslovak–Soviet Pact would come into force', and proposed a conference between Britain, France and the Soviet Union to 'show the Germans we mean business'.

From Niall Ferguson, *The War of the World*, 2006

STUDENT STUDY SECTION

QUESTION

How reliable, do you think, is Litvinov as a source for what the Soviet Union intended if Germany invaded Czechoslovakia?

By 1939, a close alliance with the French and the British looked increasingly unlikely, although in April a poll held in Britain showed that 87 per cent of respondents said they favoured an alliance with France and the Soviet Union (Ferguson, *The War of the World*, 2006). The government of Britain did eventually send a delegation to Moscow in July, but they travelled by sea, suggesting there was no sense of urgency. Turning away from the West, Stalin aimed to foster closer cooperation with Nazi Germany. Litvinov, who would have been an unlikely emissary to Berlin, was replaced as Commissar of External Affairs by Vyacheslav Molotov.

The famous (infamous) Nazi–Soviet Pact was signed in August 1939. In a decade that came to be synonymous with messianic ideologies used to justify unspeakable acts of terror, it was truly shocking to see two avowed enemies sign a pact of neutrality that agreed to carve up Poland between them. The contemporary cartoons of David Low reflect some of the disbelief and cynicism that greeted this unexpected alliance:

SOURCE B

Cartoon by David Low.

SOURCE C

Cartoon by David Low.

STUDENT STUDY SECTION

QUESTIONS – SOURCE B

Study Source B carefully and see if you can explain fully what is being depicted.

a) What is the 'tradition' being illustrated?

b) What is the significance of the maps on the wall?

c) What is in the 'parcels'?

d) Find out exactly what territories were taken by Hitler and by Stalin in 1939–40.

QUESTIONS – SOURCE C

This is another cartoon by David Low. It shows Stalin arm in arm with Peter the Great, one of the most well-known Russian Tsars. Look carefully at the boatman rowing the boat and see if you can recognize him.

a) What was David Low implying here about Stalin's ambitions?

b) What does it suggest about the terms of the Nazi–Soviet Pact?

War on the Eastern Front

For Stalin, the Nazi–Soviet Pact signed on 23 August 1939 could be seen as a win-win situation. Not only was there a guarantee of ten years' peace with Germany, the USSR also regained the land it lost in 1918 to Germany and in 1921 to Poland. This must have seemed a far better deal to Stalin than signing a treaty with two reluctant allies (France and Britain), receiving no territory and possibly being dragged into a war against Nazi Germany. Germany invaded Poland on 1 September 1939 and was followed by the Red Army on 17 September. Just over a week later, on 27 September, the Boundary and Friendship Treaty with Germany handed Lithuania over to the Soviet Union in exchange for some of eastern Poland.

Soviet rule over conquered or annexed territories was brutal and Stalin was determined to 'decapitate' Polish society. Niall Ferguson points out how, after experiencing life under Soviet rule, many Poles who had sought refuge in the east now asked to be sent home, believing that life under the Nazis could hardly be worse than under Soviet occupation (*The War of the World*, 2006). For many Poles, however, the choice was between ending up in a concentration camp under the Nazis or a gulag under the Soviets.

Source D gives some indication of the nature of the 'terror' that was carried out in Soviet-occupied Poland.

SOURCE D

Beginning on the night of February 10th, 1940, the NKVD unleashed a campaign of terror against suspected 'anti-Soviet' elements. The targets identified … were 'those frequently travelling abroad, involved in overseas correspondence or coming into contact with representatives of foreign states; Esperantists; philatelists; those working with the Red Cross; … priests and active members of religious congregations; the nobility, landowners, wealthy merchants, bankers, industrialists, hotel [owners] and restaurant owners.'

From Niall Ferguson, *The War of the World*, 2006

STUDENT STUDY SECTION

QUESTIONS

Look carefully at all the different categories of people targeted in Source D.

a) What might they all have in common, do you think?

b) What threat might they pose to Soviet occupation?

One of the most widely known wartime atrocities carried out by the NKVD was the Katyn Massacre of 1940. More than 4,000 Polish Army officers, as well as police officers, prison guards, government officials and other 'leaders' of society, were taken into the Katyn forest in Russia, shot and buried in mass graves. Meanwhile, in Estonia, Latvia and Lithuania, government representatives were required to sign 'defence treaties' and, in 1940, to 'request' that they be incorporated into the USSR.

Stalin was also concerned about security to the north and demanded that Finland relinquish territory to the USSR. When Finland refused, the Winter War broke out in November 1939 and, although some Finnish territory was lost, more than 200,000 Red Army soldiers were killed. The weakness of the post-purge Red Army had been revealed and this was noted by Hitler.

Stalin's foreign policy from 1941

Operation *Barbarossa*

Lebensraum

This was Hitler's policy of expansion eastwards to find 'living space' for the Aryan race. He believed that the Third Reich should colonize lands to the east such as Poland and the USSR where the Slav people would either be displaced or become slave workers for the Reich.

Hitler's policy of **Lebensraum** led to the invasion of the Soviet Union and the planned colonization of its territory by the German/Aryan race. According to Niall Ferguson, the timing of Operation *Barbarossa* in June 1941 may have been influenced by Hitler's concern about Stalin's encroachment on Romania and the Balkans. In the summer of 1940, Stalin demanded that Romania hand over northern Bukovina and Bessarabia (Moldova today) and this demand was followed by a 'promise of security' for Bulgaria. Hitler started to plan the invasion at this point, beginning with a meeting of his military chiefs in June 1940. Stalin was alerted many times to German invasion plans: by Richard Sorge, a double agent working in the German embassy in Tokyo; by the British who had cracked the German military ENIGMA code; and by German informants who swam across the River Bug (the border between German and Soviet-occupied Poland), but were shot as enemy agents. Ferguson estimates that there were 84 warnings in all sent to Moscow and that Stalin ignored them all. It seems Stalin trusted no one except Hitler, and was afraid that any defensive action by the Red Army would be interpreted by the Germans as preparation for an attack.

The siege of Leningrad, 1941–44

Among the most famous events of World War II on the Eastern Front were the long-drawn out efforts of the Nazi invaders to force the surrender of Leningrad and Stalingrad. Leningrad was the cradle of the Bolshevik Revolution as well as being the 'Venice of the North', a reference to its architectural and cultural prominence. It was considered imperative that the city be saved, and from 1941 to 1944 its population suffered bombardments and starvation to win through a 900-day siege. It is estimated that more than 600,000 people died out of a population of approximately 2,500,000.

The battle of Moscow, October 1941–January 1942

Known as Operation *Typhoon*, the occupation of Moscow was considered by Hitler to be vital to the success of Operation *Barbarossa*. The defence of Moscow was led by General Zhukov and, aided by extremely harsh winter conditions, he was able to prevent German victory.

The battle of Kursk, 4 July–23 August 1943

One of the largest land battles of the 20th century, the battle of Kursk was fought between the Red Army fielding 3,600 tanks and 1,300,000 soldiers and the German Army fielding 2,700 tanks and 800,000 soldiers. Although the Red Army lost 1,500 tanks and suffered 860,000 casualties, this engagement was their victory and the battle of Kursk led the way to the recovery of the city of Kharkov.

The siege of Stalingrad, 1942–43

Stalingrad could not be sacrificed because its original name, Tsaritsyn, had been changed to Stalingrad in honour of Stalin. (Today, it is Volgograd.) Sitting astride the River Volga, the city, if it could be captured, offered the Germans the possibility of severing Soviet oil supplies from the Caucasus to the Red Army force further north. The German Army

Group B nearly succeeded in capturing the city, but a Soviet counter-offensive encircled, trapped and destroyed the German Sixth Army and much of the Fourth Army. The German defeat at Stalingrad in early 1943 was seen as the turning point of the war, the beginning of Germany's retreat back to the Reich. Hitler had refused permission for General Friedrich von Paulus, the commander of German forces at Stalingrad, to break out from the encirclement in a timely manner, and thus consigned hundreds of thousands of men to either death or capture.

Figure 4.1
The German advance during Operation *Barbarossa*.

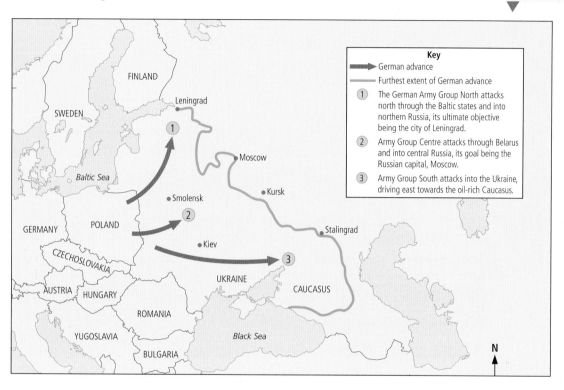

Key
German advance
Furthest extent of German advance
1. The German Army Group North attacks north through the Baltic states and into northern Russia, its ultimate objective being the city of Leningrad.
2. Army Group Centre attacks through Belarus and into central Russia, its goal being the Russian capital, Moscow.
3. Army Group South attacks into the Ukraine, driving east towards the oil-rich Caucasus.

SOURCE E

Cartoon by David Low.

NOW FOR SOME TEAMWORK, JOE

Total war

Total war is a term used to describe a war in which all the resources of the state are put at the disposal of the government to achieve victory. This will often entail the taking over of vital industries for the duration of the war; the rationing of food and other necessities; the conscription of men (and women in some cases) into the army or into factories; restrictions on access to information, on travel and so on.

STUDENT STUDY SECTION

QUESTIONS

a) **What does this cartoon suggest about the nature of the wartime alliance?**

b) **What is the significance of the objects held by Stalin and Churchill?**

c) **How does the depiction of Stalin in Source E compare with his depiction in Sources B and C?**

The end of the war

The tide turned against Germany in 1943, and over the next two years the Red Army marched westwards in the wake of the retreating Germans. The Red Army claimed to have 'liberated' the Baltic States, Poland and much of Central and Eastern Europe. Post-1989 interpretations in these countries, however, would argue that although the German Army was driven out, what followed was another occupation. Meanwhile, an estimated two million German women were raped in the areas occupied by the Red Army. The wartime conferences at Tehran, Moscow and Yalta all dealt with the borders of post-war Europe and Stalin was adamant that the next war must not be fought on Soviet soil. The German surrender to the Soviet Union took place on 8 May 1945. It was not until 9 August that the Soviet Union joined the war on Japan, occupying northern Manchuria and acquiring the Kurile Islands and South Sakhalin.

STUDENT STUDY SECTION

QUESTION

Why did the Red Army defeat Germany?

● **Examiner's hint**

Just as it is a good idea to consider why victorious countries win wars, it is also worth asking why the defeated countries lose. This kind of essay question is quite common. Here, it is worth reflecting on why the USSR, with its purged armed forces and its relatively recently industrialized economy, was able to hold off the German invasion. It is also worth asking why a vast land mass where the people had endured so much hardship in the name of 'socialism' would be prepared to wage war to save a regime that was so brutal. Some possible reasons are listed below in this chapter.

The reasons for Stalin's victory

The USSR was already a planned economy in 1941, and it made a seamless transition to '**total war**' conditions in which the government controls the production and distribution of resources. Stephen Lee in *Stalin and the Soviet Union* mentions, however, that further study of the production levels in the USSR demonstrate that with the loosening of centralized control in 1943 production levels escalated, indicating that local control of production proved more effective than central planning.

The State Committee of Defence (GOKO) was set up on 30 June 1941, with Stalin as its Chairman. He was an indefatigable war leader, taking charge of every aspect of the defence of the Soviet Union. He rarely visited the frontline, but he followed the actions of his generals closely and made it clear to them that retreat or defeat in battle was not an option. Order No. 270 of the State Committee of August 1941 decreed that 'those who surrendered to the Germans "should be destroyed by all means available, from the air or from the ground, and their families deprived of all benefits", while deserters should be shot on the spot and their families arrested' (Brown, *The Rise and Fall of Communism*, 2009).

Stalin used propaganda very effectively during the war, and the Orthodox Church was restored to a position of prominence in Russia. The conflict was labelled the 'Great Patriotic War', fought to save Mother Russia rather than an ideological war to save communism. Stalin understood that nationalism would appeal to the emotions of the people, who would fight to save their country when they may not have been inspired to fight for an ideology.

For Hitler, his was a racial war against an enemy that was considered to be 'sub-human'. It was to be a war of extermination and this was demonstrated by the brutality of the Nazi forces as they swept towards Moscow, Leningrad and Stalingrad. This treatment of the Slav population was in keeping with Nazi ideology, but strategically it was a huge error. There was support for the Germans in areas of Ukraine and in the Baltic States, for instance, as the German soldiers were often seen as liberators. This welcome soon changed, however, as the death toll of civilians mounted from German policies of extermination and eviction. Even so, an estimated two million Soviet citizens fought on the side of the Germans. To prevent any risk of further internal disturbance, Stalin 're-settled' large numbers of Chechens, people from the Balkans, Karachais, Meskhetians, Crimean Tatars, Balts, Ukrainians and Cossacks. Lee considers that this possibly thwarted the risk of more serious rebellion within the Soviet Union (Lee, *Stalin and the Soviet Union*, 1999).

The Wehrmacht (German armed forces) made swift progress towards Moscow in the first five months of the war, but stalled just short as 'General Winter' brought rain followed by frost and snow. The severe climate may not have been the main reason for the defeat of the German Army, but it halted their advance in 1941 and gave the Red Army a breathing space in which to recover. The huge expanse of the Soviet Union was also an advantage. The Soviet forces could sacrifice territory to the advancing Germans and retreat eastwards. Also, many factories could be dismantled and the infrastructure, along with the workforce, shipped east of the Urals, re-assembled and brought back into production.

External help was also important, as Stalin received very substantial aid, especially lorries and jeeps, from the US Lend-Lease arrangement that was extended to the USSR as early as the summer of 1941. Britain's Royal Navy also shipped vast quantities of equipment to the USSR along the treacherous Arctic passage to Murmansk.

The end of the siege of Stalingrad nearly coincided with the defeat of the German forces at El Alamein in North Africa. The Allied invasion of Sicily took place at the same time as the battle of Kursk, requiring German forces to be diverted to Italy. Although there can be no doubt that the brunt of the fighting in Europe took place on the Eastern Front, some of the more momentous turning points need to be placed within the context of World War II as a whole.

More than 27 million Soviet citizens (of whom at least 20 million were civilians) were killed during World War II. This was a tremendous sacrifice and made the losses of Britain and the USA seem small by comparison. This fact was not lost on Stalin, who used it to his advantage at meetings he had with Churchill and Roosevelt. Stalin's leadership, the fear of failure and the groundswell of Russian (Russian rather than Soviet, perhaps) nationalism all played an important part in the victory of the USSR.

The Soviet Union after 1945

Stalin emerged from the Great Patriotic War as the undisputed *vozhd* (leader) of the USSR. It was Stalin who, according to state propaganda, had saved the Soviet Union from the Nazi invaders. Even though Stalin visited the front only once, in 1943, he made a great deal of this theatrical appearance and referred to it in correspondence with Roosevelt. Posters and postcards were produced to herald his untiring commitment to the war effort; statues were raised to praise his role as 'liberator'; articles and books placed Stalin in the pantheon of Great Russian leaders, such as Peter the Great. Less was known inside the Soviet Union of the 'smaller fronts', as they were called, such as the hard-fought battles in the Pacific, North Africa or Western Europe following the Normandy landings in June 1944.

Stalin visits the frontline
Stalin made a visit to the Kalinin Front in August 1943. He stayed in the small village of Khoroshevo in the cottage of an old lady. He met with his generals, who travelled many miles to the meeting and who were astonished by the humble surroundings. One whispered to another that the very basic environment was intended to 'resemble the front', and so create a favourable impression for propaganda purposes.

The Soviet Union emerged from World War II with territorial gains that had restored the losses suffered in 1919. Stalin was a world statesman and the USSR was a world superpower. Despite this, its economy was devastated and Stalin lost no time in demanding more sacrifice, more unrelenting hard work and promising more lean years with no hope yet of a better standard of living for Soviet citizens.

Figure 4.2
The East–West divide after 1949.

Key

Communist countries under influence of USSR

Communist countries not under influence of USSR

Non-Communist countries

Iron Curtain

1947 Date when Communist government was established

0   1000 km

Scale

Economic recovery after 1945

To access Worksheet 4.4 on European right-wing governments, please visit www.pearsonbacconline.com and follow the on-screen instructions.

The devastation suffered during the war meant that the recovery of the Soviet economy was a gargantuan task. Some indication of the scale of the challenge is given in a book written by John Fischer, a member of the United Nations Relief and Reconstruction Agency (UNRRA) mission to Ukraine in 1946. He wrote about his experiences in *The Scared Men in the Kremlin*, published in 1947. He described daily life both in the cities and in the rural areas that he visited and repeated many times that he was at liberty to ask any questions he liked and to mix freely with ordinary members of the public as well as party officials.

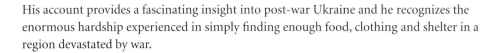

His account provides a fascinating insight into post-war Ukraine and he recognizes the enormous hardship experienced in simply finding enough food, clothing and shelter in a region devastated by war.

SOURCE F

In Kiev, least damaged of the big cities, each person was supposed to have six square metres of living space. That means a strip of floor about ten feet long and six feet wide – somewhat larger than a grave – on which to sleep, cook, eat and store one's possessions. In Kharkov … the official allocation was 4.8 square metres… If you really want to know how a typical Ukrainian family lives, pick the smallest room in your house or apartment and move your wife and children into it. Then pack in the beds, spare clothes, and furniture which you regard as absolutely indispensible. Knock off a few chunks of plaster and most of the paint… Scrap the radiators and cooking range and substitute for both a brick stove which seldom raises the winter temperature much above freezing. Break off the hot water tap in the bathroom, which you will share with several other families. Finally, invite your widowed cousin Sophie and her four youngsters to move in with you.

From John Fischer, *The Scared Men in the Kremlin*, 1947

John Fischer also explained how difficult it was for ordinary people to find fresh food, beyond the small pieces of meat, limited array of vegetables or the few eggs brought into markets by peasants who were able to cultivate small private plots. When the Fourth Five Year Plan was announced in 1946, however, it called upon the citizens of the Soviet Union, once again, to put aside any hope of increased production of consumer goods and to focus on industrial and agricultural production.

SOURCE G

Just how bad this news was did not dawn on the Russians until March 15th 1946, when the government announced the details of the first of its new Five Year Plans. This document outlined a truly back-breaking task. It called for the restoration of all industries wrecked in the war, plus an increase in output nearly fifty per cent above the pre-war level.

From John Fischer, *The Scared Men in the Kremlin*, 1947

SOURCE H

The losses were so immense that they were almost incalculable: 70,000 villages, 98,000 kolkhozi completely or partly destroyed, 1,876 sovkhozi, 17 million head of cattle and 7 million horses driven away; 65,000 kilometres of railway track, half of all railway bridges in occupied territory, over half all urban living space there, 1.2 million houses destroyed as well as 3.5 million rural homes. And then, there was the greatest loss of all, the 20 million dead, as well as the maimed in body and mind.

From Martin McCauley, *The Soviet Union 1917–1991*, 1993

Despite the enormous task that lay before the Soviet people, and despite the immense difficulties of restoring infrastructure and repairing factories and mines, the official claim was that by 1950 industrial production was 75 per cent higher than in 1940. The re-arming of the Red Army remained a priority that increased in importance as the Cold War took hold. Labour and resources were also diverted to the building of the atomic bomb, tested in 1949. Agriculture was far slower to recover and by 1950 the grain harvest amounted to only 40 per cent of that of 1940 (McCauley, *The Soviet Union 1917–1991*, 1993). The recovery of numbers of farm animals was also slow and was hampered by the pseudo-science of **Lysenkoism**.

 Lysenkoism
Named after Trofim Lysenko, this was a popular 'scientific' hypothesis that was based upon the theory of 'inherited characteristics'. Very simply, it was believed that characteristics (in animals or plants) developed in one generation could be passed on to the next. Such ideas had been popularized by Professor William McDougall who, working at Harvard University, had suggested that rats could learn to negotiate a maze and that this characteristic could be passed on to new generations. Lysenko experimented by freezing wheat grains in snow in the belief that he was developing strains of wheat that would grow in winter. He also thought that breeding cows with high milk yields with those with high beef yields would automatically produce animals with both characteristics. His ideas were, however, based on a faulty understanding of genetics, but remained popular in the USSR until the 1960s.

Domestic policies after 1945

Stalin continued to push forward his plan for 'Russification', as he wanted to introduce Russian settlers into the Baltic States and so weaken nationalism and impose Russian culture and language. This plan extended to the Baltic States and to Moldova, where the purging of the local population and the 'planting' of ethnic Russians took place. Anti-semitism also resurfaced with a crackdown on Jewish literature, journalism and culture, as well as a purging of Jewish officials from the higher levels of the party leadership.

Known as the *Zhdanovshchina*, a campaign was led by Andrei Zhdanov, the Leningrad Party leader, to remove all 'Western' influence from music and literature. Prokofiev and Shostakovich were among the composers whose music was now criticized, along with the poetry of Anna Akhmatova .There was even criticism of Einstein's theory of relativity, which was declared to be 'bourgeois' and 'reactionary'.

After Zhdanov's death in 1948, Stalin carried out a purge of the Leningrad Party known as the 'Leningrad Affair'. This was followed by another purge known as the 'Doctor's Plot' in November 1952, when the mostly Jewish doctors in the Kremlin were arrested and accused of killing their patients, including Zhdanov. It was probably Stalin's death in March 1953 that saved the lives of his closest comrades, including Beria, Molotov, Mikoyan and Malenkov. The declining health of Stalin led to increasing paranoia and he was overheard to say, 'I am finished, I trust no one, not even myself.'

Terror and propaganda after 1945

The purges of the 1930s were not repeated on the same scale after 1945, although returning prisoners of war, along with White Russians and Cossacks who Stalin had insisted be returned to the Soviet Union, were often shot or sent to a distant gulag. Stalin did not want to risk knowledge of the outside world penetrating the walls of the Soviet Union. Norman Lowe notes that an estimated 2.8 million soldiers who had survived imprisonment in German camps returned to the Soviet Union 'to be arrested and interrogated by the NKVD' (Lowe, *Mastering Twentieth Century Russian History*, 2002). Of these, some were shot, others sent to labour camps but only around 500,000 (or one-sixth) were allowed to return home.

New labour camps were built mostly to hold 'bandits', which is how Stalin referred to nationalists in Ukraine and in the Baltic States. Dmitri Volkogonov in *The Rise and Fall of the Soviet Empire* estimates that more than 90,000 'kulaks and their families, bandits, nationalists and others' were deported from the Baltic States alone. By 1947 there were more than 20 million prisoners in the gulags and 27 additional camps had been built. A law was passed 'imposing twenty years hard labour for anyone attempting to escape from exile' (Volkogonov, *The Rise and Fall of the Soviet Empire*, 1999). In all likelihood, however, the Great Terror was a grim memory and few people would have dared plot to overthrow or even to criticize Soviet rule. The show trials and the purges were resurrected in Central and Eastern Europe, however, where local communist parties were ruthlessly purged with the same random selection of victims as had plagued the USSR in the 1930s.

Within the Soviet Union, gratitude for victory in the Great Patriotic War boosted Stalin's popularity further and the suffering undoubtedly led people to believe that whatever hardship came with peace, it did not begin to compare with the suffering endured during the war.

STUDENT STUDY SECTION

In Topic 3 of Paper 2, it is not required that you study the foreign policy of single-party leaders. This means that there will not be a specific question asked about the foreign policy of Stalin, for instance. It is quite a good idea, however, to know something about this area of policy as it is bound to influence events at home. There is no doubt that the Cold War had a decisive influence on Stalin's decision to push for a rapid recovery for the war-torn USSR and to divert resources towards the building of an atomic bomb. He feared the West and galvanized the Soviet population, once again, to re-arm and to rebuild the economy.

It is also worth considering where Soviet policy towards Central and Eastern Europe fits in. Is this 'domestic' or 'foreign' policy? Countries such Poland, Romania and Hungary are not within the USSR and so need not be discussed in an answer to an exam question that asks about Stalin's post-war domestic policy. Even so, via **Cominform** and **Comecon** the USSR did have a very significant impact upon the internal policies of foreign countries and, to a lesser extent, vice versa.

For example, consider the following question:

QUESTION

Assess the success and failure of the domestic policies of two single-party leaders, each chosen from a different region.

If you chose Stalin as one of your leaders, you could go beyond 1941 (unless the question states otherwise) and you could make a reference to the extension of Soviet influence to Central and Eastern Europe (using some specific examples), linking this to Stalin's concerns about security.

Stalin's role as a world leader

Even before the end of World War II, Stalin was already a recognized world leader and his meetings with Winston Churchill and Franklin Roosevelt to determine post-war arrangements have been well documented. Unlikely allies, the 'Big Three' were in close contact throughout World War II. Historians have discussed the nature of their pre-, wartime and post-war relationships extensively, and it is still open to debate at what stage the wartime allies became post-war enemies.

How did Stalin influence the Cold War?

There is a great deal of historiography concerning the role of Stalin as one of the most important leaders at the beginning of the Cold War. His actions and motives have been carefully scrutinized by many historians. How far Stalin was responsible for the ending of the wartime alliance and the evolution of a hostile relationship with the USA is still open to debate, but the following events are worthy of investigation.

Churchill, Roosevelt and Stalin meet at Yalta in February 1945.

- In 1945, Soviet expansion into Central and Eastern Europe aroused the fears and suspicion of the USA. There was concern that Stalin was intending to extend Soviet influence over the whole of Europe.
- After the Potsdam conference in July 1945, Stalin did not meet again with the Western leaders and this contributed to a climate of suspicion. Unlike Franklin Roosevelt, President Truman did not seem to want to cooperate or compromise with Stalin.
- Stalin's 'election speech' of 1946 suggested that the USSR was, once again, using anti-Western rhetoric and this implied that the post-war peace was fragile.

Cominform (Communist Information Bureau)
Established in 1947, Cominform was a revival of Comintern, which had been disbanded in 1943. To some extent, it was a response to the development of the Marshall Plan or European Recovery Plan. Czechoslovakia and Poland had shown interest in taking part in the Marshall Plan, but Stalin wanted to ensure that there was a uniform (negative) response among the satellite states of the Eastern Bloc.

Comecom (Council for Mutual Economic Assistance)
Established in 1949 as a kind of trade organization among communist states. It was not limited to the Eastern Bloc and, in time, included Mongolia, Cuba and Vietnam.

- Hiroshima and Nagasaki brought in the atomic age and although Stalin had placed Beria in charge of a project to build a Soviet atom bomb, this was not tested until 1949. Meanwhile, the Baruch Plan of 1946 was proposed but rejected by Stalin, who was not content to have UN control over nuclear arms.

- The Marshall Plan of 1947 (European Recovery Programme) was condemned by the USSR as 'dollar imperialism' and Poland and Czechoslovakia were prevented from taking part in this US-led plan for economic recovery. The communist takeover of Czechoslovakia was prompted by this.

- When the USA and Britain united their zones of Germany in 1946, calling it Bizonia, Stalin objected as he argued that this was contrary to agreements on the administration of occupied Germany. France was persuaded to attach its zone to Bizonia in 1948, making it Trizonia. The Marshall Plan also made it imperative that the economy of the Western zones was placed on a sound footing, leading to the introduction of a new currency. Whether or not this could also be introduced into the Western sectors of Berlin led to a difference of opinion with the USSR and prompted what became known as the Berlin Blockade of 1948–49. Although Stalin's intention was to push the Western powers out of Berlin, this strategy rebounded on him, and he had to lift the blockade in May 1949.

- In many of the Central and Eastern European states that came under Soviet control, free elections were held in the post-war period. Gradually, however, 'salami tactics' (cutting something slice by slice) enabled the communist parties, which were often part of coalition governments, to control the police or the justice system. Little by little, the communists would end up in power and these countries became known as the 'satellite states'.

- The Cold War turned into a 'hot war' in 1950 with the invasion of South Korea by North Korea. At the time, the USA suspected that this had been instigated by the USSR, although later research showed quite clearly that Kim Il Sung, the leader of communist North Korea, had been the one to approach Stalin to ask for support.

To access worksheet 4.5 on the Baruch Plan, please visit www. pearsonbacconline.com and follow the on-screen instructions.

STUDENT STUDY SECTION

ACTIVITY

The list above includes most of the main events that are discussed in relation to the origins of the Cold War. See if you can rewrite each one to reflect the different historiographical interpretations of the Cold War (see Interesting Facts box).

For example: 'The USA misread Soviet concerns about security and believed that Stalin intended to expand Soviet influence beyond Central and Eastern Europe.'

The death of Stalin

Stalin ruled the Soviet Union from 1929 until 1953, longer than any other leader. He created the Soviet system of government and was the undisputed leader of world communism during his lifetime. Stalin had not been in good health for several years before his death, and in March 1953 he suffered a stroke that killed him. When he died, there was much relief but also anguish about the future of the Soviet Union. Stalin had gathered around him a small group of dedicated supporters who knew that not only their jobs but their lives depended on Stalin's goodwill. He never ceased to tell those most likely to succeed him that when he was gone, the West would challenge the Soviet Union and 'the capitalists will crush you like little kittens.' In fact, the USSR maintained its role as a world superpower, but the legacy of Stalin continued through the all-powerful secret police, the lack of political freedom and the strictly controlled command economy.

STUDENT STUDY SECTION

This chapter has looked at the rise to power of Stalin and his time as the single-party ruler of the Soviet Union. In most cases, exam questions on single-party and authoritarian states/leaders may ask about:

- The rise to power of a ruler or the establishment of a single-party state.
- The kinds of policies that were introduced, how they were implemented and how successful they were.
- How a leader consolidated his power.
- What kind of opposition he faced and the methods used to deal with it.

When you prepare for the exam be sure to revise these themes.

You may also choose to answer a question that may ask about more than one leader. Remember that if a question asks about leaders or states (plural), you have to use more than one example. Sometimes a question will ask you to write about certain leaders, but there are also 'general' questions where you get to choose who to write about. For instance, you might choose to answer a question like this.

QUESTION

Compare and contrast the methods used to consolidate power by one right-wing and one left-wing single-party leader. Suitable examples would be Hitler (right wing) and Stalin (left wing).

ACTIVITY

Plan an essay outline that addresses each of the following topics, showing the similarities and the differences in the way they were used by Stalin and Hitler to stay in power.

- **Propaganda (don't forget to consider how propaganda was communicated as well as what it conveyed)**
- **Economic policies (did they both use a planned economy?)**
- **Social policies (what was the role of education, the role of women, religion etc.?)**
- **The use of terror and the secret police (the NKVD and the Gestapo, labour camps)**
- **The use of 'scapegoats' (i.e. groups in society that could be blamed for problems, such 'Trotskyites' and Jews)**
- **Purges of the party**

Can you think of any other 'methods' you could add to this list?

REVIEW SECTION

This chapter has covered the rise to power and rule of Stalin as the leader of the USSR. In particular, it has focused upon the following:

- **How, after the death of Lenin, Stalin rose to power through the hierarchy of the Communist Party.**
- **The methods Stalin used to achieve his aim to industrialize the USSR and to consolidate his control of the Communist Party.**
- **The social and economic policies that were carried out under Stalin's leadership.**
- **The methods used by Stalin to deal with opposition within the USSR.**
- **Stalin's leadership of the USSR during and after World War II until his death in 1953.**

5 MAO ZEDONG AND CHINA

This chapter deals with the rise to power and the rule of Mao Zedong. One of the most important leaders of China during the 20th century, he established the political and economic structure that has remained in place in China until today. Mao ruled China from 1949 until his death in 1976 and was its longest-serving leader.

The sections in this chapter will address themes for detailed study as outlined in the IB History syllabus. They will cover some background to Mao and his rise to power between 1927 and 1949. They will then show how he was able to consolidate his control of China after the Chinese Civil War until his death in 1976.

Timeline – 1893–1976	
1893	Mao born in Hunan Province.
1911	Collapse of ruling Qing Dynasty.
1921	Becomes one of the founders of Communist Party of China (CPC).
1923	Mao and the CPC join the Guomindang (GMD).
1924	Formation of First United Front.
1925	Jiang Jieshi becomes leader of the GMD.
1927	Shanghai Massacre – the 'White Terror'.
1927–34	Mao creates the Jiangxi soviet.
1934–35	The Long March to Yan'an.
1935–45	Mao creates the Yan'an soviet.
1937–45	Second United Front against the Japanese.
1946–49	Mao and the CPC defeat Jiang Jieshi and the GMD in the Chinese Civil War.
1949	The People's Republic of China (PRC) is founded on 1 October.
1950	Marriage Reform Law; Agrarian Reform Law; Korean War begins.
1951	'Three Antis'.
1952	'Five Antis'.
1953–57	First Five Year Plan.
1956	Hundred Flowers Campaign is launched.
1957	Anti-Rightist Movement.
1958-62	The Great Leap Forward – Second Five Year Plan.
1961	Sino-Soviet split.
1962–66	The Socialist Education Movement is formed.
1966–76	The Great Proletarian Cultural Revolution.
1971	Death of Lin Biao.
1972	Mao meets Nixon in Beijing.
1976	The deaths of Zhou Enlai, Zhu De and Mao Zedong.

Section I:
Origins and nature of authoritarian and single-party states – the People's Republic of China

On 1 October 1949, in front of a crowd of 500,000 people, Mao Zedong proclaimed that the Chinese people had 'stood up', and he announced the establishment of the People's Republic of China (PRC). This achievement was the result of a protracted struggle for power between the Guomindang (GMD) and the Communist Party of China (CPC) through China's 'Warlord Period' (1916–27), the 'Nanjing Decade' (1928–1937) and, following the Sino-Japanese War (1937–45), the Chinese Civil War (1946–49), from which Mao emerged the winner.

What was Mao Zedong's background and why is it significant?

Mao Zedong was born in 1893 in a small farming village called Shaoshan, about 50km from Changsha, the capital of Hunan province. His parents were farmers with a smallholding of about 1.2 hectares, which was large enough to provide the family with a good standard of living. Mao's father insisted that he attend the local school, studying the traditional Confucian classics, as well as learning both to read and write. One pamphlet on 'The Dismemberment of China' was to have a strong influence on Mao. According to Jonathan Spence, 'decades later, Mao still remembered the opening line, "Alas, China will be subjugated"' (by foreign powers) and was determined that this would never happen again (*Mao*, 1999).

At the end of the 19th century, China was undergoing intense pressure both externally and internally. Externally, following the **Meiji Restoration** of 1868, Japan was emerging as the dominant Asian power. This was evident after the 1894–95 Sino-Japanese War, during which Japan rapidly defeated China, and the 1904–05 Russo-Japanese War, during which a major European power was defeated by an Asian country for the first time in centuries. Japan rapidly annexed Korea in 1910, further consolidating its grip on the region. Japan was to become a major factor in the later struggle for power in China between the GMD and the CPC in the 1930s.

Internally, partly as a result of the defeat in the 1894–95 war, China was facing increasing pressure for change, which was being rejected by the aristocracy who clung fiercely to the feudal structure of Chinese society. The Qing Dynasty had ruled since 1644, but under the leadership of the Dowager Empress, Cixi, between 1867 and 1908 it was resistant to moves for reform. Movements such as Kang Youwei's 1898 Hundred Days of Reform, which attempted to change almost every aspect of China's life, were finally rejected by Cixi. Later, by 1902, Cixi was to reverse her attitudes, but it would prove to be too late for the Qing Dynasty, which ultimately was overthrown by the Double Ten Revolution of 10 October 1911, led by Sun Yixian's Revolutionary Alliance. After having promised to change Chinese society by implementing the *Sanminzhuyi* or 'Three People's Principles' (nationalism, democracy and people's livelihood), this alliance became the Guomindang or Nationalist Party in 1912.

Wade-Giles and Pinyin
There are two commonly used systems of transliterating Mandarin into Western text: Wade-Giles and Pinyin. In this chapter, Pinyin will be used as it best approximates to how the names should be pronounced. Thus it will be Mao Zedong not Mao Tse-tung and Jiang Jieshi not Chiang Kai-shek. Also we will use Guomindang, not the Wade-Giles version, Kuomintang.

Meiji Restoration
The Meiji Restoration ended the Tokugawa Shogunate in 1867 and saw the accession of the new Emperor Meiji in Tokyo rather than Kyoto.

STUDENT STUDY SECTION

QUESTION
Look up the *Sanminzhuyi*. Explain the Three People's Principles in your own words. Which groups in China would support these ideas and why?

A further factor that was to have a crucial impact on Mao's thinking was the anti-Western attitude that pervaded the Manchu court and the peasants. Already in 1898, the USA had announced its 'Open Door Policy' in regard to foreign spheres of influence in China. In essence, it meant that the USA would not accept preferential agreements among powers, but demanded the right to trade freely within China's borders. The policy was perceived as a form of economic imperialism by China. It was followed by the German acquisition of railroad building and mining rights in Shandong, a situation that was to lead to the 1900 Boxer Rebellion, during which Beijing and Tianjin were occupied and foreign consulates burned. The German minister was killed in the Beijing attack. The Boxer Rebellion was finally suppressed when an international relief force of about 50,000 men arrived in China in August 1900.

SOURCE A

A cartoon depicts the 'carving-up' of China by Western powers.

STUDENT STUDY SECTION

CARTOON ANALYSIS

Identify each of the countries depicted. What implications could this cartoon have in the future for Mao and the PRC?

De facto
This means in practice, although not necessarily ratified by law.

Zhang Jingyao (1881–1933)
Zhang Jingyao was one of the most notorious of China's warlords, infamous for his troops' atrocities and cruelty to farmers in Hunan.

Sun's success was to be short-lived, as he too was overthrown in 1913 by Yuan Shikai (one of his generals) and was forced into exile. After Yuan Shikai's death in 1916, China lapsed into a period of anarchy dominated by its warlords. The period between 1916 and 1927 is commonly referred to as the 'Warlord Era', as China did not have an effective central government. There was a **de facto** government in Beijing but, as it had no form of enforcement, independent warlords with their own militias undermined any attempt at centralization. This situation allowed other nations, such as Japan, to reassert their attempts to make China a Japanese protectorate. The lack of central government was to lead to the problem of regionalism. Mao was to encounter this problem at first hand in Hunan when he came into conflict with **Zhang Jingyao**, its military governor.

Mao thus grew up as a young man with four major influences upon his thinking:

- An aggressive and expansionist Japanese foreign policy, which was particularly focused on acquiring raw materials for Japan's home-based industries.
- A ruling elite that ignored the needs of the rural villages and which exploited the peasants as a class.
- The perception that Western powers were attempting to exploit China for their own political and economic gain.
- The issue of regionalism.

These four influences were to remain with Mao for the rest of his life. More importantly, they would have a decisive effect on his decision-making in the future and the direction that China would take after 1949.

Mao was successful as a student and graduated from Changsha Middle School in 1918. At the age of 24, he left his family and moved to Beijing, finally finding work as a clerical assistant at Beijing University. Over the years Mao became a bookseller, a teacher, a school principal and a businessman, and he also continued to read widely. He had access to many of the Western classics of the 19th century, including books such as Adam Smith's influential economics text *The Wealth of Nations*, and started to write articles for a number of periodicals and newspapers. By 1919 he was becoming more active politically on behalf of Hunan independence, with the aim of removing Zhang from power.

The Paris Peace Settlements and their impact on China

Mao's political activities coincided with the Paris Peace Conference of 1919, which produced the peace settlement (the Treaty of Versailles) following the end of World War I in 1918. As part of the settlement, the major Western powers had agreed to Japan's claims to Shandong. China had entered World War I in 1917 with the expectation that after the war the German sphere of influence in Shandong would be ended and the province would revert back to China. On 4 May 1919, thousands of students marched in Beijing, protesting against the Treaty of Versailles and denouncing the **Twenty-one Demands**. The loss of Shandong was a reaffirmation to Mao of the treachery of the Western powers and the expansionist policies of Japan. Mao's contact with the Russian **Comintern** had also supported his xenophobia (dislike of foreigners), as accounts of Western military support for the Whites against the Reds in the Russian Civil War seemed to indicate the West's desire to overturn the Bolshevik Revolution and eliminate the communists in Russia. The direct result of the 'May 4th Movement' was the paving of the way for the emergence of the CPC, which was formally established in Shanghai in 1921 with Chen Duxiu as its Secretary-General. It numbered 12 delegates, including Mao, representing 57 members. At about the same time, another branch of the party was established in Beijing under the leadership of Li Dazhao.

SOURCE B

When the intellectuals of China understood what was happening at Versailles, they became very agitated. All over China discussion groups formed, thousands of telegrams were sent, not only by students and professors, but also by merchants, shopkeepers, businessmen, associations and guilds, and overseas Chinese communities so urgently, so seriously, did the Chinese people consider that Versailles was the testing point, the watershed; that it was democracy on trial. Were the Great Powers really going to behave as they said they would, or let China down? This was the crisis, the point of no return. Then came the terrible news. All demands by China

for readjustment of unequal treaties… had been rejected. Shandong province was allocated to Japan. In short, China, as an ally, was treated as an enemy.

From Han Suyin, *A Mortal Flower*, 1966

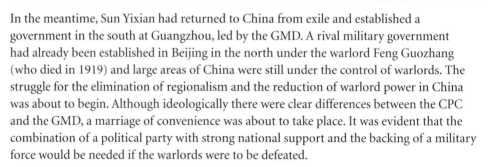

STUDENT STUDY SECTION

QUESTIONS

Han Suyin expresses herself very emotionally in the source. Find out a bit more about her background and then explain why this might be so. What were the 'unequal treaties'?

Feng Yuxiang (1882–1948)

Feng was best known as the 'Christian General', as he was a convert to Methodism. Feng's policies were inconsistent. Having been relieved of his command in the 1930s by Jiang, Feng became a harsh critic of the GMD. He was rehabilitated in 1935 and rose to play a leading role in the GMD army and government. Feng died in 1948.

In the meantime, Sun Yixian had returned to China from exile and established a government in the south at Guangzhou, led by the GMD. A rival military government had already been established in Beijing in the north under the warlord Feng Guozhang (who died in 1919) and large areas of China were still under the control of warlords. The struggle for the elimination of regionalism and the reduction of warlord power in China was about to begin. Although ideologically there were clear differences between the CPC and the GMD, a marriage of convenience was about to take place. It was evident that the combination of a political party with strong national support and the backing of a military force would be needed if the warlords were to be defeated.

With Russian Comintern support, the CPC was encouraged to form an alliance with the GMD in order to reduce foreign influence in China and eliminate warlord power. This First United Front was proclaimed in 1924. Sun's aim was to unite with the Christian warlord **Feng Yuxiang** who now controlled Beijing and who was supportive of the GMD's policies. The CPC would form a bloc within the GMD, tacitly accepting its control and discipline. The effect on CPC membership was staggering. From 57 members in 1921 it grew to 980 in 1925 and by 1927 had 58,000 members (along with another 30,000 in the Communist Youth League) (see Ranbir Vohra, *China's Path to Modernization*, 2000). The GMD had also expanded its numbers and, after the establishment of the Whampoa military academy in 1924 under the leadership of Jiang Jieshi, the First United Front now had a military force to support its political aims. Sun Yixian died in 1925 and after a brief power struggle he was succeeded as leader of the GMD by Jiang Jieshi. The decision was made to attempt a unification of China by a military campaign against the warlords. The Northern Expedition, numbering approximately 100,000 men, started out from Guangzhou in May 1926 with three main targets: the occupation of Fujian, Jiangxi and Nanjing.

◀ Mao Zedong, seen as a young man.

 Jiang Jieshi (Chiang Kai-shek) ▶

STUDENT STUDY SECTION

QUESTION

Look at the pictures of Mao and Jiang taken at about the same time. What does their choice of clothing suggest to you about their concerns and personalities?

During this time, Mao had largely confined himself to dealing with Hunanese issues, but in 1924 he duly attended the First National Congress of the GMD, as a result of which he became more active within both the GMD and the CPC in Shanghai. After a brief spell there, Mao returned to Hunan in 1926 to work with the peasants. He was ultimately given the task of organizing peasant forces in the countryside to support the United Front campaign against the warlords. What is interesting to note here is that Mao was becoming more concerned with local Hunan peasant issues than with national CPC issues, and was increasingly seen by the Hunanese as a person who represented them against both the landlords and the warlords. This positioning was to prove important in the future.

SOURCE C

'All revolutionary parties and all revolutionary comrades will stand before them [the peasants] to be tested, to be accepted or rejected as they decide. To march at their head and lead them? To stand behind them, gesticulating and criticizing them? Or to stand opposite them and oppose them. Every Chinese is free to choose among the three, but by force of circumstances you are fated to make the choice quickly.'

From a report submitted to the CPC in February 1917 by Mao, quoted in Jonathan Spence, *Mao*, 1999

STUDENT STUDY SECTION

QUESTIONS

a) **How have Mao's views been affected by his own personal background?**

b) **What does this extract show about Mao's views of the peasants?**

c) **What is the relationship between what Mao is saying and traditional Marxist-Leninist theories of revolution?**

● **Examiner's hint**
Exam questions will sometimes ask you to analyze the rise to power of a single-party leader. Although the Chinese Civil War occurred between 1946 and 1949, you would be well advised in the introduction to your essay to argue that although the war was fought between those dates, the actual long-term causes go back to the 1920s and the formation of the First United Front. This will enable you to make a far more detailed analysis of the rise to power of Mao.

The Nanjing Decade (1928–37) and the early struggle for control of China.

Figure 5.1
Map of China and its provinces.

The Northern Expedition against the warlords gained territory rapidly. By December the cities of Fuzhou, Wuhan and Hangzhou had been captured and the CPC/GMD forces were converging on Nanjing and Shanghai. However, despite the apparent unity of purpose between the GMD and the CPC, rifts were beginning to appear in the coalition. While Sun had generally supported the CPC, Jiang was much more mistrustful of its intentions. One of the major reasons behind the success of the First United Front was communist activism in the countryside and the cities. It was clear that the CPC was growing in power. A split had occurred between rival factions of the GMD as Jiang became involved in a leadership struggle with **Wang Jingwei**. Jiang needed to take some form of action to demonstrate his claim to be the leader of the GMD. He decided to get rid of the communist bloc within the GMD. He gained the support of landlords, warlords, secret societies and criminal organizations and was also supported by many Western organizations that were still in China. In the spring of 1927, Jiang suddenly attacked the communists in Shanghai. The 'White Terror' had begun. Thousands were killed in Shanghai, Wuhan and Hunan as the right wing of the GMD attacked union members, communists and peasant associations. The United Front between the CPC and the GMD collapsed. Wang decided to give up his claims to be the leader of the GMD and allied with Jiang to unite its military arm. In Beijing the communist leader Li Dazhao was killed by the Manchurian warlord **Zhang Zuolin**, who also joined forces with the GMD. Jiang was now the acknowledged leader of the GMD and was determined to eliminate the communists in China. The roots of the Civil War were set.

Wang Jingwei (1883–1944)
A member of the GMD who disagreed with Jiang's policies and emerged in the late 1920s as a potential rival.

Zhang Zuolin (1875–1928)
Zhang was the warlord of Manchuria from 1916 to 1928. He was killed in June 1928 by a bomb planted by a Japanese officer. He was succeeded by his son Zhang Xueliang. (These two men are not to be confused with Zhang Jingyao.)

SOURCE D

... we must rectify and strengthen our revolutionary ideology. In this matter of purifying the Guomindang, we should not only purge the Communists from the Guomindang ranks but also eliminate Communist ideology from our party beliefs. Since the collaboration between these two parties began, the Communists, camouflaging themselves as Nationalists, have propagated Communist ideas among different occupational groups, including agricultural, industrial, commercial and educational groups.

Wang Jingwei explains the reasons behind the 1927 terror, from D.J. Li (ed.), *The Road to Communism: China Since 1912,* **1971**

STUDENT STUDY SECTION

QUESTION

Look at Wang Jingwei's explanation for the Guomindang's actions. Why do you think he is making this statement?

The CPC Central Committee encouraged Mao to mount a peasant insurrection against the GMD in Hunan, but the task was too much and Mao was only able to mobilize a small force, which was easily suppressed by the GMD armies. Being surrounded by GMD forces, Mao decided to move his small group to Jinggangshan and later to Jiangxi province. Here Mao set up a base for the communists that became known as the Jiangxi soviet. Mao developed his aims for a peasant-based revolution. His 1928 'Land Law' clearly detailed the direction that Mao thought China should take in the future and was the precursor of the 1950 Agrarian Reform Law. By 1931 Mao had set himself up as an independent force with peasant mass support, a secure base and a strong military force using guerrilla tactics against the GMD.

SOURCE E

Confiscate all land, and turn ownership over to the soviet government, which should use the following three methods to redistribute it:

a) distribution to the peasants for them to cultivate individually;
b) distribution to the peasants for them to cultivate in common;
c) organization by the soviet government of model farms to cultivate the land

Of the above three methods, the first is to be the primary one. Under special circumstances, or when the soviet government is strong, the second and third methods may also be employed.

From Jinggangshan Land Law, 1928, quoted in Stuart R. Schram (ed.), *Mao's Road to Power: Revolutionary Writings 1912–1949,* **vol. 3, 1995**

STUDENT STUDY SECTION

QUESTION

Compare and contrast the 1928 Land Law with the extract from the 1950 Agrarian Reform Law on p.160.

Between 1930 and 1934, Jiang launched a series of five initially unsuccessful Extermination Campaigns aimed at eliminating the communists in the Jiangxi soviet. In 1931 Jiang had another threat to deal with as well. The Japanese had attacked Manchuria, installing the former Qing Emperor **Puyi** as a puppet leader and renaming the territory Manchukuo. The Manchurian warlord Zhang, who had supported Jiang in 1927, requested assistance from Jiang to repel the Japanese, but Jiang refused to give him any help against the Japanese, who he thought were too strong militarily.

The events of the late 1920s and early 1930s were to serve as the template for the 1946–49 civil war. The lines had been drawn. Mao was established as one of the few communist leaders capable of resisting the military campaigns of the GMD. Jiang had ensured that the right wing of the GMD had removed all opposition within the party and that he had emerged as the unchallenged leader of the GMD, entitling himself Generalissimo. Jiang had control over most of the major cities in China and had left the rural parts of China under the control of the landlords and pro-GMD warlords. The invasion of Manchuria in 1931 and the continued occupation of the territory, despite the League of Nations' condemnation of the action, confirmed Mao's belief that China's major external threat was to come from Japan. In Jiang's mind there was little he could do about the Japanese encroachment, as he did not want the GMD armies to oppose Japan. Jiang thought that his army was too weak and would be defeated. He therefore abandoned his warlord ally Zhang. Jiang's major concern was the elimination of the communists as a force in China, which would allow him to establish control over the whole country. To achieve this goal his armies were needed to fight the Encirclement Campaigns against the communists.

SOURCE F

A cartoon from the 1930s satirizes Japan's relationship with international treaties.

STUDENT STUDY SECTION

QUESTION

Look up the Kellog–Briand Pact and the Nine Power Treaty. What is the message conveyed in the source and why is it significant for China?

Jiang's Fifth Extermination Campaign in 1934 was more successful. Jiang changed tactics and imposed an economic blockade of the Jiangxi soviet region. At the same time he also changed his military policies and began to use 'blockhouse' tactics: building defensive fortifications and consolidating his army's position along the way as it continued its attacks on Mao's communists. The change in the GMD's tactics began to work, and a disagreement occurred within the communist ranks as to the military strategy they should follow. Finally the Revolutionary Military Council, following the advice of their Comintern advisor **Li De**, abandoned their guerrilla tactics. Mao was no longer perceived to be the leader of the communists. The combination of these changes in tactics resulted in heavy defeats for the communists and they were forced to retreat in the Long March with about 100,000 men to escape the GMD. The constant harrying of the communists and escalating casualties resulted in low morale and an increasing call for a change in the leadership. The communists were nearly at the point of elimination when, at the **Zunyi Conference** in January 1936, **Zhou Enlai** decided to join forces with Mao against Li De. Mao took over control of military matters as leader of the First Front Army and changed tactics, reverting to guerrilla warfare again. The communists marched for over a year to finally arrive at Yan'an in Shaanxi province. Figures vary, but it is estimated that approximately 90 per cent of the communist force had been lost in the march. Mao summarized its importance in December 1935.

Li De (1900–1974)
A German Comintern agent whose real name was Otto Braun.

Zunyi Conference
A conference held to analyze why the communists were losing the conflict with the GMD. It is seen as being a turning point in the history of the CPC.

Zhou Enlai (1898–1976)
A key member of the CPC, Zhou eventually became Premier and Foreign Minister in 1949. He is seen as one of the moderating influences in the Cultural Revolution (1966–76).

◀ Zhou Enlai

SOURCE G

The Long March is a manifesto. It has proclaimed to the world that the Red Army is an army of heroes, while the imperialists and their running dogs, Chiang Kai-shek and his like, are impotent. It has proclaimed their utter failure to encircle, pursue, obstruct and intercept us. The Long March is also a propaganda force. It has announced to some 200 million people in eleven provinces that the road of the Red Army is their only road to liberation.

From Mao's speech 'On Tactics against Japanese Imperialism', 27 December 1935

STUDENT STUDY SECTION

QUESTION

Explain what you understand by 'imperialists', 'running dogs' and being 'impotent'. Go back to p.145 and examine the four issues that were important determinants of Mao's background. Can you find any of them here? What events in China during the 1930s do you think Mao would include under the terms 'imperialists' and 'running dogs'?

To access Worksheet 5.1 on the Long March, please visit www.pearsonbacconline.com and follow the on-screen instructions.

Mao's consolidation

After the Long March, Mao's position as leader of the communists had been consolidated, but he was still not totally secure and he faced opposition internally. The Long March had symbolic value, as it had shown that Jiang's control was not absolute, but the communist numbers had been decimated. Yan'an was isolated enough to ensure that Mao was out of reach of the GMD and the communists gradually began to build up their base there and gather support against the Japanese.

The GMD still refused to fight the Japanese in Manchuria. Jiang ordered Zhang Xueliang, his second-in-command, to attack the Red Army in Shaanxi. Throughout China demands for a ceasefire in the civil war increased and Mao, Zhou Enlai and Zhu De personally appealed to Zhang in their 'Letter to All Officers and Men of the Northeastern Army' to join with the communists and fight the Japanese. Zhang agreed and stopped military action against the communists. Jiang went to meet Zhang in Xian to find out why they were not obeying his orders. In desperation, Zhang placed Jiang under house arrest, insisting that he join with the communists to form a Second United Front in 1937 against the Japanese. In December 1936, Jiang reluctantly agreed and preparations were started to initiate the Front. On 7 July 1937 Japan attacked China, bringing to an end the Nanjing Decade, and the Sino-Japanese War broke out. Despite the political failings of the GMD, China was more united in 1937 than it had been for many years. The GMD had control of approximately 25 per cent of China and 66 per cent of the population (Vohra, *China's Path to Modernization*, 2000). The announcement of the Second United Front had helped to unify the people against a common enemy.

Meanwhile, in Yan'an Mao had started his revision of Marxist-Leninist thought, transposing the urban based 'bourgeoisie–proletarian' model of Marxist revolutionary theory to the rural realities of China. He was aided in his creation of a Maoist ideology by **Chen Boda**, his secretary, and Mao was gradually emerging as the fully fledged leader of the communists. Jonathan Spence argues that a 'cult of Mao' was already emerging, which was consolidated in 1943 by Mao's adoption of the titles Chairman of the Communist Central Committee and Chairman of the Politburo. The preamble to the Constitution of the Communist Party published in 1945 shows how far this had developed. 'The Chinese Communist Party takes Mao Zedong's thought – the thought that unites Marxist-Leninism theory and the practice of the Chinese Revolution – as the guide for all its work and opposes all dogmatic or empiricist deviations' (Spence, *Mao*, 1999). Mao's unassailable position as leader was going to be one of the key factors behind the CPC victory in the civil war.

Chen Boda (1904–89)

Chen is seen by many observers as being influential in helping Mao to clarify his thoughts on Maoist doctrine. He became a member of the Cultural Revolution Group, siding with Jiang Qing, and was eventually removed from office in 1973.

Author's note

The Sino-Japanese War and the Chinese Civil War are covered in more detail in Chapter 13 of the companion book in this series: *Causes, Practices and Effects of War* by Keely Rogers and Jo Thomas.

Capture of Nanjing

This event is infamous for the Japanese treatment of the Chinese civilian population, hundreds of thousands of whom were murdered. It is also known for the rape of many women. Figures vary from between 30,000 to 80,000 rapes. The tragic episode is commonly known as the Nanjing Massacre or the Rape of Nanjing.

STUDENT STUDY SECTION

RESEARCH ACTIVITY

In the *Communist Manifesto* of 1848, Marx proposes a 10-step model of revolution. Find out what these ten steps are and see how many of them would apply to China in 1937.

The Sino-Japanese War (1937–45) and its consequences for China

The Japanese moved south from Manchuria and quickly seized Beijing. After the fall of Shanghai and as Nanjing became threatened, Jiang moved the GMD government initially to Wuhan and then in 1938 to Chongqing in Sichuan province, which became known as 'free China'. **Nanjing** was captured in December 1937 and the Japanese set up a puppet government under Wang Jingwei. The entire eastern seaboard of China was soon under Japanese control but, despite frequent air attacks, Chongqing did not fall. Initially the Soviet Union was the only foreign power that gave any assistance to China, but despite their control over vast areas of China, Japan had failed to destroy the nationalist government. The war became something of a stalemate until 1941, when the USA's entry into World War II began to change the military balance of power. For many Jiang seemed to be content with the policy of inaction and was waiting for the USA to win the war for the GMD, after which Jiang could carry on his fight with the communists. His attitude can be summed up in his famous quotation in 1941 that 'The Japanese are a disease of the skin, but the communists are a disease of the heart.'

STUDENT STUDY SECTION

QUESTION
What do you think Jiang means by this statement?

● **Examiner's hint**
The first sentence an examiner will see will be the first sentence of your introduction and the last sentence s/he will read will be the final sentence of your conclusion. How well these are written will inevitably have the effect, perhaps subconsciously, of labelling you as a 'good' or 'not so good' history student. Bear this in mind when practising writing them.

By 1939, Jiang had decided to break the alliance with the communists and ordered his troops to attack their forces. In 1941 the GMD army tried to annihilate the communist armies in the south and Jiang withdrew all financial support to Mao. These actions led to widespread criticism of Jiang both from within China and abroad, with the result that Jiang began to lose support. Jiang was facing other problems as well. His army was riddled with corruption. His soldiers were not receiving enough food, as their officers were selling food on the black market. Often the rice sacks would be half full of sand. The conditions of the average GMD soldier were appalling and in some units men were tied up at night to prevent their deserting. In order to have enough troops, Jiang had initiated a conscription policy that involved enlisting 1.5 million men per year. By 1944, however, Jiang only had four million soldiers after six years of war. The rest had either died in action, died through sickness, had simply deserted to the enemy or gone home. The peasantry was the group most hit by the conscription policies and Jiang's attitude towards them meant that many peasants turned to the CPC. In the countryside, Jiang was beginning to lose popular support.

Jiang's leadership was becoming more dictatorial as he became more detached from reality. He issued contradictory orders and interfered in the work of others. He ignored the reports of bribery and corruption that were being circulated about his government. Inflation spiralled out of control and Jiang's government failed to take control of the financial situation. It simply printed more money, which led to further inflation and eventually hyperinflation. There was no attempt at stabilizing the currency, with the bizarre situation in China that different cities would have different exchange rates. This situation had a devastating impact on the middle class in the cities – the main base of GMD support. The result was inevitably a shortage of money, with the consequence that the government had to increase taxes, which were mostly levied on the peasants. Expressions of discontent were met with severe repression. The press was censored. The secret police were everywhere and arrest, torture and execution became the norm. China's intellectuals were becoming disenchanted and were turning away from Jiang to support the communists. Jiang was beginning to lose support in the cities as well.

After the Japanese attack on the US Pacific naval base at Pearl Harbor in December 1941, the USA was at war with Japan. In order to assist Jiang against the Japanese, the USA had supported the GMD and it is estimated that approximately $500 million of military aid was sent to China between 1942 and 1945. President Roosevelt also sent General Joseph Stilwell to China in 1943 to make an assessment of the military situation there. Jiang and Stilwell did not get on well together, partly because of the nature of Stilwell's personality but also because of his proposal in 1943 that Jiang lift the blockade he had placed around the communist forces in the north. Stilwell also wanted to take over direct command of the GMD forces himself. The two men simply were unable to come to any form of agreement, with the result that the US Secretary of War, Patrick Hurley, was forced to recall Stilwell to the USA. He was replaced by General Albert Wedemeyer, who managed to re-establish good relations with Jiang. At about the same time (the middle of 1944), a team of military advisers, the Dixie Mission, were sent to Yan'an to evaluate the military capabilities of the Second United Front between Mao and Jiang. In November, Hurley himself was sent as Roosevelt's special envoy to meet Mao. This meeting resulted in a US proposal to arm the communists, which when relayed to Jiang was immediately rejected. It was becoming clear to the USA that the disagreements between Mao and Jiang were so fundamental that it was only a matter of time before the Second United Front would collapse.

By the end of 1944, Japanese offensives became less regular as the Japanese forces were being redeployed to fight the Americans in the Pacific. The Sino-Japanese War came to an end rather abruptly after the dropping of the two atomic bombs on Hiroshima and Nagasaki in August 1945. China rejoiced at the ending of the war after nine years of conflict and was looking forward to a period of consolidation and peace. As victor in the war, Jiang himself regained some of the prestige that he had lost earlier. A key question was – would the GMD be able to reconstruct China socially and economically? Another key consideration was – did the GMD have the strength to control the communists in the north? The answers were soon to come.

SOURCE H

Other Americans, including General Stilwell himself, were equally horrified at the campaigns of enforced conscription carried out by the Guomindang armies, and at the sight of ragged, barefooted men being led to the front roped together, already weakened almost to death by beriberi or malnutrition. Random executions of recruiting officers, occasionally ordered by Jiang Jieshi, did nothing to end the abuses. It was estimated that of 1.67 million Chinese men drafted for active service in 1943, 44 percent deserted or died on the way to join their units. Those draftees who died before seeing combat between 1937 and 1945 numbered 1.4 million, approximately 1 in 10 of all men drafted.

From Jonathan Spence, *The Search for Modern China*, 1990

SOURCE I

… The Peanut has gone off his rocker and Roosevelt has apparently let me down completely. If old softy gives in on this, as he apparently has, the Peanut will be out of control… My conscience is clear. I have carried out my orders. I have no regrets. Except to see the USA sold down the river…

From Stilwell's letter to his wife just before his recall, 1944

STUDENT STUDY SECTION

QUESTIONS
a) **Source H – what explanations can you give for the GMD's treatment of its soldiers?**
b) **What does Source I tell you about the relationship between Stilwell and Jiang? Why do you think Stilwell calls Jiang 'The Peanut'?**

For Mao and the communists, the Sino-Japanese War had several key consequences. Mao had consolidated his leadership of the CPC by 1945 through instituting a series of 'Rectification Campaigns' that eliminated many of the divisions within the party. The *zhengfeng* or Rectification Movement of 1942 aimed at purging the party of undesirable elements and revising Maoist thought. Mao had enhanced his support among the peasants following the principle of the '**mass line**' and organizing study sessions among the communists. Militarily the guerilla warfare strategies learnt in the Jiangxi period and still employed by the Red Army had been successful. The CPC, in contrast to the GMD, were now seen by many as the true nationalists, which gained it wider support. Mao's insistence on equality within the communist ranks also gave the impression of the CPC being the people's force and there was also the perception within China, carefully cultivated by Mao, that he was a superior leader to Jiang. The end result was that the GMD had lost support in China whereas the position of the CPC had been greatly strengthened, and this shift was to prove crucial in the outcome of the 1946–49 War.

Mass line
In communist thought the mass line is the means of leadership of the people, or the 'masses'. The masses are the primary force in changing a society, having identified their goals by struggles with other groups. For Mao, this force for change was to come from the peasants.

The civil war of 1946–49 and Mao's rise to power

STUDENT STUDY SECTION

QUESTION
Here are two introductions to the question: 'Why did the Guomindang lose the Chinese Civil War?' Which is better and why?

Student Answer A – *Susan*

The Chinese Civil War was a conflict between the nationalist Guomindang (GMD) under Jiang Jieshi and the Communist Party of China (CPC) ruled by Mao Zedong. The war broke out in 1927 after the Shanghai Massacre. The civil war was interrupted by two United Fronts, where nationalists and communists fought together to defeat the warlords as well as the invading Japanese. With the support of the Americans, and ultimately the dropping of the atomic bombs, China's external issues were resolved and old conflicts between nationalists and communists resurfaced. This lead to the outbreak of a full-scale war in 1946. The communists referred to the war as their revolution or the War of Liberation. The civil war ended in 1949 with a communist victory: Mao founded the People's Republic of China and the nationalist leaders fled to Taiwan.

Student Answer B – *Paul*

The Chinese Civil War 1946 to 1949 was the continuation of the conflict between the Nationalists and Communists that had started after the Qing Dynasty was overthrown in 1911 and the Guomindang (GMD), the Nationalist party, took control of China under Jiang Jieshi. That the GMD lost the Civil War even though the Chinese Communist Party (CCP) under Mao Zedong remained relatively small until long after the proclamation of the People's Republic of China in 1949, is the result of the devastated economic situation of China, and the Guomindang's general policies, especially concerning foreign affairs.

Examiner's comments

Susan's introduction starts out quite well by dating the Chinese Civil War in the second sentence and identifying the main protagonists. But by the middle of the paragraph Susan has lost direction. She is including too much detail in the introduction and it begins to lose its focus. It is almost as if she is trying to answer the question in the introduction.

Paul again starts off well, with a strong first sentence. He also focuses nicely on the question in the first part of his second sentence. However, the end of Paul's second sentence is weak. He attempts to give explanations for the reasons behind the GMD loss, but has only selected two factors. It would have been better had he left the last sentence to be a little more general. The danger here is that Paul's essay only focuses on the factors he has mentioned in the introduction, which would mean that a large number of alternative factors, such as the CPC's success in gaining popular support, could be ignored.

● **Examiner's hint**
A popular question that could be asked would be 'Why did the CPC win the Chinese Civil War?' Bear in mind that another way of looking at this question would be 'Why did the Guomindang lose the Chinese Civil War?' By taking an alternative look at the question it might well mean that you change the focus of your essay. The material for either of these questions is essentially the same, but a re-examination of the question might help you to see other aspects of the reasons behind Mao's victory. In essence, there are only so many questions that can be asked about the rise to power of any leader of a single-party state.

● **Examiner's hint**
If you cannot tell what the question is about after having read the introduction, then the introduction is probably not very strong.

As the developing Cold War in Europe began to define the relationship between the Soviet Union and the USA, both powers also had conflicting aims in China. The Soviet Union wanted to take advantage of the power vacuum after World War II to strip Manchuria of its industrial materials. The USA was concerned that Soviet influence in China would allow it to dominate Asia. The USA was also keen to broker an agreement between the CPC and the GMD to ensure a stable non-communist controlled China. Truman sent Secretary of State George Marshall to mediate, and he managed to arrange a meeting between Mao and Jiang in early 1946. A truce was arranged that lasted until July, when the civil war finally broke out in earnest. The GMD armies outnumbered those of the CPC by about 4:1. However, the communists had control of the north and used the guerrilla warfare that had been successfully applied earlier in the 1930s against the GMD, and more recently against the Japanese, constantly harrying the GMD armies. Coordination between the CPC military leaders was united in agreed goals, whereas the leadership of the GMD was disjointed. The USA provided limited assistance to the GMD, but gradually realized that by 1948 the GMD cause was lost and refused to provide further aid.

The GMD military strategy seemed to have little direction and its army suffered defeat after defeat. Ironically, one of the reasons behind the communist victory was that the CPC captured large amounts of weapons either discarded by deserting GMD soldiers or brought with them by GMD defectors to the CPC side. Realizing that defeat was inevitable, Jiang resigned the presidency in January 1949 and started to prepare for the transfer of his government to Taiwan. Fighting continued for a while, but by October Mao was ready to take the next move. He announced the establishment of the PRC on 1 October 1949.

For the first time in 50 years, China was free from major internal conflict and seemingly divorced from external involvement in its domestic affairs. Yet the country was economically weak as inflation had spiralled out of control. Measures had been taken in May 1949 to try to combat inflation. A new currency was introduced and the government attempted to reduce the amount of paper money in circulation by introducing a new price system based on the prices of five goods: oil, rice, coal, flour and cotton cloth. A new system of taxation was also introduced at the same time. Inflation was brought under control. It dropped from over 1,000 per cent in 1949 to about 15 per cent in 1951. It was clear that Mao was now in the position to undertake two of his long-promised reforms – the agricultural and social transformation of the PRC with the aim of creating a unified and cohesive socialist state.

STUDENT STUDY SECTION

Copy out the following table. Fill it in, making a list of as many reasons you can think of to explain why Jiang lost the civil war. Then rank them in order of importance.

GMD Weaknesses	CPC Strengths

Section II:
Mao Zedong in power: Domestic policies and their impact, 1949–76

The initial years of the People's Republic of China (PRC)

Most students believe that Mao immediately implemented a radical programme of repression and reform as soon as he came to power. This is not true, and he acted quite cautiously for the first few years of the PRC. In fact, a number of non-communist political parties were initially allowed to exist. It is also popularly believed that all the peasant classes welcomed Mao's accession to power, but this too is not true. Referring back to his 1926 work *How to Analyze Class Status in the Countryside* when undertaking land reform under the 1950 Agrarian Reform Law, Mao recognized several different levels of peasant status: 'rich' peasant, 'middle' peasant and 'poor' peasant. It was clear that, for Mao, the 'poor' peasants were the group that was going to benefit most from his plans. The 'rich' and 'middle peasants' were uncertain what was going to become of them.

● **Examiner's hint**
When you consider how single-party leaders rise to power there are several factors to bear in mind. What conditions exist that allow leaders to centralize power? (In other words, are there opportunities that can be taken to enable leaders to seize power?) What kind of methods do they use to achieve power? Make a list of the conditions and methods that would apply to Mao.

SOURCE A

CHAPTER I. GENERAL PROVISIONS

ARTICLE 1. The Chinese People's Political Consultative Conference … is the organization of the democratic united front of the entire Chinese people. Its aim is to unite all democratic classes and all nationalities throughout China by establishing the unity of all democratic parties and groups and people's organizations. This will enable them to put forward their combined efforts in carrying out New Democracy, opposing imperialism, feudalism and bureaucratic capitalism, overthrowing the reactionary rule of the Guomindang, eliminating open and secret remnant counter-revolutionary forces. It will also enable them to heal the wounds of war, rehabilitate and develop the people's economic, cultural and educational work, consolidate national defence, and unite with all the nations and countries which treat us on a footing of equality. All this is for the purpose of establishing and consolidating an independent, democratic, peaceful, unified, prosperous and strong People's Republic of China of the People's Democratic Dictatorship, led by the working class and based on the alliance of workers and peasants.

From 'The Organic Law of the Chinese People's Political Consultative Conference', Beijing, 29 September 1949

● **Examiner's hint**
It is important for you to understand that, even at this early stage of the PRC, Mao was already becoming isolated from the advice of others.

STUDENT STUDY SECTION

QUESTIONS

Source A is a key document that shows Mao's thinking in terms of the form of government China was going to follow. Read through it carefully and identify: a) the groups that have to be eliminated; b) the groups that were to lead the changes.

What do these tell you about Mao's thinking? Go back to p.145 and review the four major influences on Mao's life. Do these have any influence on the programme outlined in this source?

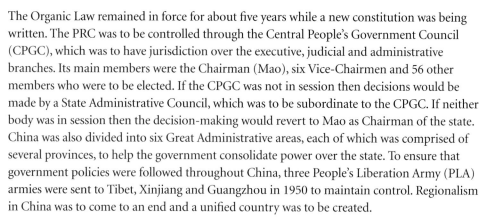

The Organic Law remained in force for about five years while a new constitution was being written. The PRC was to be controlled through the Central People's Government Council (CPGC), which was to have jurisdiction over the executive, judicial and administrative branches. Its main members were the Chairman (Mao), six Vice-Chairmen and 56 other members who were to be elected. If the CPGC was not in session then decisions would be made by a State Administrative Council, which was to be subordinate to the CPGC. If neither body was in session then the decision-making would revert to Mao as Chairman of the state. China was also divided into six Great Administrative areas, each of which was comprised of several provinces, to help the government consolidate power over the state. To ensure that government policies were followed throughout China, three People's Liberation Army (PLA) armies were sent to Tibet, Xinjiang and Guangzhou in 1950 to maintain control. Regionalism in China was to come to an end and a unified country was to be created.

At the same time the CPC, which had been reorganized in 1945, retained essentially the same structure. By 1949 about 1 per cent of the population were members (4.5 million people). Many students believe that everyone in China is a member of the CPC, but this is simply not true. Membership is very selective and applicants for membership have to have supporting statements from two other members of the party. There were three sections to it – the Politburo, the Secretariat and the Central Committee. Mao was the chair of all three bodies. The Secretariat was made up of Mao, **Liu Shaoqi** and Zhou Enlai, who were also members of the Politburo. It is clear where the power lay. Following the example of Lenin, Mao had introduced the policy of 'democratic centralism'. This is similar to the idea of the 'dictatorship of the proletariat' in Lenin's Bolshevik Russia, whereby an elite group led by a strong central figure would be entrusted with the control of the new state.

Marriage reform

One of Mao's first policies, in keeping with the promises made during the civil war, was the Marriage Reform Law of 1950. Socially, this had a very great effect on the people of China, in particular the women. For the first time, both genders were equal in a union, and both had to agree to be married. The elimination of arranged marriages had two benefits. First, Mao gained the support of many women, a group his opposition had entirely ignored during the civil war. Second, life was improved for large numbers of people within China. Younger people afraid of arranged marriages and those unhappy in their current marriage were able to choose their own spouse, or even file for divorce. In addition, other basic human rights were established: women could not be sold into prostitution, and unwanted female babies could not simply be disposed of. The government abolished practices such as **foot binding**. Later laws passed at the same time allowed women to own property and land, although this was a short-lived gain, as it would soon be replaced by the collectivization policies of the First Five Year Plan in 1953.

◀ Liu Shaoqi

Although the marriage policies seemed to be a major step forward in terms of social engineering and did rid China of many inequities of the old system, they were not without opposition. China was a patriarchal society and the traditional roles of women were entrenched in the minds of many people. Some areas of China, particularly in the west, were Muslim, and the freedom gained by women under the Marriage Reform Law went against the doctrinal policies of the Koran.

SOURCE B

▲
Chinese propaganda poster.

SOURCE C

▲
Chinese propaganda poster.

STUDENT STUDY SECTION

QUESTION

Without knowing what the captions mean, what do you think the messages are in the two sources?

The two captions are:

Source B – 'Freedom of marriage, happiness and good luck, 1953'

Source C – 'A free and independent marriage is good; there is great happiness in unified production, 1953'

How accurate were you in your analysis?

Agrarian reform

Mao now turned to agriculture in June 1950, when he passed the Agrarian Reform Law. This aimed at a redistribution of all the land in China and it was very clear from whom this land was to come.

SOURCE D

Article 1

The land ownership system of feudal exploitation by the landlord class shall be abolished and the system of peasant land ownership shall be introduced in order to set free the rural productive forces, develop agricultural production and thus pave the way for New China's industrialization.

Article 2

The land, draught animals, farm implements and surplus grain of the landlords, and their surplus houses in the countryside shall be confiscated, but their other properties shall not be confiscated.

From the Agrarian Reform Law 1950, quoted in Albert P. Blaustein (ed.), *Fundamental Legal Documents of Communist China,* **1962**

STUDENT STUDY SECTION

QUESTION

Compare this with the extract from the Jinggangshan Land Law of 1928 on p.149. How consistent are the two sources?

Peasant associations, usually led by the poorest peasants, turned against their former landlords and in a series of 'struggle meetings' or 'speak bitterness' campaigns, thousands of landlords were forced to admit their crimes against the peasantry. In many cases these meetings ran out of control as old scores were settled and in mass hysteria landlords were beaten to death or committed suicide. A reign of terror existed in the rural countryside. The exact number of deaths is not known, but some historians estimate that more than five million landlords perished. For Mao these campaigns had two aims. On the one hand, they fulfilled his promise of giving land to the poor peasants. On the other hand, the Agrarian Reform Law was a form of Rectification Campaign against the traditional powerbase of China and succeeded in eliminating one section of the Chinese population that was likely to oppose Mao's accession to power.

SOURCE E

At a struggle meeting, targeted individuals are humiliated with dunces' caps.

By the end of 1952, the reforms were completed and 700 million *mou* (1 *mou* = 666m²) had been distributed among 300 million peasants. The amount of land received by the peasants varied from 1 mou in the East and South to 7 mou in Manchuria. It was now time to turn to the second phase of the agricultural revolution.

War and the 'Antis' movements

In the meantime, China found itself involved with a war in Korea that had broken out in June 1950 when **Kim Il Sung**, the North Korean leader, attacked South Korea (see p.180). How much Mao knew about this invasion is uncertain. Most observers believed that he was taken by surprise and that Stalin had not been entirely open with Mao when they met in Moscow in February 1950 and signed the Sino-Soviet Treaty of Friendship Alliance. A war, so soon after the founding of the PRC, was certainly something that Mao was keen to avoid. Funds that were essential to China's modernization programmes had to be diverted into military expenditure.

Kim Il Sung (1912–94)
Kim was the communist leader of North Korea from its foundation in 1948 until his death in 1994.

● **Examiner's hint**
In Topic 3 of Paper 2, it is not required that you study the foreign policy of single-party leaders. This means that there will not be any specific question asked about the foreign policy of Mao. It is quite useful, however, to know something about this area of policy as it is bound to influence events at home. In Mao's case, for instance, his involvement in events such as the Treaty of Alliance with Stalin in 1950 and the consequence for China of Kim Il Sung's decision to attack South Korea, in June 1950, would have a direct effect on Mao's domestic policies.

SOURCE F

Distribution of government budget expenditures, 1950–57

Expenditure category	1950	1952	1957
Economic construction (per cent)	25.5	45.4	51.4
Social, cultural and educational outlays (per cent)	11.1	13.6	16.0
National defence (per cent)	41.5	26.0	19.0
Government administration (per cent)	19.3	10.3	7.8
Other	2.6	4.7	5.8
Total in per cent	100.0	100.0	100.0
Total in millions of yuan	6,810	16,790	29,020

Source: Jonathan Spence, *The Search for Modern China*, 1990

On the other hand, the Korean War gave Mao several advantages. First, it brought the new state together as people united against foreign encroachment. Second, after the PRC had successfully fought UN forces, which included the might of the US Army, to a standstill, the reputation of China globally and Mao personally increased. Third, it gave Mao an excuse to take action against elements of Chinese society that might have been opposed to Mao's accession to power. In other words, the Korean War allowed Mao to carry out a series of Rectification Campaigns in the rest of China. The targets of these campaigns were lumped together under the title of 'reactionaries' or 'counter-revolutionaries', terms that were vague enough to include a wide range of groups and potential opponents.

The first of these took place in late 1951 against the 'evils' of corruption, waste and bureaucracy (inefficiency). It was known as the *sanfen* or the 'Three Antis' movement and was directed against party members, government officials and business owners. This was followed in 1952 by the *wufan* or 'Five Antis' movement, which targeted cheating on government contracts, stealing state economic information, tax evasion, theft of state property and bribery. Employees in private businesses were encouraged to denounce their bosses, who were then required to undertake a thought reform programme to eliminate 'wrong thinking'. These movements followed the same methods as those taken against the landlords in the rural areas through struggle meetings and self-confessions, and were focused on the bourgeoisie and capitalists. Businesses were categorized according to the seriousness of their crimes and punishments were meted out accordingly. The result was that state revenue increased and inflation was reduced. More importantly, the government had brought yet another section of Chinese society directly under its control.

SOURCE G

Results of the Five Antis movement in Shanghai, 1952

	Small firms		Medium firms	
Law-abiding	59,471	(76.6%)	7,782	(42.5%)
Basically law-abiding	17,407	(22.4%)	9,005	(49.1%)
Semi law-abiding	736	(0.9%)	1,529	(8.3%)
Serious lawbreakers	2		9	
Total	77,616		18,325	

Source: Jonathan Spence, *The Search for Modern China*, 1990

STUDENT STUDY SECTION

QUESTION

What is the message conveyed in the source? Is the government targeting 'small firms' or 'medium firms'? Explain your answer

While the Three and Five Antis movements were continuing, another section of Chinese society was being targeted – the intellectuals. These could be defined as the 'educated elements' of Chinese society and included journalists, teachers, lawyers, writers, artists etc. Almost by definition, these groups of people within China were not part of the peasantry, the vanguard of the revolution, and therefore must have been exposed to ideas that went against Mao's socialist revolution. Much of their knowledge was not related to manual labour; it came from books and therefore, to Mao, they lacked the credentials of true revolutionaries. There is a slight contradiction here, as without these members of society it is almost impossible to undertake meaningful progress towards change, so by eliminating this section of society the government was actually taking a step away from reform. During this campaign many 'intellectuals' were 'struggled' against so that they would see the error of their ways. The Korean War, therefore, assisted Mao in eliminating opposition through the three campaigns described above and strengthened the control that the CPC had on the people of China. This was further enhanced by the party's registration system, which took a triangular structure. It worked through the introduction of residence permits (*hukou*), work permits (*danwei*) and secret personnel files (*dangan*). Of these, the latter were the most important as they contained all of the details about an individual's life, which determined whether or not a *hukou* or a *danwei* would be issued. Thus, the government had a centralized system of control based on an individual's duty to register familial details. By the beginning of 1953, Mao was ready to take the next step. The Korean War was at a stalemate, the agricultural revolution had taken place, 'counter-revolutionaries' had been brought under control and opposition had been largely crushed. The movement had come to turn to industrialization and to move the transition to socialism forward.

The First Five Year Plan

It was now time to launch a new phase of the land revolution. Despite the changes made under the Agrarian Reform Law, the structure of Chinese agriculture, divided into large numbers of peasant-owned plots, was not appropriate for the modern economic development of the nation. Mao had studied Stalin's Five Year Plans in the Soviet Union and his move towards collectivization and industrialization. He decided to implement the same sort of programmes in China. Why he did so is unclear, as the nature of China in 1953 was very different to the Soviet Union in 1928. One problem was that the vast majority of the population in China was based in the countryside. Some observers have commented that China's use of the Soviet model was perhaps one way of emphasizing the non-Western nature of the new Chinese state. Mao's main intention was to industrialize as rapidly as possible, and for this to work Soviet technical and financial aid was necessary. The PRC had to take out a series of high-interest loans to finance their industrial programme. The aims were to double the amount of industrial output and complete a 'socialist transformation' of China as quickly as possible. The results were impressive, as most of the targets had been achieved by December 1956, but the successes were achieved at some cost to the people. All private businesses and commercial enterprises were nationalized under state control. A total of 58.2 per cent of government investment was to go to industrial development, but only 7.6 per cent would go to agriculture. This imbalance was to have a crucial effect on the relative productivity of both sectors (see Sources H, I, J and K below).

The land reform programme would take place in three phases. The first phase was the introduction of 'mutual aid teams' of between three and 30 persons, whereby small groups of peasants would work together on a small area of land. The idea was to introduce an '**economies of scale**' model whereby all of the tools, labour and materials would be jointly owned and worked. Peasants without tools could exchange labour for the loan of tools and animals, particularly during the spring planting season and autumn harvest time. The transition to collectivization was not without its difficulties. Better-off peasants were not always willing to share with poorer peasants, and much to the horror of Mao and the CPC class divisions began to appear among the peasants. The harvests of 1953 and 1954 were not good and productivity was low. By the end of 1954, the CPC decided to move to the next level.

The second stage was the merging of these 'mutual-aid' teams into larger cooperatives, working on the same principles whereby theoretically individual ownership was still retained but land would be pooled as well. In a 1955 speech, Mao reiterated the importance of the peasantry. As in 1927, in his Hunan Report, in which he saw the peasants as leading China forward towards socialism, he called upon the rural population of China to be

Economies of scale
A microeconomic term which implies that concerns become more efficient as they grow by reducing costs.

Dekulakization
The Stalinist campaign against the better-off peasants and their families in the Soviet Union between 1929 and 1932.

the means by which his socialist revolution could move ahead. But there was opposition to these policies in some quarters. The Central Committee was fully aware of the effects that Stalin's **dekulakization** policies had had upon the Soviet Union in his forced collectivization of agriculture in the 1930s. Some members were afraid that the same slaughter of animals and famine that led to the loss of so many lives in the Soviet Union might happen in China. But Mao was determined to go ahead with the next phase. He believed that, while the peasants were leading the way forward, the CPC was becoming too reactionary and that many members 'were tottering along like a woman with bound feet, always complaining that others were going too fast' (Meisner, *Mao's China and After*, 1999). Mao forged ahead with the move to small-scale cooperatives. Any resistance to the new programme was overcome by the state 'assisting' the better-off peasants to join the scheme through the withholding of capital loans, which virtually forced them into the cooperatives. Families were paid for the amount of resources they had contributed to the cooperative – almost a semi-capitalist system as the more a family owned the more it received from the collective's profits.

The final phase started in 1956, with the intention of creating Soviet-style collective farms in which the land was owned by the state and private ownership was almost completely eliminated. Although there was some minimal opposition to the change as some peasants emigrated to the cities, it went ahead with little resistance. A major change from the system of small-scale cooperatives to the larger-scale cooperatives was that the amount of money that a peasant received was to be determined by the amount of labour that s/he contributed to the collective. By the end of 1956 this shift was well under way, and the smaller cooperatives began to shrink in number as the larger-scale cooperatives gained (see Source H). The 'mutual-aid teams' became less and less important in rural life, finally dying out in 1957. By the end of 1957 about 700,000 cooperative farms had been created each of which contained up to 300 families (600–700 people) (Hsu, *The Rise of Modern China*, 2000).

SOURCE H

Share of peasant household in different types of ownership units, 1950–57

Year	Mutual aid teams (%)	Agricultural producer cooperatives (%)	
		Lower stage	Higher stage
1950	10.7	negl.	negl.
1951	19.2	negl.	negl.
1952	39.9	0.1	negl.
1953	39.3	0.2	negl.
1954	58.3	1.9	negl.
1955			
End of autumn	50.7	14.2	0.03
Year end	32.7	63.3	4.00
1956			
End of January	19.7	49.6	30.70
End of July	7.6	29.0	63.40
Year end	3.7	8.5	87.80
1957	None	negl.	93.50

Source: Jonathan Spence, *The Search for Modern China*, 1990

QUESTIONS

Source analysis

Compare and contrast the Sources I, J, K and L below. What evidence can you find to indicate whether the First Five Year Plan was a success or a failure? To help you, draw a table like the one below and fill it in with as much detail as possible. Remember that you need to understand what the aims of the Five Year Plan were before you can make any judgements.

First Five Year Plan 1953–57

Successes	Failures

● **Examiner's hint**
Whenever you are analyzing the economic successes or failures of any single-party state try to use statistics to support your statements. Do not be afraid to quote figures to make your point. Examination essays are often very weak in this area and often contain unsupported assertions.

SOURCE I

The First Five Year Plan, 1953–57

Indicator (unit)	1952 Data	1957 Plan	1957 Actual	1957 actual as percentage of plan
Gross output value (in million 1952 yuan)				
Industry (excluding handicrafts)	27,010	53,560	65,020	121.4
Producer sector	10,730	24,303	34,330	141.0
Machinery	1,404	3,470	6,177	178.0
Chemicals	864	2,271	4,291	188.9
Producer sector less machinery and chemicals	8,462	18,562	23,862	128.5
Physical output				
Coal (mmt)	68.50	113.00	130.00	115.0
Crude oil (tmt)	436	2,012	1,458	72.5
Steel ingot (mmt)	1.35	4.12	5.35	129.8
Cement (mmt)	2.86	6.00	6.86	114.3
Electric power (billion kWh)	7.26	15.90	19.34	121.6
Internal combustion engines (thousand hp)	27.6	260.2	609.0	234.2
Hydroelectric turbines (kW)	6,664	79,500	74,900	94.2
Generators (thousand kW)	29.7	227.0	312.2	137.5
Electric motors (thousand kW)	639	1,048	1,455	138.8
Transformers (thousand kva)	1,167	2,610	3,500	134.1
Machine tools (units)	13,734	12,720	28,000	220.1
Locomotives (units)	20	200	167	83.5
Railway freight cars (units)	5,792	8,500	7,300	85.9

ToK Time
'History – among many other and more important things – is the record of the crimes and follies of mankind' (Eric Hobsbawm, *Age of Extremes*, 1994). To what extent do you think history is this?

Indicator (unit)	1952 Data	1957 Plan	1957 Actual	1957 actual as percentage of plan
Merchant ships (thousand dwt tons)	21.5	179.1	54.0	30.2
Trucks (units)	0	4,000	7,500	187.5
Bicycles (thousand units)	80	555	1,174	211.5
Caustic soda (tmt)	79	154	198	128.6
Soda ash (tmt)	192	476	506	106.3
Ammonium sulphate (tmt)	181	504	631	125.2
Ammonium nitrate (tmt)	7	44	120	272.7
Automobile tires (thousand sets)	417	760	873	114.9
Sulphuric acid (tmt)	149	402	632	157.2
'666' insecticide (tons)	600	70,000	61,000	87.1

Note: mmt = million metric tons; tmt = thousand metric tons; kva = kilovolts-amperes; dwt = deadweight tonnage; kWh = kilowatt hour; kW = kilowatt

Source: Jonathan Spence, *The Search for Modern China*, 1990

SOURCE J

Despite the speed of compliance with the call for higher-level cooperatives, agricultural production figures for 1957 were disappointing. Grain production increased only 1 percent over the year, in the face of a 2 percent population rise. Cotton-cloth rations had to be cut because of shortages. Indeed although the First Five-Year Plan had met its quotas well enough, it had also revealed disturbing imbalances in the Chinese economic system. While industrial output rose at about 18.7 percent per year during the plan period, agricultural production rose only about 3.8 percent. Per capita grain consumption grew even less, at just under 3 percent per year. With rural markets booming, local purchasers bought up most of the grains, edible oils, and cotton that was for sale, decreasing the amount available for state procurement or for urban consumers.

From Jonathan Spence, *The Search for Modern China*, 1990

SOURCE K

Per capita annual consumption, Shanghai, 1929–30 and 1956 (in catties, except as noted)

Commodity	1929–30	1956	% increase
Rice	240.17	270.74	12.5
Wheat flour	15.17	15.68	3.4
Pork	9.78	16.21	65.7
Beef, mutton	1.89	2.29	21.2
Chicken, duck	0.76	2.70	255.3
Fish, shellfish	10.17	27.39	169.3
Eggs	1.85	7.02	379.5
Vegetables	159.57	193.50	21.2
Vegetable oil	612.58	10.20	-18.9
Animal oil	0.47	0.71	73.2
Sugar	2.40	4.17	73.8
Cigarettes (20)	24.21	32.36	33.7
Alcoholic beverages	13.43	6.46	-51.9

Commodity	1929–30	1956	% increase
Tea	0.55	0.15	-72.3
Cotton fabrics (m²)	6.43	14.00	117.7
Kerosene	19.17	0.40	-91.9
Coal and charcoal	43.14	228.17	428.9
Combustible grasses	242.77	78.24	-67.8
Leather shoes (pair)	0.17	0.27	58.8
Rubber shoes (pair)	0.10	0.51	410.0
Stockings (pair)	1.26	2.08	65.0
Living space (m²)	3.22	4.78	48.5
Units: 1 catty = 0.5kg			

Source: Jonathan Spence, *The Search for Modern China*, 1990

SOURCE L

'*National income grew at an average annual rate of 8.9 percent (measured in constant prices), with agriculture and industrial output expanding annually by about 3.8 and 18.7 percent respectively.*' *On top of the large increase recorded from 1949 to 1953, this was a stunning rise. Since population growth was 2.4 percent and output grew at 6.5 percent per person, the growth rate, if sustained, would double national income every eleven years.*

From Lee Feigon, *Mao: A Reinterpretation*, 2002

While the First Five Year Plan was under way, Mao finally decided to introduce the new Chinese constitution in 1954, which formally centralized state control and replaced the 1949 Organic Law. The state was to be overseen by a National People's Congress (NPC) that would be elected every four years and was at the top of a pyramidal system through which the lowest level of local and regional congresses elected representatives to the next level until they reached the NPC. Mao was to be the Chairman of the NPC and he would be supported by a single Vice-Chairman (in 1954 this was Zhu De), replacing the six chairmen that had previously existed under the Organic Law. In 1956, the CPC was similarly reorganized, with a National Party Congress whose members were elected for five years. A Central Committee controlled the executive power chaired by Mao and with five chairmen (originally four, but a fifth was added in 1958). A Politburo also existed which had a Standing Committee of seven men. (Until the Cultural Revolution these were Mao, Zhou Enlai, Deng Xiaoping, Zhu De, Liu Shaoqi, Lin Biao and Chen Yun.) 'Democratic Centralism' was still the basis of government, and Mao was clearly the undisputed leader of China as Chairman of the NPC, the Central Committee and the Politburo.

SOURCE M

September 20 1954

ARTICLE 40 The Chairman of the People's Republic of China, in pursuance of decisions of the National People's Congress or the Standing Committee of the National People's Congress, promulgates laws and decrees; appoints or removes the Premier, Vice Premiers, Ministers, Heads of Commissions and the Secretary-General of the State Council; appoints or removes the Vice-Chairmen and other members of the Council of National Defence; confers state orders, medals and titles of honour; proclaims general amnesties and grants pardons; proclaims martial law; proclaims a state of war; and orders mobilization.

From the constitution of the People's Republic of China, quoted in Albert P. Blaustein (ed.), *Fundamental Legal Documents of Communist China*, 1962

In the early and mid 1950s, events outside China began to have an effect on Mao's thinking within China. Following the East German uprising in 1953, China, represented by Zhou Enlai, attended a conference in Bandung, Indonesia, in 1955. Despite Mao having proclaimed that there would be no '**third way**' in 1950, at the end of the Bandung Conference it was evident that China was seen by many Third World countries as the nation that could represent a '**non-aligned**' movement. In 1956 two events were to prove crucial in determining the future direction of China. In February 1956, at the 20th Party Plenum, Khrushchev launched his 'destalinization' speech, attacking Stalin for his 'cult of personality' and his 'crimes against the party'. Not only did it seem as if the Soviet Union was changing direction ideologically, which seemed to be confirmed by its announcement of a policy of 'peaceful coexistence' with the West, but it also seemed to imply a direct criticism of Mao's own style of leadership within the CPC. The second event was the sudden anti-Soviet uprisings in Poland and Hungary, which Mao took as indicating the loss of control that Moscow now had on its satellite states. It seemed clear that open criticism against Moscow was a sign of reactionary movements within the communist bloc.

In April 1956, *The People's Daily* published an editorial commenting on Khrushchev's speech. While admitting that Stalin had made mistakes, the article went on to reinforce the importance of following the 'mass line' and went on to say: 'Marxist-Leninists hold that leaders play a big role in history. The people and their parties need forerunners who are able to represent the interests and will of the people, stand in the forefront of their historic struggles and serve as their leaders. It is utterly wrong to deny the role of the individual, the role of forerunners and leaders' (quoted in *The Historical Experience of the Dictatorship of the Proletariat*, 1956). The message was clear: Mao would never make the same sort of mistakes that had been made by Stalin and Mao's style of leadership was entirely the means by which the transformation of China into a truly socialist state would occur. But events in China were going to cast doubt upon Mao's effectiveness as a leader.

The Hundred Flowers Campaign and the Anti-Rightist Movement 1956–57

The first mention of the phrase 'to let a hundred flowers bloom and a hundred schools of thought contend' was made at a speech to the Politburo in April 1956. Its context was to encourage debate in fields of art, literature and science. The idea behind it was to promote progress in these fields by allowing criticism and some freedom of expression, through which the clashing of new ideas would bring improvements that would move China forward. It is a classic example of the Marxist **dialectic** in action. By February 1957, after the events in Europe in 1956, this encouragement of criticism had spread to the CPC itself. The party would find out from the people how it could improve. In the Rectification Campaigns that had already taken place, 'self-criticism' was seen as the way forward. By recognizing and admitting mistakes, an individual could improve him/herself. If this worked for an individual then why not apply the same principles to the CPC and the government? In one of his most famous speeches, which influenced the ideological direction China would take until his death in 1976, Mao showed the direction that China should follow:

Third way
A term used to describe the creation of a political ideology somewhere between the two superpowers in the Cold War.

Non-aligned movement
An international organization of states considering themselves not formally aligned with or against any major power bloc.

Dialectic
Where one idea is met by an opposing idea and a synthesis is produced which lies somewhere between the two opposing ideas.

SOURCE N

… Towards the people … it uses the method of democracy and not of compulsion, that is, it must necessarily let them take part in political activity and does not compel them to do this or that but uses the method of democracy to educate and persuade. Such education is self-education for the people, and its basic method is criticism and self-criticism… Literally the two slogans – let a hundred flowers blossom and let a hundred schools of thought contend – have no class character; the proletariat can turn them to account, and so can the bourgeoisie or others. Different classes, strata and social groups each have their own views on what are fragrant flowers and what are poisonous weeds. Then, from the point of view of the masses, what should be the criteria today for distinguishing fragrant flowers from poisonous weeds? In their political activities, how should our people judge whether a person's words and deeds are right or wrong? On the basis of the principles of our Constitution, the will of the overwhelming majority of our people and the common political positions which have been proclaimed on various occasions by our political parties…

From Mao's speech 'On the correct handling of contradictions amongst the people', 27 February 1957

STUDENT STUDY SECTION

QUESTION

This is one of Mao's most important speeches. Write out, in your own words what Mao is saying in the source.

Despite initial doubt about Mao's intentions behind the Hundred Flowers Campaign, particularly amongst the intellectuals, thousands of articles appeared criticizing all manner of CPC actions. All over China criticism was levelled at individual members of the CPC, at CPC authoritarian attitudes, at the economic situation and the poor standard of living in China, at corruption, at the closing off of China from foreign contacts and at the extensive privileges party members were given, among many other things. The CPC was horrified that Mao would allow people outside the party to criticize members within it. Both Mao and the party were shocked at the volume and nature of the criticisms that followed and within a month it had been decided to end the Hundred Flowers Campaign. Mao's February speech was published for the first time in June with major revisions, one of which was the means by which 'fragrant flowers' could be distinguished from 'poisonous weeds'. The result was the Anti-Rightist Campaign, led by **Deng Xiaoping**, that swung into action in July 1957. The exact numbers it affected are not known but, using the familiar methods of 'struggle meetings', hundreds of thousands of intellectuals were identified as 'rightists'. Many party members committed suicide or were executed and millions of people were sent into the countryside to 'learn' from the peasants or were sent to labour camps. The Anti-Rightist Movement taught China that criticism of the party, and particularly of Mao himself, was not permitted.

Deng Xiaoping (1904–97)
A member of the Long March who was Party Secretary-General between 1954 and 1966. He was purged in the Cultural Revolution, but eventually came to power in 1978, dying in 1997.

Deng Xiaoping
▼

● **Examiner's hint**
What does the title of Source O tell you about the position the writers will be taking towards Mao?

STUDENT STUDY SECTION

QUESTION

There is considerable disagreement about the motives for the introduction of the Hundred Flowers Campaign. Two views are expressed below. Which one do you support and why?

SOURCE O

The Party, he [Mao] said needed to be accountable and 'under supervision'. He sounded reasonable, criticizing Stalin for his 'excessive purges', and giving the impression there were going to be no more of these in China…

Few guessed that Mao was setting a trap, and that he was inviting people to speak out so that he could use what they said as an excuse to victimize them. Mao's targets were intellectuals and the educated, the people most likely to speak out.

From Jung Chang and John Halliday, *Mao: The Unknown Story*, 2005

SOURCE P

The Hundred Flowers campaign was not a simple plot by Mao to reveal the hidden rightists in his country, as some critics later charged and as he himself seemed to claim in the published version of his speech… It was, rather, a muddled and inconclusive movement that grew out of conflicting attitudes within the CPC leadership. At its center was an argument about the pace and type of development that was best for China…

From Jonathan Spence, *The Search for Modern China*, 1990

The Great Leap Forward, 1958–62

The success of the First Five Year Plan encouraged Mao to start thinking about a second plan. There was the feeling that some peasants were not putting enough effort into the land revolution and were quite content to reap the benefits of collectivization. After returning from Moscow in November 1957, Mao was convinced that the way forward was best achieved by a massive increase in steel production. He also believed that by creating new and larger types of communes, through which industrial productivity could be increased, the nation would also move ideologically closer to his own goals of a socialist state. China's massive population would be directed into labour-intensive industries that did not need much capital investment. In February 1958, in 'Sixty Points on Working Methods', Mao initiated the next stage. Reviewing the PRC's progress since 1949 he wrote:

SOURCE Q

… The party has become more united, the morale of the people further heightened, and the party–masses relationship greatly improved. We are now witnessing greater activity and creativity of the popular masses on the production front than we have ever witnessed before. A new high tide of production has risen, and is still rising, as the people of the whole country are inspired by the slogan – 'Overtake Britain in Iron and Steel and Other Major Industrial Production in Fifteen or More Years'. To meet this new situation certain methods of work of the party Centre and local committees have to be modified…

From Mao Zedong, 'Sixty Points on Working Methods', 1958

This modification was to be achieved by a Great Leap Forward, which would merge together all of the collectives into even larger-scale People's Communes. By the end of 1958, almost all of the peasants had been merged into about 27,000 communes, each with approximately 5,000 households. Private ownership of land was abolished. The communes were like small towns, as they included nurseries, banks, schools, care for the elderly, health care and communal kitchens. The commune managed all the agricultural and industrial materials and tools that had formally belonged to the collectives. The communes were run almost in a military manner. Targets were set by the state, but these were not based on any economic principles and the projected figures were unrealistic. In order to help achieve targets, 'backyard furnaces' were set up in every village to produce home-made steel and all metal tools and utensils were smelted down in order to make the new steel. The problem was that the temperature of these 'backyard furnaces' was not high enough to produce good-quality steel for industrial use, which could only come from traditional steel production methods in large foundries. More than a quarter of the steel produced in China in 1959 was unfit for industrial use. The government announced that steel output had doubled in 1957 and with this tremendous evidence of success there was no reason not to introduce even larger-scale communes.

It is clear that progress was made, but it was never going to be sustainable. Quality was sacrificed for quantity. Standards were not being maintained and there was no overview of the needs of the country. This situation resulted in shortages of some items and oversupply of others. Many of China's forests were cut down to provide the fuel for the backyard furnaces. Without an efficient infrastructure, China simply could not develop its industry at the rate needed for sustained economic growth. The state demanded higher and higher steel quotas, which were unachievable. The creation of the people's communes did not have the effect on productivity Mao expected. The impersonal nature of the communes contributed to a spiral of decline as the destruction of private ownership and the family meant that there was less enthusiasm among the people. This led to large numbers of disaffected workers, and the need for workers in the factories meant the mobilization of peasants into production-brigades, resulting in many people being taken away from their fields to work in the communes or in factories, with terrible consequences for agriculture.

SOURCE R

Chinese backyard furnace, part of Mao's failed experiment in steel production.

SOURCE S

The Communist Party is really wonderful.

In three days more than a thousand furnaces were built.

The masses' strength is really tremendous.

The American imperialists will run off, tails between legs.

The Chinese people will now surpass Britain.

The East wind will always prevail over the West wind.

Song composed by workers in Hsinhua County in 1958, quoted in Jonathan Spence, *The Search for Modern China*, 1990

STUDENT STUDY SECTION

QUESTIONS

a) **Describe what you see in Source R.**

b) **Write out in your own words the message of Source S. What is the purpose of the song?**

Deep ploughing
A technique whereby a field is ploughed into deep triangular trenches with the aim of creating more grain per square metre.

In agriculture, the same failures were occurring. Based on the claims of Trofim Lysenko, a Soviet scientist, China tried to produce 'super-crops' with extremely high production yields. They attempted to produce higher yields of grain by '**deep-ploughing**' and close planting. Sometimes these worked, but in the vast majority of cases they exhausted the soil and produced lower crop yields. In 1958 the harvest was exceptionally high, producing about 200 million tons of grain, but the reported grain figures were said to be 375 million tons. The exaggerated reports by the cadres, who were afraid of reporting shortfalls in their grain quotas, led to a never-ending cycle that was bound to lead to disaster. Local officials tried to 'reach for the moon' and reported production figures that were inflated. They were afraid that by reporting the real levels, which were significantly less, they would be branded as defeatists or counter-revolutionaries. The real disaster was that the state would then take their quota from the exaggerated figures, leaving the peasants with little or nothing to eat. Ironically much of this grain was shipped to the Soviet Union or North Korea.

SOURCE T

Statistical analysis of China 1957–61

Grain output (million metric tons)

	Total grain	Rice	Wheat
1957	185	86.8	23.6
1958	200	80.8	22.6
1959	170	69.3	22.2
1960	143.3	59.7	22.2
1961	147.5	53.6	14.25

Other crops (million metric tons)

	1958	1961
Sugar cane	12.50	4.27
Beets	3.00	0.80
Oil-bearing plants	4.77	1.80
Cotton	1.97	0.80

Livestock (millions)

Pigs	138.29	75.50
Draught animals	53.60	38.10

Industrial output (billions yuan)

1958	1959	1960	1961	1962
121	163	183	113	94

Steel, coal and cement (million metric tons)

	1958	1959	1960	1961	1962
Steel	8.8	13.87	18.66	8.70	6.67
Coal	270.0	369.00	397.00	278.00	220.00
Cement	9.3	12.27	15.65	6.21	6.0

Source: Jonathan Fenby, *The Penguin History of Modern China*, 2008

STUDENT STUDY SECTION

QUESTION

What evidence is there in Source T that the Great Leap Forward was a failure?

The CPC announced that steel output had more than doubled, from 5.35 million metric tons in 1957 to 10.7 million tons in 1958. Similarly, cereals were said to have risen from 196 million tons in 1957 to 375 million tons. On this evidence it seemed logical to increase the number of people's communes. By October 1958, it was apparent that the Great Leap Forward's targets were unrealistic. After concerns being raised at the Wuhan Conference in November 1958, even by Mao himself, the government reduced the steel and grain targets for 1959. But it was too little, too late. The outcome was catastrophic, particularly when the 'three bad years' of 1959–61 brought drought, floods and famine which worsened the plight of the peasants, who began to starve. In Hunan and Anhui provinces in 1960 the situation was desperate. Some villagers were forced into cannibalism and one family strangled and ate their eight-year-old daughter. In Gansu it is estimated that one third of the people died. Estimates vary, but it is thought that more than 50 million people died as a result of the Great Leap Forward.

A split was also beginning to take place within the CPC that would ultimately result in Mao stepping down as head of state in 1959. At the **Lushan Conference** one of Mao's longest standing supporters, Peng Dehuai, explained what he had seen when he went to visit the province of Hunan and complained about the shortcomings of the Great Leap Forward. In a private letter to Mao, he expressed his concerns about the economic disasters befalling China. Mao distributed the letter to all the members of the conference and turned on Peng. Mao took his comments as a personal attack on himself and removed Peng from his post as Minister of Defence. He turned on the CPC and threatened to 'go to the countryside to lead the peasants to overthrow the government. If those of you in the Liberation Army won't follow me, then I will go and find a Red Army, and organize another Liberation Army (quoted in Zhisui Li, *The Private Life of Chairman Mao*, 1994).

Lushan Conference
The Lushan Conference of the Central Committee of the CPC was convened in July 1959 to discuss developments in China since 1958.

Peng Dehuai

This silenced his critics and it was obvious to everyone that criticism of Mao, even from within the CPC, was not to be tolerated. Many observers see events at the Lushan Conference as the precursor to the Great Proletarian Cultural Revolution of 1966.

SOURCE U

Millet is scattered all over the ground,
The leaves of the sweet potatoes are withered.
The young and the strong have gone to smelt iron,
To harvest the grain there are children and old women.
How shall we get through next year?
I shall agitate and speak out on behalf of the people.

Poem written by Peng Dehuai, 1959, from R. MacFarquhar, *The Origins of the Cultural Revolution*, 1983

To access Worksheet 5.2 on the Cultural Revolution, please visit www.pearsonbacconline.com and follow the on-screen instructions.

STUDENT STUDY SECTION

QUESTION

Compare and contrast Sources S and U above. How do you account for such radically different views?

Towards the Cultural Revolution

By 1961 relations between China and the Soviet Union had deteriorated to the point of no return and the Sino-Soviet split occurred. Part of this was due to ideological differences and part was due to the Soviet removal of all its technicians and support personnel in 1960. China had supported Albania in its split from the Warsaw Pact and in October 1961, in Moscow, Khrushchev attacked both Stalin and Albania with the result that the Chinese representative, Zhou Enlai, walked out of the conference. The two countries had finally broken off contact between each other but, more importantly, China was now completely isolated from the outside world.

Within China, the failures of the Great Leap Forward had at last been recognized and a new programme was needed to unify the party and consolidate Mao's position within it. Mao had stepped down as leader of the state after the Wuhan Conference in 1959 and had been replaced by Liu Shaoqi. Liu and Deng had supported the return to private ownership of land, which Mao thought was leading China away from socialism and collectivism. The Socialist Education Movement (1962–66) aimed at fostering the three 'isms' of collectivism, patriotism and socialism. These were to be achieved by the implementation of the 'Four Clean-ups', focusing on politics, the economy, the organization of the CPC and ideology. Once again, cadre members were to be sent to learn from the peasants and reinforce their understanding of the mass line. In 1965, in his 'Twenty-Three Articles', Mao stated that there was a conflict within the CPC between ideologies and that socialism was being threatened by 'capitalist-roaders'.

At the same time, Mao consolidated his control over the army. Lin Biao was rising in importance within the party and had been appointed Minister of Defence, replacing Peng Dehuai. He fully supported Mao and with Chen Boda in 1963 helped to compile

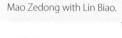

Mao Zedong with Lin Biao.

the 'Little Red Book', the unofficial title of *Quotations from Chairman Mao Zedong*. By 1965 the army had been turned into a propaganda organ, extolling Mao's virtue and helping to create the cult of Mao. Lin abolished all ranks and insignia in the PLA and shifted its political stance further to the left. He also took over control of public security. The split between Mao and the party was initiated by an attack from a relatively unknown writer, Yao Wenyuan. He wrote an article criticizing a play called *The Dismissal of Hai Rui from Office*, which had been written by Wu Han, the Deputy Major of Beijing. The play was an obvious attack on Mao, and Yao's article accused Wu Han of ignoring the masses and attempting to subvert the socialist revolution. This seemingly trivial affair brought to light the divisions within the CPC and it was now that Jiang Qing, Mao's wife, entered the conflict.

She was a traditionalist and became important among those communists who represented the hard-line group within the CPC. It was Jiang along with Lin Biao who helped to launch the Great Proletarian Cultural Revolution (GPCR) in 1966, as they began to move against those members of the CPC who had been identified as counter-revolutionaries, such as Liu and Deng. In August 1966, Jiang helped to set up the Central Cultural Revolution Group (CCRG), which was going to be the means by which Mao would carry out the GPCR.

In May 1966, with the support of Lin Biao and the PLA, students at Beijing University rebelled against the university administration. Wall posters were put up attacking the Chinese educational system. Mao supported the students and promised wide-ranging changes in the educational structure to ensure that it carried out the Maoist revolution. Liu and Deng sent 'work teams' into schools and universities to try to keep the students under control. During all of this time, Mao had remained in the background, but suddenly in July 1966 he reappeared in a carefully stage-managed event, swimming in the Yangtze River for over an hour. The message was clear. Mao was very much alive and was going to return to the political scene and take control of events. At a meeting of the Central Committee, Mao elevated Lin to be its first Vice-Chairman, essentially identifying Lin as his second-in-command. The GPCR swung into gear with Mao's 5 August poster 'Bombard the headquarters', which called on students to attack the CPC, and this was followed on 8 August with Lin Biao's speech based on the '16 Points', ordering students to attack the 'four olds'.

Jiang Qing

> **Jiang Qing (1914–91)**
> Jiang met Mao in Yan'an and became his third wife. She kept out of the political scene until the mid 1960s but took on a leading role in the radicalization of the Cultural Revolution. After Mao's death she was arrested, tried for 'counter-revolutionary crimes' and jailed. She died in jail in 1991.

SOURCE V

Although the bourgeoisie has been overthrown, it is still trying to use the old ideas, culture, customs, and habits of the exploiting classes to corrupt the masses, capture their minds, and endeavor to stage a comeback. The proletariat must do just the opposite: It must meet head-on every challenge of the bourgeoisie in the ideological field and use the new ideas, culture, customs, and habits of the proletariat to change the mental outlook of the whole of society. At present, our objective is to struggle against and crush those persons in authority who are taking the capitalist road, to criticize and repudiate the reactionary bourgeois academic 'authorities' and the ideology of the bourgeoisie… so as to facilitate the consolidation and development of the socialist system.

From the Central Committee's 16 Points, 1966, from Michael Schoenhals (ed.), *China's Cultural Revolution, 1966–1969: Not a Dinner Party,* **1996**

To access Worksheet 5.3 on Mao's famous swim and the power of mass support, please visit www.pearsonbacconline.com and follow the on-screen instructions.

STUDENT STUDY SECTION

QUESTION
What are the key phrases in the source? Who or what is the source aimed at?

At the Eleventh Plenum of the CPC, meeting in August, the 'Red Guards' – students wearing red armbands and carrying the 'Little Red Book' – were to be formed as the vanguard who would carry out the Cultural Revolution. These 'Red Guards' were assisted by the PLA, and followed the motto 'To rebel is justified'. They wrote wall posters, attacked private property and aimed at ridding China of all 'bourgeois' practices.

SOURCE W

'Criticize the old world and build a new world with Mao Zedong Thought as a weapon' (1966). Wall poster from the Great Proletarian Cultural Revolution.

凡是错误的思想，凡是毒草，凡是牛鬼蛇神，都应该进行批判，决不能让它们自由泛滥。
毛泽东

In the first stage of the GPCR, as the cult of Mao steadily grew, millions of students rampaged across China. They caused a tremendous amount of damage to churches, libraries, museums and temples, and effectively closed down schools and universities for months. The CPC itself was targeted by Jiang Qing, and Liu was dismissed from his post and placed under house arrest. Others such as Zhu De and Deng Xiaoping were denounced as reactionaries and sent to work camps. Liu finally died in prison in 1969, having being labelled a 'counter-revolutionary revisionist' and as being a reactionary 'bourgeois' element. By the end of 1966, Mao had begun to lose control of the situation as the Red Guards themselves split into factions and began to fight each other. In January 1967, workers in Shanghai overthrew the city government and even foreign embassies were attacked in scenes reminiscent of the Boxer Rebellion of 1900. Eventually, in February 1967, Mao called upon the PLA to restore control. Major unrest continued throughout the year and finally, in September, Mao told the PLA to restore order using lethal force if necessary, as China was on the verge of civil war.

SOURCE X

沿着毛主席的革命文艺路线胜利前进

'Advance victoriously while following Chairman Mao's revolutionary line in literature and the arts' (1968). Wall poster from the Great Proletarian Cultural Revolution.

STUDENT STUDY SECTION

QUESTION

What is the message in Source X?

Eventually the Red Guards were brought under control, but they were replaced by the PLA who, following the instructions of Jiang Qing and Lin Biao, started their own campaign of terror, persecuting 'counter-revolutionaries' all over China. This campaign lasted from 1968 until 1971 and some historians believe that almost as many people were killed by the PLA as were killed in the first phase of the Cultural Revolution. At the same time, millions of people (some estimates are as high as 12 million) were sent into the countryside to learn from the peasants how to be revolutionary.

The cost to China of the Cultural Revolution economically and socially was incalculable and up to 100 million people suffered as a result of it. Today most people in China consider that the GPCR lasted from 1966 until 1976, only ending with Mao's death. Immanuel Hsu maintains that the GPCR almost made China bankrupt. It damaged the CPC, purging many of its leaders. Zhou Enlai survived but was to die in 1976. Deng Xiaoping was dismissed, but by the middle of the 1970s he had been rehabilitated and was later to become Premier of China. Agriculturally and industrially, China suffered reversals that multiplied the failings of the Great Leap Forward. Education was disrupted and many intellectuals, teachers and scientists were sent into the countryside, taking away from them any possibility of undertaking research. Hsu argues that the GPCR affected three generations and was 'anticultural, anti-intellectual and antiscientific' (Hsu, *The Rise of Modern China, 2000*).

In June 1981, the CPC gave its own assessment of the GPCR. 'The Great Cultural Revolution from May 1966 to October 1976 caused the most devastating setback and heavy losses to the party, the state, and the people in the history of the People's Republic, and this Great Cultural Revolution was initiated and led by Comrade Mao Zedong' ('Resolution on Certain Questions in the History of our Party Since the Founding of the People's Republic', *Beijing Review*, no. 27, 6 July 1981).

To access Worksheet 5.4 on Mao and 'correct ideas', please visit www.pearsonbacconline.com and follow the on-screen instructions.

Women enact a political drama for a large crowd during the Cultural Revolution.

The aftermath of the Cultural Revolution

The obvious question is – what was Mao's motivation for initiating the GPCR? Mao himself never gave any explanation behind his orchestration of it or what he intended to accomplish by it. During its course, Mao rarely spoke in public at mass rallies. Shortly before his death Mao said that he had achieved two great victories. The first was defeating the Japanese and Jiang Jieshi; the second was the introduction of the Cultural Revolution which Mao thought was still unfinished. Opinions among historians naturally differ. One opinion is simply that Mao wanted to re-establish his position as leader of China after the failures of the Great Leap Forward. Others see him observing the direction that the Soviet Union was heading ideologically under Khrushchev, and fearing that China was going in the same direction, Mao felt the need to stabilize the socialist revolution. Peng's removal from office in 1959 was the first step in this lengthy process that would ultimately result in the elimination of Liu Shaoqi as a political force. In order to achieve this result, Mao had to circumvent the CPC and his permanent revolution would be continued by appealing to the masses.

By 1971 the Cultural Revolution was beginning to wind down, although it would take a few years to finally come to an end. The cult of personality that Mao had developed was now at its height, although Mao was taking steps to cool it down. The re-establishment of a Young Communist League was intended to keep the youth of China under control. Lin Biao began to believe that Mao was becoming disenchanted with him and that he was concerned about the growing influence that Lin had acquired as a result of the Cultural Revolution. The exact details of what actually happened in 1971 are unclear, but it appears as if Lin and some members of the army hatched a plot to assassinate Mao and take over the government. An informant alerted Mao to the attempted *coup d'etat* and Lin fled for his life. Apparently heading for the Soviet Union, his plane crashed in September 1971, killing everyone on board.

Mao's reaction to the news of the plot was surprising. He took to his bed and remained there for days. Rather than celebrating the removal of a rival, Mao seemed to be shocked by the betrayal of one of his closest supporters. Lin's death had several consequences for China. Lin was now identified as a traitor to China with the result that people in China started to lose faith in the CPC. They asked themselves how someone who had been seen as Mao's successor and one of the key supporters of the Cultural Revolution could now be seen as a 'capitalist-roader' reactionary himself.

Another consequence of Lin's downfall was the rehabilitation of Deng Xiaoping, who had been dismissed during the Cultural Revolution. Deng had never been treated as harshly as Peng or Liu, and had been sent into Jiangxi province to work. It was evident that Zhou Enlai was suffering from cancer and could not be expected to live much longer. In 1973 Mao recalled Deng, which had the effect of creating a split between Jiang Qing, who despised Deng, and Mao. Mao wrote in a letter to Jiang in 1974 that 'it would be better for us not to see each other. For years I have advised you about many things, but you have ignored most of it. So what use is there for us to see each other?' (Spence, *Mao*, 1999). Jiang and the **Gang of Four** started a campaign to radicalize the Cultural Revolution that was eventually to lead to their arrest after Mao's death in 1976.

Gang of Four
The most radical of the revolutionaries, this group comprising Jiang Qing, Wang Hongwen, Zhang Chunqiao and Yao Wenyuan. They wanted to continue the GPCR after Mao's death, but were arrested by Mao's successor, Hua Guofeng.

The death of Mao Zedong

1976 was to prove to be a significant date in the history of the PRC. In January, Zhou died of lung cancer. He had been a moderating factor during the Cultural Revolution and was one of China's most respected leaders. Deng gave the funeral oration, as Mao was too ill to attend, and there were mass demonstrations in Tiananmen Square to commemorate Zhou. These demonstrations were attacked by the Gang of Four as being counter-revolutionary and a campaign of repression was launched against the demonstrators. The Politburo dismissed Deng from his position within the party. Mao named a relatively unknown member of the CPC, Hua Guofeng, the Hunan Party Secretary, to be his successor. A power struggle began between Hua and the Gang of Four. In July Zhu De, the builder of the Red Army, died at the age of 90. The Chinese believe that, historically, natural disasters signify the end of a dynasty. On 28 July one of the worst earthquakes in the history of China happened in Hebei. The city of Tangshan was almost wiped off the map. The end of the dynasty came on 9 September 1976, when Mao died after a lengthy illness. He was mourned by the nation, but interestingly there was no large display of spontaneous grief as there had been after the death of Zhou.

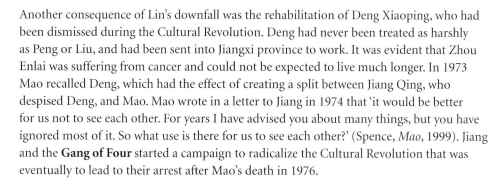

STUDENT STUDY SECTION

Here is a typical IB question:

QUESTION
Analyze the successes and failures of Mao's domestic policies between 1949 and 1976.
This one is specifically on Mao and is quite general. Look at the two introductions below. What do you like about them? How could they be improved?

Student Answer A – *Kevin*

On the 1st October 1949, after Mao proclaimed the People's Republic of China (PRC), he became its unquestionable leader, destined to change its future forever in an attempt to industrialize and transform China into a modern superpower. The following years from 1949 to 1976 which became known as the 'Mao years', are characterized by huge economic programmes as well as very controversial social policies. However, the assessments of Mao as well as those of his policies vary greatly.

Examiner's comments

A catchy start that identifies the context (e.g. time and place). The second sentence is solid, but the last sentence does not really belong there and spoils what is, up to then, a reasonably sound introduction.

● **Examiner's hint**
Other types of questions will specify the policies, e.g. social and economic. These might also ask for a comparison of Mao with another leader – either 'right wing' (Hitler or Mussolini) or 'left wing' (Castro or Stalin).

Student Answer B – *Anna*

Throughout history many great leaders have walked this planet with leadership qualities such as a deep understanding of business, charisma, willingness to admit mistakes etc. The communist leader of China, Mao Zedong, who ruled from 1949 to 1976 is arguably both a successful and unsuccessful leader. He managed to save the previously corrupt China, but also created great poverty and more violence in his country. His successes and failures are what defined him as a person and as a leader of China.

Examiner's comments

The first sentence attempts to set the essay in a global context. The 'etc.' should not be there and the choice of leadership qualities is somewhat strange. The second sentence repeats the question, although the third sentence is OK. The final comment is fairly obvious. A satisfactory but not inspiring introduction.

● **Examiner's hint**

Remember the advice about foreign policy given on p.161.

Section III:

Mao Zedong in power: Foreign policies and their impact, 1949–76

Mao had one clear goal in his foreign policy. He wanted to make the PRC recognized as a powerful independent state throughout the world. Based on his experiences in the early years of the 20th century, he wanted to ensure that China was never dependent on any foreign power. This attitude also helps to explain Mao's insistence that the PRC be able to stand on its feet economically. After October 1949, the natural ally was certain to be the Soviet Union. Despite deep ideological differences between China and the Soviet Union and frosty relations between the two leaders, who disliked each other from the first meeting, there were times of cooperation. In 1950, after the signing of the Sino-Soviet Treaty, the USSR supported China through a $300 million loan, which allowed the country to start developing economically. However, this debt was eventually repaid entirely and Mao kept the country free of foreign debts or other constraints.

The Korean War, 1950–53

Korea had been under Japanese control since its annexation in 1910. As a result of the 1943 Cairo Conference, it was decided that at the end of World War II Korea would be divided along the 38th parallel. In the north a pro-communist government was set up under Kim Il Sung, while in the south a pro-US democratic state was created under the leadership of Syngman Rhee. Both leaders wanted to establish a united and independent Korea, but under the control of one government. After Mao's victory in the Chinese Civil War, a speech by US Secretary of State Dean Acheson defining the American Defence Perimeter in the Pacific in January 1950 excluded both Taiwan and South Korea from its remit. It seemed as if the USA was willing to surrender Taiwan to the PRC in line with Truman's policy of 'disengagement'.

This suddenly changed on 25 June 1950, when North Korean troops crossed the 38th parallel and invaded the South, rapidly advancing to the city of Pusan. The PRC's response was muted apart from condemning the aggression of South Korea. South Korea appealed to the United Nations (UN) Security Council that, following the boycott of the USSR (which protested against the PRC being denied a seat as one of the permanent members) condemned the invasion and gave instructions for a UN force to intervene. This force was largely made up of US soldiers (although 15 other nations sent troops) under the command of General Douglas MacArthur. Afraid that China might attack Taiwan, MacArthur met with Jiang in August 1950 and affirmed US support for his government. After the Inchon landings in September 1950, the UN and South Korean troops pushed the North Koreans north over the 38th parallel and began a policy of 'rolling back' the communist forces. The UN troops began to move towards the Yalu River, which was the border between North Korea and the PRC.

In December the Chinese suddenly attacked across the Yalu River and pushed the UN troops south again. MacArthur was dismissed by Truman for wanting to escalate the conflict, and the war finally came to an end in July 1953 when an armistice was signed establishing the 38th parallel as the borderline between the two states. Casualties were high on both sides, with the Chinese losing almost one million men. The war was seen by the PRC as yet another attempt by Western powers to interfere in China and as more evidence, following its support for Jiang Jieshi in the Chinese Civil War, that the USA was determined to overthrow Mao and the PRC. In foreign affairs the Korean War turned Chinese political and public opinion firmly against the USA. For China, Korea was a double-edged sword. On the one hand it had shown the world that the PRC could defeat the West and the war had been used as a rallying cry to unify China. On the other hand, China lost many lives and the financial and economic cost to the embryonic PRC was enormous. China had to repay more than $1 billion to the USSR for military aid it had received during the war.

Sino-Soviet Relations, 1953–61

The Korean War severely tested the relationship between the PRC and the Soviet Union. Mao was convinced that Stalin had not told him the truth about his relations with Kim Il Sung and the planned invasion of South Korea. After Stalin's death, relationships between the two powers steadily improved as Khrushchev was more willing to supply aid and technicians to the PRC. But, as we have seen, this rapidly changed after Khrushchev's destalinization speech in 1956. Mao was concerned about developments among the Warsaw Pact countries and Khruschchev's policy of 'peaceful coexistence' with the West. When he visited the Conference of Communist Parties in Moscow in 1957, Mao attempted to redirect the Soviet Union ideologically, asking them to abandon 'revisionism', but was ignored by Khrushchev. Deep down Mao suspected that Khrushchev's shift in policy towards 'peaceful coexistence' was a deliberate attempt to isolate the PRC globally.

The final breakdown of relationships between the two powers occurred as a result of the 1958 Great Leap Forward. The following year was to prove a difficult one for the PRC. Soviet criticisms of Mao's policies at home were supported by internal party criticism at the Lushan Conference. Externally there were difficulties with Tibet, Laos, India and Indonesia, with Khrushchev seemingly supporting the latter two countries diplomatically and financially. Disagreement between Mao and Khrushchev over policies towards Albania and Yugoslavia led to the withdrawal of all Soviet experts and advisors from the PRC in mid 1960 and, following Zhou Enlai's withdrawal from the 1961 Moscow Congress, the Sino-Soviet split was complete. Relations between the PRC and the Soviet Union finally reached their lowest point in 1969, when a relatively minor incident led to actual fighting between the two sides along the Sino-Russian border, which was only brought to an end by the realization that this might escalate into a nuclear conflict. One of the consequences of this dispute was the easing of tensions between the PRC and the USA, as Mao gradually began to embrace the USA in the early 1970s.

Sino-American relations, 1971–76

In 1971 the world was shocked at Mao's extraordinary turnaround in foreign policy and his apparently sudden decision to invite President Nixon to China. Mao's decision amazed the Chinese people. Their traditional Western imperialist enemy, the USA, which had been vilified for decades, was now seen as a friend. US Secretary of State Henry Kissinger and Zhou Enlai had been preparing the ground since 1971. Part of the reason behind Nixon's visit to Beijing in February 1972 was China's determination to create a Sino-American relationship that would undermine the Soviet Union's position as a world power. Another key factor was the USA's decision to allow the PRC to replace Taiwan as a permanent member of the UN Security Council. This change had been long in coming, as the PRC had great support from the non-aligned nations in the General Assembly, the majority of whom had in 1970 already voted for the transfer of the Security Council seat to the PRC.

SOURCE A

Meeting betwen Mao Zedong and Richard Nixon, 1972.

● **Examiner's hint**
Sometimes an apparently very simple photo can be full of meaning. Study the photo carefully, looking at what is included and excluded, and interpret it in its full historical context. Looking at Source A, for example, what can you deduce about the relationship between Mao and Nixon? Give evidence to support your assertions.

SOURCE B

Cartoon by Pat Oliphant in the *Denver Post*, 1971.

Nixon's 1972 visit to the PRC was a great success and the USA's recognition of the PRC ultimately led to the two countries finally establishing full diplomatic relations with each other in 1979. The motivation behind recognizing the PRC from the US point of view was its intention to isolate the USSR. For Mao, having veto power in the UN Security Council meant that the PRC could block Soviet-initiated resolutions. It also had the effect of relaxing tensions with Japan, with the result that in 1978 a friendship and trading treaty was signed between the two countries. The PRC was finally coming out of isolation and beginning to be recognized as an important member of the global marketplace.

Relations between the PRC and other nations

During the PRC's early years, Mao also had successful interactions with India, which had recognized the PRC in 1950. They came to an agreement over Tibet, initiating the Five Principles of Peaceful Coexistence. Border disputes resulted in a short war between the two countries in 1962 and the relationship gradually worsened in the 1960s, as China supported Pakistan in the 1965 war. It took until 1976 before India and the PRC stabilized the relationship between the countries by exchanging ambassadors.

In terms of interactions with the West, there was very little mutual respect. In the East relations were also strained. The UN criticized Mao heavily for invading Tibet and ruthlessly suppressing the 1959 rebellion that led to the exile of the Dalai Lama and caused thousands of Tibetans to flee their country. China's relations with Taiwan were probably the most controversial, as neither wanted to recognize the other as the legitimate government of China. Mao made continual efforts to regain Taiwan for the Chinese mainland, but eventually recognized that he did not have the military strength to do so.

Initially, at the Bandung Conference of Afro-Asian states in 1955, Mao had been keen to accept a leadership role for the non-aligned nations, but by the 1970s Mao believed that China had joined the Second World along with countries such as West Germany and Japan. He gradually lost interest in Third World matters as the PRC's status as a world power became consolidated. Historians are rather ambivalent about whether or not Mao's foreign policies were a success. One fact is certain – the PRC was never entirely consistent in its relationships with other powers, but its policies did maintain China's independence as a nation.

Mao: An assessment

Throughout his life, Mao remained true to his beliefs. The decisions that he made were rooted in his own experiences. By 1949 the regionalism that had existed in the time of the warlords was no longer evident – a strong new nation had been unified under one central government and internal divisions had been overcome with his victory in the Chinese

Civil War. Similarly the fear of Japanese encroachment on Chinese territory was no longer present after their defeat in 1945 in the Sino-Japanese War. During his time as leader of the PRC, Mao was ever mistrustful of overseas contact and this distrust was a key factor that influenced Mao's foreign policies. Mao remained loyal to his roots and continually returned to his conviction that the peasants and the 'mass line' were the means by which China's movement towards socialism could be achieved. However, China's isolation from foreign contact and Mao's refusal to delegate authority to his fellow party members meant that he became increasingly divorced from reality. This shift resulted in Mao replacing the ruling elite that he had despised in his youth with another elitist and authoritarian figure – himself. It is not the intention of this section to offer a definitive analysis of Mao. What it will do is to point out what some respected historians and writers have said and allow you to make your own judgements.

Many social successes for the Chinese people can be attributed to Mao's policies. Although there is debate about the extent of their successes, the rights of women established in the Marriage Reform Law, the liberation of peasants in the Agrarian Reform Law and cultural development in later policies cannot be denied. In 1949, 50,000 scientists had been working in China. By 1966, the number had increased to 2,500,000. The increase in scientists was a success in that China was again able to compete with the most modern nations of the world (Meisner, *Mao's China and After*, 1999). In addition, a population that had mostly been illiterate was now largely literate with basic reading and writing skills, from 20 per cent in 1949 to more than 70 per cent in 1976, although the numbers attending university were still very low. Some of the gains here were also lost as a result of the Cultural Revolution. There were also improvements in the healthcare system with the creation of '**barefoot doctors**' in the late 1960s. Unfortunately, doctors were often the victims of Rectification Campaigns which reduced their numbers and effectiveness. The improvement in living conditions for the people of China can be seen by the life expectancy rate. In 1949, the average person lived to 35. But by 1978, life expectancy had risen to 68 years of age. Although some of the conditions created under Mao's rule were atrocious, people did begin to live healthier, longer, more cultured lives.

On the negative side, the government attacked religion, denouncing it as superstition although it did allow the creation of some 'patriotic churches', which were really under state control and the members of the clergy had to openly support Mao and the CPC. Creative artists were also singled out for attack if their work seemed to go against the revolutionary movement towards a socialist state; they were 're-educated' in labour camps. Whenever Rectification Campaigns such as the Hundred Flowers or the Cultural Revolution took place, they impacted negatively on the social and economic gains that had been achieved previously, as the campaigns resorted to force. For Mao individuals were unimportant; the state was paramount.

Barefoot doctors

'Barefoot doctors' were introduced into China in 1965. They were farmers who had received basic training in primary care services such as immunization and delivering births. The aim was to bring health care to rural areas using both traditional Chinese and modern Western medical practices.

One writer summed up Mao's regime in the following way: 'historians will agree that Mao was supremely successful as a revolutionary but extremely erratic as a nation builder. His great achievements before 1957 may serve as an inspiration to others, but his major mistakes thereafter must serve as a lesson to all' (Hsu, *China Without Mao*, 1982). When assessing Mao, most historians run through a catalogue of Mao's policies, evaluating their relative success. Hsu, on the other hand, takes a more holistic approach in his writing. In an 'objective assessment', he maintains that one of Mao's greatest blunders was his rejection of any form of population control. The population almost doubled from 500 million in 1949 to 925 million by 1976. Hsu argues that Mao saw this as a problem that only existed under capitalism. He sees Mao's paralleling of the Soviet model, by emphasizing industrial development over agriculture, as inappropriate for a nation that was over 80 per cent rural in nature. This resulted in the neglect of agriculture in favour of industry. Hsu quotes the figure of $50 per capita farm production between 1978 and 1979 as evidence to support his claim. A second error, for Hsu, was the isolation of the PRC from external contact. China needed to develop relations with the outside world in order to advance technologically and culturally. Admittedly, relations with the Soviet Union did exist for little over a decade, but Hsu considers that this was not enough and that the cost of Mao's failure to establish contact with the West was 'incalculable'. Hsu then criticizes Mao's economic policies and his 'total disregard of objective economic realities', specifically targeting the Great Leap Forward, the Cultural Revolution and the 1976–85 Ten Year Plan. Finally, Hsu turns to Mao's personal style of leadership, comparing him to the feudal rulers of the past and spotlighting his creation of a cult of personality. Supported by the army and the security systems, the PRC's policy of 'democratic centralism', as outlined in the 1954 constitution, was meaningless. Hsu comments that 'Like the emperors of the past Mao was a patriarch, helmsman, and even god-hero, who could do no wrong'.

Other writers are even more dismissive: 'While feeling deeply discontented at having failed to achieve his world ambition, Mao spared no thought for the mammoth human and material losses that his destructive quest had cost his people. Well over 70 million people had perished – in peacetime – as a result of his misrule, yet Mao felt sorry only for himself' (Chang and Halliday, *Mao: The Unknown Story*, 2005).

SOURCE C

Backed by the immense cult of his personality, the charismatic, narcissistic Son of Heaven, who thought himself capable of changing human nature through his mass campaigns, could demand complete loyalty to the cause of revolution as he chose to define it. Nobody and nothing could be excused from utter dedication and readiness to contribute whatever was demanded. Private life meant nothing. People were a blank sheet of paper, mere numbers to be used as the leader saw fit. Maoist autocracy reached heights of totalitarianism unparalleled by Hitler or Stalin, accompanied by massive hypocrisy as the leader who preached simplicity, morality and proletarian values …

A potent terror organization ensured obedience, a huge gulag swallowed up real or imagined opponents, and a massive propaganda machine fed the myths. Yet it is hard to argue that Mao did not inspire adulation. He was a monster, but a monster whom people revered as the symbol of a new China that would wipe away all the suffering and weakness of the hundred years before 1949 and who offered at least a promise of an 'iron rice bowl' of food and welfare however much it was contradicted by his actions.

From Jonathan Fenby, *The Penguin History of Modern China*, 2008

SOURCE D

Not only did Mao begin the process of opening up China to the outside world, he also created the industrial infrastructure that laid the basis for the resuscitation of the Chinese economy during the Deng years. Chinese industrial output increased thirty fold from 1949 to 1976. By 1952 Mao had restored China from the devastation of Japanese occupation and the war between Chinese Communists and Nationalists to the highest level it had achieved in the pre-war, pre-revolution years. Between 1952 and Mao's death in 1976, industrial output increased an average of 11.2 percent per year, an amazing rate of growth by any reckoning. Even during the so-called wasted decade of the Cultural Revolution, the country had almost no inflation and an industrial growth rate of between 8 and 10 percent.

From Lee Feigon, *Mao: A Reinterpretation*, 2002

 To access Worksheet 5.5 on Chinese propaganda, please visit www. pearsonbacconline.com and follow the on-screen instructions.

QUESTION

Compare and contrast the views about Mao's leadership expressed in Sources C and D.

Feigon is supported by Maurice Meisner, who cites an Australian economist: 'This sharp rise [of almost 30 per cent] in industry's share in China's national income is a rare historical phenomenon. For example, during the first four or five decades of their drive to modern industrialisation, the industrial share rose by only 11 per cent in Britain (1801–41) and 22 per cent in Japan (1878/82–1923/27)' (Kueh, 'The Maoist Legacy and China's New Industrialization Strategy', *The China Quarterly,* September 1989). Meisner comments that these figures are even more remarkable as they were achieved with very little outside assistance and with China's limited resources. Meisner gives convincing statistical evidence to support his claims that Mao was a great modernizer for China between 1949 and 1976.

He does, however, criticize Mao for his inability to create a socialist state. The reality that was China in 1976 was far away from the Maoist vision of a society conceived in Yan'an. The PRC was neither capitalist nor socialist and the promised 'transition to socialism' did not take place. Meisner's final judgement on Mao is that he 'was far more successful as an economic modernizer than as a builder of socialism' (*Mao's China and After*, 1999).

● **Examiner's hint**

Remember that the success or failure of a policy may change over time. What could be considered to be an initial failure may turn out in the end to be an ultimate success.

STUDENT STUDY SECTION

Here are two conclusions to the same essay question on p.179. What are their strengths and weaknesses?

QUESTION

Analyze the successes and failures of Mao's domestic policies between 1949 and 1976.

Student Answer A – *Denise*

A leader of a country can never be perfect and fulfil all the people's expectations. Mao is a memorable leader who helped China, but he also made several mistakes that harmed the people and the country. It can be concluded that he had the people's best interest at heart and fought for what he believed in. Up until 1957 Mao managed to save China from corruption and gain the support and admiration of his people. This was his greatest success. However from 1958 onwards, the economy declined and millions of deaths were caused due to the Second Five Year Plan and his Cultural Revolution. Whether he was an unsuccessful or successful leader is still debated, but what he will be remembered by is his love for his people and the people's love for him.

Examiner's comments

This is a reasonably sound conclusion, although the writer sees Mao's actions as being predominantly altruistic, which is debatable.

Student Answer B – *Risa*

Chairman Mao achieved a great deal during his rule of the People's Republic of China. Though he celebrated many successes, failures followed often too. Some of his greatest achievements include the rapid increase in production during the first Five Year Plan and the unification of his country during the Agrarian Reforms. However, many of his foreign affairs were not successful, and campaigns such as the Proletarian Revolution and the Great Leap Forward caused great losses.

It seems that, in retrospect, Mao's greatest successes lie in the development of China's economy, the introduction of healthcare, and rights for women. His greatest failures lie in unrealistic goals, leading to the famine during the Great Leap Forward, and the oppression of millions. Regardless of this, however, Mao was a unique leader who made a great deal of difference in Chinese history. His biggest blunder was forgetting the wellbeing of the people he was serving, but the country benefited from his rule.

Examiner's comments

A soundly written, well-balanced conclusion. But do you agree with it?

Copy out the following table. Fill it in, making a detailed list of the policies Mao introduced in the PRC and whether you consider them to have been a success or a failure. Then, using the table, write a concluding paragraph that would apply to the essay question on p.186.

Successes	Failures

the essay question on p.186.

REVIEW SECTION

This chapter has examined the rise to power of Mao and his years as the single-party ruler of the People's Republic of China. It has focused on the following six points:

- The major influences on Mao's early life.
- How Mao rose to power and established a single-party state.
- An analysis of how Mao consolidated his power after the Chinese Civil War.
- The nature, implementation and consequences of the types of policies that Mao introduced, both domestic and foreign.
- The nature of the opposition that Mao faced and an analysis of how he dealt with it.
- A discussion of how historians' assessments of Mao have differed over time.

ToK Time

'The socialist revolution is a revolution for the complete abolition of the exploiting classes and private ownership; it is incomparably more profound and incomparably broader than the democratic revolution.' (Extract from the *Peking Review*, vol. 9, no. 27, 1 July 1966, commemorating the 45th Anniversary of the founding of the CPC).

'Long live the world socialist revolution' (Lenin, 1917).

Class discussion: Try to find two or three definitions of the term 'socialist revolution'. Has there ever been a true socialist revolution in the 20th century?

JULIUS NYERERE AND TANZANIA

Julius Nyerere

This chapter deals with the rise to power and the rule of Julius Kambarage Nyerere. Seen by many observers as one of the most important African leaders, he established the political and economic structure that still remains in place in Tanzania today. Nyerere was Tanzania's leader from 1960 until his retirement in 1985, and was its longest-serving leader to date.

The sections in this chapter will address themes for detailed study as outlined in the IB History syllabus. They will cover some background to Nyerere and his rise to power in 1960. They will then show how he was able to consolidate his control of Tanzania until his retirement in 1985. A section is devoted to Nyerere's foreign policy and a final section will make an assessment of his successes and failures in Tanzania and Africa. As well as information and analysis, the chapter also has extracts from many sources, maps, cartoons and photographs. These will help build an overview of the main areas that you will need to prepare to answer essay questions using Nyerere as an example of a single-party ruler.

Timeline – 1922–99

1922	Julius Nyerere is born in Butiama, near Lake Victoria.
1949	Goes to study history and economics at Edinburgh University in Scotland.
1952	Returns home to Tanganyika and becomes a teacher (mwalimu).
1954	Launches the Tanganyika African National Union (TANU).
1960	Agrees on terms with Britain and becomes Chief Minister of the British colony of Tanganyika.
1961	Becomes first Prime Minister of an independent Tanganyika.
1962	On the country's first anniversary, Tanganyika becomes a republic, with Nyerere as its President.
1963	Nyerere helps to create the Organization of African Unity (OAU).
1964	Zanzibar unites with Tanganyika to become the Republic of Tanzania, with Nyerere as its President.
1965	Tanzania officially becomes a single-party state under Nyerere's leadership.
1967	The Arusha Declaration commits Tanzania to a programme of socialism and self-reliance.
1977	Nyerere's ruling party (TANU on mainland Tanzania) merges with Zanzibar's Afro-Shirazi Party to become the Chama Cha Mapinduzi (CCM) party; the East African Community (EAC) of Tanzania, Kenya, Rwanda, Burundi and Uganda collapses in the same year.
1978	Tanzania is invaded by Uganda.
1979	Idi Amin is ousted from power by the Tanzanian Army.
1985	Nyerere retires as President of Tanzania.
1999	Nyerere dies.

Section I:
Origins and nature of authoritarian and single-party states – Tanganyika/Tanzania

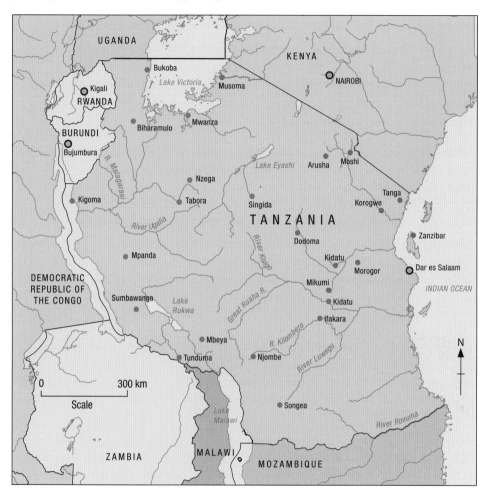

Figure 6.1
Map of Tanzania and surrounding countries.

Background

In 1885, as a consequence of the Berlin Conference, the colony of German East Africa was established. In 1891 Germany took over direct administration of the area from the German East Africa Company and set up a governor in its largest city, Dar es Salaam. As a result of the Paris Peace Conference after World War I, German East Africa was taken away from Germany and put under the control of Britain as a mandated territory under the auspices of the League of Nations, and renamed Tanganyika. Following World War II, Tanganyika became a trusteeship under the United Nations (UN) and continued to be a British colony.

In the early years of the trust territory there seemed to be a contradiction in the policies carried out by the British. The Colonial Office recognized the fact that eventually there would be a demand for self-government by African colonial states and recommended that moves be taken to allow Africans more authority within these territories to enable a smooth transition of power. In East Africa, however, the policies pursued by the colonial government were aimed at the exact opposite – to prevent Africans from increasing their power in the territories. The position was summed up by Philip Mitchell, then Governor of Kenya, in the following way:

SOURCE A

[We must] persevere in the task to which we have set our hands which I conceive to be no less than to civilize a great mass of human beings who are at present in a very primitive moral, cultural and social state … how primitive the state of these people is and how deplorable the spiritual, moral and social chaos in which they are adrift are things which can perhaps only be realized by those who are in close personal touch with the realities of the situation.

The only way the multitude of East African tribes can enjoy the benefits of civilized governments both central and local now and for generations to come, before they become themselves civilized is under the forms of colonial government administered by a strong and enlightened colonial power.

From a letter to the Secretary of State, 25 February 1947

Despite strong opposition from the colonial government in Tanganyika, the UN trusteeship council encouraged the move towards a constitutional government and began to pressure Britain to invest more in Tanganyika's infrastructure, building more schools and increasing investment. One of the results of these policies was to raise the political awareness of Tanganyikans, who began to campaign for a more equitable form of government.

The majority of Tanganyikans worked in agriculture and felt that they were overburdened with taxation and had little or no political representation. The major question to be resolved was: what would be the nature of a new government? The Colonial Office wanted to ensure that any government would be based on the ratios of comparative political power of the major racial groups in the territory: European, Asian and African. The British thought that the formation of any government should also follow a similar policy to the governments in Kenya, Southern Rhodesia and Uganda, and be based on similar racial parity. In Kenya it was 2:1:1(European, Asian and African); in Uganda it was 1:1:2. In Tanganyika, however, the ratio of the racial groupings in the population was predominantly African. Cranford Pratt estimates the ratio to be approximately 1:4:430 (*The Critical Phase in Tanzania 1945–1968*, 1976).

Tribalism
In Tanzania there are more than 120 different tribes, each with its own traditions and customs. In order for Tanganyika to become unified, it was important that the concerns of the individual tribes be reconciled to create a united country.

Formed from the earlier African Association in 1948, the Tanganyikan African Association (TAA), under the presidency of Julius Nyerere, wanted to ensure that the African majority had the major voice in any new government. Yet the TAA had little or no political power, and so in July 1954 Nyerere merged a larger number of TAA branches into a more politically oriented Tanganyikan African National Union (TANU). This organization had the express political aims of preparing the country for independence and ensuring African control of the new country by awarding the majority of seats in councils and committees to Africans. TANU wanted to restrict **tribalism**, which was comparatively easy to achieve as Tanganyika did not have the conflicting ethnic groups present in other African colonies, such as Nigeria. Nyerere also insisted on the adoption of Kiswahili as the language of TANU, which helped to unify Tanganyika linguistically and politically.

Julius Nyerere himself had been born close to Lake Victoria in 1922. He went to Tanganyika's only secondary school and from there attended Makerere University College, at which he earned his teaching certificate in 1945. He began teaching, and in 1949 became the first Tanganyikan to attend a British university after receiving a scholarship to study at Edinburgh University. After World War II, Nyerere became active in local politics as a member of the TAA, a step that began his steady political rise.

To access Worksheet 6.1 on Julius Nyerere, please visit www. pearsonbacconline.com and follow the on-screen instructions.

The move to independence

TANU received tacit support from the UN as an apolitical party that would help to move Tanganyika towards national self-determination. By 1955, both the UN and the British government had indicated that it was time for elections to be held for the Tanganyika Legislative Council (LEGCO), which traditionally represented non-African interests. Anticipating these elections, Governor Edward Twining had encouraged a group of Europeans and Asians to form the United Tanganyika Party (UTP) in order to provide TANU with organized electoral opposition. The UTP favoured the continuation of British colonial rule and ran its election campaign under a programme that would elect equal numbers of Asians, Europeans and Africans to LEGCO. The UTP leaders thought that TANU might boycott the elections, but ironically this tactic backfired as Nyerere and TANU decided to compete nationally and campaigned vigorously against the UTP. The result was an overwhelming victory in the 1958 elections for TANU, which received massive African support. It won all 15 seats in the Legislative Council, thus demonstrating that the multi-racial policies of the British colonial government were unacceptable to the Tanganyikans. Twining was quickly replaced by a new governor, Richard Turnbull, who, in his opening address in 1959, rejected the former multi-racial stance of the colonial government and stated that:

SOURCE B

In terms of population the Africans are and always will be an overwhelming majority in Tanganyika and, as the country progresses, it is right and proper, as indeed it is natural and inevitable, that African participation both in the legislature and in the executive should steadily increase. It is not intended and never has been intended that parity should be a permanent feature of the Tanganyikan scheme.

From Tanganyika Legislative Council Official Report, 34th Session, 14 October 1958

STUDENT STUDY SECTION

QUESTION

Compare Source B with Source A. In your own words, explain why this change of policy has occurred.

Under Turnbull, Tanganyika moved rapidly towards independence. There were now two nationalist parties – TANU and the African National Congress (ANC). TANU had a much wider appeal nationally and racially, being supported by both Asians and Europeans, who had been guaranteed a certain number of seats in the National Assembly, as well as by Africans. New elections were held in 1960 and TANU won easily. In October 1960, Tanganyika was granted self-government with Nyerere as Chief Minister. Finally, on 9 December 1961, Tanganyika became fully independent with Nyerere as its Prime Minister. The newly independent country's motto was *uhuru na zaki* or 'freedom and work'. The transition from British colonial rule to an African-dominated, self-governing, independent Tanganyika had taken place very smoothly without any direct violence between two competing sides and with almost no conflict between the tribal, ethnic or religious groups within its borders. This peaceful shift was to be rare in African history.

The British hoped that the status quo would be preserved and thought that Tanganyika would continue to rely heavily on Britain for economic and social support. They were also well aware that Nyerere lacked the infrastructure needed to administer the country and assumed that there would still be a need for British civil servants to ease the transition of power. The speed of change was impressive, however. It had taken Tanganyika only 39 months from its first national elections in October 1958 to full independence in December 1961. In Nigeria this had taken 38 years and in the Gold Coast 32 years (see Pratt, *Critical Phase in Tanzania*, 1976).

ToK Time

Is it possible to write an accurate history of a country if the writer has never been there, does not speak the language and has no experience of its culture? Give examples to support your answer.

STUDENT STUDY SECTION

Tanzania is an excellent example to include in Topic 3, 'The rise and rule of single-party states' in Paper 2. Whatever opposition to change there was internally was overcome through constitutional means. There is ultimately no major conflict between the former colonial power Britain and its colony. There is no revolution or military coup. Tanganyika's independence came about peacefully. These facts make Tanzania a good contrast with other 20th-century single-party states. Mao comes to power through victory in the civil war by 1949; Castro overthrows Batista in the Cuban Revolution in 1959; Lenin replaces the Romanovs in the October Revolution in 1917 and so on.

Another type of question relates to a leader coming to power because of a 'crisis'. In the case of Tanzania, there is neither an economic nor a political crisis. There is a difference of opinion between the Africans and the colonial power, Britain, but this is not of 'crisis' proportions. Tanzania thus contrasts well with the leadership 'crisis' faced after Lenin's death or the political and economic crises faced by the Weimar Republic in the early 1930s.

QUESTION

'While it is certainly true that single-party states are authoritarian and oppressive, it is not always true that they have come to power because of a crisis.' How true is this of Nyerere?

Here is an introduction and a conclusion to this question

Student Answer (Introduction) – *Jamie*

Julius K. Nyerere was one of Africa's most significant leaders. He was the founder of the Tanganyika African National Union (TANU) in 1954 and in 1964, he became the first President of the United Republic of Tanzania, which was formed of the former two countries Zanzibar and Tanganyika. Under his leadership, Tanzania became a country marked by a strong sense of national unity and an expanding educational system, which should serve as a role model for other African countries. This essay will examine to what extent the quotation above applies to Julius K. Nyerere's rise to power and his two-decade enduring rule over the Republic of Tanzania.

Examiner's comments

The first sentence is a short but effective attention catcher. The second sentence sets the essay in context, although it is a little long. The final sentence really should not use the format 'to what extent the quotation above' – it is too general and might lead to an essay that does not focus on the key words in the quotation. It would be much better to use the key words 'authoritarian', 'oppressive' and 'crisis' somewhere in the introduction. Remember that if a reader cannot tell what the question is by reading your introduction, then you need to change your style of writing.

Student Answer (Conclusion) – *Jamie*

In conclusion, it is true to say that in most aspects the quotation is applying to Julius K. Nyerere's rise to power and his dictatorship over Tanzania. He certainly was to some extent authoritarian and oppressive by suppressing capitalist institutions, but nevertheless, he tried to help the Tanzanian population by introducing an educational programme and by giving them a sense of nationalism. Furthermore, the quotation is right as it says that single-party states don't need to come to power because of a crisis, which is also the case for Nyerere's rise to power. Although there were some political disputes between the TANU and the British colonial power, it wasn't to such an extent a crisis as for example in Russia under Lenin and Stalin. Additionally, due to the British colonial rule, there was no economic crisis in Tanganyika which could have been a reason for Nyerere's rise to power.

QUESTION

Do you think that the reference to Lenin and Stalin is appropriate in the conclusion? Explain your answer.

Section II:
Political structure and foreign policy developments

In Tanganyika, the intention was to base the new governmental structure on the Westminster constitutional model, which allowed for the creation of a democratic parliamentary system similar to the political system of the United Kingdom. This was the form taken by most **Commonwealth** nations after having being granted independence. It would have a head of government, usually a Prime Minister. This position would devolve to the leader of the elected party in parliament with the greatest number of seats and there would be a multi-party system that would include a parliamentary opposition.

It soon became clear to Nyerere that this type of system might not be the best model for Tanganyika. He resigned as Prime Minister in early 1962, aiming to restructure TANU and examine ways of changing the Tanganyikan constitution. He believed that the classic Western liberal-democratic basis of government did not apply to an African state. Nyerere, a firm believer in socialist principles, argued that democracy did not need a multi-party system, but that true democracy could occur through a single-party system in which the people would select their representatives themselves, thus preventing the danger of factional grouping. In 1962 a new constitution was introduced, making Tanganyika a republic and replacing the position of Prime Minister with that of President. In December 1962, Nyerere ran for President of the new republic, winning with 97 per cent of the vote and intending to proceed towards the establishment of a single-party state.

Nyerere's socialism was based on his criticism of capitalism, and had as its basis the following fundamental principles:

Commonwealth
The Commonwealth (or British Commonwealth) is a group of nations consisting of the United Kingdom and several former British colonies that are now sovereign states (such as Canada and New Zealand), but still pay allegiance to the British Crown.

To access Worksheet 6.2 on Nyerere and international relations, please visit www.pearsonbacconline.com and follow the on-screen instructions.

SOURCE A

The foundation, and the objective, of African socialism is the extended family. 'Ujamaa,' then, or 'familyhood,' describes our socialism. It is opposed to capitalism, which seeks to build a society on the basis of the exploitation of man by man; and it is equally opposed to doctrinaire socialism which seeks to build its society on a philosophy of inevitable conflict between man and man. In our traditional African society we were individuals within a community. We took care of the community, and the community took care of us. We neither needed nor wished to exploit our fellow men. To us in Africa land was always recognized as belonging to the community. Modern African socialism can draw from its traditional heritage the recognition of 'society' as an extension of the basic family unit. Tanganyika, today, is a poor country. The standard of living of the masses of our people is shamefully low. But if every man and woman in the country takes up the challenge and works to the limit of his or her ability for the good of the whole society, Tanganyika will prosper; and that prosperity will be shared by all her people.

Adapted from an essay by Julius Nyerere, 'Ujamaa: The Basis of African Socialism' in *ChickenBones: A Journal for Literary & Artistic African-American Themes*

STUDENT STUDY SECTION

QUESTIONS

Nyerere's idea of a democratic single-party state based on communal support, which he saw as being far more appropriate to the tribal communities that have always existed in Africa, is a rather unusual model of government. Is the concept of a 'democratic single-party state' an **oxymoron**? In groups of three, discuss the advantages and disadvantages of this form of government.

Oxymoron
An oxymoron is a phrase that combines two normally contradictory terms. A 'loud silence' would be an example.

Zanzibar
Located off Tanzania's coast, the territory of Zanzibar includes the main island, Unguja (usually called Zanzibar), Pemba and a number of smaller islands in the Zanzibar archipelago.

Afro-Shirazi Party
The Afro-Shirazi Party was created by the merging of the Persian Shiraz Party and the mostly African Afro Party.

Unity with Zanzibar

In December 1963, **Zanzibar** became independent from Britain, with the Arab-led Zanzibar Nationalist Party (ZNP) in power. After little over a month, the ZNP was itself overthrown by a revolution and an African nationalist and member of the **Afro-Shirazi Party** (ASP), Abeid Amani Karume, took control. The uprising seemed to the Soviet Union and China to give them the possibility of establishing a foothold in Africa. The new government was quickly recognized by a number of communist countries, who supported Karume and his Revolutionary Council. Nyerere was quick to see the danger for Tanganyika if foreign powers were to gain a foothold on an island so close to the mainland, and he moved rapidly to form an alliance with Karume. The result was that in April 1964 the first voluntary joining of two African states took place when Nyerere announced the creation of the United Republic of Tanzania with Nyerere as its President and Karume as Vice-President. Although united together, the two states retained a considerable amount of internal autonomy over their own political affairs.

SOURCE B

The Tanzanian coat of arms. ▶

RESEARCH ACTIVITY

What do all the symbols signify? There about 12 of them!

The coat of arms has a warrior's shield in the centre. This is divided into four sections. The top, golden section signifies mineral resources; the second one is the **Tanzanian flag**; the third one is red, which links to Tanzania's soil and agricultural resources; and the fourth one signifies the sea, lakes, rivers and coast of Tanzania. The **burning torch** means *uhuru* (freedom), while the crossed axe and hoe are the tools that are used to cultivate the soil. The spear signifies defence. The shield is flanked by elephant tusks, each held by a man and a women, indicating equality. They are standing on a representation of Mount Kilimanjaro and a clove bush surrounds the feet of the man, while a cotton bush is at the woman's feet. The woman appears to be wearing a head scarf. The words in Swahili mean 'Freedom and Unity', the title of a book by Nyerere.

Did you get all of these? What is interesting about them is that you could use the coat of arms to almost write an outline of the aims and objectives of the newly created state of Tanzania. The symbols reflect the beliefs of the leaders and their priorities in the formation of the new republic.

Tanzanian flag
In this flag, green means land, blue means the sea, black signifies the people and gold indicates mineral wealth.

Burning torch
The *uhuru* or freedom torch is a national symbol of Tanzania and was first lit on the top of Mount Kilimanjaro in 1961 to celebrate Tanganyika's independence.

The Zanzibarian revolution of 1964 was one of the reasons that prompted some members of TANU to consider the creation of a Tanzanian single-party state. Its Secretary-General, Oscar Kambona, maintained that internal security would be easier to maintain if there were no alternative opposition parties. Nyerere agreed, in principle, with the idea of the establishment of a single-party state, but insisted on fair and open elections. Another reason for the change in government style was the mutiny of the army in January 1964. This involved a dispute over pay scales and the perceived inequity between Tanzanian and British soldiers in the officer corps. Many of the army's members were part of the old colonial order and, with British assistance, a new army was created made up from TANU members.

Until 1992, all members of the Tanzanian armed forces were required to be members of TANU and the combination of the mutiny and the newly formed army certainly contributed to the decision to move forward towards a single-party state. In order to ensure TANU's stability as a political party, Nyerere merged private trade unions into the National Union of Tanganyika Workers (NUTA) and cooperative societies into the Cooperative Union of Tanzania (CUT). These were then ideologically aligned with TANU and were required to follow its political orientation. In order to suppress any vocal opposition to TANU from trade union leaders and tribal chiefs, the 1962 Preventive Detention Act was used to detain suspected opponents of the party. By early 1965, several hundred people had been arrested and jailed.

SOURCE C

Take the question of detention without trial. This is a desperately serious matter. It means that you are imprisoning a man when he has not broken any written law, or when you cannot be sure of proving beyond reasonable doubt that he has done so. You are restricting his liberty, making him suffer materially and spiritually, for what you believe he intends to do, or is trying to do, or for what you believe he has done. Few things are more dangerous to the freedom of a society than that. For freedom is indivisible, and with such opportunity open to the Government of the day, the freedom of every citizen is reduced. To suspend the Rule of Law under any circumstances is to leave open the possibility of the grossest injustices being perpetrated.

From Julius Nyerere, *Freedom and Unity*, 1966

The single-party state

In 1965, under the new constitution, Nyerere announced the establishment of a single-party state that he believed would allow for open debate and a proper democratic system. The candidates who stood for election had to meet several conditions. Each had to be a member of TANU, which was open to anyone who accepted its aims, and have the support of 25 people who could vote. At a district party conference all candidates would be interviewed and a number of these would be recommended as candidates to TANU. The National Executive Committee (NEC) of TANU would select two candidates in each constituency and voters had to choose between them. No one could spend his own money on an election campaign. No one could campaign on the basis of race, tribe or religion and all candidates had to campaign in Kiswahili. TANU elders were to supervise the elections.

When elections were held in October, it appeared as if Nyerere's philosophy had been successful – voters removed politicians with whom they were dissatisfied and TANU was seen as a party that had arranged a truly democratic election. There were 807 candidates for 107 seats. In 97 out of the 107 seats there were more than two candidates, which meant that the NEC had to make a choice to select two of them. Out of the 107 new members of the National Assembly, 86 were new. This single-party system was further consolidated later when, in 1977, TANU and the ASP merged to form Chama Cha Mapinduzi (CCM; the Party of the Revolution). At the time of writing, in 2010, this party is still in power, although Tanzania has been a multi-party state since 1992.

SOURCE D

Its enactment indicates the new power of the single ruling party and total disregard of constitutional process. No Constituent Assembly was ever convened to pass this Constitution. It was adopted by the parliament in its constituent capacity as if it was amending an existing constitution…

… It is worth noting that in the process of bringing this new Constitution into operation the people had been clearly and deliberately by-passed. No attempt was made to involve them. It was party leaders who were busy preparing documents and using the state machinery to see them though the legal processes in order to avoid criticism. Little effort was taken to ensure the legitimacy of the new constitution.

From Chris Maina Peter, 'Constitution-making in Tanzania: The role of the people in the process', 2000

SOURCE E

In Tanzania the several tiny parties which appeared in 1962 were harassed out of existence, their leaders deported or detained and their right to register and to hold meetings severely restricted. When Nyerere first suggested that there could be competitive elections within a single-party system there was little support for the idea within the leadership ranks of TANU…

David Lamb, in his book, The Africans, *notes that until 1979 Tanzania had more political prisoners in detention than even South Africa. Lamb comments that Nyerere 'granted amnesty to 6,400 prisoners that year and freed another 4,436 in 1980'. He also writes that Nyerere allowed no opposition to his policies and had censored most of the media by 1980.*

From Cranford Pratt, *The Critical Phase in Tanzania 1945–1968,* **1976**

STUDENT STUDY SECTION

QUESTION
Find a definition of the word 'oligarchy'. Re-read Sources D and E. Do you believe that Nyerere's government in Tanzania is an example of an oligarchy or a democracy? Explain your answer.

Foreign policy in Tanzania, 1961–85

Since its independence, Tanzania has generally followed consistent aims in its foreign policy. Although there was no clearly identifiable aim in Tanganyikan foreign policy before 1963, events elsewhere made it necessary to develop a position on external security issues once independence had been consolidated. The assassination of **Patrice Lumumba** in the Congo and a *coup d'état* in Togo were seen as the result of foreign involvement in Africa, and Nyerere had to decide on what foreign policy objectives he would follow. He decided on three main areas. One of these was to ensure national security through diplomatic means; the second was to give support to the liberation movements in Africa and work for African unity; the third was the pursuance of non-alignment linked to the policies of the Organization of African Unity (OAU) and the UN.

In order to strengthen national security, one of Nyerere's first objectives was to formalize the old East African High Commission, established in 1948, into a more effective Eastern African Federation of states. He wanted to merge Tanganyika, Kenya, Zanzibar, Rwanda, Burundi and Uganda into a regionally unified group. Initially, his attempts to do so were unsuccessful, partly due to these areas' need to consolidate their own internal stability. The turning point was the announcement by Nyerere and Karume of the creation of Tanzania in April 1964. This soon led to closer economic and trade agreements between Kenya, Uganda and Tanzania that were to facilitate the 1967 Treaty for East African Cooperation, which included the formation of the **East African Community** (EAC).

The EAC was to last for ten years until 1977, by which time disagreements between Nyerere and Jomo Kenyatta, President of Kenya, over their conflicting economic development philosophies led to a split between the two leaders. Kenya preferred a modified capitalist growth model, whereas Tanzania was pushing forward with self-reliance, as outlined in the 1967 Arusha Declaration. As neither country could agree on the amount that each country should contribute financially to the EAC, it simply collapsed in July 1977. This situation then led to a dispute between Kenya and Tanzania over economic policy, with the result that Nyerere closed the border between the countries, thus severely restricting access to Tanzania's northern game parks from Nairobi. He hoped that this measure would result in safari park visitors flying directly into Tanzania, thus stimulating the tourist industry. The end effect was a major fall in tourist numbers, resulting in a huge drop in revenue. The border remained closed until 1982 (see p.206).

A second key area for Nyerere's foreign policy was support for the liberation struggles in southern Africa. Nyerere targeted what he saw as racist regimes in Mozambique, Southern

ToK Time
The IB has divided its World History Course into four regions. Nyerere obviously fits into the African region on Paper 3. Divide yourself into groups of four and discuss the issues involved in studying the history of a region such as Africa. Is it any easier to study Europe and the Middle East? To help you, have a look at what the content of the courses are by looking at the IB History Guide.

Patrice Lumumba (1925–61)
Patrice Lumumba was the first Prime Minister of the Republic of the Congo when it became independent from Belgium in 1960. After only a short time in power, his government was overthrown in a *coup d'etat* led by Colonel Mobutu. Lumumba tried to escape, but was soon captured and executed.

East African Community
The EAC aimed at strengthening the trading links between its members through a common market and a common customs agreement, with the objective of increasing economic growth within the region.

To access Worksheet 6.3 on Tanzania's economy, please visit www.pearsonbacconline.com and follow the on-screen instructions.

Rhodesia and South Africa. In 1965, following the Rhodesian unilateral declaration of independence, Nyerere was annoyed by Britain's failure to bring the illegal government into line and broke off diplomatic relations with Britain for two years. Nyerere also recognized the independence of Biafra in 1967, a decision that was opposed by almost all African nations. An alliance of Front Line States (FLS) was later formed between Tanzania, Zambia and Botswana with the objective of supporting southern African liberation movements. The freeing of Mozambique and Angola in 1975 and the independence of Zimbabwe in 1980 showed the success of this alliance, which took a position that coincided with Nyerere's own stance on colonialism, apartheid and racism. Tanzania allowed political refugees to enter Tanzania and also permitted independence-supporting groups such as the Pan-African Congress (PAC), the South West African People's Organization (SWAPO) and the Front for the Liberation of Mozambique (FRELIMO) to establish offices there. Support for these liberation groups from socialist nations caused friction with traditional Western aid donors such as Britain and the USA, but Nyerere was adamant in supporting these groups.

Cold War positioning

Tanzania traditionally maintained a non-aligned position during the Cold War, preferring not to be linked to any ideological bloc, and Nyerere was also a keen supporter of the OAU, helping to establish it in 1963. Up until the end of 1963, Tanganyika had aligned itself with Britain, partly as a result of the development aid that Britain was supplying. Nyerere's move towards non-alignment and the union with Zanzibar were to have a crucial effect on the relationship between the two countries in 1964 and 1965. The **independence of Zanzibar**, with its resultant uprisings, attracted interest externally. East Germany, China, the Soviet Union and other communist countries recognized the new state and, following the creation of Tanzania in April 1964, Nyerere was forced to rethink the direction of his foreign policy. US and Belgian support for **Moise Tshombe** in the Congo further pushed Nyerere to seek alternative means of obtaining foreign aid.

Tanzania began to explore the idea of moving closer to other socialist states, while still remaining non-aligned. There was little direct support from the USSR and other Eastern European countries, but the People's Republic of China (partly because of its support for the liberation movements globally) began to supply economic and financial aid to Tanzania. Nyerere was determined to reduce Tanzania's dependence on West Germany and Britain, with the result that China began to play a more important role in funding Tanzania's development programme. One project that **Kenneth Kaunda**, the President of Zambia, and Nyerere were keen to complete was the building of the Tanzam railroad, linking Dar es Salaam and Lusaka. When Tanzania broke off relations with Britain over the situation in Rhodesia, China stepped in with an offer of $400 million of aid. Pragmatically, Nyerere still kept Tanzania's links with the West, receiving aid from the US-backed Agency for International Development (AID) and the International Development Association (IDA). Although Tanzania seemed to be moving closer to China economically, Nyerere was determined that it would still be non-aligned ideologically. He argued that rather than contradicting a non-aligned policy, the close cooperation between the two countries actually reinforced Tanzania's non-aligned status.

By 1967, Tanzania was globally recognized as non-aligned and was receiving support from a large number of external sources, including the USA. Nyerere was now thinking about the direction in which he wanted to take Tanzania economically. Non-alignment invites a state to determine its own future direction and it is hardly surprising that Nyerere's foreign policies, linked to his own thinking about the nature of a socialist state, would lead to the next development in Tanzania – the adoption of the *ujamaa* villagization programme (see below p.201).

Independence of Zanzibar

Following its independence in 1963, the Arab-led government in Zanzibar was overthrown in 1964 by an African nationalist leader, John Okello. In March of the same year, Okello was exiled by Karume, whom he had appointed President after the coup.

Moise Tshombe (1919–69)

After losing the national elections to Patrice Lumumba in 1960 in the Congo, Tshombe declared the province of Katanga independent. When the UN intervened in 1963, he was forced into exile. Tshombe returned the following year as premier only to be dismissed in 1965. Tshombe was kidnapped in 1967 and extradited to Algeria, where he died in 1969.

Kenneth Kaunda (b. 1924)

Kenneth Kaunda was the first President of Zambia, from 1964 to 1991.

In the meantime, relations between Uganda and Tanzania had been deteriorating seriously since 1971, when **Idi Amin** overthrew a longtime friend of Nyerere, **Milton Obote**, in a *coup d'état*. The disputes between Amin and Nyerere gradually escalated, ultimately culminating in the outbreak of war between Uganda and Tanzania in 1978, when Ugandan soldiers attacked the province of Kagera. Nyerere appealed to the OAU to intervene and impose economic sanctions against Uganda. When the OAU did not take any direct action and suggested that both parties stop fighting, Nyerere ordered the Tanzanian Army to attack Uganda, which resulted in the occupation of Kampala and the end of Idi Amin's government in April 1979. Nyerere imposed himself as the de facto leader of Uganda, removing potential Amin successors from power. The cost to Tanzania of the 1978 war was immense, estimated at almost $500 million, and was to have a tremendous impact on the economic situation in a country trying to implement Nyerere's programme of socialist reforms.

Idi Amin

SOURCE F

PRINCIPLES
Article III
The Member States, in pursuit of the purposes stated in Article II solemnly affirm and declare their adherence to the following principles:

1. *The sovereign equality of all Member States.*
2. *Non-interference in the internal affairs of States.*
3. *Respect for the sovereignty and territorial integrity of each State and for its inalienable right to independent existence.*
4. *Peaceful settlement of disputes by negotiation, mediation, conciliation or arbitration.*
5. *Unreserved condemnation, in all its forms, of political assassination as well as of subversive activities on the part of neighbouring States or any other States.*
6. *Absolute dedication to the total emancipation of the African territories which are still dependent.*
7. *Affirmation of a policy of non-alignment with regard to all blocs.*

From the Charter of the Organization of African Unity, 1963

Idi Amin (c.1925–2003)
Idi Amin was the military dictator and President of Uganda from 1971 to 1979.

Milton Obote (1925–2005)
Milton Obote was Prime Minister of Uganda from 1962 to 1966 and its President from 1966 to 1971 and from 1980 to 1985.

STUDENT STUDY SECTION

QUESTION
In your opinion, how far did Nyerere's policies in Tanzania adhere to the principles of the Organization for African Unity?

Section III:
Economic developments, 1961–85

In 1961, directly after becoming independent, Nyerere identified three main issues that needed to be addressed in Tanganyika if rapid economic development was to be achieved. These were poverty, disease and ignorance. To deal with these problems, the government introduced the Development Plan for Tanganyika 1961–64, which aimed at promoting rural development. Under this plan, three sectors of Tanganyikan society would be targeted to receive priority financing. These were to be: Agriculture (24 per cent), Communication, Power and Works (28.8 per cent), and Education (13.7 per cent). The plan was actually prepared by British civil servants and aimed at developing import substituting industries (ISI) in order to modernize Tanzania and reduce external borrowing. The Tanzanian government under Nyerere then introduced a series of Five Year Plans (1964–69, 1969–74, 1976–81, 1981–86), following the Stalinist and Maoist models, to supplement the earlier Development Plan. The plans actually encompass six years chronologically.

The First Five Year Plan (1964–69) aimed at stimulating the economy to produce a projected 6.7 per cent increase in **gross domestic product** (GDP). Nyerere admitted in his speech proposing the plan that much of the investment needed for it to be successful would have to come from foreign investment. The plan was not able to achieve the target it set for itself, although economic growth did reach 5.3 per cent. Despite the financial support given to business and industry by the Tanzanian government, the growth rates of the economy were disappointing and did not bring about the desired results. Between 1961 and 1967, the population increased at about 2.3 per cent, while the economic rate of growth was between 4.3 and 5 per cent. The consequence was an economic growth rate of about 2.7 per cent, which was insufficient to create and sustain real economic growth. One factor that was to play an important part in Nyerere's thinking was the question of foreign aid.

By 1966 it had become clear to Nyerere that Tanzania could not depend on foreign sources for the sort of capital development that it wished to undertake. Foreign loans required repayment with interest and were often linked to political interdependency, restricting Tanzania's ability to take independent action. Tanzania's experiences between 1961 and 1966 had shown that loans from external sources did not always arrive when they were promised or when they were needed. Nyerere began to develop the idea that Tanzania should determine its own economic future without being tied to foreign investment. He did not intend that Tanzania should cut itself off from the rest of the world. He stated this clearly: 'The doctrine of self-reliance does not mean isolationism. For us, self-reliance is a positive affirmation that for our own development, we shall depend upon our own resources' (*Freedom and Socialism*, 1968).

Gross domestic product

An index for measuring a nation's economic output, based on the market value of all final goods and services made within the borders of a country in a year.

SOURCE A

Tanzanian Population Growth, 1948–2000

Year	Total population	Average annual growth rate (per cent)
1948*	7,981,120	–
1957*	9,600,852	2.25
1967	12,313,469	2.82
1978	17,527,564	3.30

*Excluding Zanzibar and Pemba

Sources: Tanzania, Ministry of Economic Affairs and Development Planning, *Statistical Abstract, 1965*, Central Statistical Bureau, 1967; Bureau of Statistics, Ministry of Finance and Planning, *1978 Population Census Preliminary Report*, n.d.

Adapted from Rodger Yeager, *Tanzania: An African Experiment*, 1989

Ujamaa villages and self-reliance

The First Development Plan had not been successful in meeting the targets that had been set. Yet Tanzania's experience with it was significant, as it had not only shown that the country need no longer depend upon external aid and loans, but also that, in economic terms, Tanzania had been able to generate a sufficient amount of cash and enough food crops to be almost self-sustaining. It was in light of these achievements that Nyerere began to think about the policy of 'self-reliance', by which the country could stand on its own two feet. He believed that development should be based on the three principles of 'freedom, equality and unity'.

In the Arusha Declaration of 1967, Nyerere proposed the creation of *ujamaa* villages that would focus on traditional African values of community and family and make Tanzania a socialist, self-reliant nation. Previously, the private sector had been seen as the main mechanism for development in Tanzania. Now this changed, as Nyerere proposed to nationalize all of the banks and large industrial concerns, including agricultural processing plants, and put them under government control. He believed that capitalism was inappropriate for poor African countries, and Nyerere introduced a system of '**parastatals**' that were to oversee the buying of foreign goods, and regulate the selling of export crops such as **sisal**, coffee and cotton. The number of parastatals increased significantly from 64 in 1967 to 380 in 1981, showing the rapidly increasing state control of the economy.

The Second Five Year Plan (1969–74), incorporating the socialist principles laid down at Arusha, was intended to put Tanzania on the path to self-reliance by focusing on agriculture. It aimed at reducing the **balance of payments deficit**, stabilizing wages and achieving a growth rate of between 5 and 6 per cent.

SOURCE B

From now on we shall stand upright and walk forward on our feet rather than look at this problem upside down. Industries will come and money will come but their foundation is THE PEOPLE and their HARD WORK, especially in AGRICULTURE. This is the meaning of self-reliance.

Our emphasis should therefore be on:
(a) The Land and Agriculture
(b) The People
(c) The Policy of Socialism and Self-Reliance, and
(d) Good Leadership…

…TANU believes that everybody who loves his nation has a duty to serve it by co-operating with his fellows in building the country for the benefit of all the people of Tanzania. In order to maintain our independence and our people's freedom we ought to be self-reliant in every possible way and avoid depending upon other countries for assistance. If every individual is self-reliant the ten-house cell will be self-reliant; if all the cells are self-reliant the whole ward will be self-reliant; and if the wards are self-reliant the district will be self-reliant. If the districts are self-reliant, then the region is self-reliant, and if the regions are self-reliant, then the whole nation is self-reliant and this is our aim…

From the Arusha Declaration, 5 February 1967

Parastatal
A parastatal is a partially or fully state-owned enterprise or corporation.

Sisal
Sisal is a plant that yields a stiff fibre used in the production of rope, twine and dartboards. The word can be used to describe both the plant and the fibre.

Balance of payments deficit
A balance of payments deficit exists when a country imports more goods than it exports.

ToK Time
'Life must be lived forward, but it can only be understood backward' – Søren Kierkegaard. What do you understand by Kierkegaard's statement? Can we only know anything after looking back on it?

STUDENT STUDY SECTION

QUESTION
Divide your class into groups of four and discuss the following question among yourselves: Do you think that Nyerere's proposal for self-reliance could work? Explain your answer.

In order to make Tanzania self-reliant, Nyerere proposed the introduction of the *ujamaa* villagization scheme (*ujamaa vijijni*). Investment and education would be focused on the rural, agricultural sector and 'rural economic and social communities where people would live together for the good of all' (Nyerere, *Freedom and Socialism*, 1968) would be created. The *ujamaa* villages would be based on a similar model to the cooperatives set up by Mao in his First Five Year Plan (1953–57). Families would move together into communities rather than farm their own individual plots, working together around a common centre, with the expectation that these collective villages would result in a more efficient, and therefore more productive, method of farming the land. Nyerere also believed that centralized villages would make it possible for the government to provide the community with better access to services such as education and medicine, thus improving the general standard of living. He further hoped to eliminate what he saw as a divisive class split among the villagers, whereby some wealthier farmers were beginning to exploit the landless villager. This situation almost resulted the creation of a 'kulak' class of peasant. At the same time, taxes were increased in order to redistribute Tanzania's national income.

As the table below shows, the transfer of people into these centralized villages took place rapidly.

SOURCE C

The Rate of Ujamaa Villagization in Tanzania, 1969–74

	December 1969	December 1970	December 1971	December 1972	March 1973	January 1974
Number of villages	650	1965	4484	5556	5628	5008
Number of members	300,000	531,200	1,545,240	1,980,862	2,028,164	2,560,470

Source: Michael F. Lofchie, 'Agrarian Crisis and Economic Liberalization in Tanzania', *The Journal of Modern African Studies*, vol. 16, no. 3, 1978

In 1970, 531,000 people, less than 5 per cent of the population, were living in 1,956 villages, with an average occupancy of 271 inhabitants. When the *ujamaa* villagization experiment ended in October 1977, more than 13 million people, representing an estimated 79 per cent of the society and 85 per cent of all rural dwellers, were relocated in 7,300 villages, at an average occupancy rate of about 1,850 (see Yeagar, *Tanzania: An African Experiment*, 1989).

SOURCE D

Workers in an *ujamaa* collective.

Despite the apparent success of the villagization movement in terms of the movement of the agricultural population into the villages, ultimately the *ujamaa* experiment in self-reliance turned out to be an economic disaster for Tanzania. By 1977 the economy was in a catastrophic state with a growth rate of only about 1.5 per cent per annum. What went wrong?

Initially the scheme went well, as there was general enthusiasm for the idea of creating *ujamaa* villages. However, when villagers discovered the reality of the programme, opposition began to grow. The peasants preferred to work their own individual plots of land, and did not put as much effort into their work as there were no personal incentives to do so. Similarly, there was no direct profit from the peasants' investment of capital and labour, as everything belonged to the *ujamaa* village. Violent confrontations began to occur between government troops and rebellious villagers. The result was that the government began to use force to move peasants to new settlements. This was in direct contradiction to what Nyerere had previously stated in an essay entitled 'Socialism and Rural Development':

SOURCE E

Ujamaa villages are intended to be socialist organizations created by the people, and governed by those who live and work in them. They cannot be created from outside, nor governed from outside. No one can be forced into an Ujamaa village, and no official – at any level – can go and tell the members of an Ujamaa village what they should do together, and what they should continue to do as individual farmers

Julius Nyerere, *Freedom and Socialism,* **1968**

By the early 1970s, the government had introduced forced migration of peasants into *ujamaa* villages, such as in Operation *Rufiji* and Operation *Dodoma*, if they did not move voluntarily. Nyerere's position was clear. In November 1973, he was quoted as saying 'there was a need for every Tanzanian to change his mode of life if rapid progress was to be achieved. People who refused to accept development changes were stupid, if not ignorant or stubborn' (*Daily News*, 7 November 1973, quoted in Kjell J. Havnevik, *Tanzania: The Limits to Development from Above*, 1993). Opposition grew and by 1974 very few of the *ujamaa* villages had developed to the point where they were producing at the levels of output needed for the Tanzanian economy to grow. The government's own economic survey in 1975 showed that 8 per cent of villages were at this stage.

Michael Lofchie argues that the *ujamaa* villagization programme created such a disaster that the amount of grain produced in Tanzania was not enough to feed the country's own population. In addition, a crisis in maize production, which led to a decline in cash crop exports, meant that Tanzania had to import huge quantities of maize. Tanzania's cotton exports fell at the same time, with the result that an enormous deficit in its balance of trade was created. Somewhat ironically, considering one of the objectives of the Arusha Declaration, Tanzania became more and more dependent on overseas loans.

SOURCE F

Tanzania's external trade in maize, 1968–76 (million metric tons)

	1968–69	1969–70	1970–71	1971–72	1972–73	1973–74	1974–75	1975–76
Imports	0	46.9	0	92.3	78.9	183.6	317.2	42.3
Exports	51.8	0	53.4	0	0	0	0	0

From Marketing Development Bureau, Ministry of Agriculture, *Price Policy Recommendations for the 1977/78 Agricultural Price Review*, vol. 1, 1976

SOURCE G

Cotton production, Tanzania 1964–85

	Area harvested (hectares)	Beginning stocks (mt)*	Production (mt)	Imports (mt)	Total imported from USA (mt)	Total supply (mt)	Exports (mt)
1964	202,000	1,524	54,432	0	0	55,956	53,343
1967	273,000	1,089	69,672	0	0	70,761	61,617
1971	283,000	11,757	65,318	0	0	77,075	40,062
1975	380,000	29,393	42,457	0	0	71,850	39,409
1985	370,000	28,304	30,917	0	0	59,221	26,998

*mt = metric tons
Source: Adapted from www.indexmundi.com

STUDENT STUDY SECTION

QUESTION

What do the figures in Sources F and G tell you about Nyerere's programme of villagization?

Another key factor that contributed to the worsening economic situation was the stagnation in price of one of Tanzania's main cash export crops – sisal. In 1963/64, Tanzania was producing a total of 233,500 metric tons of sisal, contributing to more than 35 per cent of total export earnings, and was the largest single employer in the country. By 1998, however, Tanzania was producing less than 28,000 tons of sisal and export earnings had dropped to less than 1 per cent. This decline resulted from a number of factors, including the nationalization of the sisal industry after the 1967 Arusha Declaration, the discovery of alternative synthetic means of manufacturing rope and a lack of investment capital being available. The government analyzed the situation thus:

SOURCE H

The single most serious problem which has afflicted the sisal industry in the last twenty years has been the advent of synthetic substitutes (polypropylene) which have taken more than 55 per cent of market share... Synthetic spinning was backed up by low prices from large petrochemical companies and new technology which made it easier for them to grab market share from sisal products.

Tanga: Tanzania Sisal Authority, *Tanzania Sisal Authority Corporate Plan, 1996–2000*, 1996

The result was a serious economic slump as the growth of Tanzania's GDP dropped to about 2.2 per cent in 1974. As population growth between 1967 and 1978 was between 2.8 per cent and 3.3 per cent (see Source A above on p.200), the standard of living in the country was dropping overall. The crisis in the production of cash and food crops led to a rapid increase in inflation. The government was threatened with bankruptcy when Nyerere decided to modify the *ujamaa* villagization scheme by the passing of the Villages and *Ujamaa* Villages Act in 1975. This act increased the minimum size of an *ujamaa* village to 250 families.

The failure of the *ujamaa* programme was due to a combination of internal and external factors. Not least of these was the 1973 global oil crisis that resulted from the 1973 Yom Kippur War between Egypt and Israel. This conflict resulted in an additional drain on Tanzania's **capital reserves**, as insufficient grain and commodities were produced for export. The cost of importing oil rose from 10 per cent of export earnings in 1973 to nearly 40 per cent by the middle 1980s following a second global oil price increase in 1979. By 1980, the Tanzanian economy was on the edge of bankruptcy. The 1978–79 war with Uganda had cost $500 million and the removal of Idi Amin came at a terrible price for Tanzania, exhausting **foreign reserves**. Domestically food production was at crisis levels due to poor weather and corruption. Factories were seriously under-utilized, operating well below their full capacity. The collapse of the EAC in 1977 had also meant that Tanzania had to invest heavily in its own infrastructure in areas like aviation and the building of new harbours. Tanzania desperately needed an injection of foreign capital if its economy was going to recover.

> **Capital reserves**
> 'Capital reserves' refers to the value of the capital resources a country holds at a certain point in time.
>
> **Foreign reserves**
> 'Foreign reserves' means the amount of foreign currency held by a government at a certain point in time.

SOURCE I

Cartoon by Masoud Kipanga, Government of Tanzania's Poverty Reduction Strategy Paper, 2000.

STUDENT STUDY SECTION

QUESTION

What is the message conveyed by Source I? Sources I and N (below, p.209) are published in 2000 and 2002 respectively. What relevance do they have for the study of Tanzania under Julius Nyerere?

Nyerere had planned to retire in 1980, but because of the economic crisis he agreed to stay on for one more term as President. His victory in the previous presidential elections was something of a foregone conclusion. Nyerere received 99 per cent of the 'yes' vote in 1970; 93 per cent in 1975 and 93 per cent in 1980. However, there was only one candidate in the elections – Nyerere – and voters could either vote yes or no! (see David Lamb, *The Africans*, 1987).

International Monetary Fund
An international economic organization, founded in 1944. Its activities include working towards stabilizing international exchange rates and providing major national loans.

It was during this period, between 1981 and 1985, that Tanzania began to negotiate with the **International Monetary Fund** (IMF) and other international aid givers for loans to help rejuvenate the stagnating economy. Nyerere realized, however, that heavy external indebtedness, and the consequences this would have for Tanzania, would mean an end to his experiment in creating an African socialist state. The IMF conditions required a liberalization of the economy and that Tanzania reduce its government expenditure, devalue the currency and close down the parastatals. Nyerere would not abandon *ujamaa* and refused to comply with the IMF's conditions. As a result, the Tanzanian economy continued to spiral downwards for another five years.

A contributory factor towards Tanzania's economic decline was the policies it followed in regard to its tourist industry. There was some question whether such a Western-dominated industry was ideologically compatible with an African socialist state, with the result that the tourist infrastructure was allowed to fall into neglect. Extortionate fees for hotel accommodation and entry fees for the game parks resulted in a severe decline in tourist numbers in the 1970s and 1980s, causing the tourist industry virtually to collapse. The closing of the border with Kenya in 1977 also caused a massive decline in tourist numbers. Despite the eventual reopening of the border, visitor numbers had dropped from 300,000 in 1976 to 58,000 in 1985, resulting in a tremendous loss of hard currency for the economy.

SOURCE J

▲ 'Universal Brotherhood' – Cartoon from Anna Paczuska, *Socialism for Beginners*, 1986.

● **Examiner's hint**
When analyzing cartoon sources, make sure that you have identified all of the images in the cartoon. Do not include this descriptive part of the process in your answer. The question will normally ask 'What is the message in the cartoon?' Describing all of the images is not answering the question. In Source J what can you see? An African woman with a hoe in her hand who has been working on the land. She is wearing traditional African dress; her hand on the hip indicates that her attitude is one of dissatisfaction or frustration about something. This cartoon is unusual as it contains a great deal of text and the tone of what she is saying will help you to understand the message of the cartoon. The frustration has to do with the clash between ideal of 'universal brotherhood', which promises equality for all, and the reality of someone working in the fields. The woman is complaining that she has to grow cash crops to pay off Western companies rather than food crops to feed her children. She is also complaining that the amount that she has to produce is increasing every year to pay off the loans. Equality therefore has different meanings according to a person's position in society.

STUDENT STUDY SECTION

QUESTION
What is the message conveyed in Source J?

By 1985 wages were declining, inflation was running at 40 per cent, the peasants were abandoning the *ujamaa* villages and Tanzania was forced to devalue the shilling by 25 per cent in 1984. It was clear that Tanzania was approaching economic ruin, but Nyerere still refused to agree to the IMF's demands for change. Its GDP averaged about 1.7 per cent between 1980 and 1987 and its external debt had snowballed from $250 million in 1970 to approximately $3.7 billion in 1986. In the same year, Tanzania imported more than $1 billion worth of goods while its export earnings accounted for only $343 million (Yeagar, *Tanzania: An African Experiment*, 1989). It was only after Nyerere resigned the presidency in 1985 that the new President, Ali Hassan Mwinyi, realized that Tanzania had to change its policies. He agreed to adopt the measures required by the IMF in exchange for a massive injection of financial aid from foreign donor agencies.

SOURCE K

Tanzania – Economic indicators for 1967–84

	1967–73	1974–78	1979–81	1982–84
Growth rate of real GDP	5.2%	2.5	2.1	0.6
Growth rate of GDP per capita	2.5	-0.9	-1.1	-2.9
Growth rate of real output in agriculture	2.3	4.7	-1.0	1.8
Growth rate of real output in industry	7.8	4.7	-1.2	-9.9
Growth rate of exports	3.6	-6.8	7.1	-16.7
Growth rate of imports	3.6	2.8	14.3	-8.3

Source: Adapted from U. Lele, 'Agricultural Growth, Domestic Policies, the External Environment and Assistance to Africa. Lessons of a Quarter Century', 1989, in Kjell Havnevik, *Tanzania: The Limits to Development from Above*, 1993

STUDENT STUDY SECTION

QUESTION

Source K is extremely revealing. Take each row one by one and summarize in your own words what it shows. Then write a paragraph answering the following question – What does this source tell you about economic growth in Tanzania between 1967 and 1984?

Section IV:
Nyerere's social policies

In 1977, Nyerere made an assessment of how far Tanzania had progressed ten years after the announcement of the plans outlined in the Arusha Declaration. In particular, he pointed to some impressive achievements in the social sector as a result of the Second Five Year Plan. He reported that the number of children in primary education had risen from 825,000 in 1967 to 1,532,000 by 1975. He also commented that further improvements had occurred in 1976, with 665,621 children entering school for the first time compared to 187,537 in 1967. Nyerere further announced that 1.9 million people had passed a basic reading and writing test in August 1975, after taking part in a national programme to combat adult illiteracy. He then turned to health issues and pointed to an increase in the number of rural health centres, from 42 in 1967 to 152 in 1976. He also claimed that the average life expectancy in Tanzania had risen from 35–40 in 1961 to 47 in 1976.

Just before retiring in 1985, Nyerere proudly detailed his accomplishments as leader of Tanzania since 1961. He also summarized what improvements had been made in the life of Tanzanians, even since his interim report in 1977. The number of primary school enrolments had risen from 86,000 in 1961 to 3.6 million in 1985, an achievement that he considered was 'unmatched elsewhere in Africa'. Adult literacy now stood at 85 per cent, the highest in Africa. Life expectancy was over 50 as a result of dramatic improvements in a number of areas. There had been a significant increase in the number of qualified doctors available nationally; the number of hospitals had also increased; clean water was now far more widely available and infant mortality had been halved. Nyerere also reported that annual per capita income had more than doubled from $120 to $250 (see Yeagar, *Tanzania*).

Interestingly, a World Bank Report published in 1994 seemed to corroborate many of Nyerere's claims (see Source L).

SOURCE L

Expansion of the education sector between 1971 and 1991

Inputs and enrollees	1971	1981	1991
Civil servants working in education	21,131	93,318	101,042
Primary school enrollees	902,619	3,530.622	3,512,437
Secondary school enrollees	43,352	67,002	166,812
Students per civil servant	41	39	36

From Ministry of Education and Culture (Tanzania), *Tanzania Public Expenditure Review: The Role of Government*, World Bank, 1994

The figures quoted by Nyerere were similar to those published by the World Bank, which also showed that enrolments in secondary education had increased and that the number of teachers and support staff had increased markedly in Tanzania since the 1967 Arusha Declaration. The report also showed an impressive rise in the number of health centres and pharmaceutical dispensaries (see Source M).

SOURCE M

Expansion of the health sector in Tanzania between 1969 and 1992

Inputs	1969/70	1978/79	1992
Civil servants	12,400	17,036	32,650
Health centres	50	183	267
Dispensaries	1,444	2,282	2393
Civil servants per unit	8.7	6.6	12.3

From Ministry of Health (Tanzania), *Tanzania Public Expenditure Review: The Role of Government*, World Bank, 1994

Yet the World Bank report went on to say that, while acknowledging there had been improvements, there were still areas within the social sector of the country that had been neglected or had not been dealt with adequately by the government. It concluded that: 'None of the problems were insoluble. However the Government of Tanzania did relatively little to improve the situation during the 1980s… As a result the quality of most social services declined … textbooks and basic teaching materials were in short supply as were qualified and motivated teachers in rural primary schools.'

The findings of the report were corroborated by Kjell Havnevik: 'The quality of education deteriorated after the introduction of universal primary education in 1976. From the early 1980s onwards, lack of school books, pupils' desks, teachers' housing and poor school maintenance had eroded much of what Tanzania had gained during its first two decades of independence. From the early 1980s most rural health stations had only a very limited supply of medicine to offer, if any at all' (Havnevik, *Tanzania: The Limits to Development from Above*, 1993).

The report also commented on the issue of gender equality and access to education. Interestingly, the gross enrolment rate for girls in primary schools was found to be higher than that for boys, standing at about 81 per cent in 1991. However, it reported more negatively on equality for females within Tanzania, as a result of its traditional patriarchal and paternalistic society. It pointed to four areas of discrimination. Women were not usually allowed to own land as part of the household, as legally and practically it belonged to the male. Women could not inherit land either. Females were seldom put in charge of cash crops, being relegated to the providing of all food for the family. It also found that as the labour costs for women were higher due to maternity leave (12 weeks every three years under the Employment Act, with time off for breastfeeding as well), and as the number of children per family was high (on average 6.1), women were less likely to be hired than men. Finally it deplored the continual existence of a bride price (dowry) that had to be repaid by women in case of divorce.

At the end of 1985, in both economic and social terms, the quality of life for Tanzanians had made improvements, particularly in the areas of education and health, but it was still a long way from the achievements promised by Nyerere at Arusha. When questioned about *ujamaa* by Ikaweba Bunting, a journalist, in 1999, shortly before his death, Nyerere made the following comment: 'The Declaration is still valid: I would not change a thing… The Arusha Declaration was what made Tanzania distinctly Tanzania. We stated what we stood for, we laid down a code of conduct for our leaders and we made an effort to achieve our goals. This was obvious to all, even if we made mistakes – and when one tries anything new and uncharted there are bound to be mistakes' (Ikaweba Bunting, *New Internationalist Magazine*, Issue 309, January–February 1999).

SOURCE N

Cartoon by Kijasti (Nathan Mpangala) a Tanzanian artist, 2002.

STUDENT STUDY SECTION

QUESTION
What is the message in Source N?

Section V:
An assessment of Julius Nyerere

SOURCE A

'Julius Kambarage Nyerere', cartoon by Fred Halla, a Tanzanian artist, date not known.

STUDENT STUDY SECTION

QUESTION
What is the message conveyed by Source A? Is it complimentary or critical of Nyerere – or both? This type of question is worth two marks in the exam.

SOURCE B

Julius Kambarage 'Mwalimu' Nyerere was an outstanding leader, a brilliant philosopher and a people's hero – a champion for the entire African continent. He shall always be remembered as one of Africa's greatest and most respected sons and the father of the Tanzanian nation.

Throughout his long life he enjoyed respect and popularity that extended far beyond the borders of Tanzania. His wise counsel was sought from around the globe, even after he resigned from the presidency in 1985. A legacy in his own lifetime; he served as a symbol of inspiration for all African nations in their liberation struggles to free themselves from the shackles of oppression and colonialism.

From a statement by the African National Congress of South Africa, Johannesburg, 14 October 1999

SOURCE C

Nyerere No Great Leader, But Ensured Poverty For Tanzania
*Some would excuse his infantile utopianism and the lives it destroyed on the ground that his army overthrew Uganda's Idi Amin in 1979. Not much of an excuse, given that all Mwalimu did was reinstall Milton Obote, a creature just as vicious as Amin, if not quite as ostentatious a butcher. If Nyerere is really an exemplar of Africa's best, as **Albright** would have us believe, God help Africa. But then Albright probably did not have the faintest clue what she was talking about. What was this hero who would not, once in power, ever subject himself to a popular plebiscite and who relied upon westerners to keep his economy solvent? A traitor to Africa, I would say.*

From a South African daily newspaper, *Business Day*, by Simon Barber, October 27, 1999

 Madeleine Albright (b. 1937)
Madeleine Albright was US Secretary of State between 1997 and 2001. She was the first women to hold the office.

STUDENT STUDY SECTION

QUESTION
How can you reconcile the two totally contradictory viewpoints on Nyerere expressed in Sources B and C?

Julius Nyerere's leadership of Tanzania between 1961 and 1985 has, as you can see from the above comments, been viewed in many different ways. The majority of writers would see the means by which Nyerere led Tanzania to its independence from Britain as a major success. Contrary to many other African nations, the transition of power was peaceful and relatively smooth. It was accomplished in a very short time span as well. What is perhaps more impressive is that Tanzania is one of the very few countries in Africa that have been relatively stable politically since it became independent in 1961. Nyerere gave Tanzania a common language, a sense of unity and years of peace. It is also worth noting that Nyerere voluntarily relinquished the presidency in 1985, a rare action in 20th-century single-party states. Politically, Nyerere was a committed socialist and a Pan-African. His vision for Tanzania was clear for all to see in the 1967 Arusha Declaration, with its programme of education for self-reliance and the establishment of *ujamaa* villages. Nyerere was determined to try to make Tanzania more self-sufficient by utilizing what he saw as traditional African values.

 To access Worksheet 6.4 on assessments of Nyerere, please visit www. pearsonbacconline.com and follow the on-screen instructions.

But Nyerere's experiment in collectivization was ill-conceived and ultimately had a devastating effect on the Tanzanian nation; by 1985 the country was virtually bankrupt. The replacement of local communes by the overly bureaucratic and inefficient state-controlled parastatals and the forced relocation of millions of Tanzanians meant that Tanzania's agricultural production was unable to provide its people with either food crops or cash crops. Nyerere's dream of economic independence was over, as Tanzania plunged into debt and became almost totally dependent on foreign aid. As opposition to his policies increased and his political position became more precarious, Nyerere resorted to coercion and his single-party state began to resemble that of a dictatorship. He did not hesitate to use the Preventive Detention Act, which allowed him to lock up his opponents virtually at will.

In East African affairs, Nyerere was not entirely successful, as the EAC he helped to create collapsed in 1977. Nyerere's role in Africa was similarly controversial. His policies diverged from those of the OAU, the organization he had helped to form. In 1979, he rejected the principle of non-interference in the internal affairs of OAU member states, and sent the Tanzanian Army to end Idi Amin's regime in Uganda. Nyerere was prominent as a supporter of the liberation of southern Africa and allowed hundreds of thousands of refugees to enter Tanzania. An obituary in *The Nation*, a Kenyan newspaper, summarized Nyerere's accomplishments as follows:

SOURCE D

Most Western judges of Julius Nyerere have concentrated on his economic policies and their failures. Ujamaa and villagization have been seen as forces of economic retardation which kept Tanzania backward for at least another decade. Not enough commentators have paid attention to Nyerere's achievements in nation-building. He gave Tanzanians a sense of national consciousness and a spirit of national purpose.

The Nation, 17 October 1999

However, in 1996 Stanley Meisler made a slightly different assessment of Tanzania under Nyerere when he summed up the time period between 1961 and 1985. 'But the Tanzanian experiment offers good evidence that saints do not really make very good presidents' ('Saints and Presidents: A Commentary on Julius Nyerere', 1996).

● **Examiner's hint**
Make sure you know which single-party states you have studied are considered to be left wing and which right wing.

STUDENT STUDY SECTION

QUESTION

What do you think Meisler means by this statement? Explain it in your own words.

How would you use Tanzania under Nyerere to answer each of the following questions? Make a brief outline using bullet points to help you organize your essay.

QUESTIONS

a) **'Single-party states have rarely succeeded in providing economic and social benefits for their people.' With reference to at least two single-party states taken from two different regions, how far do you agree with this statement?**

b) **Compare and contrast the successes and failures of the leaders of one right-wing and one left-wing single-party state taken from two different regions.**

These are the sort of essay questions you can expect to see in Paper 2. You should have noticed that no country or leader is named, which means that you have to set up the essay in the introduction indicating which two single-party states you have selected. This is what makes Paper 2 so challenging, as you will only have 45 minutes in which to write your answer. In both of these questions, a thematic rather than a chronological approach will be more successful. For each of the questions identify the single-party states you will choose and select three or four themes, each of which will be the basis of a paragraph in your essay. Your essay will therefore have either five or six paragraphs – an introduction, three or four themed paragraphs and a conclusion. Now have a look at the following question.

QUESTION

'In order to achieve and retain power, a leader of a single-party state needs to be ruthless, blind to human suffering and yet charismatic.' To what extent do you agree with this statement when evaluating Nyerere as leader of Tanzania between 1961 and 1985?

This is the type of question that scares students when they see it in an IB exam. They take one look at it during the reading time and then quickly try to find another question. In fact, this question is much easier than the two you have already looked at. Why? Because the single-party state is already identified for you. It could have been Castro, Stalin, Mao or any other single-party state – but this question has chosen to focus on Nyerere. Another reason why this type of question is relatively straightforward is that the essay structure is already set. There must, by definition, be an introduction and a conclusion to any IB History essay and the three paragraphs that you must focus on will deal with Nyerere's rise to power and consolidation of power, examining whether or not he was 'ruthless', 'blind to human suffering' or 'charismatic'. A great deal of the hard work is already done for you.

REVIEW SECTION

This chapter has examined the rise to power of Julius Nyerere and his years as the leader of Tanzania between 1961 and 1985. It has focused on the following five points:

- How Nyerere rose to power and established a single-party state.
- An analysis of how Nyerere consolidated his power after Tanganyika's independence from Britain.
- The nature, implementation and consequences of the types of policies that Nyerere introduced, both domestic and foreign.
- •The nature of the opposition that Nyerere faced and an analysis of how he dealt with it.
- How historians' assessments of Nyerere have differed over time.

7

GAMAL ABDEL NASSER AND EGPYT

◀ Gamal Abdel Nasser

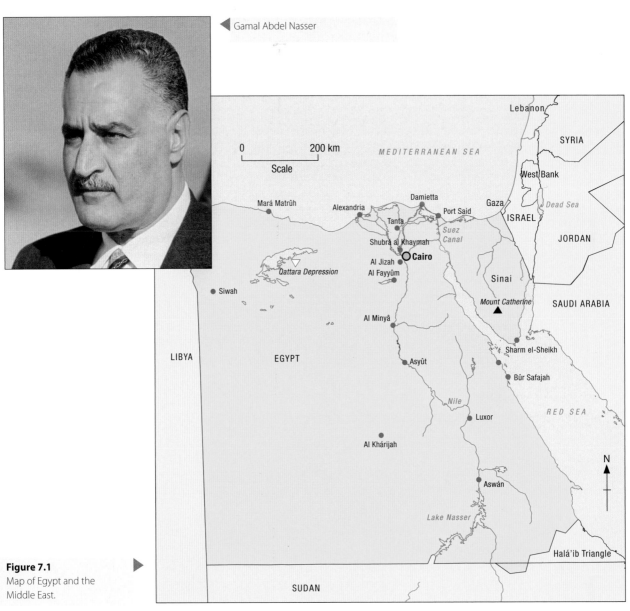

Figure 7.1
Map of Egypt and the Middle East.

This chapter will focus on the rise to power and the rule of Gamal Abdel Nasser, the President of Egypt from 1955 until his death in 1970. A hugely charismatic leader, Nasser was an avowed anti-imperialist and a strong supporter of Egyptian and Arab nationalism. The chapter will give background information on: Egypt prior to the coup that brought Nasser and the Free Officers to power in 1952; the emergence of Nasser as the sole leader of Egypt; and the introduction of his own brand of 'Arab Socialism' that included land reform and some state ownership of industry. Extracts from both primary and secondary sources will be included, as well as maps, cartoons and photographs along with samples of student work and hints on how to use Nasser as an example of a single-party leader for IB exam questions.

1918	Gamal Abdel Nasser is born on 15 January in Alexandria.
1926	Fahima Mahad, Nasser's mother, dies while Nasser is away at school.
1936	Nasser is involved in an anti-British demonstration in Cairo; the Anglo-Egyptian Treaty is signed with Britain.
1937	Nasser completes his schooling at Nahda School in Cairo; Nasser is admitted to the Military College in Cairo.
1939	World War II breaks out in Europe.
1948	The first Arab–Israeli conflict breaks out.
1949	The Free Officers' Movement is set up by Nasser and like-minded army officers.
1952	The Free Officers carry out a military coup; King Farouk leaves for exile in Europe; in July a government is set up with General Mohammad Naguib as President.
1953	The monarchy is abolished; Egypt becomes a republic.
1954	An assassination attempt on Nasser fails; President Naguib is removed from office, and then reinstated; Nasser becomes Prime Minister; a new treaty is signed with Britain regarding the Suez Canal.
1955	Nasser becomes President.
1956	Nasser nationalizes the Suez Canal, resulting in an international crisis.
1958	The United Arab Republic (UAR) is established with Syria.
1962	Nasser introduces the National Charter.
1967	The Six Day War ends with the defeat of Egypt and the loss of Sinai and Gaza to Israel.
1969	The War of Attrition leads to continual low-level conflict in Sinai.
1970	Nasser dies of a heart attack on 28 September.

Section I:
Origins and nature of authoritarian and single-party states – Nasser and Egypt

Nasser was the first Egyptian leader of Egypt since the time of the pharaohs. As Anthony Nutting, one of Nasser's best known biographers, states, 'After two and a half thousand years of taking orders successively from Persian, Greek, Roman, Byzantine, Arab, Kurdish, Turkish, French and British pro-consuls, the people of Egypt were at long last to regain their national statehood' (*Nasser*, 1972).

Although this chapter will examine the rise to power of Nasser, and analyze the methods by which he consolidated his control over Egypt, it will begin with an overview of the political events that shaped the development of Nasser's political philosophy.

A brief overview of Egypt up to 1945

Egypt before and after World War I

Nominally a part of the Ottoman Empire, Egypt was a **British protectorate**. The British Governor was hugely influential in Egyptian politics alongside a ruling class whose origins were Turkish rather than Egyptian. In 1914, the outbreak of World War I led to a crisis in which Turkey allied itself with Germany and declared war on Britain. To secure its position, Britain declared Egypt a British protectorate, although in practice the same dynasty of Turkish rulers continued to occupy the throne. By the end of the war, as in so many other 'colonies', Egyptian nationalism was given a boost by the ideology outlined in President Wilson's Fourteen Points embraced at the Paris Peace Conference of 1919.

British protectorate
Egypt became a protectorate of the British government in 1882. This action was prompted by a nationalist uprising that threatened the rule of the Sultan (Khedive) Taufiq Pasha. The British government did not want direct rule over Egypt or to make it into a British colony, but wanted to ensure its stability, as this was crucial for British control over the strategically important Suez Canal. The method of government chosen was that of a 'protectorate', which ensured influence but without removing the ruling family.

Fourteen Points

In January, 1919, President Woodrow Wilson of the USA made a speech in which he described Fourteen Points outlining the landscape of post-war Europe. Among them was the right of self-determination. Although this was not to be applied to the colonial states of the European powers, Egyptian nationalists were nevertheless keen to try to gain independence from Britain.

A group of nationalists, led by Saad Zaghlul, planned to go to Paris to plead the case for Egyptian independence. This, in 1919, was the beginning of the Wafd Party, a name derived from *al-wafd al-misry* meaning 'Egyptian delegtion'. At first, Zaghlul was forbidden from leaving Egypt, but this decision was revoked after a series of strikes and demonstrations by his supporters. In Paris, rather predictably, Britain proved unsympathetic to calls for early Egyptian independence.

Egyptian independence

In February 1922, however, Egypt was given recognition by Britain as a sovereign state with a constitutional monarchy. The nephew of Khedive Abbas was crowned as King Fuad and a new constitution, drawn up in 1923, allowed the King to appoint the Prime Minister, dismiss his ministers and, if he so wished, to dissolve parliament. Full independence was limited, however, by four provisions:

- Britain retained control of 'imperial communications' (Robert Stephens, *Nasser*, 1971), which effectively meant the **Suez Canal**.
- Britain had the right to defend Egypt in the event of an invasion, which meant it could continue to have its army stationed there.
- Britain had the right to defend the rights of foreigners and minorities.
- Britain had the right to determine the status of **Sudan**.

The Wafd Party grew in popularity, but was limited in its influence not only by the British High Commissioner (the highest-ranking British official now that Egypt was officially independent) but also the King, who suspended the constitution and ruled by decree. Stephens comments on how the political landscape in Egypt revolved around the three power blocs of the King, the British and the Wafdists. In addition, the 'Young Egypt' (*Misr el Fatat*) movement – or 'Green Shirts', as they became known – conducted paramilitary parades in support of the King.

To add to the mix, a new party, the **Muslim Brotherhood**, was established in 1928. Founded by Hassan el-Banna, the Sheikh (leader) of the al-Azhar University in Cairo, it was both a nationalist and an Islamic party. Its manifesto demanded the restoration of the Islamic Caliphate, to be based in Cairo, and for a 'holy war' to be declared against the British.

STUDENT STUDY SECTION

QUESTION
After reading the first part of this chapter, what had the Egyptian nationalists achieved by the end of the 1920s and what obstacles did they continue to face?

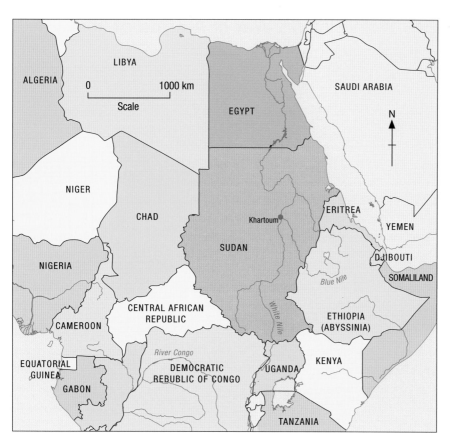

Figure 7.2
Map of north-east Africa.

The Italian invasion of Abyssinia

Under the leadership of Mussolini, Italy invaded Abyssinia in 1935. This ancient Christian kingdom was the only independent nation in Africa, although Italy had attempted to occupy it in 1896 from its neighbouring colonies in Eritrea and Somaliland. The League of Nations applied sanctions in response to Italy's invasion, but the Italians fought a cruel and bitter campaign and defeated Abyssinia in 1936. The British did not oppose Mussolini with any real determination because they were concerned about the emergence of Nazi Germany and feared driving Italy into the arms of Hitler.

King Farouk, Queen Narriman and Crown Prince Ahmed Fuad II. King Farouk had divorced his first wife, the popular Queen Farida, an event that added to his unpopularity by the time of his abdication.

The Anglo-Egyptian Treaty of 1936

Following the death of King Fuad in 1936, there were increasingly strident calls for the restoration of the 1923 constitution. King Fuad was succeeded by his young nephew, Farouk, who was studying at a boarding school in England at the time. Concerns about growing threats to peace in Europe and the **Italian invasion of Abyssinia** contributed to British readiness to negotiate a treaty with the Wafd Party, which had won the election in 1936. This 'treaty of alliance', as it came to be known, guaranteed the right to station up to 10,000 British troops in the Canal Zone for at least another 20 years; allowed Egyptian troops to be stationed in the Sudan; and permitted Egypt to become a member of the League of Nations.

Most sources refer to this treaty as a false dawn for Egyptian independence, as Britain continued to occupy the country. Certainly, many nationalists were disappointed by the negotiations that had been led by the Wafd Party and, as we shall see, a schoolboy by the name of Gamal Abdel Nasser was among those who demonstrated their opposition. The Wafd Party's negotiations with the British made them less popular, but boosted the public approval of the young King Farouk, who succeeded to the throne shortly before the treaty was signed and was widely believed to be a nationalist. The Muslim Brotherhood, who took a strongly anti-British stance, also gained popular support.

Egypt and World War II: A state of limited independence

World War II began in 1939, and the European conflict spread to North Africa in 1940 when Italian forces launched an attack on the British in Egypt. German reinforcements drove the British back to El Alamein before that siege was lifted in 1943. Many Egyptian nationalists supported the Germans in the hope that they would finally get rid of the British. A political crisis in 1942, however, led to the British High Commissioner, Sir Miles Lampson, insisting that King Farouk appoint the Wafdist, pro-British Nahas Pasha as Prime Minister. Although there was tacit agreement to the appointment, the government protested that this act challenged the independence of Egypt. British tanks surrounded the palace and the King was told either to agree or to abdicate. This episode, known as the Abdin Palace coup, not only humiliated the King but also gave the impression that the Wafdists were no more than puppets of the British. Was Egypt a sovereign state or was it a British colony? This was the question asked by a group of army officers, including Gamal Abdel Nasser. There were further stirrings of rebellion in the army when General Mohammad Naguib wrote to King Farouk stating, 'I am ashamed to wear my uniform … and request permission to resign.'

It was not until 1945 that Egypt officially declared war on Germany and Japan, partially in order to gain a seat in the United Nations. So Egypt ended the war 'neither victor nor vanquished nor neutral' (Stephens, *Nasser*, 1971). The declaration of war was widely disliked and resulted in the assassination of Prime Minister Aly Maher by a young nationalist lawyer. There was considerable frustration at being theoretically independent but, in practice, still subject to a domineering Britain.

Section II:

The rise to power: Conditions that produced a single-party state

Nasser's early years

Gamal Abdel Nasser was born on 15 January 1918, in Alexandria. His father came from the south of Egypt (or Upper Egypt) and was a low- to middle-level civil servant. His mother came from a better-off family, and she had been born and brought up in Alexandria. Nasser, therefore, had family connections in both **Upper and Lower Egypt**, although he is often described as having the physique and the temperament of his father's people.

In 1924, at the age of six, Nasser went to live with his uncle so that he could attend primary school. Two years later, his mother passed away and, according to his biographers, the loss of a deeply loved parent had a lasting impact upon the boy. When his father remarried in 1928, Nasser went to stay with his grandparents in Cairo before returning to live with his father in Alexandria a year later. His ambition was to join the army, a career that had become possible for a young man from a humble background only after the Treaty of 1936, when the British government agreed to an expanded Egyptian Army being placed under the command of its own officers. At first, Nasser's application to enter the Military Academy was unsuccessful. This rejection was possibly because he lacked the social connections still required of the less well-off, or perhaps because he had a police record from when he was arrested in 1936 for participating in an anti-British demonstration. Before he made another application to the Academy, Nasser approached the Secretary of State, Ibrahim Kheiry Pasha, who gave him his support. This tale, along with other anecdotes, is mentioned by many of Nasser's biographers, who also relate how he devoured books on military strategy and the lives of great warriors from Alexander the Great to Napoleon. Interestingly, in his biography of Nasser, Robert Stephens emphasizes that Nasser was 'not so much a soldier who went into politics as a politician who went into the army' (Stephens, *Nasser*, 1971).

A photograph of Captain Gamal Abdel Nasser in the Egyptian Army.

Note on sources
There are rather limited sources available on the life of Nasser, and many depend on each other, so the same stories are repeated by several biographers. Given that the anecdotes tend to be rather flattering, it is best to be rather cautious in their use and to be aware of the limitations as well as the value of these sources.

ToK Time
It is said that Nasser, like two other single-party leaders, Stalin and Hitler, was deeply attached to his mother. Do you think that studying the psychology of single-party leaders helps us to understand them better? How important is it to historians that the three leaders mentioned above were said to have adored their mothers but had cool, even unfriendly relations with their fathers? How far, do you think, is this kind of information useful to an historical assessment of the careers of these leaders?

The Free Officers' Movement

Nasser rose quickly within the army and had been promoted to captain by 1942, when he became involved in what would become the Free Officers' Movement. This organization, if it can be referred to as such in 1942, arose out of frustration with the failure of the King and the government of Egypt to stand up to the British. Although its members, who were army officers, wanted King Farouk to be more assertive towards the British, they were also careful to remain loyal. This, they hoped, would widen their support base in the army and among a population that was mostly pro-monarchist.

The Muslim Brotherhood was also vocal in their opposition to the British, although they, too, supported the King. Said Aburish describes the group as 'right wing' and says that its members '…did not object to the ways of the King and the landlords, provided they toed an Islamic line' (*Nasser: The Last Arab*, 2004). Another political faction with communist leanings that came to the fore at this time was the **Democratic Movement for National Liberation (DMNL)**.

The ideology of the Free Officers was fairly moderate or, as Aburish suggests, both 'diluted' and 'naïve'. Their Six Point Plan, as it was known, can be summed up as follows:

- The liquidation of colonialism and the Egyptian traitors who supported it.
- The end of domination of power by wealth.

The DMNL
The Democratic Movement for National Liberation united the Egyptian Movement for National Liberation with Iskra. Both parties had been set up in 1943 and both were communist. The DMNL was also known by its Arabic acronym, Haditu.

- The liquidation of **feudalism**.
- The establishment of social equality.
- The building up of a powerful army.
- The establishment of free elections and a healthy democratic atmosphere.

SOURCE A

But at the outset, Nasser's aims and ambitions were strictly limited to the eviction of the British. Far from being directed against the throne, his initial object was, so he subsequently told me, to try to put some stuffing into the King and, by creating a militant opposition to British imperialism within the army, to strengthen Farouk's resistance to further encroachments on Egypt's sovereignty. Neither Nasser nor any of his fellow conspirators had any love for the King as a man, still less for the corrupt palace clique…

From Anthony Nutting, *Nasser*, 1972

STUDENT STUDY SECTION

QUESTIONS

a) **In Source A, Nutting writes 'so he subsequently told me', indicating that his information came directly from Nasser. How does this affect the reliability of this source?**

b) **So far, this chapter has mentioned three different 'nationalist' groups in Egyptian politics: the Wafd Party; the Muslim Brotherhood; and the Free Officers' Movement. How would you explain their similarities and also their differences?**

Post-war Egypt

Social and economic conditions

Egypt had suffered badly in the economic depression during the 1930s and most of its population lived at just above the poverty level. Robert Stephens in *Nasser* notes that the average per capita income was £42 p.a. or one-tenth of what it was in Britain at this time. Farmers earned an average income of £22 p.a. and landless labourers, whose income was also dependent on seasonal work, earned an average of £7 p.a. (All amounts are given in Egyptian pounds.) Fewer than 6 per cent of landowners owned 65 per cent of all cultivable land and the remaining 94 per cent owned just 35 per cent. More than 77 per cent of the population over five years old was illiterate and life expectancy was just 36 years, compared with 69 years for American males at this time. In an attempt to escape the poverty of the countryside, peasants would go to the cities, where they lived in sprawling slums. Living conditions were poor and lack of housing led to overcrowding, especially as the urban population started to increase. Workers' rights were almost non-existent and trade unions were either controlled by the state or banned. The gap between the lives of the rich and the poor was enormous and Stephens compares conditions with those of pre-revolutionary France.

In addition to the tension that arose from economic hardship, there was always the shadow of an ever-present imperialism. Economically, World War II brought some prosperity to Egypt, but after it was over, the economy faltered, unemployment increased and there was increasing discontent with the government. The balance of payments deficit in 1952 was £38 million and there was a budget deficit of £81 million.

Political conditions

Inevitably, demands for complete independence were voiced again once the war was over. Mahmoud Fahmi al-Nuqrashi, the Prime Minister, called for a re-negotiation of the Treaty of 1936 and the complete withdrawal of British troops. In addition to this, there was a call for the unification of Sudan with Egypt, a subject very dear to the hearts of the nationalists and the King, who included 'King of Sudan' among his titles. According to Stephens, the British did not respond enthusiastically to these proposals and believed that the invasion of Egypt by the Axis Powers in 1940 more than justified the cautious terms of the 1936 treaty. Popular demonstrations broke out and in 1946, at the Abbas Bridge in Cairo, 170 casualties resulted from a clash with police. Amid this tense atmosphere, Anglo-Egyptian talks began under the leadership of Ismail Sidky Pasha, the new Prime Minister.

Post-war Palestine and the 1948 Arab–Israeli War

The British mandate over Palestine was returned to the United Nations (UN) in 1947, but events were unfolding that would have an impact throughout the Middle East and would soon culminate in the first Arab–Israeli conflict. Discussions at the UN in November 1947 led to the partition of Palestine into an Arab and a Jewish state, but with direct UN control over Jerusalem. The birth of Israel in May 1948 led, almost immediately, to conflict with the **Arab League**. Said Aburish claims that King Farouk seized this opportunity to pose as King of all the Arabs, partially to divert attention away from economic problems in Egypt.

For Nasser, this first taste of war was a formative experience. The King, it seemed, cared little for the lives of his soldiers, who were ill-equipped and badly led by high-ranking officers often promoted not for their military skill but because of family connections. In 1949, Egypt retreated from a humiliating war that established the statehood of Israel but not Palestine. In the opinion of the anti-imperialist Nasser, the outcome of the war had been decided not on the field of battle but in the corridors of Washington, Paris and London where, he suspected, decisions had been made to support Israel (Stephens, *Nasser*, 1971).

Nasser's biographers agree that the 1948 war was an important step in the radicalization of the Free Officers' Movement with its aim to '…uphold the honour of the army and to liberate Egypt'. Political tension worsened in December 1948, when a member of the Muslim Brotherhood assassinated Prime Minister al-Nuqrashi, who had returned to power. His successor, Ibrahim Abdel Hadi, called for the suppression of the Brotherhood. When elections were held in 1950, it was the Wafd Party that won and Mustafa Nahhas became Prime Minister. Calm was not restored, however, and although, on the surface, the Free Officers shared many of the same aims as the Wafdists, the army's frustration remained. The **Tripartite Agreement** placed a ban on the purchase of arms by Egypt and this added to its humiliation and sense of injustice.

The coup of 1952

A failure to reach an agreement with the British government over the continued presence of British troops in Egypt led to the 'abrogation' of the 1936 treaty by Prime Minister Nahas Pasha in October 1951. The British government responded with a proposal to replace the treaty with a Middle East Defence Organization (MEDO), of which Egypt would be a founding member. This was intended to be the equivalent of the North Atlantic Treaty Organization (NATO), but specifically for the Middle East. It was rejected by the Egyptian government, who saw it as a proposal for the occupation of the Canal Zone not by one power (Britain) but by four (USA, Britain, France and Turkey).

A policy of non-cooperation with the British followed, with a boycott imposed on the use of Egyptian labour in the Canal Zone and a refusal to allow the movement of supplies. Conflict with the British troops in the Canal Zone erupted in Ismailia when General Erskine, the British Army commander in the region, ordered tanks to fire on the headquarters of auxiliary police suspected of supporting 'liberation commandos' or guerrilla fighters. As well as three British soldiers, 41 auxiliary policemen were killed and 71 wounded. This excessive use of force caused public outrage, and demonstrations in Cairo led to widespread unrest. The 25th of January 1952 became known as 'Black Saturday', as more than 700 buildings were attacked or looted and an estimated 17 Europeans and 50 Egyptians were killed. Afraid of 'turning the clock back seventy years' (Stephens, *Nasser*, 1971), the British ambassador held off calling in British troops. The King, unsure of the loyalty of his officers, also hesitated before finally calling in the army to restore order. 'The King, the Wafd and the British who between them had ruled Egypt for the previous thirty years had now between them made Egypt ungovernable' (Stephens, *Nasser*, 1971).

Stephens maintains that the army now became the most powerful element in Egyptian politics, as the Free Officers met to plan a coup that would remove the King from power. The Free Officers were encouraged by elections on 6 January 1952 for the President and Committee of the Army Officers' Club in Cairo. The King had put forward his own candidate for the presidency, but it was General Mohammad Naguib, the candidate of the Free Officers, who won a resounding victory.

After the debacle of Black Saturday, Prime Minister Nahas Pasha was dismissed, but his three successors lacked the confidence of either the government or the King. The last of these, Hussein Sirry, appointed General Naguib as the Minister of War, but the King insisted on the appointment of General Hussein Sirry Amer. Yet another Prime Minister was appointed and he chose the King's brother-in-law, Colonel Ismail Sherin, as Minister of War. Measures were put in place to get rid of the Free Officers, whom the King dismissed as 'that bunch of pimps'. All of these events brought matters to a head and the Free Officers conducted a coup on the evening of 22 July 1952.

When asked to abdicate in favour of his baby son, King Farouk agreed and prepared to leave for exile in Europe. At the port of Alexandria, the King embarked on the royal yacht along with his young wife, baby son, three daughters and large quantities of luggage. It had been agreed that he could take this last voyage aboard the royal yacht but, as it was the property of the Egyptian people, it would have to return as soon as its royal passengers disembarked at Naples. King Farouk also took with him gold from the Bank of Egypt, although this was not discovered until after he had left. In his place, a Regency Council was appointed to govern until the Crown Prince was old enough to succeed to the throne. This Council was composed of: Brigadier Rashad Muhana, sympathetic to the Muslim Brotherhood; Bahieddine Barakat Pasha, a judge and member of an aristocratic family; and Prince Mohammad Abdel Munim. In reality, the Revolutionary Command Council (RCC), composed of members of the Free Officers' Movement, was now in charge.

Why was the coup successful?

Black Saturday had shown that there was considerable discontent amongst the Egyptian people, and that the King and his government were not confident about using the army to suppress popular demonstrations. Reasons for the coup's success included:

- The Muslim Brotherhood and the Wafdists agreed not to oppose the coup.
- The British and the USA did not oppose the coup and agreed to the removal of King Farouk.

- The Free Officers had the support of General Mohammad Naguib, who was well known and had widespread support among the population.
- The King, widely seen as a corrupt and decadent monarch, did not have the support needed to oppose the coup.
- The population in general welcomed a government that they hoped would finally remove British occupation of the Canal Zone, improve social and economic conditions and restore national pride.
- This was not a legal revolution! Unlike many other single-party leaders, Nasser and the Free Officers were part of a political/military faction that used the threat of force to persuade a monarch to abdicate.
- Nasser was adamant that the role of the RCC was that of a 'commando vanguard' to rule as a '…guardian for a definite period of time.'

Because of the 1948 war, Nasser had been able to set up the Free Officers' Movement and these soldiers wanted to help to get rid of feudalism in Egypt. What they meant by this was that there was a class of people who were very rich and who also managed to win elections. Nasser thought that because of this, the system would never change unless the poor people were helped to improve their lives. King Farouk was also unpopular and the Free Officers thought it was important to get rid of him although, at first, they were not sure if they would have enough support to do this.

Examiner's comments

Jenny has rushed into her second paragraph and does not seem to have planned very effectively. Here she mentions not only the living conditions of the people but also the 1948 war and the unpopularity of King Farouk. She could have linked them together but does not do so, and so it appears to be a list rather than a combination of facts and analysis. Also, she fails to mention whether she is discussing 'conditions' or 'methods'.

Student Sample B – *Iris* (this is also the second paragraph of Iris' essay)

Among the conditions that Nasser and the Free Officers were able to use to come to power in 1952 were the poor living conditions of the vast majority of the people in Egypt. In the countryside, less than 6 per cent of the landowners owned 65 per cent of all cultivable land, there was a 77 per cent illiteracy rate and the life expectancy was just 36 years. This meant that for most people, life was very hard. In their Six Point Plan, Nasser and the Free Officers spoke about ending what they called 'feudalism' and they now set about gathering support for political change. This proved to be a very effective method as there was considerable discontent with the way the King and the leading politicians were linked to corruption and an extravagant lifestyle.

Examiner's comments

Iris has written a well-focused paragraph that has good use of supporting evidence and links economic conditions to the methods of the Free Officers. The terms 'conditions' and 'methods' are used and so an examiner would be reminded that Iris knew what the question was asking. There could be a little more on why there was discontent with the political system, but this paragraph suggests that the essay will be focused, analytical and well supported with relevant evidence.

● **Examiner's hint**

Exam questions on Paper 2, Topic 3, will often ask for comparisons and contrasts. If, for instance, you consider the rise to power of a single-party leader, are there comparisons to be made with similar events elsewhere. In Egypt in 1952, it could be said that you have the following conditions:

● Defeat in a war
● Rejection of colonialism
● An unpopular monarch
● Complaints about corruption
● The need for radical land reform
● The lack of organization of the government
● Failure to introduce social and economic reform

Do some or all of these conditions also apply in the cases of other single-party leaders you have studied?

As with most revolutions, there will always be people who feel that the level of change has been insufficient or incomplete. In August 1952, communist groups, who had hoped for changes similar to those of October 1917 in Russia, led riots in the port city of Alexandria. In some cases, soviets were set up in factories and, after these were suppressed, the leaders were arrested and two were condemned to death. The application of the death penalty was a serious matter and Nasser, along with a few of his colleagues, protested that this punishment was too harsh, but they were in a minority on the RCC. After the two leaders were hanged, the Communist Party withdrew its support from the RCC.

Despite having earlier described the Free Officers' Movement as 'the blessed movement', the Muslim Brotherhood had withdrawn their support from the RCC by October 1952, when their hopes for an Islamic constitution had not been fulfilled and their request for four ministerial positions in the government had been rejected.

The military coup that took place in 1952 was not a legal method of taking power. The threat of violence was used to intimidate the King into leaving and to impose the authority of the Free Officers on the government. Eric Hobsbawm, the British historian, wrote about the nature of military involvement in revolutions in his book *Revolutionaries*, and noted

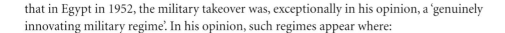

that in Egypt in 1952, the military takeover was, exceptionally in his opinion, a 'genuinely innovating military regime'. In his opinion, such regimes appear where:

SOURCE B

the necessity of social revolution is evident, where several of the objective conditions of it are present, but also where the social bases or institutions of civilian life are too feeble to carry it out. The armed forces, being in some cases the only available force with the capacity to take and carry out decisions, may have to take the place of the absent civilian forces, even to the point of turning their officers into administrators.

From Eric Hobsbawm, *Revolutionaries*, 2007

STUDENT STUDY SECTION

QUESTIONS

a) Can you think of other occasions when military coups provided the base for a single-party state?

b) How far would you agree with Hobsbawm that these take place where civilian institutions are 'too feeble' to carry out necessary social change?

c) Eric Hobsbawm is a Marxist historian: in what way(s) does knowing this make a difference to how you respond to his opinions?

Domestic policies up to 1955

Economic change – land reform

The Free Officers were determined that land reform was essential to improve Egypt's impoverished, agrarian economy. Out of a population of around 22 million, 16 million Egyptians were dependent upon farming and land shortage was a significant problem, especially with rapid population growth. There were calls to end what the Free Officers' Six Points had termed 'feudalism', but was Egypt really a 'feudal' country? In the following source, Anne Alexander argues that it was not.

SOURCE C

At an economic level, Egyptian agriculture was anything but feudal. It was highly capitalised, mechanised and well-integrated into the world economy. At a social and political level, the officers' campaign against 'feudalism' struck a chord with millions of Egyptians. As a contemporary observer noted: 'when an Egyptian economist was asked what he meant by a feudal estate, he replied, "It means that the landowner keeps a private army to defend his house and his person; and that armed men stand guard over the crops."'

From Anne Alexander, *Nasser*, 2005

STUDENT STUDY SECTION

QUESTIONS

a) What does this source tell you about the way 'feudalism' was perceived in Egypt?

b) Why, do you think, did the Free Officers use the term 'feudalism'?

The Free Officers were not the first group to attempt land reform in Egypt, as attempts had been made to pass bills through parliament in the 1940s. These were intended to limit the size of farms, but the King, as the owner of large estates, had not wanted land reform and neither had the Wafdists, who represented the middle class. The extent of the reforms was rather modest, however, although both prominent Marxists and the US government had been consulted on how the reforms should be carried out. Ultimately, only 10 per cent of cultivable land was set aside for redistribution and large landowners could keep up to 300 *feddans* (acres) as well as being compensated for any land that was expropriated. Anne Alexander notes that only between 15 and 20 families had land taken away from them and royal estates alone accounted for one-third of all expropriations. Nevertheless, this was a highly symbolic reform and was a very important method to show that the Free Officers meant to push through social and economic change.

Political change – the road to a single-party state and a republic

The Liberation Rally

The Wafd Party, the Muslim Brotherhood and the communists were still popular political parties in Egypt and, initially, the RCC had intended to include what they called 'purged' parties to be part of the government. By January 1953, however, all political parties with the exception of the Muslim Brotherhood (whose religious affiliation made it too sensitive to be treated too harshly) were abolished, along with independent trade unions and student political groups. In their place, the Liberation Rally was set up to become a mass movement of the people. Nasser became its Secretary-General and he promised that the Rally would deliver 'unity, discipline and work' (Alexander, *Nasser*, 2005). This was to give Nasser a strong position from which to launch his own bid for power.

The Philosophy of Revolution

By 1953, Nasser, the leading member of the Free Officers' Movement, if not its public figurehead, was grappling with the challenge of how to achieve social and economic change in Egypt. He saw the dangers of a military government evolving into a dictatorship and expressed his determination that the military officers should only lead the way. Stephens notes, however, that Nasser 'had been dismayed to find that the masses did not follow the army's desperate charge but hung back as onlookers' (*Nasser*, 1971). In his 'manifesto' **The Philosophy of Revolution**, which was written in 1953 and published in 1954, Nasser spoke of his concern that creating a truly democratic system was proving difficult in a land where a class system was so entrenched. Over the next 17 years, he would struggle to turn Egypt into a state where his vision of political freedom and economic progress could be realized. Nasser also wrote about his view that Egypt was central to the Arab, African and Islamic worlds. These three, he argued, were linked together and Egypt played a role that went beyond its national borders. According to Aburish, this was a hint of the role Nasser would aspire to a few years later as that of a pan-Arab leader suggesting that, in this case, ideology preceded action.

The Philosophy of Revolution

Said Aburish claims that it was Nasser's close friend, the journalist Mohammad Heikal, who actually wrote *The Philosophy of Revolution* and that he was 'an ardent Arab nationalist, (*Nasser*, 2004), which is why this booklet signalled a shift away from Egyptian to pan-Arab nationalism.

The abolition of the monarchy and the entry of Nasser into the government

In the summer of 1953, the monarchy was abolished and Egypt officially became a republic. General Naguib became President and Prime Minister. Nasser now entered the government as Deputy Prime Minister, and his close friend, Abdel Hakim Amer, became commander-

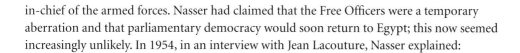

in-chief of the armed forces. Nasser had claimed that the Free Officers were a temporary aberration and that parliamentary democracy would soon return to Egypt; this now seemed increasingly unlikely. In 1954, in an interview with Jean Lacouture, Nasser explained:

SOURCE D

In a year and a half we have been able to wipe out corruption. If the right to vote were now restored, the same landowners would be elected – the feudal interests. We don't want the capitalists and the wealthy back in power. If we open the government to them now, the revolution might just as well be forgotten.

Nasser quoted in Anne Alexander, *Nasser*, 2005

STUDENT STUDY SECTION

QUESTION

In this source, Nasser seems to be saying that the Free Officers have to stay in control because to give up power now would imperil the whole revolution. Can you think of other single-party leaders who would have used a similar excuse to justify their refusal to relinquish power? You might like to turn to the ToK chapter to see how different single-party leaders wrestled with the problem of appearing democratic when such a political system could not be guaranteed to support their policies.

Nasser – steps to power

Step one: Naguib is undermined

By 1954, Nasser was growing in confidence and was less prepared to wait patiently for reforms that seemed too radical for President Naguib. There were growing divisions that Anne Alexander in *Nasser* summarizes as follows:

- Naguib wanted a return to parliamentary democracy, but Nasser did not.
- Naguib wanted better relations with the Muslim Brotherhood, but Nasser did not.
- Naguib wanted an end to military rule in Egypt, but Nasser wanted to continue to use the army to achieve his goals.
- Naguib called the events of July 1952 a 'coup', but Nasser called them a 'revolution'.

In February 1954, Naguib offered his resignation, having lost the struggle for support within the RCC. His resignation was accepted because, it was claimed, he had wanted to establish a dictatorship.

SOURCE E

We had to break with Naguib who aimed at dictatorship, criticised in public and to foreigners decisions that had been made by a majority, and with no thought but his own popularity, played a double game by coming to an understanding with the opposition.

Salah Salem, a member of the RCC, quoted in Anne Alexander, *Nasser*, 2005

It was not so easy to remove a popular President, however, and crucially there was a pro-Naguib faction within the army. Aware of the dangers posed by this group, the reinstatement of Naguib was agreed to by Nasser, but with himself as Prime Minister.

Step two: Popular unrest is used to call for change

Nasser had suffered a temporary setback by reinstating Naguib, but he did not give up. On 25 March, Nasser made a speech in which he pledged: to restore parliamentary government by July 1954; to lift the ban on political parties; to end censorship; and to facilitate the gradual release of political prisoners. 'The Council of the Revolution will surrender its powers to a constituent assembly on 24 July 1954, at which time it will declare the end of the Egyptian revolution.'

As anticipated by Nasser, this caused consternation among many sections of the Egyptian population, especially those who supported the Liberation Rally and feared that democracy would lead to the return of pre-revolutionary social and political elites. Nasser now used his position as Secretary-General of the Liberation Rally to organize strikes and demonstrations that called for the continuation of the revolution. He was supported not only by workers in the cities, but also by peasants who feared the end of land reform and members of the middle class who wanted the continuation of strong government.

Step three: Nasser's response to attempted assassination

A crucial event was the attempted assassination of Nasser in October 1954 by Mahmud Abdul Latif of the Muslim Brotherhood. A swift crackdown followed with, according to Aburish, as many as 700 members of the Brotherhood rounded up, although Stephens quotes the official figure as having been 1,800. After being tried in a hastily established 'People's Court', eight of the conspirators were sentenced to death and six of them were executed (two had their sentences commuted to life imprisonment). Prison camps were built to contain any suspects and the Muslim Brotherhood was dissolved. Meanwhile, accused of conspiring with the Muslim Brotherhood and the communists, Naguib was finally removed from office.

Step four: The presidency

In January of 1955, Nasser was appointed President by the RCC.

> If you have studied the rise to power/consolidation of power of Hitler, Mussolini or Stalin, can you think of similar moments when an event is used as a turning point towards stronger centralized government?

FACTORS IN THE RISE TO POWER

Below is a list of factors that may contribute to the rise to power of a single-party leader, with a specific example of how they can be applied to Nasser. You could use the same template for other leaders you have studied to help you analyze how they got into power.

The creation of a revolutionary organization:
The Free Officers' Movement

The deposition of head of state:
The abdication of King Farouk

The appointment of a public figurehead:
General Mohammad Naguib

The introduction of popular reform:
Land Reform

The revolutionary ideology:
The Philosophy of the Revolution

The seminal moment:
The attempted assassination of Nasser

● **Examiner's hint**
Dividing the period from 1952 to 1955 into different stages will give you a structure to remember how Nasser came to power. Using these six points as headings, see if you can add a paragraph briefly under each one to explain what happened. You would not include a narrative of events in an exam, but it really helps to place events into chronological order so that you can then develop an analysis, explaining how each event follows on from the last.

An overview of Nasser's rise to power

Points to remember:
- The establishment of the Free Officers' Movement; its programme; its choice of leader.
- The political, social and economic conditions that led to the coup of 1952.
- The setting up of the Revolutionary Command Council and preliminary reforms.
- The establishment of the Republic, after which Nasser joins the government.
- The attempted assassination of Nasser and the removal of President Naguib.
- Nasser is appointed President.

Section III:

Nasser in Power: The consolidation of an authoritarian and single-party state

Foreign policy: Non-alignment, the Cold War and the Suez Crisis

STUDENT STUDY SECTION

Examiner's comments

The foreign policies of single-party leaders are not included in the 'themes' for Topic 3 of Paper 2. It is, however, difficult to assess the role of Nasser without placing his policies in the context of the Middle East and of the Cold War.

To access Worksheet 7.1 on Nasser and Ben Gurion, please visit www.pearsonbacconline.com and follow the on-screen instructions.

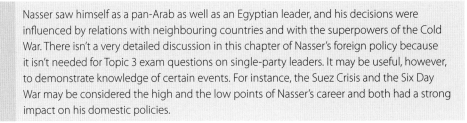

Nasser saw himself as a pan-Arab as well as an Egyptian leader, and his decisions were influenced by relations with neighbouring countries and with the superpowers of the Cold War. There isn't a very detailed discussion in this chapter of Nasser's foreign policy because it isn't needed for Topic 3 exam questions on single-party leaders. It may be useful, however, to demonstrate knowledge of certain events. For instance, the Suez Crisis and the Six Day War may be considered the high and the low points of Nasser's career and both had a strong impact on his domestic policies.

Nasser and the Non-Aligned Movement

Nasser attended the African–Asian Bandung Conference in Indonesia in 1955 where, according to Aburish, 29 countries represented half of mankind. Among the world leaders present were Prime Minister Nehru of India; President Sukarno of Indonesia; President Nkrumah of Ghana; Premier Zhou Enlai of China; and Marshal Tito of Yugoslavia. For Nasser, the concept of non-alignment fitted easily with his anti-imperialist policies and he wholeheartedly embraced the concept of 'positive neutralism'. When he returned to Egypt, he began his quest to obtain arms and approached the Soviet embassy. This began a series of events that led to the Suez Crisis, a huge gamble that, nevertheless, paid off. In 1961, Nasser attended the Non-Aligned Conference in Belgrade and became good friends with Marshal Tito. Like many members of this movement, Nasser embraced 'socialism', but he was also staunchly anti-imperialist and wanted to make Egypt truly independent of external control, not easy to achieve in a bi-polar world where smaller countries fell under the influence of either the USA or USSR.

Nasser and the USA

When the Free Officers staged their coup in 1952, as long as they were clearly anti-communist they were accepted by the USA. Scott Lucas in *Divided We Stand* (1996) suggests that the Central Intelligence Agency (CIA) was keeping a close watch on events in Egypt well before the coup. Nasser gradually formed a friendship with Kermit Roosevelt, the son of Franklin Roosevelt and one of the CIA's Middle Eastern specialists. Nasser was repeatedly disappointed, however, by the refusal of the USA to sell arms to Egypt so that they could tackle the problem of Israeli cross-border raids in response to attacks by Palestinian *fedayeen*. Despite the Tripartite Agreement, France was selling Mystère jets to Israel, but refused to sell them to Egypt as long as Nasser supported the Front de Libération Nationale (FLN) in Algeria.

Although encouraged to bring Egypt into the **Baghdad Pact** in 1955, Nasser refused to consider this move, as he considered this alliance to be too 'colonial', because it would be led by Britain, on behalf of the USA. Nasser strongly believed that if there were to be a mutual defence pact in the Middle East, it should be organized independently by the Arab states, a view that reflected Nasser's anti-imperialism.

Nasser and the USSR

After attending the Bandung Conference in 1955, Nasser was encouraged to assert his independence of the West by approaching the USSR for arms. Nikita Khrushchev had more or less assumed the leadership of the USSR by this time (he was to become Prime Minister officially in 1958) and agreed to provide Egypt with arms from Czechoslovakia. This was the beginning of a relationship that was not as close as the Soviet Union would have liked. Nasser was never a communist and had imprisoned and executed Egyptian communists. Inevitably, there were tensions in the relationship between the Soviet Union and those of

ToK Time

How important, do you think, is the naming of organizations like the Non-Aligned Movement, or the wording of the phrase 'positive neutralism'? Can you think of other examples of names given to political movements or policies that were meant to convey a positive image? How important, do you think, is 'naming' in gathering popular support?

Fedayeen

'Freedom fighters'. These were Palestinian refugees living in Gaza and Sinai who launched surprise attacks on Israeli border posts or settlements.

The Baghdad Pact

In 1955, Britain, Iraq, Turkey, Iran and Pakistan joined together in a NATO-style alliance with the aim of preventing the spread of Soviet influence into the Middle East.

its client states that did not embrace communism. This did not prevent generous aid being given to Egypt, for instance, which was made to sound ideologically closer by being referred to as a 'state of socialist orientation'.

The Suez Crisis, 1956

Egypt took over Gaza after the 1948 war and had Palestinian refugees living under its administration. Border raids staged by *fedayeen* into Israel were commonplace and often met with reprisals. In 1955, 39 Egyptians and Palestinians were killed in an incident that worsened relations between Israel and Egypt. As we have seen, Nasser turned to the USSR for arms in an act described by John Foster Dulles, the American Secretary of State, as 'the most dangerous development since Korea'. This growing concern led to the withdrawal of Western funding for the construction of Nasser's most important project, the building of the **Aswan Dam**. Nasser now made the most controversial, but also the most popular, decision of his career by announcing on 4 August 1956 that the Suez Canal would be nationalized. More an act of bravado than of economic necessity, as the income from the canal was insufficient to build the dam, it won Nasser huge acclaim at home, in neighbouring Arab states and elsewhere in Africa. If Egypt was indeed at the heart of the intersecting circles of Islam, Arabia and Africa, then Nasser now came close to proving this.

When it was announced that the Suez Canal would be nationalized, the reaction in London and Paris was one of outrage. In September 1956, Israel, Britain and France hatched a secret plot to recover control of the canal. Israel would invade Egypt, and Britain and France would sent troops to 'protect' the canal on the pretext that it was an important international waterway. The plan went ahead in October, but failed partly due to poor planning and partly due to the loud condemnation issued by the USA towards its allies. Lester Pearson, the Prime Minister of Canada, brokered a peace and UN peacekeeping forces were sent to patrol the border with Israel. According to his memoirs, Khrushchev, the leader of the USSR at this time, told the British, French and Israeli governments: 'You have attacked Egypt, knowing that it is considerably weaker than you are, that it does not have much of an army, and that it does not have many weapons. There are other countries which are entirely capable of coming to Egypt's defence… I have been told that when Guy Mollet received our note, he ran to the telephone in his pyjamas and called Eden. I don't know if this story is true, but whether or not he had his trousers on doesn't change the fact that twenty-two hours after the delivery of our note the aggression was halted' (*Khrushchev Remembers*, 1970).

Nasser emerged as the hero who had faced down this last gasp of imperialism, and his reputation reached new heights. Buoyed by this level of support, both at home and abroad, he was ready to take the revolution a stage further.

The results of the Suez Crisis

The results of the Suez Crisis can be summarized as follows:
- Nasser's popularity in Egypt was well and truly established.
- Nasser's fame spread beyond Egypt to neighbouring states in the Middle East and Africa.
- The USA criticized British intervention but became increasingly suspicious of Nasser.
- In 1957, the Eisenhower Doctrine expressed US interest in the Middle East as a sphere of influence.
- Relations between Egypt and the USSR grew warmer.
- UN peacekeepers moved in to patrol the border between Egypt and Israel.
- Relations with Israel deteriorated.
- Nasser's increased popularity contributed to the establishment of the UAR.

To access Worksheet 7.2 on the Suez Crisis, please visit www.pearsonbacconline.com and follow the on-screen instructions.

The Aswan Dam
More correctly known as the Aswan High Dam (the Low Dam was an earlier construction), this structure was built on the River Nile near the town of Aswan. The intention was to increase by 30 per cent the amount of cultivable land, to store water and to make flooding and also drought less likely. It was also a hydroelectric project to provide power to thousands of small villages. Some 60,000 people were moved from areas that were submerged in the building of the dam and UNESCO financed the removal and rebuilding of the Temple of Abu Simbel, one of the great historical sites of Ancient Egypt. The building of the dam began in 1960 and was completed in 1970.

How the canal was nationalized
The actual takeover of the offices of the Suez Canal Company was carried out by Colonel Mahmoud Younes, who was told to listen to the broadcast of Nasser's speech on the evening of 26 July and to go ahead with the plan if Nasser mentioned Ferdinand de Lesseps (the French architect who had built the canal). Nasser had decided to go ahead with the nationalization and was so anxious that, according to Nasser's friend, Mohammad Heikal, 'It was de Lesseps this and de Lesseps that until he had repeated it about ten times and people began to wonder why he was making such a fuss about de Lesseps, for the Egyptians had no real love for him.'

Figure 7.3
Map showing the movement of troops during the Suez Crisis of 1956.

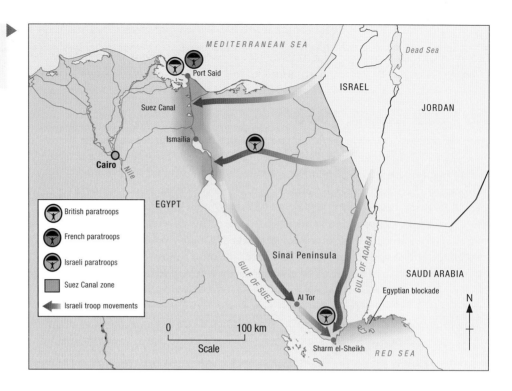

Domestic policies: Nasser after Suez

Political change

In June 1956, Nasser introduced a new constitution for the Egyptian republic. This stated that Islam was the state religion and that Egypt was part of the 'Arab nation'. Meanwhile, the structure of the government was changed and was now led by a President (who would hold office for a six-year term), a council of ministers and a National Assembly to be elected by universal suffrage. The Liberation Rally was replaced in 1957 by the National Union, which was intended to replace all political parties. Nasser was reluctant to grant political freedom because he still feared that voters would be drawn to the Muslim Brotherhood and the communists. He was also convinced that a more democratic system would only result in the restoration of a political system that acted in the interests of the bourgeoisie.

The National Assembly became the 'national representative body' (Aburish, *Nasser*, 2004) and when elections were held in July 1957, women voted for the first time. Although it was intended that this body would have a majority of representatives from the lower classes, including workers and poor peasants, in fact it was full of middle-class professionals. There were very few peasants, possibly because £50 was charged as a deposit to all candidates standing for election. Stephens argues that, for all its restrictions, the National Assembly was a dynamic and often critical institution where different political opinions were aired. It was closed down in March 1958, after the declaration of the UAR, but during its lifespan, significant changes did come about, including: a ban on the employment of children under the age of 12; increased measures taken to improve working conditions; the provision of health care; and the distribution of free food to the needy.

Nasser wanted to take Egypt into a new future and embraced what can be described as 'Islamic modernism'. He began by secularizing the religious courts and advancing women's rights, although both of these measures were criticized by the Muslim Brotherhood. Undeterred, Nasser pressed on with measures to make primary education compulsory, as he considered this to be fundamental to the process of modernization.

The National Union is one means for us to enforce our internal conditions and the necessities of our foreign policy. It is the cadre through which we will realize our revolution, for the security of the homeland and to safeguard its independence. It is a form of peaceful co-existence between the social classes.

From an article by Nasser published in *al-Ahram* in 1959, quoted in Anne Alexander, *Nasser*, 2005

STUDENT STUDY SECTION

QUESTIONS
a) What did Nasser mean by 'peaceful co-existence between the social classes'?
b) What does this tell us about his political ideology?

Economic change

The success of the nationalization of the Suez Canal led to further confiscation of foreign-owned businesses. In 1957, Nasser had already spoken of the 'Egyptianization' of all foreign banks, insurance companies and import–export agencies in order to reduce the dependence of Egypt on foreign investment. To organize this change, a National Planning Committee was set up as well as an institution known as the Economic Organization, which would deal with the nationalized property. A Five Year Plan was set in motion in 1958 to increase the growth of industrial output from around 6 per cent p.a. to 16 per cent p.a. It was intended that although the bulk of investment would come from the government, private investment would also be encouraged.

Nasser was disappointed at the limited success of this mixed public–private investment plan and we shall see that this pushed him towards further nationalization after 1960. Meanwhile, he recognized that corruption was becoming endemic in the system, as officials directed grants and contracts towards friends and family or in exchange for bribes.

In agriculture, Nasser was disappointed that the land reform had achieved so little. Production levels had risen, but it was estimated that only 5 per cent of the peasantry had actually benefited from the redistribution of land.

SOURCE B

The laws controlling rent and fixing minimum agricultural wages were being widely evaded, often with the connivance of the tenants and farm workers themselves, owing to the acute shortage of land and jobs. There was criticism in the press of the amount that farmers had to pay the government in interest and annual repayments for the land they acquired under the agrarian reform… There was also evasion of the law limiting the amount of land that could be owned by one person or his family. By exploiting the allowance made for relatives and the use of 'straw men' (a fictitious person who could be the nominal owner of land but who didn't really exist), it was possible for a former big landowner whose personal holding should not have exceeded 200 feddans to control effectively as much as two or three thousand feddans. Thus, he was able to maintain in his district the kind of power and influence over the peasantry that the revolution had branded as 'feudalism' and had tried to eradicate.

From Robert Stephens, *Nasser*, 1971

Ba'athist Party
Meaning 'renaissance' or 'resurrection', the first Ba'athist Party was founded in Syria in 1940 and began as a secular anti-imperialist political party that aimed to unite the Arab countries.

Plebiscite
A plebiscite means that voters are given the opportunity to express their support of or opposition to a single issue.

STUDENT STUDY SECTION

QUESTIONS

a) **How successful, would you say, were Nasser's economic reforms?**

b) **What do you think were the main obstacles to the 'eradication of feudalism'?**

The nationalization of major companies took place, although two-thirds of businesses continued to be privately owned. Aburish says that Nasser wanted total government control of the economy, but this was not achieved. Agricultural production gradually increased, and there was higher investment in industry with the expansion, in particular, of the Helwan steelworks, but progress was disappointing.

If we consider anti-imperialism to be at the core of Nasser's political ideology, then the Suez Crisis was his defining moment. He had acted audaciously to challenge the former Great Powers of Britain and France and they had been humiliated at the hands of a former colony. Such moments fed into the development of a cult of personality that made Nasser well known not only throughout Egypt, but also beyond its borders. This led to the establishment of a pan-Arab experiment in 1958, when Nasser was asked if Egypt would unite with Syria to establish the UAR.

The UAR 1958–61: 'Three and a half years of troubles'

On 1 February 1958, Egyptian President Gamal Abdel Nasser and Syrian President Shukri al-Quwatli signed a union treaty. Syria and Egypt became united under the United Arab Republic (UAR). The union lasted until 1961, when a military coup in Damascus precipitated Syria's withdrawal from the UAR.

There were strong similarities between the Free Officers' Movement and the **Ba'athist Party** in Syria. Both used the slogan 'unity, freedom and socialism' and the Syrian Ba'athists looked to Egypt for support against the growing influence of Syria's Communist Party. In January 1958, a group of Syrian army officers asked Nasser if he would agree to a union of the two countries. By embracing this opportunity to put his dream of a pan-Arab state into practice, Nasser sought increased security for Egypt plus an improved economy with the provision of new markets for Egyptian goods and jobs for Egyptian workers. The UAR was set up on 1 February 1958, and was approved by a **plebiscite** on 22 February. Although this was a step towards closer unity among the Arab states, Aburish suggests that Nasser may not have fully considered the many significant differences between Syria and Egypt. With a population of only five million, Syria was far smaller than Egypt and was also more heavily influenced by the Muslim Brotherhood and the Communist Party, two groups that Nasser placed under strict control in Egypt.

1 February 1958: Egyptian President Gamal Abdel Nasser and Syrian President Shukri al-Quwatli sign the union treaty. Syria and Egypt become united under the United Arab Republic (UAR). The union lasted until 1961, when a military coup in Damascus precipitated Syria's withdrawal from the UAR.

Nasser's appointment of Abdel Hakim Amer, his commander-in-chief, as Governor-General of Syria, possibly made it seem that this was less a union than an annexation, as suggested by this British cartoon from 1961.

Cartoon by Michael Cummings, published in the *Daily Express*, 29 September 1961.

The assassination of King Faisal of Iraq and his Prime Minister, Nur al-Said, in July 1958, was followed by an attempted coup in Lebanon that led to US intervention. There was no doubt that, for the USA, Nasser was seen as a profoundly destabilizing force in the Middle East. Nasser responded by visiting Moscow to consult with Khrushchev who, eager to prevent war, suggested a summit. Stephens emphasizes that Nasser, too, wanted tempers to cool and did not want the Middle East to be embroiled in a superpower conflict that could result in the use of nuclear weapons. He was, nevertheless, gratified that Iraq had broken away from the Baghdad Pact and was now allied with Syria and Egypt. By the end of the year, US troops had been withdrawn from Lebanon and the crisis was over. According to Nasser, 1958 had been a 'year of victory' for Arab nationalism, but differences among the Arab states remained a serious obstacle to unity. Nasser clashed with General Abdel Karim Kassim, the leader of Iraq, amid concerns that communism would infiltrate the Middle East through Syria and Iraq. In 1959, Nasser carried out a purge of suspected communists in Syria and Egypt and arrested 280 leaders. Stephens states that many were sent to the 'notoriously brutal desert concentration camp of Abu Zaabal and to military prisons, where several were reported to have died as a result of torture' (*Nasser*, 1971). It is remarkable to consider that while Nasser imprisoned communists, he continued to promote socialist policies and maintain a close relationship with the USSR. Khrushchev said, 'Abdel Nasser is a young man, passionate and hot-headed', but he still chose to lend him a helping hand and Soviet aid flowed into Egypt to help finance the building of the Aswan Dam.

Eventually, the UAR foundered on Nasser's socialist and political policies. He wanted a tightly controlled single-party state with increased levels of nationalization and socialism, and when the UAR ended in 1961 Nasser described it as having been 'three and a half years of troubles'.

● **Examiner's hint**
In exam questions that ask you to consider the leadership or ideology of a left- and/or a right-wing leader, it may seem a little difficult to decide where to place Nasser. He was not a communist but he was anti-capitalist and he described his policies as 'socialism'. So, he belongs with other left-wing leaders such as Stalin, Mao, Castro and Nyerere. His ideology, as you can see, was not fixed by any allegiance to a predetermined political manifesto. He was very pragmatic and driven, it would seem, by a desire to rid Egypt of all the trappings of imperialism and to improve the lives of the poorest people. His biggest problem lay in knowing how best to achieve these goals.

Post-UAR: From the National Union to the Arab Socialist Union

The failure of the UAR resulted in a period of radical reform in Egypt. According to Anthony Nutting, Nasser blamed the collapse of the UAR on the Egyptian 'business community' or bourgeoisie. Egyptian businessmen had done very well out of the expulsion of foreign interests in 1956 and had been very much in favour of the UAR, as they felt it might open up access to trade with France. Nasser suspected that once these business interests realized that the UAR meant further socialization of both the Egyptian and Syrian economies, they worked to undermine it.

When the UAR collapsed, Nasser was determined to show that the implementation of socialism had not come to a halt, and in October 1961 he confiscated the property of 167 'reactionary capitalists'. This step was followed in December by further confiscations and the seizure of more than 80 banks and corporations now put under 'emergency administration'. Aburish comments on how difficult it was for Nasser to move the economy along in the direction he wanted, as he was against 'extreme socialist measures such as collective ownership', but was opposed by the influential 'old bourgeois and industrial bloc' who advised foreign investors to stay away (*Nasser: The Last Arab*, 2004). Meanwhile, Nutting maintains that 'Nasser's evolution to socialism was thus an essentially pragmatic process, based largely on reaction to the collapse of the union with Syria and with little, if any, ideological motivation' (*Nasser*, 1972). He cites as an example Nasser's nationalization of the press in 1960, because he feared that the capitalists had succeeded in dominating the 'political and social media'. Furthermore, Nasser feared that Egypt was on the brink of a counter-revolution, and so he pushed onwards to socialism as the only way to proceed with his revolution.

What Nasser seized upon now as the key to change was termed 'Arab Socialism'. In October 1961, he stated in a radio broadcast that 'Socialism is our only road to justice … the national income must be shared among citizens, to each according to the efforts he makes to produce it. But there also had to be equal opportunities' (Stephens, *Nasser*, 1971). In the new structure, Nasser claimed, room had to be made for peasants and workers, but not for 'reactionary forces'. Individual ownership was acceptable, but not what Nasser described as 'exploitative ownership'.

The National Charter, introduced in May 1962, is considered by Stephens to be 'the key document' in understanding Nasser's political ideology post-UAR. Once again, he saw political reform in Egypt as the lynch-pin for change elsewhere.

SOURCE C

The Egyptian revolution was set apart from both capitalism and the Marxist class struggle. The Egyptian people said the Charter resisted capitalism because it attempted to exploit national independence and national economic development needs for its own interests. At the same time, they 'rejected the dictatorship of any class and decided the dissolution of class differences should be the means of real democracy for the entire people's working forces.' One of the 'guarantees' of the revolution was the decidedly un-Marxist one of 'unshakeable faith in God, His Prophets and his Sacred Messages.'

From Robert Stephens, *Nasser*, 1971

STUDENT STUDY SECTION

QUESTION
Explain briefly how Source C would help you to argue that Nasser was not a Marxist?

Arab socialism?

Economic change

In 1958, Nasser announced the First Five Year Plan which embraced more radical land reform. Once again, there would be a limit on the amount of land owned by an individual farmer and there would also be a system of cooperatives to boost production by providing better access to irrigation projects financed by the state. There would also be access to credit and cheap technology to help the *fellahin*. Again, however, vested interests made it difficult for him to push through the practical application of land redistribution, as only 17 per cent of cultivable land was redistributed and only 8 per cent of the *fellahin* benefited.

Mazrui and Tidy maintain, however, that despite the limited success of the land reform programme, the cooperative system did bring considerable benefit to the Egyptian countryside (*Nationalism and New States in Africa*, 1984). For Nasser, capitalism was not the answer for Egypt because, for him, it was inextricably linked to imperialism. He drew the line, though, at total nationalization of the means of production and the state ownership of land. These, he argued, were not necessary for socialism, Egyptian-style. Nasser argued for the nationalization of infrastructure and financial institutions, along with heavy industry and mining, although there could be private ownership of light industry. Some progress was made, with economic growth averaging between 6.4 per cent and 6.6 per cent p.a. in the years 1960 to 1965. This compared with a lower rate of 4.7 per cent p.a. between 1945 and 1952. Manufacturing output grew by 15.5 per cent in 1960–61 and by 10 per cent in 1963–64.

Political change

Following the collapse of the UAR, the government was restructured in 1963 based on the National Charter, the Arab Socialist Union and the National Assembly. The National Assembly had 350 elected and ten appointed members, half of whom had to come from the peasant and worker class. It met for the first time in March 1964 and although martial law was lifted the day before, new emergency measures were introduced the day after, so the internal security system barely changed. Nasser was nominated for re-election as President by the Assembly and this was confirmed by a 99.9 per cent vote in a plebiscite. Nasser reorganized the army, stating that half the officers would continue as professional soldiers and the remainder would transfer into civilian posts either in the government or in private business. Biographers of Nasser comment on this system of government as a military-bureaucracy. Aburish calls it a 'military-bureaucratic society' made up of the old clique of the Free Officers who were promoted or demoted according to Nasser's wishes. 'Neither democratic nor military, Egypt became a military-bureaucratic society' (Aburish, *Nasser: The Last Arab*, 2004).

Economic problems and solutions

Population

A constant source of worry was the relentless growth in the Egyptian population. Like all single-party leaders, Nasser relished a large population that would support a large army, but the 2.5 per cent p.a. growth rate in population also meant more mouths to feed, a significant concern when agriculture was impeded by the shortage of arable land. Nasser knew that Egypt could not support this population growth rate, but this was a subject that was difficult to address in an Islamic country that did not, in theory, support birth control.

Fellahin
The name given in Egypt to the poor peasant farmers who worked the land. The land reforms carried out after the 1952 revolution were intended to benefit the *fellahin*.

Divisions between the rich and the poor

Plans to bring more of Egyptian industry under the control of the state were overly ambitious and, in practice, production fell short of the intended goals of a 16 per cent growth p.a. In reality, much of the planned expansion of industry did not take place and expensive imported machinery lay idle. As there was a shortage of basic goods, Egypt came to depend increasingly on imported goods. This led to grumblings about the economy and a sharp criticism of the 'elite' who seemed to live very well indeed. These included the former Free Officers and those who had secured well-paid jobs in the government bureaucracy. A social class had appeared, similar to the **nomenklatura** of the Soviet Union, leading privileged lives immune to the economic problems that accompanied a startling 10 per cent inflation rate. The high inflation rate was partially due to higher indirect taxes, which were levied instead of a rise in income tax that Nasser did not feel able to impose on an already heavily taxed population.

The Aswan Dam

In 1964, the first stage of the Aswan Dam, Nasser's most important project, was completed (it would be finished in 1970) and Premier Khrushchev of the Soviet Union attended the opening ceremony. More than £500 million worth of Soviet aid had been granted to Egypt and Khrushchev now pledged another £100 million to help with the industrialization programme of the Second Five Year Plan. Nasser was also awarded the Order of Lenin and the Hero of the Soviet Union and relations were amicable, made better by his having arranged parole for all who had been imprisoned for communist activities. (Oddly enough, among the many allegations of misbehaviour levelled against Khrushchev in 1964 when he was removed from office was this very fact, that he had made Gamal Abdel Nasser a Hero of the Soviet Union! See Archie Brown, *The Rise and Fall of Communism*, 2009.)

Gamal Abdel Nasser and Nikita Khrushchev at the opening of the first stage of the Aswan Dam in 1964.

Grain

Egypt was dependent on the USA for 50 per cent of its wheat imports, under a deal negotiated with President Kennedy, but this deal was in danger of not being renewed in 1965. Nasser also obtained grain from the Soviet Union and China, but Egypt needed US wheat. A new agreement was finally reached with the Johnson administration. In 1966, however, when there were serious grain shortages, the USA sent its surplus to India instead of Egypt, and Nasser, in a fit of anger, decided that his relationship with the USA would never improve as long as Lyndon Johnson was President.

More foreign policy: Entanglement and defeat

Once again, for a good understanding of Nasser's rule, there needs to be some reference to foreign policy. Nasser felt that Egypt had a duty to fulfil to its neighbours, although his enemies saw his policies as ambitious and expansionist. In what became known as 'Egypt's Vietnam', Nasser became involved in a civil war in Yemen that cost the Egyptian people dearly in money and troops. The involvement of Egypt in Yemen not only made Egypt an enemy of Saudi Arabia, but it also tied up soldiers at the time of the Six Day War in 1967.

The Yemeni Civil War

By 1960, Yemen was divided into two regions: a theocracy ruled by Imam Ahmad based in Sanaa and the British protectorate of Aden that bordered the Red Sea. Although the Imamate was not opposed to closer unity amongst the Arab states, as proposed by Nasser, Egypt's socialist policies were denounced by the deeply conservative Imam as 'ungodly'. When the Imam died in 1962, there was hope among the growing Yemeni middle-class for change. A revolt broke out and the Imam's son and heir, Mohammad al-Badr, was presumed killed. The Yemen Arab Republic was officially declared, under the leadership of Abdallah al-Sallal, Chief of Staff of the army, and recognized by both the USSR and the USA. Mohammad al-Badr was alive, however, and with help from Saudi Arabia he raised enough support to hold on to around one-third of the country. Nasser, in an attempt to shore up the Yemen Arab Republic, sent Egyptian troops to Yemen and by 1963 there were 15,000 soldiers based there fighting in a civil war of great brutality.

The Six Day War

A disaster for Egypt and for Nasser, the Arab–Israeli War of 1967 was the low-point in his political career. Aburish suggests that Nasser had no intention of attacking Israel, but more orthodox interpretations indicate that an escalating war of words and actions aroused Israeli fears. In May 1967, Syrian attacks on Israeli farmers ploughing land that was officially 'demilitarized' resulted in a quick and decisive Israeli response, including the closing of the Straits of Tiran and the dismissal of the UN forces from the Egyptian border. The USA refused to pledge to Israel that an attack on Israel's borders would be viewed as an attack on the USA and, furthermore, Israel was warned not to launch any kind of pre-emptive action.

General Moshe Dayan, however, joined the Israeli cabinet as Minister of War in June 1967 and he began to plan a surprise attack, which he considered essential if Israel, a country small enough to be overrun in a day, were to survive a war with its neighbours. On 5 June 1967, an air attack was launched on Egyptian, Syrian and Jordanian air bases, giving Israel vital control of the skies. This caught the coalition of Egypt, Syria and Jordan unprepared and a rout followed, leading to the Israeli occupation of Gaza, Sinai, the Golan Heights, East Jerusalem and the West Bank. Following this deeply humiliating defeat, Nasser offered his resignation on 9 June, but withdrew it the following day when his supporters took to the streets shouting, 'No leader but Gamal!'

Nasser remained tied to the USSR, an ally he needed now more than ever, as Egypt's armed forces needed to be rebuilt. President Podgorny of the Soviet Union visited Cairo just two weeks after the end of the war and Nutting describes how Nasser had 'to beg' for free arms

 How defeat was handled

At the beginning of the Six Day War, the devastating air attacks by the Israeli Air Force were kept from the public and Eugene Rogan mentions how one Egyptian intelligence officer, hearing news of the war on the radio, recalled, 'The whole world thought that our forces were at the outskirts of Tel Aviv'. When the time came for the people to be told about the defeat of their army, Nasser, along with King Hussein of Jordan, blamed US and British planes 'for taking part against us from aircraft carriers'. Finally, on 9 June, Nasser told the people of *al-Naksa* ('the reversal') and offered his resignation.

and also for instructors and technicians to be attached to the Egyptian Army (*Nasser*, 1972). A cartoon in the British newspaper the *Evening Standard* commented wryly on President Podgorny's visit:

Cartoon by Raymond Jackson (Jak), *Evening Standard*, 23 June 1967. The caption to the cartoon has Podgorny saying: 'As far as Russia is concerned, we will fight – to the last Egyptian!'

The conflict with Israel did not end with the ceasefire, and a War of Attrition followed in 1969–70. This low-level but continuous conflict with Israel required arms, and these could only come from the USSR.

ToK Time

SPHINX!

This is a British cartoon of Nasser published during the Six Day War in 1967. How is Nasser portrayed here? What kind of emotional response do you have to this? How important, do you think, are political cartoonists in influencing public opinion? See if you can compare this cartoon to cartoons published today about current politicians.

> **The attack on the USS *Liberty***
> Nasser's propaganda campaign alleged that the USA was behind the Six Day War and that it was a staunch ally of Israel. Israel had, in fact, attacked the USS *Liberty*, an American surveillance ship, killing 34 servicemen and wounding 171.
>
> **Abdel Hakim Amer (1919–67)**
> Nasser and Amer had been young officers together in the Egyptian Army during the 1940s. One of the founding members of the Free Officers' Movement, Amer became commander-in-chief of the armed forces in 1953, a position he retained until the defeat of Egypt in the Six Day War in 1967.

The political and economic impact of the war

Blame for the disastrous outcome of the war was placed on the army, and on 11 June Nasser sacked his Chief of Staff, **Abdel Hakim Amer**, along with 50 senior commanders. Amer committed suicide before his trial by taking poison, and although there were rumours that he had been 'allowed' to do so, these were not substantiated. Nasser had arisen from a powerbase within the army and his fellow officers had played a central role in the administration and ideology of the Arab Revolution. Now that many of his former compatriots had been purged, Nasser was increasingly isolated.

The Egyptian economy was not so badly affected by the war, despite the loss of the Sinai oilfields and the closure of the Suez Canal. By 1969, the discovery of new fields increased oil production to 14 million metric tons. An increase in world prices for cotton and a fall in the price of wheat also helped the trade balance between imports and exports, and by 1969 there was a trade surplus of £43 million, the first surplus since 1930 (Stephens, *Nasser*, 1971). At the same time, the USSR provided support in the form of arms and aid vital for the completion of the Aswan Dam in 1970.

Nasser tried to keep inflation under control through the implementation of what were called 'austerity measures', meaning cuts in government expenditure, including subsidised food prices, but with limited success. In July 1969, Nasser pushed forward plans to place under state ownership the 283,000 hectares of cultivable land made available as a result of the construction of the Aswan Dam. New limits were placed on the maximum acreage that could be owned by an individual (20 hectares) or a family (40 hectares).

Though industry's share of national output rose by 50 per cent by around 1970, the price of Nasser's over-ambitious economic plans was inflation, shortages of basic essential commodities, debt, an inflated public-sector payroll, stifling controls and urban overcrowding (Meredith, *The State of Africa*, 2006). Nasser was increasingly aware of criticism levelled against those who had done well out of the 'revolution'. He was also aware that the limited purge of the military after the 1967 war had not satisfied workers and students, who took to the streets to protest in early 1968. The sentences given to the officers who had been put on trial were considered too lenient, while the students, in particular, were strident in their demands for greater freedom of the press. There was no liberalization, however, and it was foreign affairs that once again entangled Nasser through the summer of 1970.

The successful hijacking of three commercial airlines by members of the **Popular Front for the Liberation of Palestine (PFLP)** in September 1970 led to a major international crisis. Nasser was asked by the USA to broker negotiations between King Hussein of Jordan and Yasser Arafat of the **Palestine Liberation Organization (PLO)**. A ceasefire was agreed but Nasser, already suffering from heart problems aggravated by diabetes, died late in the evening of 28 September 1970. The news of his death brought crowds onto the streets of Cairo to lament the loss of a leader who had come to symbolize Egypt.

The PLO and the PFLP

At an Arab summit in Alexandria in 1964, the decision was taken to establish the Palestine Liberation Organization (PLO) and a Palestine Liberation Army (PLA). Syria and Egypt were the strongest supporters of these organizations, although their motives were quite different. Nasser saw the PLO as a necessary way to structure and to discipline the many different *fedayeen* groups, whose attacks on Israel often led to retaliation against Egypt. Syria, meanwhile, urged on the revolutionaries and encouraged more radical groups such as al-Fatah and the Popular Front for the Liberation of Palestine (PFLP).

SOURCE D

The years 1956 to 1959 marked the high tide of Nasserism as he seemed to sweep all before him. His appeal to the Arabs – and especially to the younger generation, who formed the majority – was overwhelming. They saw him as a modern Saladin who would unite them in order to drive out the Zionists – the crusaders of the twentieth century. The danger for Nasser was that he was raising expectations which neither he nor Egypt could fulfil.

From Peter Mansfield, *A History of the Middle East*, 1991

The personality cult of Nasser

Despite the disaster of 1967 and the economic crises, Nasser remained extremely popular both in Egypt and elsewhere in the Arab world. He was a very persuasive orator who spoke to the Egyptian people using a language that the ordinary 'man in the street' could understand. He knew how to express his ideas in different registers of language and this was a skill he perfected over time.

Aburish claims that Nasser was not guided by a strong ideology but that he listened to the people, following rather than leading popular opinion.

The Voice of the Arabs (Radio Cairo)

The radio broadcasts of the Voice of the Arabs (or Radio Cairo) were an important propaganda tool for Nasser. Broadcast not only in Egypt but throughout the Middle East and Africa, programmes and speeches were, according to Stephens, Nasser's 'most powerful political weapons' (*Nasser*, 1971). Nasser used them not only to criticize any vestiges of imperialism, but also to target any leaders with whom he disagreed, appealing directly to the people of countries such as Jordan and Iraq or Syria.

STUDENT STUDY SECTION

QUESTION

Populist policies can often be an important method used by single-party leaders to stay in power. How far, do you think, is this true of the leaders you have studied?

A man of the people, Nasser lived in a modest suburban villa rather than a presidential palace and would regularly go home for lunch, just as though he were a low-ranking civil servant. He would even invite visiting heads of state to eat dinner with him at his home, where his wife would prepare simple dishes.

Also, unlike many other single-party leaders, he did not create a 'dynasty' and had no plans for his children to follow him into political power. The CIA noted that Nasser was a very difficult target as, 'he is too clean, he has no vices'. Mohammad Heikal, editor of *al-Ahram*, called him the 'pious President'. There was nothing they could find to use against him. Aburish does claim, however, that the British and the CIA planned to get rid of Nasser and that there were at least ten British and two French plots to assassinate him.

Nasser at home introducing his son to Prime Minister Nehru of India.

Nasser with his family outside his home.

SOURCE E

There is no escaping the conclusion that Nasser represented an odd type of dictator. He manifested a need to be loved … which most other dictators do not have. His dictatorial ways were a mixture of populism and a need to be accepted as a man of principle.

From Said Aburish, *Nasser: The Last Arab*, 2004

SOURCE F

He preferred plain Egyptian food and his friends with more sophisticated palates regarded it as a culinary penance to have to dine at the President's house; the menu seemed never to vary, nearly always the same dish of chicken, rice and vegetables – the Cairo middle-class equivalent of meat and two veg. ['Meat and two veg' refers to a British cliché that sums up very conservative British meals consisting of plainly cooked meat and two vegetables.]

From Robert Stephens, *Nasser*, 1971

Yet, whatever disasters befell Egypt, Nasser never lost his popularity with the masses. When, after the 1967 defeat, he announced his resignation, popular protests propelled him back into office. His reputation as the man who had stripped the old ruling class of their power, nationalised their wealth, booted out foreigners, restored to Egypt a sense of dignity and self-respect and led the country towards national regeneration – all of this counted for far more than the setbacks.

From Martin Meredith, *The State of Africa*, 2006

STUDENT STUDY SECTION

QUESTION

How far do Sources E, F and G convey a similar impression of Nasser as a single-party leader? How would you sum him up?

Nasserism

It is difficult to define Nasserism. It was often explained as a kind of Arab socialism, although Meredith describes it as a 'system of personal rule' and one of Nasser's biographers, Professor P. J. Vatikiotis, says that Nasser 'managed to abolish the difference between state and government and between those two and himself'.

Nasserism was aimed at improving the lives of ordinary people while being anti-imperialist and firmly against external involvement in Egyptian policy-making. In some ways, Nasser's relations with Israel were always influenced by his belief that Zionism was a manifestation of Western imperialism.

Nasser's membership of the Non-Aligned Movement sums up his left-leaning but independent foreign policy.

Section III:
Nasser: Social policies

Education

Nasser knew that the high level of illiteracy and inadequate access to education was a major stumbling block to political reform in Egypt. Of course, what he wanted was for the population to be educated in such a way that they would support and follow his political aspirations. He made primary schooling compulsory, and between 1952 and 1957 the number of students attending technical and vocational schools increased by 40 per cent. Literacy reached 50 per cent by 1970, an improvement on the 80 per cent illiteracy rate measured in 1952. In his attempt to modernize Islam, he encouraged the teaching of science and technology, a change that had a significant impact upon the curriculum at the al-Azhar University in Cairo, the seat of Islamic learning not only in Egypt but throughout the Arabic-speaking world. Numbers receiving both primary and secondary education rose significantly, and out of 80,000 secondary school graduates in 1969, 34,000 went on to higher education.

University tuition was free and there were small grants for students who could not afford to support themselves.

The role of women

Nasser also tackled the role of women in Egypt. The **veil** was banned, which affected the towns more than the countryside where, traditionally, women had been unveiled. Girls had better access to education and professions were opened up to them. Nasser was a man of his times and he was accustomed to women being mothers and wives rather than having careers. According to Nutting, however, Madam Tito 'talked him round' to including in the National Charter a pledge to recognize the equality of women. He was persuaded that this was needed to push forward the economic growth of Egypt. Along with this came a realization that family planning was necessary. As we have seen, the population of Egypt, which stood at 26 million in 1960, was growing quickly and Nasser was concerned about the ability of the economy to keep pace. Nasser appointed Hikmat Abu-Zayd to the post of Minister of Social Affairs in 1962, the first time a female had held a cabinet post in Egypt. Generally, the role of women did not change so much. In Cairo and Alexandria, the two main cities, the role of women was not so dissimilar to that of their European or North American counterparts. In the countryside, however, especially in Upper Egypt, women still led traditional lives and young girls were often removed from school at an early age. Even so, the overall number of children receiving primary school education rose from 1,300,000 in 1952 to 3,400,000 in 1966 and more than 1,300,000 of these were girls (Stephens, *Nasser*, 1971). There were also 30,000 women in higher education in 1969 out of a total student population of 120,000.

The veil
The veil here refers to the *niqab* or the short veil worn to cover the face. The *hijab* or headscarf was more common in the countryside than the cities where, during much of the 20th century, the middle class especially were less likely to adopt either the *hijab* or the *niqab*.

Religion

Nasser was a devout Muslim, although he did not espouse the political Islam of the Muslim Brotherhood. Even so, his relations with this group were not entirely consistent. Before the coup, he had links with them as, indeed, did many army officers, but once in power he saw the Brotherhood as opponents and rivals for the support of the people. Aburish describes Nasser's attitude towards the Brotherhood in this way: 'Nasser was an observing Muslim and following the tenets of his religion came naturally to him. But his opposition to political Islam was rock solid, and from that he never deviated, nor did he consider compromise. He believed that you could not run a moderate state on the basis of the Koran'. Aburish mentions an incident at one of the prisons in 1957 when the police killed 21 members of the Muslim Brotherhood held there, but 'Nasser never expressed regret over the handling of this incident' (Aburish, *Nasser: The Last Arab*, 2004).

Sayyed Qutub, the chief 'ideologue' of the Muslim Brotherhood, repeatedly criticized Nasser for imposing a state of *Jahiliya* ('ignorance' or the state of a pre-Islamic movement) on Egypt. He was imprisoned several times by Nasser and, in 1966 having been linked to a Saudi plot, was sentenced to death and executed. In return, Aburish states that the Brotherhood 'passed a death sentence on Nasser.' Nasser had always been a 'modernist', someone who believed that Muslim societies could embrace new technology and social change without ceasing to be Islamic. This brought him into conflict with the 'fundamentalists', who wanted to reject modernity.

ToK Time
How far, do you think, are values and beliefs something that we are born with or are they shaped by our social or political environment? Can single-party leaders change our values and beliefs? Discuss these issues in groups and see if you can come up with examples of leaders who have tried to impose new values or, perhaps, have attempted to suppress religious belief. Were they able to achieve this?

The media and culture

Egyptian newspapers came under state ownership in 1960, and there was strict censorship. Nasser was greeted enthusiastically at first by writers such as Nobel Prize winner Naguib Mahfouz, but encountered their opposition when there was so much suppression of the right to freedom of speech and expression. Nasser was not an avid reader, despite his fondness for military biographies when he was a schoolboy. He is said to have enjoyed films, however, but mostly of the sentimental kind that may have given him a release from the stresses of leadership. Nasser's closest friend was said to be Mohammad Heikal, Minister of National Guidance and editor-in-chief of the national newspaper, *al-Ahram*. Having met in 1952, Heikal and Nasser remained in close contact and had a good mutual understanding. For foreign diplomats and journalists, reading Heikal's column in the daily edition of *al-Ahram* was considered to be the surest way to keep abreast of Egyptian politics.

Egyptian cinema was important for entertainment not only in Egypt but throughout the Middle East. The film industry was nationalized in 1963 and class struggle became the theme of many popular films. One example of this genre was *al-Haram* (*The Sin*), produced in 1965.

SOURCE A

[The film's] protagonist, a poor agricultural seasonal worker who had been raped, dies after having to deliver the resulting child in secret. Yet, contrary to the structure of a regular family melodrama in which the individual would have to bear their plight alone, the death of the woman incites the inhabitants of the village to develop solidarity with the seasonal workers to which the woman belonged.

From Viola Safik, 'Egyptian Cinema: A Report by Viola Safik', February 2007

Another example of social realism in the cinema was *al-Mutamarridun* (*The Rebels*) produced in 1966.

SOURCE B

…the extraordinary al-Mutamarridun / The Rebels *(1966), directed and written by Taufik Salih, addressed the issue of class struggle most intensely. [It] focused on peasants versus feudal authorities and workers versus capitalists. In* al-Mutamarridun *the conflict was depicted in an entirely allegorical and pessimistic way by following the story of a rebellion. A group of infected people, who are kept in a desert camp in quarantine, take over the camp's direction but build up the same unjust and authoritarian structure as the former administration.*

From Viola Safik, 'Egyptian Cinema: A Report by Viola Safik', February 2007

STUDENT STUDY SECTION

QUESTION
Read the plots of the two films discussed in Sources A and B and consider how these may have actually reflected the themes of class struggle to an Egyptian audience. Which of the two films, do you think, would have been more 'politically correct'? Give reasons to support your answer.

Nasser and opposition

External opposition

Externally, the emergence of a charismatic *al-Rayyes* (The Captain) who appealed to the people of Arab states led, inevitably perhaps, to a reaction from their leaders. Nur al-Said, the Prime Minister of Iraq, saw Nasser as a dangerous rival, likely to incite Iraqis to demand union with Egypt. King Hussein of Jordan allowed the creation of a pro-Nasser

● **Examiner's hint**
In the IB History Guide, 'opposition' is one of the themes linked to the study of single-party states. You may be asked to consider the 'nature' of opposition, which means, 'What kind of opposition existed?' as well as its 'extent', meaning 'How much of it was there?' If you are asked to discuss how a leader dealt with opposition, don't forget that many leaders took measures to halt opposition by the imprisonment or even the execution of those considered enemies. Propaganda as well as popular policies that could fend off opposition by winning the support of the people could also be mentioned.

government, but was equally nervous about where this would lead. In Lebanon, President Camille Chamoun leaned even further to the West to counter the threat from Egypt.

In January 1957, the USA issued the Eisenhower Doctrine that declared communism to be the greatest threat to the Middle East and offered aid to any government that would help resist its encroachment. In many ways, this was a reaction to the tide of Nasserism and its suspected links to the USSR.

Internal opposition

Inside Egypt, opposition came from the Muslim Brotherhood, who considered Nasser un-Islamic, and from the communists, who considered him un-socialist. Both groups were targeted and suppressed, with their members filling prisons and concentrations camps.

The communists

Even when Nasser was close to the USSR, he maintained a ruthless policy of suppression towards the communists. He was adamant that receiving aid from the Soviet Union would not mean the ascendancy of communism in Egypt and that it would not 'tie us to the wheel of dependency'. In January 1959, especially concerned about the activities of communist groups in both Syria and Iraq, Nasser carried out a purge of the Egyptian Communist Party when 280 of its leaders were arrested and imprisoned. For many of those arrested, this meant years of hardship at the desert 'concentration camp' of Abu Zaabal. Ultimately, this harsh policy towards the communist opposition did not harm Nasser's relations with the USSR, because he outlasted General Kassim of Iraq. Khrushchev realized that there would not be a Soviet-sponsored government in Iraq and so became accepting of Nasser's anti-communism. Although banned, the Communist Party finally dissolved itself in 1965 and joined the National Committee, but the Muslim Brotherhood continued to be a source of concern for Nasser.

The Muslim Brotherhood

Nasser had cracked down on the Muslim Brotherhood after the attempt on his life in 1954. In 1965, there was a further spate of arrests when Nasser claimed that another plot to overthrow the government had been discovered. More than 400 suspects, including intellectuals, doctors, army officers and lawyers, were rounded up. Amongst those now arrested was Sayyed Qutub, the chief ideologue of the movement. He was tried, sentenced to death and executed and, in return, the Brotherhood passed a death sentence on Nasser. There is no doubt that, for Nasser, the Brotherhood represented a threat to the success of the revolution. They opposed socialist policies, secularization and women's rights, and Nasser would not consider any compromise with a movement that promoted a form of political Islam. According to Aburish, Nasser would not accept that it was possible to form a moderate government 'on the basis of the Koran' (*Nasser: The Last Arab*, 2004).

Nasser's secret police, the *mukhabarat*, were relentless in chasing down conspiracies both real and imagined, and one of Nasser's ministers stated 'Their main task – and source of livelihood – comprised in suggesting to their chief, Nasser, the existence of conspiracies against him, and that they were protecting him from them' (Meredith, *The State of Africa*, 2006).

Nutting claims that 'suspicion was Nasser's besetting sin and principal weakness' and claims that he would tap the telephone lines of his ministers to keep track of their misdemeanours. One minister was astonished when, asked for his resignation, he was played a recording of a telephone call to a mistress made many years before. Nasser himself was 'incorruptible', but seized upon faults that could be used, if necessary, to remove his 'enemies' from office (Nutting, *Nasser*, 1972).

Aburish blames General Amer for creating a 'state within a state based on a vicious security apparatus' (*Nasser: The Last Arab*, 2004), implying that Nasser was 'out of touch' and did not know about the oppressive methods used to maintain the single-party state. This is a characteristic associated with many single-party leaders such as Stalin and Hitler, who were also believed by their supporters to be unaware of the oppression carried out in their name. Aburish says that Nasser was never going to realize his dream of leading the Arab world because, quoting Heikal, 'He [Nasser] hated the idea of violence, of blood', but such moderation, while admirable, was not suitable 'for people who wanted to control and run the Arab Middle East' (Aburish, *Nasser: The Last Arab*, 2004).

To access Worksheet 7.3 on tributes to Nasser, please visit www.pearsonbacconline.com and follow the on-screen instructions.

STUDENT STUDY SECTION

QUESTION
Why is it, do you think, that this claim that the leader is unaware of what is being done in his name is common to many single-party states across regions and time spans?

Conclusion: How successful was Nasser?

Gamal Abdel Nasser, unlike many single-party leaders, was not inward-looking. He was strongly nationalist, but he also viewed Egypt within the context of the Middle East. Entranced by the concept of a pan-Arab union of states, Nasser tried many different ways to unite the disparate countries that had emerged from centuries of Ottoman rule only to become 'mandates' of Britain and France. It was not until the 1950s that opportunities arose for true independence, and once Nasser and the Free Officers led the way similar military coups took place in Syria and Iraq.

The Cold War, however, meant that whether or not an attempt was made to consolidate independence through membership of the Non-Aligned Movement, reality meant that one side had to be chosen over the other. With the granting of aid and security, obligations to accede to the requests of the chosen superpower were unavoidable. Despite Nasser's avowed anti-imperialism, under his rule Egypt moved from the British sphere of influence briefly to that of the USA and, ultimately, to that of the USSR.

At home, Nasser attempted to improve the lives of the impoverished masses, but came up against the obstacles of a weak economy and limited education. He tried to remove the bourgeoisie from power, but in many ways the expulsion of foreign businessmen and investors opened new opportunities that benefited the very class that Nasser tried to undermine. In trying to nationalize and democratize Egypt, he created a vast bureaucracy and a new class of managers and administrators, many of whom had come up through the ranks of the army. Time and again, foreign policy intruded to impact on domestic policy, and from the Suez Crisis through the UAR to the Six Day War, Nasser tried one method after another. He always met opposition to his plans. High inflation along with an economy that never seemed to improve the lot of the poorest classes left him frustrated and, increasingly, suffering from ill health. Despite all this, he remained overwhelmingly popular and his death in 1970 was mourned across not only Egypt but throughout the Arab world. The foreign dignitaries who attended the funeral were prevented from following the coffin, for fear they would be trampled by the estimated five million distraught mourners who filled the streets.

In the opinion of Aburish, Zhou Enlai, the Chinese Premier, who had met Nasser at Bandung in 1955, delivered the ultimate judgement: 'He died of sorrow; he died of a broken heart.'

Photo of Nasser's funeral procession, from the *al-Ahram* newspaper.

● **Examiner's hint**

It is possible that you will be asked to compare and contrast the policies of two or more single-party or authoritarian leaders. This type of question requires careful planning, as you will need to use what is called a 'comparative structure'. In other words, you will need to compare the policies, in this case, of Stalin and Nasser, and then to contrast them (or vice versa). What is important is that you don't describe the policies of Nasser and then the policies of Stalin. This is what is called an 'end-on' response and although it may be perfectly appropriate for some questions, it would not be a very good structure to use to answer a comparative question. When you plan this answer, a good idea is to make a list of all the relevant policies and then to jot down how these are similar or different. Perhaps the aims are the same but the methods are different or some may succeed in one state but fail in the other. Don't forget that 'social policies' refer to ways in which he tried to influence education, culture, the role of women, religion and the media. Be careful not to confuse 'social' with 'political'.

STUDENT STUDY SECTION

QUESTION

Compare and contrast the economic and social policies of Nasser and Stalin.

Here is an extract from a student answer to this essay question:

Student Answer – *Wyn*

Both Stalin and Nasser had a similar aim with regard to economic policy as both wanted their countries to develop and to prosper. Stalin wanted the Soviet Union to catch up with the West and to have industrial growth that would allow it to re-arm effectively. In order to do this, Stalin introduced the collectivization of agriculture in 1929 so that food exports could finance industry that would grow by applying Five Year Plans. Nasser also wanted Egypt to grow quickly and to develop its industry. Nasser also introduced central planning, but Nasser did not bring everything under state control and he did not introduce collectivization of farming. Unlike Stalin, Nasser was not a communist and although he did nationalize some industry and also foreign businesses, he also wanted private business and production to develop. Stalin was prepared to use slave labour to build canals and railways but Nasser, although he was often disappointed because economic growth and investment were difficult to achieve, never used methods like this.

Examiner's comments

You can see here that Wyn has used a comparative structure quite effectively. He begins the paragraph by comparing the economic aims of the two leaders and then goes on to show how they differ. He could go on to add some statistics to support his argument, but this extract shows a clear understanding of what the question requires.

REVIEW SECTION

This chapter has covered the rise to power and the rule of Nasser as the leader of Egypt.

In particular, it has focused upon the following:

- How Nasser along with the Free Officers' Movement came together to organize and carry out the coup against King Farouk and to establish a new government.

- The social, economic and political reforms that were carried out by the Revolutionary Command Council.

- The emergence of Nasser as the President and single-party leader of Egypt.

- The period from the Suez Crisis to the United Arab Republic and how these events had an impact upon Nasser's popularity and policies.

- The implementation of pan-Arabism and Arab nationalism.

- The methods used by Nasser to remain in power; what he aimed to achieve; and an assessment of his successes and failures as a single-party leader.

Chapter 8
Theory of Knowledge

Introduction

This book is about single-party and authoritarian leaders. These were men (all the examples are men) who came to power either legally or illegally and who proceeded to establish control over the state and the people. In this chapter, each of the leaders is looked at from a ToK perspective that will help you to assess the resources that are available. This chapter will help you to build critical awareness and link history to other areas of knowledge, such as art, politics and ethics. The leaders will be looked at from a different perspective, focusing on their public image and how this can be manipulated and can change over time.

Study this sculpture. What do you think it represents?

The role of art and theatre in promoting nationalism

This is an example of Makonde (an ethnic group) artwork that comes from northern Mozambique and south-eastern Tanzania. The style was originally known as *dimoongo* (Bantu for 'power' or 'strength'), but after an exhibition in Tanzania in the 1960s it became known as *ujamaa* (Swahili for 'extended family' or 'familyhood'). Why do you think that this happened? (Read pp.250–53 to help you answer this question.) The artists were supported in their work by **Frelimo**, who saw the sculptures as helping to perpetuate traditional African values.

> **Frelimo**
> Frelimo stands for Frente de Libertação de Moçambique (Liberation Front of Mozambique). It was a political movement aimed at promoting Mozambique's independence.

One of the key objectives of the political party the Tanzanian African National Union (TANU), was the elimination of what it saw as cultural imperialism by the colonial powers' domination of art and theatre. These powers suppressed African performing arts, as they realized that art and culture were a means of encouraging tribalism. To combat this threat, an African cultural group was started in Tanzania in the 1950s called Hiari ya Moyo, whose aim was to retain the nation's tribal and ethnic traditions. Their first performance was entitled *Amka Msilale* (*Wake up, don't sleep*).

◀ A Makonde sculpture

> **Questions**
> Why is the title of the performance significant?

The group leader (*Mwinamila*) compositions and the *Hiari ya Moyo* dance style became one of TANU's methods of mobilizing Tanzanians for independence. What other examples can you find to support the idea that art and theatre can be used by a country to promote cultural imperialism? Give specific examples to support your argument.

Mwalimu (Swahili for 'teacher'), as Nyerere was more generally known, also aimed at introducing the Tanzanians to Shakespeare. He translated two plays into Swahili: *Julius Caesar* (*Juliasi Kaizari*) and *The Merchant of Venice* (*Mabepari wa Venisi*). It is interesting to analyze the importance of the role of translation in history by looking at the words that Nyerere used. Nyerere translated 'Merchant' in the title of the play as *mabepari*, which is a plural word and can be translated as 'capitalists'. There is another Swahili word, *Mfanyabiashara*, which is more literally 'merchant'. The *Merchant of Venice* became *The Capitalists of Venice*, which implies an exploitation of the workers or proletariat by the bourgeoisie. Nyerere made the translations between 1963 and 1969. Remember that Nyerere was a committed socialist and his translations give Shakespeare's play a clear political message to those people reading it in Swahili.

Julius Nyerere

Activity

Divide yourself into groups of four and brainstorm the motives that Nyerere might have had for choosing these two plays and his reasons behind his choice of words.

Che Guevara

Question

Can you think of other examples in history where art and theatre have been used to reinforce a country's nationalism? Give specific examples.

The issue of the political usage of translation is an interesting topic. Find a partner who is bilingual and discuss, with examples, how word choice can become a political tool when translating from one language into another.

Che Guevara – Art in History

Background

The image here shows Cuban photographer Alberto 'Korda' Díaz holding a very famous photograph of Ernesto 'Che' Guevara, the photo known as *Guerrillero Heroico* or 'Heroic Guerrilla Fighter'. Korda took the photograph during a mass funeral for victims of an explosion in Havana harbour. At the time the photograph was taken, Guevara was listening to a speech by Fidel Castro. The photograph was not published until the following year, when it appeared in the newspaper *Revolución*, but it only became internationally popular after Guevara died in 1967. It is now considered the most reproduced image in the history of photography.

Questions

Study Korda's photograph and discuss it with your group. How many of you are familiar with this photograph? Can you remember the context in which you have seen it? What do you think it represents? To what extent does your knowledge of the Cuban revolution affect the way in which you interpret and appreciate this photograph?

Do you consider it a work of art? Explain your views by making reference to what you consider a work of art to be.

Korda said about the photograph: 'This photograph is not the product of knowledge or technique. It was really coincidence, pure luck.' Can works of art be the result of 'pure luck'? How important are knowledge and technique to the appreciation of a work of art? What other factors play a part?

Some of the applications of the photograph include the 3 peso Cuban banknote, the image of the vodka Smirnoff, tattoos worn by superstars, T-shirts, underwear, watches, cigar cases and mouse pads, among other uses worldwide. It has also gone from the language of protest to merchandizing and museum exhibitions. This has certainly contributed to making people more aware of Che Guevara and events in Cuba. How do you think this diffusion has affected what is known and believed about the history of the Cuban revolution?

Questions

'Korda's image has worked its way into languages around the world. There isn't anything else in history that serves in this way.' Do you agree with this view? To what extent has this image affected the way the history of the Cuban revolution and the role of Che Guevara are studied? Can you think of other examples where works of art have become symbols of events or people?

'Heroic Guerrilla Fighter' has been a source of inspiration to other artists. Study the images on this page.

◀ Che Guevara, as depicted by James Fitzpatrick

◀ Andy Warhol's p[...] art depiction of [...] Guevara.

▲ 'Last Supper of Chicano Heroes', mural by Tony Burciaga. Burciaga carried out a survey asking Chicanos (Mexican-American people) who their heroes were and painted the 13 most popular choices at the table; other less popular choices stand behind.

Questions

'A work of art is enlarged by its interpretation.' To what extent do these re-enactments of Korda's photographs contribute or change the interpretation of his work? What light do they throw on how Guevara is perceived as a leading figure of the Cuban revolution? Explain your answer fully.

The role of government posters in promoting propaganda

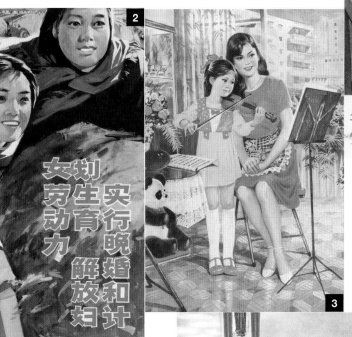

These are all posters published by the Chinese government between 1953 and 1987. It may well be that you know very little about Chinese history, but even with no background information you can make some assumptions about what the government is attempting to communicate to its people.

Questions

a) What is the significance of the way in which the women are dressed in each of the posters on p.253? How do the features of the women differ? What are the reasons behind this?

b) Study each poster and identify the main features and symbols in each of them. Be as detailed as you can. What do you think the message is in each one?

c) These are the dates of the posters: 1953, 1954, 1964, 1975, 1986, 1987. (The posters are not in chronological order.) Try to identify correctly which date belongs to which poster.

Activity

Here are the titles for each poster, without the date. Try and identify which title belongs to which poster.

- Have culture
- We are proud to participate in the industrialization of our nation
- Expectations
- Good sisters at the conference of outstanding workers
- New view in the rural village
- Realizing [the policy of] marrying late and birth control to liberate the labour power of women

Here are the correct answers:

1) We are proud to participate in the industrialization of our nation (1954)
2) Realizing [the policy of] marrying late and birth control to liberate the labour power of women (1975)
3) Expectations (1987)
4) New view in the rural village (1953)
5) Good sisters at the conference of outstanding workers (1964)
6) Have culture (1986)

These are all examples of propaganda posters from an authoritarian society that is attempting to influence the actions of the people who live in it. Can you find any examples of a democratic government using propaganda to influence the actions of its citizens? Be specific.

Are there any restrictions on a government's use of propaganda? If not, should there be? Find out what restrictions there are in any two countries of your choice.

Perón – Reconstructing History

The Perón novel

Argentine writer and journalist Tomás Eloy Martínez wrote in 1985 *The Perón Novel*, which describes aspects of the life of Juan Domingo Perón. After his fall in 1955, Perón spent 18 years in exile. The novel starts with Perón preparing to leave his exile in Madrid to return to Buenos Aires to become President in 1973.

The Perón Novel brings together different methods of research on Perón: journalistic investigation, the conversations between Perón and Eloy Martínez, as well as the memories read to the author by López Rega (Péron's private secretary who became Minister of Welfare in his third presidency).

Eloy Martínez said about this novel:

This is a novel where everything is true. For ten years, I gathered thousands of documents, letters, eyewitnesses' voices, newspaper pages, photographs. Many of these were unknown. During my exile in Caracas [Venezuela], I reconstructed the memoirs which Perón dictated to me between 1966 and 1972 and those which López Rega read to me in 1970, telling me that they belonged to the General even when López Rega had written them. In Maryland, I decided that the truths of this book did not admit a language other than that of imagination. That is how a Perón no one had wanted to see appeared: not the Perón of History but the intimate Perón.

From Tomás Eloy Martínez, *La Novela de Perón*, 1985 (trans. by Daniela Senés)

Questions

a) Discuss each of the methods used to reconstruct the life of Perón in *The Perón Novel*. In what ways are they a) similar and b) different to the methods used by an historian? What are their strengths and limitations?

b) What do you understand by Eloy Martínez's comment above, in which he says that everything in the novel is true while he also claims that the book did not admit a language other than imagination?

c) What light can research on the 'intimate Perón' throw on your understanding of the events and circumstances that explain his rise and fall? To what extent do you agree with the view that an historian should expand his or her research with creative imagination to build a living account of events? Should an historian limit himself to the scientific analysis of evidence?

d) 'Reality cannot be told nor repeated. The only thing one can do with reality is to invent it again.' To what extent do you agree with this view? How may it influence the way we study and understand history?

'A fly lands on the General's stiff, liver-spotted hand. It has a blue back, transparent wings, avid eyes.

'A housefly', the General notes as he chases it away. 'Flies here, this high up?'

They see it fly towards the lights in the ceiling and then land. It rubs its legs together.

'Oh, my,' the señora sighs.

'Look at it.' The General points. 'Look at those eyes. They cover almost its entire head. They're very strange eyes, with four thousand facets. Each one of those eyes sees a thousand different pieces of reality. My grandmother Dominga was very impressed by them. Juan, she used to say to me, what does a fly see? Does it see four thousand truths, or just one truth divided into four thousand pieces? And I never knew what to answer her...'

From Tomás Eloy Martínez, *The Perón Novel*, 1998

Questions

a) Do you think we see and understand things as we are rather than as what they are? What would the implications of this situation be for the study of history?

b) To what extent can we see different truths when a) we speak different languages, b) we have a different religious or ideological background? Can you think of examples where cultural/linguistic differences have proved to be a difficulty for historical study?

c) In what ways does the passage above help you understand why there are different and conflicting interpretations of Peronism?

How does the present influence our knowledge of the past?

Where does historical knowledge come from? How do we separate fact from opinion?

Winston Churchill famously said, 'History will be kind to me, for I shall write it.' Of course, he was rather optimistic, as although he did write about his own career and his role as a war leader, alternative interpretations have been argued by historians and many have been less generous about Churchill than Churchill was about himself.

History is a dynamic subject and historians rarely leave the past alone. They tug and pull at it, looking for new and different ways of looking at events and leaders. It is not only historians who rewrite the past, however. In single-party states, especially, the past can be very dangerous, especially if it is remembered 'incorrectly'. For example, Josef Stalin went through many incarnations after his death in 1953.

An elderly Russian man embraces a portrait of Josef Stalin.

Stalin died in 1953 and yet only three years later in February 1956, his reputation was savaged by Nikita Khrushchev in a speech made to a meeting of the Congress of Soviets. The Congress was only open to delegates to the Communist Party of the Soviet Union, but news of the attack spread quickly.

The BBC reported Khrushchev's speech in this way:

SOURCE A

In a sensational speech to the 20th Congress of the Communist Party Mr. Khrushchev painted a graphic picture of a regime of 'suspicion, fear, and terror' built up under the former dictator who died three years ago. He said he wanted to break the 'Stalin cult' that has held Soviet citizens in its thrall for 30 years. The prime minister described the purges during the period of 1936–38.

BBC News

When Leonid Brezhnev became Secretary-General of the Communist Party of the Soviet Union in 1964, there was a more sympathetic approach to Stalin and plans were made to commemorate in 1969 the 90th anniversary of Stalin's birth.

SOURCE B

They were not proposing a reversion to the terror of the 1930s and 1940s; but as they grew old in office, their unpleasant memory grew dimmer and they became nostalgic about their own contribution to the glorious past… Only strenuous representations to the Politburo by foreign communist parties brought about a last-minute reversal of the decision on Stalin's rehabilitation.

From Robert Service, *A History of Modern Russia*, 2003

In Source C below, Volkogonov mentions Mikhail Gorbachev's ambivalence about Stalin. Whereas in speeches Gorbachev was careful to acknowledge Stalin's contribution to the building of the USSR through the Five Year Plans and the victory over Nazi Germany, he was also aware of the mythology that surrounded Stalin.

SOURCE C

It took time and effort for Gorbachev to free himself of the Stalinist mythology. If it was so hard for him to change himself, how much harder was it going to be for him to change society. The applause at the mention of Stalin's name shows how painful even the best informed Soviet citizens were finding their self-emancipation. The published pamphlet of Gorbachev's speech states that Stalin's name was greeted with 'prolonged applause'. That understates the case. Even the editors of the minutes were ashamed to write that the applause had, in fact, been a stormy ovation, and they downgraded it to 'prolonged'.

Reference to speech made by Mikhail Gorbachev on the 70th anniversary of the revolution in 1987; from Dmitri Volkogonov, *The Rise and Fall of the Soviet Empire*, 1998

This poster is called 'Stainless Stalin' by Syarhei Voivchanka, Uladzimir Tsesler, Andrei Shalyuta and Krysztof Ducki (1987). If you look carefully, you can see Stalin's profile on the knife blade. The poster's title cleverly plays with a reference to Stalin's name. It works as an indication of Stalin's terror, and also the way in which the personality cult of Stalin is almost indestructible.

Today, Stalin's place in Russian history continues to be controversial. Dmitry Medvedev, the President of Russia, speaking in December 2009, had this opinion of Stalin:

SOURCE D

'Stainless Stalin', a poster by Syarhei Voivchanka, Uladzimir Tsesler, Andrei Shalyuta and Krysztof Ducki (1987).

SOURCE E

'Millions of people died as a result of terror and false accusations... But we are still hearing that these enormous sacrifices could be justified by certain ultimate interests of the state,' Mr. Medvedev said. 'I am convinced that neither the goals of the development of the country, nor its successes or ambitions, should be achieved through human suffering and losses. It is important to prevent any attempts to vindicate, under the pretext of restoring historical justice, those who destroyed their own people.'

From The Times Online, 4 December 2009

'History is past politics and politics is present history.'

E.K. Freeman 1823–92

Questions

What, do you think, did Freeman mean by this? He said this in 1886, so does it still apply today?

A new history textbook introduced to schools in Russia in September 2009, however, was described in *Prospect* (a British journal) in the following way:

SOURCE F

The whole postwar period in Russian history is viewed through the prism of the cold war 'initiated by the United States of America.' The textbook does not deny Stalin's repressions; it justifies them. The concentration of power in Stalin's hands suited the country; indeed, conditions of the time 'demanded' it. 'The domestic politics of the Soviet Union after the war fulfilled the tasks of mobilisation which the government set. In the circumstances of the cold war ... democratisation was not an option for Stalin.'

From Arkady Ostrovsky, 'Flirting with Stalin', *Prospect*, 28 September 2008

The article also notes that Vladimir Putin, now the Prime Minister of Russia, had met with history teachers in 2007 (when he was President) to discuss how the past was represented to Russian schoolchildren. He is quoted as saying, 'We can't allow anyone to impose a sense of guilt on us'. We can see that the same article (Source G) notes that the textbook offers a particular view of Mikhail Gorbachev:

SOURCE G

But if Stalin mobilised the country and expanded the Soviet empire so that it reached parity in power-status with the US, Mikhail Gorbachev surrendered those hard-won positions. Stupidly, from the textbook's point of view, Gorbachev considered western partners to be his political allies. He gave up Central and Eastern Europe, which meant Russia lost its security. America and the west instigated revolutions in Ukraine and in Georgia, which turned the former Soviet territories into western military bases. These revolutions 'set a task for Moscow to pursue a more ambitious foreign policy in the post-Soviet space,' the textbook says.

From Arkady Ostrovsky, 'Flirting with Stalin', *Prospect*, 28 September 2008

Stalin, it seems, is just too important to be forgotten in Russian history.

Images of revolutionary or communist figures can be highly controversial – Poland, for instance, banned images of Che Guevara (see p.259).

Questions

Reading Sources A–G, consider the following questions:

a) 'He who controls the present controls the past.' How far do Sources A–G support this statement by George Orwell?

b) Source B suggests that during the 1960s, there was an attempt to rehabilitate Stalin. Why, do you think, did the Politburo of the time feel 'nostalgia' about such a harsh leader?

c) As President of Russia, why did Dmitri Medvedev take such a critical view of Stalin (Source E) despite the publication of the textbook described in Source F?

d) When Prime Minister Putin says, 'We cannot allow anyone to impose a sense of guilt on us', who is the 'anyone' he is referring to? How important is history in the creation of a sense of national unity, especially in a new or newly independent country?

e) In Source G, Gorbachev is looked at critically. Can you think of any circumstances in which he may be 'rehabilitated' in the future?

f) Sources C and D both indicate how a) party officials and b) a group of artists responded to the memory of Stalin in 1987. In what way do these sources give a different point of view?

g) Do we get the history we deserve? Do governments impose their version of history on society or does society want a feel-good account of its past?

h) Do you think it is important to teach the 'good' aspects of your country's history? Give reasons for your answer.

i) There must be many people still living in Russia who lived through the 1930s and 1940s and who experienced Stalin's rule at first hand. How, do you think, would they react to a positive assessment of Stalin's rule? Can our memories of the past be influenced by what we are told happened?

The new law [to ban Che Guevara images] has drawn criticism from left-wing lawmakers and other observers who say it is ill-defined and will be hard to implement. The law does not list the banned symbols and it also exempts from punishment their use for artistic, educational or collectors' purposes. The legislation was initiated by Law and Justice, a right-wing opposition party that President Lech Kaczynski helped found and which has sought to purge Poland of the legacy of four decades of communist rule.

The European Union Times online

Tom Burns, 'The Communist Party'. ▶

A Stalin look-alike poses for the camera.
▼

Question

How significant, do you think, are symbols of single-party regimes? Poland may ban the wearing of a t-shirt with the image of Che Guevara but in most countries, a t-shirt with the image of 'The Communist Party' by Tom Burns (see below) would be considered amusing. (Note Stalin in the background.) Would you wear a t-shirt printed with this image? Give reasons for your answer.

There are Stalin look-alikes in Russia who make a living posing as the dictator. Generally they are greeted warmly, although this may not be a reliable indication of Stalin's continuing popularity.

Question

Can you imagine a Hitler look-alike walking around Berlin? Give reasons for your answer!

Single-party leaders and democracy

The term 'democracy' is a very familiar one in the 21st century and a general definition would be that it is a form of government composed of representatives of the people of a state. These representatives are chosen in free elections by secret ballot and hold office for a fixed term. In addition, a democracy will usually uphold the right of the people to freedom of speech, freedom of assembly and the freedom to form political parties.

Question
Do you agree with this definition? What would you add or take out?

A t-shirt depicting Latin American 'revolutionaries'. (How, do you think, would the wearer define democracy?)

A Nasser supporter brandishes his leader's image on placards.

◀ Posters promote the cult of Eva Perón on the Argentine streets.

▲ Vladimir Lenin

In the 20th century, especially after 1945, democracy was viewed by many people as the best form of government and the most likely to protect basic freedoms and to improve living/working conditions for the majority of the population. Many of the single-party leaders included in this book chose not to restore democracy in the states they controlled, but even they felt compelled to explain why they took this position. Here are two reasons given for Gamal Abdel Nasser's reluctance to restore democracy in Egypt:

Overall, the original inclinations toward re-establishing democracy were fading because Nasser had decided that the country would revert to its former corrupt self and because he relished his status as spokesman for all the Arabs.

From Said Aburish, *Nasser: The Last Arab*, 2004

By January 1954, Nasser was admitting openly that he had no intention of allowing the restoration of parliamentary government… He told Jean Lacouture, 'No, it wouldn't make any sense. In a year and a half we have been able to wipe out corruption. If the right to vote were now restored, the same landowners would be elected – the feudal interests. We don't want the capitalists and the wealthy back in power. If we open the government to them now, the revolution might just as well be forgotten.'

From Anne Alexander, *Nasser*, 2005

Questions

a) According to these sources, what did Nasser consider to be the risks of restoring democracy in Egypt?

b) Do you think such reservations were justified?

This was the opinion of Julius Nyerere:

In advocating a strong State, I am not advocating an overburdened State, nor a State with a bloated bureaucracy. To advocate for a strong State is to advocate for a State which, among other things, has power to act on behalf of the people in accordance with their wishes. And in a market economy, with its law of the jungle, we need a State that has the capacity to intervene on behalf of the weak.

Julius Nyerere, 'Good Governance for Africa', 13 October 1988

Questions

a) When Nyerere refers to a 'strong state', what, do you think, does he have in mind?

b) Why does he think a 'strong state' is a good idea?

c) Does a 'strong state' mean a 'democratic state', do you think? Give reasons for your answer.

d) To what extent do Nasser and Nyerere share the same view of democracy?

The best argument against democracy is a five minute conversation with the average voter.

Winston Churchill

This is how Lenin summed it up!

Democracy for an insignificant minority, democracy for the rich – that is the democracy of a capitalist society.

From V. Lenin, *State and Revolution*, 1917

Question

Why did Lenin consider the 'democracy of a capitalist society' not to be a true democracy?

And Perón said:

'Man is good, but when he is watched over, he is better.'

Juan Peron

Question

How far does Perón's opinion as expressed agree with those of Nasser, Lenin and Nyerere?

Many of the single-party leaders of the 20th century claimed to be 'democratic'. The names of communist states established after 1945 mostly began with the prefix 'The People's Democratic Republic of…' although, during elections, the voters could only choose from a list of candidates published by the ruling communist party. Examples of such states would include Kampuchea, North Korea, East Germany and China.

Democracy is two wolves and a lamb voting on what to have for lunch. Liberty is a well-armed lamb contesting the vote!

Benjamin Franklin

▲ Women voting in an Iranian election.

Questions

a) Would you consider the countries listed above to be democratic? Give reasons for your answer.

b) Why, do you think, was it considered so important to include 'democratic' in the name of the states mentioned above?

c) In his book *The End of History*, Francis Fukuyama stated that after the collapse of the USSR in 1991, all countries wanted to be 'democratic' even if they weren't, and still wanted to be called 'democratic'. Do you agree with this assertion? Give evidence to support your answer.

Group discussion

Consider the following questions and give reasons for your answers.

a) Should all adult citizens of a state (men and women over the age of 18) be allowed to vote? Would you exclude anyone? Why? Why not?

b) In some countries, prisoners cannot vote. Do you agree with this?

c) Should the voting age be reduced to 16?

d) Should it be a legal obligation to vote in elections?

e) During wartime, democracies have been known to suspend elections. Why have they done so and do you agree with this action?

f) How would you define a 'democratic' state? (You can start or end with this question!)

g) We often associate democracy with economic growth, but post-Mao China is not a democracy, yet its economy is growing very rapidly? What kind of state is it? To what extent should China be considered a model for developed and/or developing countries that want to achieve economic prosperity?

▲ The Greeks were the founders of the democratic system of government.

FURTHER READING

Books and Articles

Juan Perón and Argentina

Bethell, Leslie, *Argentina Since Independence,* Cambridge University Press, 1993

Brennan, James P., *Peronism and Argentina*, Scholarly Resources Inc., 1998

Crassweller, Robert D., *Perón and the Enigmas of Argentina*, W.W. Norton & Company, 1987

del Campo, Hugo, *Sindicalismo y Peronismo: Los comienzos de un vínculo perdurable,* CLACSO, 1983

Elena, Eduardo, 'What the People Want: State Planning and Political Participation in Peronist Argentina, 1946–1955', *Journal of Latin American Studies*, 37, Cambridge University Press, 2005

Foster, David William, Melissa Fitch Lockhart and Darrell B. Lockhart, *Culture and Customs of Argentina*, Greenwood Press, 1998

Goddard, Victoria Ana (ed.), *Gender, Agency, and Change: Anthropological Perspectives,* Routledge, 2000

Lewis, Daniel K., *The History of Argentina*, Palgrave Macmillan, 2003

Luna, Félix, *A Brief History of Argentina*, Planeta, 1995

MacLachlan, Colin M., *Argentina: What Went Wrong?*, Greenwood Publishing Group, 2001

Nouzeilles, Gabriela and Graciela Montaldo (eds), *The Argentine Reader: History, Culture and Politics*, Duke University Press, 2002

Page, Joseph, *Perón: A Biography*, Random House, 1983

Plotkin, Mariano Ben, *Mañana es San Perón: A Cultural History of Perón's Argentina,* Scholarly Resources Inc., 2003

Rein, Mónica Esti, *Politics and Education in Argentina, 1946–1962*, M. E. Sharpe, 1998

Rock, David, *Authoritarian Argentina: The Nationalist Movement, Its History and Its Impact*, University of California Press, 1993

Shannon, William, 'Evita and Propaganda: Selling an Argentinian Dictatorship', 2000

Fidel Castro and Cuba

Balfour, Sebastian, *Castro*, Longman, 1990

Baloyra, Enrique A. and James A. Morris (eds), *Conflict and Change in Cuba*, University of New Mexico Press, 1993

Batista, Fulgencio, *Cuba Betrayed*, Vantage Press, 1962

Benjamin, Jules, *The United States and the Origins of the Cuban Revolution*, Princeton University Press, 1990

Bethell, Leslie (ed.), *Cuba: A Short History*, Cambridge University Press, 1993

Bunck, J.M., *Fidel Castro and the Quest for a Revolutionary Culture in Cuba,* Pennsylvania University Press, 1994

Chomsky, Aviva (ed.), *The Cuba Reader: History, Culture, Politics*, Duke University Press, 2003

DePalma, Anthony, *The Man who Invented Fidel: Cuba, Castro and Herbert L. Matthews of the New York Times*, PublicAffairs, 2006

Domínguez, Jorge I., *Cuba: Order and Revolution*, The Belknap Press of Harvard University Press, 1978

Farber, Samuel, *The Origins of the Cuban Revolution Reconsidered*, University of North Carolina Press, 2006

Fernández, Damián J. (ed.), *Cuban Studies since the Revolution*, University Press of Florida, 1992

Garcia, Luis M., *Child of the Revolution: Growing Up in Castro's Cuba*, Allen & Unwin, 2006

Goldstone, Jack A., *Revolutions: Theoretical, Comparative and Historical Studies*, Wadsworth Publishing, 2003

Guevara, Ernesto, *Episodes of the Cuban Revolutionary War 1956–58*, Pathfinder Press, 1996

Halperín Donghi, Tulio, *The Contemporary History of Latin America*, Duke University Press, 2003

Huberman, Leo and Paul Sweezy, *Cuba: Anatomy of a Revolution*, Monthly Review Press, 1960

Kapcia, Antoni, *Cuba in Revolution*, Reaktion Books, 2008

Kapcia, Antoni, *Cuba: Island of Dreams*, Berg, 2000

Kirk, John M., *Between God and the Party: Religion and Politics in Revolutionary Cuba*, University of South Florida Press, 1989

Lewis, Paul H., *Authoritarian Regimes in Latin America*, Rowman & Littlefield Publishers, 2006

Luis, William, *Culture and Customs of Cuba*, Greenwood Press, 2001

Pérez, Louis A., *Cuba: Between Reform and Revolution*, Oxford University Press, 1988

Pérez, Louis A., *On Becoming Cuban: Identity, Nationality and Culture*, HarperCollins, 1999

Pérez-Stable, Marifeli, *The Cuban Revolution: Origins, Course, and Legacy*, Oxford University Press, 1993

Quirk, Robert E., *Fidel Castro*, W.W. Norton and Company, 1993

Rosendahl, Mona, *Inside the Revolution: Everyday Life in Socialist Cuba*, Cornell University Press, 1997

Selbin, Eric, *Modern Latin American Revolutions*, Westview Press, 1993

Smith, Lois M. and Alfred Padula, *Sex and Revolution: Women in Socialist Cuba*, Oxford University Press, 1996

Thomas, Hugh, *Cuba or the Pursuit of Freedom*, Da Capo Press, 1998

Josef Stalin and the USSR

Brown, Archie, *The Rise and Fall of Communism*, HarperCollins, 2009

Corin, Chris and Terry Fiehn, *Communist Russia under Lenin and Stalin*, Hodder Murray, 2002

Deutscher, Isaac, *Stalin: A Political Biography*, Penguin, 1966

Ferguson, Niall, *The War of the World*, Allen Lane, 2006

Figes, Orlando, *The Whisperers*, Penguin, 2007

Fischer, John, *The Scared Men in the Kremlin*, Hamish Hamilton, 1947

Fitzpatrick, Sheila (ed.), *Stalinism*, Routledge, 2000

Getty, J. Arch and Oleg V. Naumov, *The Road to Terror*, Yale University Press, 1999

Gill, Graeme, *Stalinism*, Palgrave Macmillan, 1998

Hobsbawm, Eric, *Revolutionaries*, Abacus, 2007

Hosking, Geoffrey, *A History of the Soviet Union 1917–1991*, Fontana, 1992

Kershaw, Ian and Moshe Lewin (eds), *Stalinism and Nazism*, Cambridge, 1997

Lee, Stephen J., *Stalin and the Soviet Union*, Routledge, 1999

Lewin, Moshe, *The Soviet Century*, Verso, 2005

Lowe, Norman, *Mastering Twentieth Century Russian History*, Palgrave, 2002

McAuley, Mary, *Soviet Politics 1917–1991*, OUP, 1992

McCauley, Martin, *The Soviet Union 1917–1991*, Longman, 1993

Montefiore, Simon Sebag, *The Court of the Red Tsar*, Phoenix, 2003

Nove, Alec, *The Soviet Economic System*, George Allen and Unwin, 1980

Service, Robert, *A History of Modern Russia*, Penguin, 2003

Service, Robert, *Comrades*, Macmillan, 2007

Volkogonov, Dmitri, *The Rise and Fall of the Soviet Empire*, HarperCollins, 1998

Mao Zedong and China

Blaustein, Albert P. (ed.), *Fundamental Legal Documents of Communist China*, F.B. Rothman, 1962

Chang, Jung and John Halliday, *Mao: The Unknown Story*, Cape, 2005

Chieng, Peikai and Michael Lestz, *The Search for Modern China: A Documentary History*, W.W. Norton & Company, 1999

Feigon, Lee, *Mao: A Reinterpretation*, Ivan R. Dee, 2002

Fenby, Jonathan, *The Penguin History of Modern China*, Penguin, 2008

Gittings, John, *The Changing Face of China*, Oxford University Press, 2006

Green, James, *China*, Oxford, 1989

Hobsbawm, Eric, *Age of Extremes: The Short Twentieth Century, 1914–1991*, Michael Joseph, 1994

Houn, Franklin, *A Short History of Chinese Communism*, Prentice-Hall, 1973

Hsu, Immanuel, *China Without Mao*, Oxford University Press, 1982

Hsu, Immanuel, *The Rise of Modern China*, Oxford University Press, 2000

Kueh, Y.Y., 'The Maoist Legacy and China's New Industrialization Strategy', *The China Quarterly*, no. 119, September 1989

Lawrance, Alan, *China Since 1919*, Routledge, 2004

Li, D.J. (ed.), *The Road to Communism: China Since 1912*, Van Nostrand Reinhold, 1971

Li, Zhisui, *The Private Life of Chairman Mao*, Random House, 1994

'Long Live Mao Zedong's Thought', *Peking Review*, vol. 9, no. 27, 1 July 1966

Lynch, Michael, *The People's Republic of China 1949–1976*, Hodder Education, 2008

MacFarquhar, R., *The Origins of the Cultural Revolution*, Columbia University Press, 1983

Meisner, Maurice, *Mao's China and After*, The Free Press, 1999

Morcombe, Margot and Mark Fielding, *China in Revolution*, McGraw Hill, 2007

'Resolution on Certain Questions in the History of our Party Since the Founding of the People's Republic', *Beijing Review*, no. 27, 6 July 1981

Schoenhals, Michael, *China's Cultural Revolution, 1966–1969: Not a Dinner Party*, M.E. Sharpe, 1996

Schram, Stuart (ed.), *Mao's Road to Power: Revolutionary Writings 1912–1949*, vol. 3, M.E. Sharpe, 1995

Snow, Edgar, *Red Star over China*, Random House, 1968

Spence, Jonathan, *The Search for Modern China*, W.W. Norton & Company, 1990

Spence, Jonathan, *Mao*, Viking, 1999

Suyin, Han, *A Mortal Flower*, Jonathan Cape, 1966

Vohra, Ranbir, *China's Path to Modernization*, Prentice Hall, 2000

Julius Nyerere and Tanzania

Bryceson, Deborah Fahy, 'Peasant Commodity Production in Post-Colonial Tanzania', *African Affairs*, vol. 81, no. 825, 1982

Government of Tanzania's Poverty Reduction Strategy Paper, 2000

Havnevik, Kjell J., *Tanzania: The Limits to Development from Above*, Nordiska Afrikainstitutet, 1993

Ibhawoh, Bonny and J.I. Dibua, 'Deconstructing *Ujamaa*: The Legacy of Julius Nyerere in the Quest for Social and Economic Development in Africa', *African Journal of Political Science*, vol. 8, no. 1, 2003

Lamb, David, *The Africans*, Vintage, 1987

Lofchie, Michael F., 'Agrarian Crisis and Economic Liberalization in Tanzania', *The Journal of Modern African Studies*, vol. 16, no. 3, 1978

Mwakikagile, Godfrey, *Life under Nyerere*, Dar es Salaam, 2006

Mwakikagile, Godfrey, *Nyerere and Africa*, New Africa Press, 2007

Mwakikagile, Godfrey, *Tanzania under Mwalimu Nyerere*, New Africa Press, 2006

Nyerere, Julius, *Freedom and Unity*, New Africa Press, 1966

Nyerere, Julius, *Freedom and Socialism*, New Africa Press, 1968

Nyerere, Julius, *The Arusha Declaration: 10 Years After*, New Africa Press, 1977

Paczuska, Anna, *Socialism for Beginners*, Unwin, 1986

Peter, Chris Maina, 'Constitution-Making in Tanzania: The Role of the People in the Process', University of Dar es Salaam, August 2000

Pratt, Cranford, *The Critical Phase in Tanzania 1945–1968*, Cambridge University Press, 1976

Rasmussen, P. Kent, *Modern African Political Leaders*, Facts on File, 1998

Sabea, Hanan, 'Reviving the Dead: Entangled Histories in the Privatization of the Tanzanian Sisal Industry', *Africa*, vol. 71., no. 2, 2001

Vinokurov, Y.N. (ed.), *Julius Nyerere – Humanist, Politician, Thinker*, New Africa Press, 2005

World Bank, *Tanzania: Social Sector Review*, World Bank, 1994

Yeager, Rodger, *Tanzania: An African Experiment*, West View, 1989

Gamal Abdel Nasser and Egypt

Aburish, Said, *Nasser: The Last Arab*, Duckworth, 2004

Alexander, Anne, *Nasser*, Haus Publishing, 2005

Brown, Archie, *The Rise and Fall of Communism*, HarperCollins, 2009

Freedman, Lawrence, *A Choice of Enemies*, Phoenix, 2008

Hobsbawm, Eric, *Revolutionaries*, Abacus, 2007

Lucas, Scott W., *Divided We Stand*, Hodder and Stoughton, 1996

Mansfield, Peter, *A History of the Middle East*, Penguin, 1991

Mazrui, Ali and Michael Tidy, *Nationalism and New States in Africa*, Heinemann, 1984

Meredith, Martin, *The State of Africa*, The Free Press, 2006

Nutting, Anthony, *Nasser*, Constable, 1972

Rogan, Eugene, *The Arabs: A History*, Allen Lane, 2009

Stephens, Robert, *Nasser*, Simon & Schuster, 1971

Websites

To visit the following websites, go to www.pearsonhotlinks.com, enter the title or ISBN of the book and click on the relevant weblink.

Juan Perón and Argentina

Eva Perón Historical Research Foundation
A major site for the study of Eva Perón – click on Weblink 1.

Argentine Sourcebook
Numerous primary sources relating to Argentine history – click on Weblink 2.

Modern History Sourcebook; Juan Domingo Perón
Documents relating to Juan Perón – click on Weblink 3.

Evita and Propaganda: Selling an Argentinian Dictatorship
Online article by William Shannon – click on Weblink 4.

The Transformations of Peronism
A downloadable article on Peronism by Torcuato Di Tella – click on Weblink 5.

Fidel Castro and Cuba

The Economic History of Cuba
Documents relating to Cuba's economic and social history – click on Weblink 6.

Latin American Studies
Provides useful links to other websites. Links are classified by category – clink on Weblink 7.

The International Institute for the Study of Cuba
A London-based organization devoted to studying the 'social experience' of Cuba – click on Weblink 8.

Castro Speech Database
Includes some of the most important speeches and press conferences given by Castro between 1959 and 1996 – click on Weblink 9.

Magnum photos
Online exhibition of photographs to commemorate the revolution's 50th anniversary – click on Weblink 10.

Fidel Castro – PBS
Contains maps, timelines, original footage and articles on the history of Cuba under Fidel Castro – click on Weblink 11.

Josef Stalin and the USSR

History of the Soviet Union
A very useful and comprehensive site with good links to primary and secondary sources – click on Weblink 12.

Collectivization and Industrialization
Lots of great archive material on many aspects of Soviet society, economy and culture – click on Weblink 13.

Old posters about Stalin and the Soviet people
A good site for propaganda posters published in the Soviet Union – click on Weblink 14.

Marxists.org

A useful site to browse for more information on 'socialist realism' and with good links. Be a little wary of the source, however – click on Weblink 15.

Holocaust Research Project

Information on the German invasion of the Soviet Union – click on Weblink 16.

Cold War – National Archives

Useful archives or links to the role of Stalin in the Cold War – click on Weblink 17.

Mao Zedong and China

The Historical Experience of the Dictatorship of the Proletariat

Full text of the book by the Foreign Languages Press – click on Weblink 18.

Stefan Landsberger's Chinese Propaganda Poster Pages

Stefan Landsberger's book and website are invaluable sources for anyone studying China under Mao. The series showing how China's perception of the role of women changed over time is well worth viewing – click on Weblink 19.

Selected Works of Mao Tse-Tung

Extensive collections of writings by Mao Zedong from Marxists.org – click on Weblink 20.

Julius Nyerere and Tanzania

OAU Charter

Full text in a single PDF document – click on Weblink 21.

Tanzania without Poverty

A 'plain language' guide to Tanzania's important Poverty Reduction Strategy Paper – click on Weblink 22.

Constitution-making in Tanzania

An article by Chris Maina Peter – click on Weblink 23.

Arusha Declaration

Full text of this important document – click on Weblink 24.

Ujamaa **– The Basis of African Socialism**

By Julius Kambarage Nyerere – click on Weblink 25.

Saints and Presidents: A Commentary on Julius Nyerere

Article by Stanley Meisler – click on Weblink 26.

Gamal Abdel Nasser and Egypt

Six Day War

Website about the 1967 conflict, which includes some analysis of Nasser's handling of the situation – click on Weblink 27.

Mid East Web

A major website on Middle Eastern affairs. Search the website with the term 'Nasser' to bring up primary and secondary sources – click on Weblink 28.

Suez Crisis

In-depth BBC history of this episode in Egyptian history – click on Weblink 29.

INDEX

The arrangement is word-by-word.
Italic page numbers indicate illustrations not included in the text
     page range.
Bold page numbers indicate interesting facts boxes.